THE SOCIALIST REGISTER 1989

SOCIALIST REGISTER 1989

Edited by
RALPH MILIBAND
LEO PANITCH
JOHN SAVILLE

THE MERLIN PRESS
LONDON

First published in 1989
by The Merlin Press Ltd
10 Malden Road
London NW5 3HR

British Library Cataloguing in Publication Data

The Socialist Register.–1989/
  1. Socialism – Serials
  I. Miliband, Ralph   II. Saville, John   III. Panitch, Leo
  355'.005

ISBN 0-85036-376-4
ISBN 0-85036-377-2 Pbk

Printed in Great Britain
by Biddles Ltd, Guildford, Surrey

Typesetting by Selectmove Ltd
Tech West Centre, Acton Vale, London W3

TABLE OF CONTENTS

PREFACE

1989 marks the bi-centenary of the French Revolution. Rather than add to the torrent of writing engendered by this anniversary, we are devoting this year's volume of *The Socialist Register* to the theme of revolution at the end of the twentieth century. 1989 marks an anniversary for the Register itself – our 25th – and the exploration of this year's theme is well in line with the purposes which this annual has tried to serve since its inception in 1964, namely the discussion and elucidation of questions which, in both theoretical and practical terms, concern socialists everywhere.

The question of revolution is clearly one of these, perhaps the most important of all such questions. The socialist aspiration to create a cooperative, egalitarian, democratic and classless society entails, for its realization, a fundamental transformation of the social and political order, in a word, a revolution. But what does the idea of revolution itself entail today? To ask this question as we approach the end of this century immediately raises a host of issues concerning whether and how socialist aspirations can be realized, and poses problems and dilemmas over the very ways we can think about these issues, as well as over the ways in which they might be resolved.

These problems and dilemmas present themselves differently for socialists in the countries of advanced capitalism, in the 'third world', and in the Communist countries; and even within each of these global arenas. The decade of the 1980s has witnessed a sustained capitalist reaction in the West against many of the reforms, and indeed against the very notion of a gradualist reform agenda, whose achievement had long inspired the practice of socialist, and most communist, parties in the West. The 1980s have also witnessed the challenges mounted to 'actually existing socialism' in the East by movements like *Solidarnosc* from below, and by *perestroika* from above. At the same time, new revolutionary regimes in the Third World have displayed an extremely wide range of experiences and outcomes; and such diversity is inscribed again in the practices and ongoing struggles of revolutionary movements. What this indicates is that, even if socialist aspirations may be essentially the same, the problems of realization – of revolution – are never exactly the same and can never be addressed in uniform fashion.

The articles in this volume testify to this diversity. But they also testify to the fact that reflections on the meaning of revolution (and its always-present nemesis, counter-revolution) in 1989 means far more than reawakening the ghosts of 1789. Revolution – for all its problems and dilemmas – remains very much a contemporary issue.

We wish to pay tribute here to Raymond Williams, whose appreciation of 'the long revolution' only enhanced his commitment to the need for fundamental change, for searching new ways of renewing the revolutionary agenda and making socialism more effective and influential in the modern world. Raymond Williams was a contributor to the Register, and we had invited him to write an essay on the meaning of revolution today shortly before his untimely death in January 1988. We feel his loss acutely, as must all those who have been instructed by his insight and inspired by his commitment to the spirit of revolution. This insight and commitment are well-reflected, we believe, in the quotation that opens the first essay in this volume which addresses a topic which Raymond Williams helped so much to elucidate, that is, the importance, as well as the difficulties, of revolutionary socialist change in the advanced capitalist countries.

Among our contributors, Carlos Vilas is an Argentinian who has until recently been the Co-ordinator of the Centro de Investigaciones y Documentacion de las Costa Atlantica in Nicaragua. John Saul is an editor of *Southern Africa Report* and teaches in Atkinson College, York University, Toronto. Val Moghadam is at the Pembroke Centre of Brown University, Rhode Island, and David Mandel is in the Department of political science at the Université du Québec à Montreal. Tony Benn, who was for eleven years a Cabinet Minister in the Wilson and Callaghan Governments, is M.P. for Chesterfield and a member of the National Executive of the Labour Party. Victor Kiernan is Emeritus Professor of History at the University of Edinburgh. Ernest Mandel teaches political Economy at Brussels University, and Norman Geras is in the Department of Government, Manchester University. Michael Lowy is Research Director at the Centre National de la Recherche Scientifique, Paris, and Frieder Otto Wolf is a Member of the European Parliament for the German Green Party. Johanna Brenner is in the Department of Sociology at the University of Oregon, Portland, and Lawrence Littwin is in the Department of Political Science at California State University, Northridge. Saul Landau is a Senior Fellow at the Institute for Policy Studies in Washington, D.C.

We are grateful to our contributors for their collaboration; and we also want to thank Martin Eve and Norman Franklin of Merlin Press for their cooperation in the production of this volume. Many thanks also to Mike Gonzales for his translation of Carlos Vilas's article.

February 1989

R.M.
L.P.
J.S.

CAPITALISM, SOCIALISM AND REVOLUTION: THE CONTEMPORARY MEANING OF REVOLUTION IN THE WEST*

LEO PANITCH

> . . . there must be something in every socialist, from the very values involved in wanting social-
> ism at all, wanting a revolution to bring about socialism rather than just wanting a revolution,
> that continually pulls towards precisely the compromises, the settlements, the getting through
> without too much trouble and suffering. . . It is only when people get to the point of seeing that
> the price of the contradictions is yet more intolerable than the price of ending them that they
> acquire the nerve to go all the way through to a consistent socialist politics. . .
> Once you have decided for revolutionary socialism, not because it is quicker or more exciting,
> but because no other way is possible, then you can even experience defeat, temporary defeat,
> such as a socialist of my generation has known, without any loss of commitment.
>
> Raymond Williams[1]

I

What meaning can we give to the notion of socialist revolution in the advanced capitalist countries today? It is appropriate to raise this question in the year of the bi-centenary of the French Revolution. 1789 is usually taken as marking the historical moment when the concept of revolution, as we understand it today, emerged; when the idea of revolution passed from its ancient connotation – cyclical, revolving movements in the political order – to its modern connotation: the creation of an entirely new social and political order. With 1789 we can date '. . . the revolutionary spirit of the last centuries, that is, the eagerness to liberate *and* to build a new house where freedom can dwell, [which] is unprecedented and unequalled in all prior history'.[2] Few would dispute that this eagerness for fundamental social transformation was carried into the world of the twentieth century by socialism, with its aspiration for liberation from the paradoxical freedom of the bourgeois revolution, that is, from the competition and exploitation upon which capitalist social relations are founded; and with its aspiration to build a fully democratic, cooperative and classless society where freedom and equality might realize rather than negate the sociability of humankind.

Yet as we approach the end of the century, it is clear that great uncertainty

---

*I would like to thank Ralph Miliband for having inspired this essay, and for his substantive contribution to it.

and confusion, hesitation and even pessimism, has come to attend the socialist project. The question of what the very concept of socialist change actually
means in terms of objectives, social forces, agencies, etc., let alone in terms
of methods or immediate or long-term possibilities, may well be more open
now than it has ever been in this century. Such reflection on the contemporary meaning and prospects of socialist revolution as the anniversary of 1789
spawns must, in these conditions, be sober and careful. It must be mindful
of past failures and disappointments. But it must above all look to the future
even as it reexamines the past. For the main point of the exercise, as Marx
once put it, is that of 'finding once more the spirit of revolution, not of making
its ghost walk about again.'[3]

II

The theme of revolution has hardly been absent from political discourse in
recent years in the countries of advanced capitalism. But it has been a
theme far more confidently sounded on the Right, where it has taken on
the colouration of a revolution *from above*, than it has been on the Left.
'We were all revolutionaries', Ronald Reagan told his White House staff on
his last day in office, 'and the revolution has been a success.' We may be
sure that when Mrs. Thatcher finally leaves 10 Downing Street she will say
much the same thing. It is tempting, of course, simply to characterize such
rhetoric as the ad-man's cover for counter-revolution, equivalent to Reagan's
earlier designation of the Nicaraguan *contras* as 'freedom fighters'. Not only
a healthy degree of scepticism regarding this 'revolutionary' rhetoric is justified, but considerable rage and dismay at explicitly counter-revolutionary
actions abroad against socialist regimes and movements; the reactionary
turn even against the limited achievements of social democratic and liberal
reformism at home; and the manifest disdain for those who seek to draw
on the egalitarian and democratic legacy of 1789 as a means of defending
the poor, extending women's, workers' and minorities' rights, challenging
authoritarian tendencies in the state, and so on.

   Yet there is a sense in which the self-characterization of contemporary
capitalist politicians like Reagan or Thatcher as 'revolutionaries' might well
be taken more seriously. Merely to dismiss such rhetoric as mendacious
nonsense misses an important dimension of what they have been about.
For they have sought to reinfuse their societies with the very kind of bourgeois norms and values that were identified in the *Communist Manifesto*
where Marx and Engels affirmed that '[the] bourgeoisie, historically, has
played a most revolutionary part'.[4] Can we not in fact say that Reagan
and Thatcher have sought to immerse their societies 'in the icy water of
egotistical calculation' and to leave remaining 'no other nexus between man
and man than naked self-interest, than callous "cash payment"'? Have they
not endeavoured to resolve 'personal worth into exchange value and, in

place of the numberless indefeasible chartered freedoms. . . set up that single, unconscionable freedom – free trade'? And, 'for exploitation, veiled by. . . political illusions' have they not tried to substitute 'naked, shameless, direct, brutal exploitation'? Whether or not their drive to prosecute the bourgeoisie's long revolution into the world of the twenty-first century has been or will prove nearly as successful as Reagan or Thatcher would like to think, surely we must nevertheless admit that the bourgeoisie in a great many western countries in the 1980s seems to have 'conquered for itself, in the modern representative state, exclusive political sway.'

Today's bourgeois revolution from above is not the same thing as the heroic historic moment that 1789 represented. But setting aside what capitalist political leaders themselves say or do, there is a deeper sense in which it is still appropriate to see the contemporary bourgeoisie as continuing to play 'a most revolutionary part.' In the world of the micro-chip, of computer technology, of numerical control of production, of instant global communication and capital transfers; in an era of global restructuring of industry, occupation, finance and control, of workplace relations as well as the relations between gender and work, culture and household, we are perforce reminded of the essential meaning of the *Manifesto*'s designation of the bourgeoisie as revolutionary. 'The bourgeoisie cannot exist without constantly revolutionizing the instruments of production, and thereby relations of production, and with them the whole relations of society.' Consider, moreover, the very contemporary ring that our present day experience of the globalization of capitalism lends to a description penned a century and half ago:

> The need of a constantly expanding market for its products chases the bourgeoisie over the whole surface of the globe. It must nestle everywhere, settle everywhere, establish connections everywhere. . . [It] has drawn from under the feet of industry the national ground on which it stood. All old-established national industries have been destroyed or are daily being destroyed. They are dislodged by new industries, whose introduction becomes a life and death question for all civilized nation. . . [We] have intercourse in every direction, universal interdependence of nations. And as in material, so also in intellectual production. . . [The bourgeoisie] compels all nations, on pain of extinction, to adopt the bourgeois mode of production; it compels them to introduce what it calls civilization into their midst, i.e. to become bourgeois themselves. In one word, it creates a world after its own image.

To be sure, such developments in our own time also accompany and, to some significant extent, emerge out of the renewal of capitalist crises in our time. We live under the mark of a kind of global financial speculation that makes what Marx described in 1850 in France seem like small change. This rampant speculation, together with the Third World debt crisis and unwieldy deficits of advanced capitalist states, stands astride the revolutionary era of the micro-chip in production and communication. The return to the heartlands of the bourgeois order of mass unemployment in the course of the crisis of the mid-1970s and early 1980s remains all too visible over our shoulders. State macroeconomic planning and domestic and international trade and commerce regulation are still under assault just when they appear to be most needed to ensure a modicum of stability. The edifice appears precarious indeed not only to Marxist economists but to *The Wall Street Journal*. They watch, whether with bated breath or wringing hands, for another 'great crash', even as they marvel at the stock exchange recovery from October 1987. And all this invites us to ask of the bourgeoisie's 'revolutionary part' in our own time whether it is not still, again in the words of the *Manifesto*, 'paving the way for more extensive and more exhaustive crises', all the while 'diminishing the means whereby crises are prevented.' Is it not now more than ever possible that the bourgeoisie 'is like the sorcerer who is no longer able to control the powers of the nether world whom he has called up by his spells'?

Perhaps. To say the bourgeoisie continues to play a revolutionary part, in the sense we have drawn from the *Manifesto*, is at the same time to say that the renewed dynamism of the bourgeoisie in every epoch emerges out of the contradictions that spawn capitalist crises. 'Constant revolutionizing of production, uninterrupted disturbances of all social conditions, everlasting uncertainty and agitation distinguish the bourgeois epoch from all earlier ones.' All these are present together, and to say the bourgeoisie remains revolutionary is really just to say that we continue to live in the bourgeois epoch. The reemergence of capitalist crises, the demise of Keynesianism, the class war from above prosecuted in the name of market freedom has undermined the post-war social democratic notions of an eternally stable, harmonious, 'mixed-economy', 'organized' capitalism. But must we not also cast aside such notions as 'capitalism in its death throes' or even 'late capitalism'? For even as the bourgeoisie increasingly merges and conglomerates, concentrates capital and socializes production and communication on a global scale, and even as this very concentration and socialization seems to lay the bases for new capitalist crises, so it remains the case that capitalism is still driven by competition over rates of profit, even among global giants. It is this competition that is the source of the contemporary evidence that to exist the bourgeoisie must be revolutionary in production, and in the changes it brings to relations in society more generally. It is one thing to say that capitalist development is inherently rent by its own contradictions: that remains the great insight of Marxism. But what is wrong about fatalistic breakdown expectations is not just that capitalism has consistently outlived them, but that they ignore the fact that the bourgeoisie is distinctive among ruling classes historically precisely because it cannot exist without 'constantly revolutionizing. . .'

The bourgeoisie's continuing 'revolutionary part' should certainly not be associated with unadulterated notions of 'progress'. The ecological damage being visited on the globe demonstrates how market competition pushes us against the limits of nature in a manner that is more horrific than it is 'progressive'. Barbaric social conditions, moreover, exist not only in the Third World's all too common combination of degrading poverty and brutal dictatorship. They also exist in the heartlands of capitalism, above all in the social and physical devastation of the inner cities, in the combination of unemployment and racism and the culture of violence, drug gangs and police repression that attends them. Across the river from the new palace of gold that is the Trump Tower in Manhattan lies the inhumane devastation of the Bronx. The point to be drawn from this, however, is not that capitalism is closer to 'barbarism' than it was in the 1840s when Marx and Engels celebrated the wonders accomplished by the bourgeoisie even as the conditions of inhumane life in Manchester were fresh in their minds. Both the wonders and the degradation existed simultaneously as evidence of the bourgeoisie's being the first class 'to show what man's activity can bring about'. The point is that both characteristics still simultaneously exist. In the bourgeois epoch, the bourgeoisie is always both revolutionary and barbaric. The market freedom that unleashes the wonders of the micro-chip upon Wall Street, and much more generally on production and communication, is the same market freedom that devastates the Bronx. And the rich and the poor remain equally free to sleep under the exit ramps of the Expressway.

III

In relation to this, what can we say about the socialist 'spirit of revolution' as we approach the end of the twentieth century? The longing for a humane capitalism that would avoid the upheavals of revolution has predominantly defined the practice of the Left in the advanced capitalist countries for most of this century. But the politics of reformist compromise, however understandable, left in place a society in which the bourgeoisie continued to play the main part in production and communication, a society therefore subject to the competitive and contradiction-laden dynamic of capitalism. Even the social democratic state, or the state of the New Deal, was condemned to riding that tiger, and as that state expanded, in its bureaucratic fashion, to meet the minimal requirements of what was taken to define a humane capitalism, it became, for capital, a source of contradiction itself.

The discourse that defined the politics of compromise went as follows: why insist on the old revolutionary means, when the ends of socialism can be secured without them? Yet the politics of compromise could have no other effect than leaving the commanding heights of the economy in capitalist hands, and leaving the state itself far too insulated from popular pressures and controls beyond the electoral and lobbying devices of liberal democracy to be able to resist the bourgeoisie's assertion of its primacy. After decades of searching for a bourgeoisie that would meet the requirements of a humane capitalism, that discourse now is threadbare: the bourgeoisie's continuing revolutionary part demonstrates that the ends cannot be achieved without the means. The case for trying to define and practise a consistent socialist politics, and for marshalling the nerve to go all the way through with it –

that is, of *taking capital away from the bourgeoisie and democratizing control over the instruments and processes of production and communication to the end of transforming their content and function* – is reinforced by the bourgeois revolution from above in our time. As Raymond Williams suggested, this is not because it can now be shown to be quicker or more exciting, and certainly not because capitalism is about to succumb to its own contradictions so that all socialists need to do is proclaim the fact, but because *no other way is possible*.

But to say that no other way is possible is not to say that socialism itself is possible. We are often given to think today of socialism's failures in terms of the record of post-revolutionary regimes, their disappointment of original aspirations and promises, if not much worse; or in terms of the less heroic, indeed often abject, entrapment of social democracy within the capitalist framework. But from another perspective, socialism's failure stands out in the sense of the absence, especially in the advanced capitalist countries, of that *conscious, organized and creative movement for a democratic, cooperative and classless society which, in so far as it is an expression of massive popular support, is the* sine qua non *of realizing socialist aspirations, of the making of a socialist revolution*. To recognize this is to come face to face with one of the most sobering facts that must confront socialists at the end of the twentieth century.

Such frustration is only partially tempered once viewed in a more global perspective. Socialist revolutions there have been in the Third World in our time, from Angola and Mozambique to Grenada and Nicaragua. Indeed it has been argued, quite plausibly, that the determination of capitalist politicians like Reagan and Thatcher to redouble the effort to create a world after their own image can be seen to derive, to no small extent, from the 'explosive impact of the new wave of Third World revolutions in the seventies. . .' From 1974, after a decade of containment and/or defeat of anti-imperialist struggles, '[a] cascade of Third World revolutions, some socialist, some radically nationalist in orientation, broke out. In the space of six years some fourteen states witnessed seizures of power by insurrectionary movements.'[5] The international solidarity that has been shown to Angola or Nicaragua right through the 1980s – not only by Cuba, but by many people in the advanced capitalist countries that go well beyond the left as traditionally defined – has been admirable. In the Americas the impact of Liberation Theology and common opposition to Reagan's counter-revolutionary 'freedom fighters' has created a renewed sense of interdependence among those struggling for fundamental change, and the beginnings of dialogue regarding complementary and mutually enriching forms of struggle.[6] But it cannot be denied that the impact of such an awareness and dialogue on the advanced capitalist societies remains small; while the new revolutionary regimes themselves, even where they have survived counter-revolutionary attacks and pressures, stand cramped as well as besieged, with their fate linked to the infinitely arduous and painful climb out of the abyss of dire poverty and underdevelopment. Not to mention, of course, the fact that some of the revolutions in the Third World, from the Pol Pot regime in Cambodia to Khomeini's regime in Iran, have themselves provided their own gruesome meanings to what we must understand by 'barbarism' today.

Viewing socialist possibilities in a global perspective also means taking into account the historic developments currently taking place in the Communist world. In particular, Gorbachev's 'revolution from above' seems to be leading the Soviet Union towards recovering through *glasnost* some of the spirit of revolution of 1917, and it is deservedly being watched closely by socialists everywhere. An image of 'actually existing socialism' which is more humane and democratic may help to liberate socialist aspirations in the West from the totalitarian connotions spawned not only by the rhetoric of the Cold War but by the terrible reality of Stalinism. But optimism must be tempered by the implications of a new era of detente for leaving revolutionary socialist movements and regimes in the Third World bereft of support in the face of repression and counter-revolution. And it must be tempered as well by the predominantly top-down nature of *perestroika* so far, as well by those aspects of it that are more inspired by norms of market efficiency than by democracy. Not only does this complement ideologically the free market practices and rhetoric that have emanated from a resurgent bourgeoisie in the West; it may also, especially if capital markets are the outcome of the reform in the East, presage a large-scale penetration by international capital of areas of the globe that have been heretofore closed off to it. The revolution from above in actually existing socialism is deeply ambiguous in many respects; but one of these is the difficulty of clearly distinguishing between those developments that are leading to a recovery of the socialist spirit of revolution and those that involve embracing the bourgeois one.

Neither revolutionary developments in the Third World nor in the Communist countries, then, provide an escape from directly addressing the difficult and sobering question of the all-too-visible crisis of socialism in the West. To put this problem in perspective, two things must immediately be said about this. First, that a distinction between two meanings of revolutionary socialism, of which many socialists in the West have long been cognizant, must still be borne in mind today. On the one hand, it may be taken to mean a fundamental transformation in the social order, however that transformation is brought about. On the other hand, it may also mean the overthrow of a system of government, the word 'overthrow' being intended to convey the notion of a sudden and violent political convulsion outside the existing constitutional channels. The two notions may be related, in so far as fundamental transformation may be impossible without such a political convulsion. But however this may be, the two meanings need to be differentiated; and it is undoubtedly true that the overwhelming majority of the population of advanced capitalist countries, including the overwhelming majority of the working classes, has shunned revolutionary change in the second meaning of the term. There have very occasionally been circumstances when something approximating to a revolutionary situation has occurred in one or another such country. But, even then, an essential ingredient to the overthrow of the system of government has usually been missing, namely the presence of a revolutionary party capable of developing extensive popular sympathy and support, and determined to use the situation to take power. Social democratic parties in this century never had such an intention: this has been unambiguously clear since World War One, at least. And the Western Communist parties, certainly from the thirties onward, have also rejected out of hand what they denounced as ultra-left adventurism or petty bourgeois romanticism. Moreover, the attempts that were made to build such revolutionary parties by groups of a Trotskyist or Maoist persuasion in recent decades have proved largely barren.

In other words, revolutionary agencies with popular support have not existed in any significant sense for revolution-by-overthrow in these countries; and there is little reason to think that this will change in any relevant perspective. The fact may be deplored, viewed as the most blatant example of false consciousness in the people and of parliamentary cretinism and rank opportunism in the leadership of socialist and communist parties. Or it may be applauded as a demonstration of maturity and wisdom, a recognition of the fact that, given the relation between state and civil society in the West, given the very nature of hegemony, the notion of revolution by 'seizing' and 'overthrowing' the 'state' is meaningless, absurd. But deplored or applauded, so it nevertheless is.

The second point that needs to be made, however, is that the absence of significant popular support for revolution-by-overthrow cannot be taken to mean absence of popular support for socialist aspirations altogether, even in our time. It is worthwhile recalling, at the end of this decade, that the 1980s opened with the programmes for socialist change figuring centrally on the political agenda in a good number of western countries: Mitterand's and the Common Progamme's 1981 victory in France; the Wage Earners' Fund proposals in Sweden; the short 'march to power' of PASOK in Greece; the strength of the socialist left in the Labour Party in Britain, with that Left occupying governmental office in Europe's largest city. These developments did not appear out of thin air. They were the indirect products of the spirit of 1968, of the post-Cold War generation that spawned the New Left and the industrial militancy of the late 1960s and early 1970s. Such developments, connected as they were in the bourgeois mind with the apparent 'ungovernability' of this generation and with a rekindling of their old fears that they might lose any control over the state, were another factor in inducing the bourgeoisie's renewed determination to create the world in their own image.

Yet what is now all too evident is that there was a severe underestimation, on the one hand, of the hegemonic capacity of capitalist forces; and, on the other hand, an overestimation of the enthusiasm of the masses and the solidarity and/or commitment of the leadership. The recently renewed disappointments regarding an electoral road to socialism in the West in the 1980s have combined with a growing disaffection from classical revolutionary approaches, even among those elements on the Left that put so much effort into reviving them in the 1970s, to produce, in the face of the bourgeois revolution from above in this decade, the confusion and hesitancy among socialists which we identified at the beginning of this essay.

Less weight may be given to the claims that there has taken place a great and irreversible ideological shift among the bulk of the population of a kind that betokens massive and deep popular support for the bourgeois revolution from above. It is probably the case that the socialist electoral options put forward in a number of European countries were unable to garner positive support from more than a quarter of the electorate at the very most (with the rest of their support coming in the form of a negative vote against the bourgeois options). But it is worthwhile setting against this the fact that even the most ardent and successful of the bourgeois 'revolutionaries' could hardly claim anything like absolute majorities. The Reagan victories in 1980 and 1984, of Bush in 1988, of Thatcher in 1979, 1983 and 1987, were all won with the support of something in the order of one-third of the population entitled to vote. And they took place against the backdrop of the failures and retreats of earlier liberal or social democratic parties in government in the 1970s.

Still, there is small comfort to be drawn from this as matters now stand. In many countries of Europe, there has occurred a distinct loss of support for, and commitment to, traditional parties of the Left in the eighties: and even where such parties have been able to stage an electoral recovery, this has certainly not occurred on the basis of their seeking popular endorsement for socialist aspirations and programmes. At best, they have presented themselves as offering a moderate defence of the welfare state against the radical excesses of the renewed bourgeois spirit of revolution. Meanwhile, in places like Australia or New Zealand, such parties really do seem determined in government to prove that they can make the market economy run better than can the bourgeois parties.

Where does this then leave the socialist aspiration for fundamental change in the West? It is hardly surprising that one of the most notable characteristics of much of the Left in recent years has been the deep pessimism which the question evokes. Again and again, the same theme in different versions is heard, namely that even the advocacy of socialism is politically damaging and doomed to relegate its advocates to a marginal and ineffectual ghetto. The tactical and strategic accent, on this view, has to fall on a moderate pragmatism and on the defence and possible extension of old reforms in a manner that does not offend the sensibilities of those seduced by the appeal of the bourgeois revolution from above of the 1980s. Where Reagan and Thatcher proclaim 'we were all revolutionaries' in the bourgeois meaning of the term, large sections of the Left think it best to disclaim emphatically any association at all with revolutionary aspirations, even if these are conceived as being realized within existing constitutional channels. Are we to be left, then, with nothing other than the kind of opposition than that offered by Dukakis who, accused in the first televised debate by Bush of being a card-carrying member of the American Civil Liberties Union, could offer no more eloquent defence of the tradition of American liberalism than to say this was, after all, an organization which defended Ollie North? Are we merely to follow social democratic politicians such as Neil Kinnock in promising, as he did to the 1988 Labour Party conference, 'to run the market economy better than the Tories?' Better, to be fair, is intended to mean in a less barbaric and more just, less privatized and more state-interventionist, manner. And the liberal tradition does accord the right of defence even to the likes of Ollie North. But the debate is conducted on the terms set by the 'revolutionaries' of the Right. The socialist 'spirit of revolution' in the West is marked largely by its absence, or at least by its extreme marginality.

IV

Here, then, lies a great paradox of our time. The continuing revolutionary part played by the bourgeoisie has undermined the politics of compromise that sustained social democracy and liberal reformism in their search for a humane capitalism. This ought to make the ethical and logical basis for socialist aspirations and commitment stronger than ever. But at the same time, even the advocacy of socialism is more than ever marginalized within the societies of advanced capitalism.

What this means, first of all, is that the major political formations on the Left, which altogether dominated the labour movements and progressive intelligentsia of the advanced capitalist countries, are in the grips of a deep crisis of ideology, programme and policy, with all the tensions and uncertainties this is bound to engender. Moreover, the global competitive thrust of the bourgeoisie and the restructuring of industry that goes with it, has exposed anew the trade union constituencies of these parties to that competition, weakening the institutional base that provided support to the old politics of compromise. The leaders of these parties, and the intellectuals associated with them, desperately cling to the example of the Scandinavian societies, especially Sweden, as evidence that their project is still feasible. But to do this they must ignore the pull that the new era of bourgeois revolution, ideologically as well as materially, has had on the Swedish bourgeoisie itself, and which is causing much concern to Swedish social democrats. They must pretend, moreover, that all that is needed to replicate Sweden's social democratic state elsewhere in the West is to adopt this or that Swedish 'policy', technocratically conceived. They forget that the dense institutional organization of the working class and cooperative movements that nurtured and sustained such policies emerged out of a cultural and political matrix, and a half-century of struggle and confrontation, which could only be now replicated elsewhere in the West with something very like a revolution. Many activists in these parties understand very well that a remobilization of support cannot be achieved on the basis of dry explanations of the detailed structure of the Swedish Labour Market Board. Even if that is where they too hope eventually to arrive, many of them understand that the first step in this direction entails, as it did originally in Sweden, promoting the capacity for self-organization and activism at the base, a process that requires some renewal of the 'spirit' of socialist revolution. But they are thwarted at every turn by the immediate-term electoral pragmatism that dictates the actions of those – and there are many at the base as well at the leadership levels – who still long to cling to the politics of compromise.

In the absence of any alternative, however, the weakening of the old political and industrial institutions that practised the politics of compromise only further exposes people to the vagaries of the ethos and reality of competition. To be sure, it provides an opening for remobilization and reorganization, but the immensity of the task – do we need to start all over again from scratch? – is daunting. Moreover, the failure of the Communist parties of the West, as well as of the Trotskyist and Maoist groups, promotes further ground for pessimism. Have not only the politics of liberal reform and social democracy proved a failure, but all possible variants of a consistent socialist politics?

To affirm this would be to retreat from the creative political role that socialist intellectuals can play. We are not confined, in recognising the inability of social democracy or liberal reformism to tame the capitalist tiger, to jump backwards towards the practice of the Communists or Trotskyists or Maoists in the West, just because they too discerned the limits of the politics of compromise. There is no reason why socialists in the West today cannot reconsider the strategic possibilities of a consistent socialist politics free of the old preoccupations with sectarian debates over the lessons to be drawn from 'classical' revolutions which occurred in societies where the peasantry still formed the bulk of the population; free of the stultifying organizational structures of democratic centralism; free of the rigid teleological theories that posited an inevitable and imminent capitalist breakdown matched by an equally inevitable proletarian 'seizure' of the state; and indeed, free of the simple positing of 'soviet democracy' in stark opposition to representative democracy.

In early 1919 (at what appeared to many then and, looking back, also to many today to be the high water mark of socialist revolutionary possibilities in this century), the founder of modern social democracy in Canada, J.S. Woodsworth, entered into the debate then raging among Canadian socialists – the same debate that was raging elsewhere in the West – over Bolshevik versus Social Democratic strategy. Inspired by the British Labour

Party's explicit adoption of socialist objectives in 1918, Woodsworth took the latter side in the debate, but he nevertheless averred:

> Our ultimate aim must be a complete turnaround of the present economic and social system. In this we recognise our solidarity with the workers of the world over. . . Such a change, we hope, will be accomplished by means of education, organization, and the securing by workers of the machinery of government.
>
> Revolution may appear to come more slowly [in Britain than in Russia] but there will be no counter-revolution. . . It may take a few years to work out, but when its done its done for good.[7]

In light of what Thatcher has undone in respect to the reforms that Labour Governments had introduced, some will now find it tempting to mock Woodsworth's words. Yet to see these words as nothing but a cover for the merest reformist ambitions would be a mistake. While some would point to the explicitly counter-revolutionary behaviour of the German Social Democratic leaders in the very year the above words were written, there are no good grounds to taint thereby the sincere intentions of a great many of those who set out on the path of fundamental social change within the existing constitutional framework of liberal democracy. Indeed, in one crucial respect, and for the reasons we have already indicated, the premise that underlay the social democratic position, that an insurrectionary strategy was impossible in the West, must be recognized as having been fundamentally correct.

We must surely, finally, escape from the simplistic dualisms that have bedevilled the Left throughout this century. The Left has beaten itself up, sometimes quite literally, with debates over parliamentarism *versus* extra-parliamentarism, reform *versus* revolution, and most notoriously even today, party *versus* movement, as if one ruled out the other, black and white, or, rather, grey and red. Such dualisms are terribly misleading. Posing the issues this way gets us nowhere. The question is not parliamentarism *versus* extra-parliamentarism, but what kind of parliamentarism will not give rise to the illusion that all people need to do – all they ought to do – is vote for representatives who will then put everything right. The real problem regarding parliamentarism occurs when the point of seeking election becomes only to offer a 'team' of leaders who refuse to use their platform to engage in socialist mobilization and education. The question is not, by the same token, reform *versus* revolution, but what kinds of reforms, including reform in 'the machinery of government' itself, produce the structural changes that can be said to be revolutionary, i.e. that can not be so readily undone as to tempt one to mock the aspiration that 'when its done its done for good'. And most important, the question is not party *versus* movement, but what kind of party, in what relationship to the state, on the one hand, and to party members and supporters, on the other, can sustain an organized thrust for education, organization and participation over the broadest possible range of popular struggles for social justice; so that the intellectual and organizational capacities that are nurtured thereby yield the popular resources and support which are, in the end, the essential condition for revolutionary change – even when elections are won.

V

All this, of course is more easily said than done. We noted at the outset of this essay that the very meaning of socialist change was probably more open today in terms of objectives, social forces and agencies than it has ever been in this century. This is less a cause for alarm or pessimism than it is an opportunity for creative socialist thinking and action. Although most recent reflections and polemics on the crisis of socialism in the West have focused on the question of what is wrong about traditional socialist conceptions in terms of objectives and social forces, it may be more pertinent to focus on the problem of agency, in particular of party. This is because agency is the mediating variable between social forces and objectives, the nodal point through which the two intersect. It is also because the crisis of socialism, posed in terms of whether there is any longer a significant constituency for socialist change, is bound up with the crisis of agency, i.e. the role parties and movements play not just in the representation of pre-given identities with 'objective' interests, but in the very formation of identities and in the articulation of interests of social groups.

It is appropriate in this context to turn back, for a moment, to the *Communist Manifesto*. There is clearly much irony in the fact that the claims it made regarding the revolutionary vocation of the working class look quite shop-worn alongside the insights that text still affords on the revolutionary part played by the contemporary bourgeoisie. Marx and Engels, while predicting ever greater and more insoluble capitalist crises, and incapable of imagining themselves in 1848 that the bourgeoisie would still play 'a most revolutionary part' at the end of the twentieth century, did not, of course, expect that socialism would emerge like a phoenix from the ashes of capitalist breakdown. On the contrary, the key to a socialist future lay in the organization of the working classes that developed on the basis of the wage labour called into existence by the bourgeoisie as the essential condition for the augmentation of its capital. The argument that in calling into existence these modern proletarians the bourgeoisie had produced 'its own gravediggers' did not rest on any notion (as it has recently become quite fashionable to argue in today's confused intellectual climate on the Left) that these modern proletarians carried revolutionary consciousness in their genes. What gave the bourgeoisie its historically revolutionary part was *competition*; what gave the proletarians their revolutionary part was *organization*. The conditions for such organization were in part established by the bourgeoisie itself, as it brought many workers together under one roof, and subjected them to similar conditions of life. It also provided means of communication that laid the basis for contact among workers of different localities, whereby they connected together their numerous local struggles against low or fluctuating wages, against appalling working conditions and despotism in production, against restraints on workers' freedom of association, and against the exclusion of the propertyless from the new structures of representative government that the bourgeoisie had fashioned for itself in relation to the state.

The *Manifesto*'s prediction on the revolutionary implications of working class organization long appeared to be remarkably prescient. Imagine what bells it rang for people at the turn of the century to come across the *Manifesto* and to read: 'Now and then the workers are victorious, but only for a time. The real fruit of their battle lies not in the immediate result, but in the ever expanding union of the workers. . . . And that union, to attain which the burghers of the Middle Ages, with their miserable highways, required cen- turies, the modern proletarians, thanks to railways, achieve in a few years.' Even if 'a few years' had to be taken metaphorically, can we not understand why it appeared to socialists that 'every class struggle is a political struggle' just when the earlier local and craft organization of workers seemed indeed to be giving way to the 'organization of the proletarians into a class, and consequently into a political party. . .'?

Someone reading the Manifesto in South Korea today – or watching the rise of COSATU in South Africa – might be excused it that idea sounded very fresh indeed. Why does it sound so stale, then, in the advanced capitalist countries? The clear passage, through the post-war years, of the overwhelm- ing majority of the population of *all* the western capitalist countries to the status of people who have to sell their labour to gain a livelihood within capitalism is incontrovertible. The feminization of the labour force is a most notable contemporary dimension of this, as is the growing absolute and rela- tive number of women in the membership of trade unions. Yet none of this any longer conjures up the image that 'what the bourgeoisie produces, above all, is its own gravediggers', at least in the advanced capitalist countries. It is not just that the metaphor of 'a few years' has been so badly stretched out of shape. Nor is it just that vast and growing sections of the 'white collar sector' remain unorganized, while the old industrial unionized sector is itself declining. The point is rather that it was wrong to claim *ever* that 'the advance of industry. . . replaces the isolation of the labourers, due to competition, by their *revolutionary* combination, due to association' and that it 'therefore, cuts from under its feet the very foundation on which the bourgeoisie produces and appropriates products.' The isolation overcome via collective bargaining simply does not do this, in and of itself. Trade unions are not by themselves 'schools for socialism'. Association for the purpose of collective bargaining is just that, i.e. it is about bargaining over the price and conditions of wage labour, not over its abolition. And if this is what makes it compatible with the continuation of the bourgeois epoch, it also is what makes it subject to assault in a new era of capitalist competition and restructuring, the kind of era we are living through today.

This would not have been news to Marx and Engels, of course: their revolutionary aspirations often carried them away in their rhetoric, especially in 1848. Indeed, even in the face of such rhetoric, the *Manifesto*'s deep insight into what continuing capitalist competition and restructuring means for working class organization still jumps out at us: 'This organization of the proletarians into a class, and consequently into a political party, is continually being upset again by the competition between the workers themselves.' Our confidence must be shaken in the notion, however, that 'it constantly ever rises up again, stronger, firmer, mightier.' Our confidence in this must be shaken not only because of the bourgeoisie's continually revolutionary part, but because of what else has been disconfirmed alongside the confirmation of what the *Manifesto* had to say about the development of the working class. The identity of workers, even organized workers, even politically conscious workers, has not been something that has erased other identities, sometimes, indeed often, more immediately compelling identities in social and political terms. The *Manifesto*'s notion that '[d]ifferences of age and sex have no longer any distinctive social validity for the working class' is plainly wrong, if it was meant to be taken as an empirical statement. The same must be said, *a fortiori*, about race and about national identity, and, to some extent as well, about ethnicity and religion.

The point is not only, moreover, that significant differences have always persisted in terms of wages and conditions of work along many of these dimensions even in common places of work as well as across job ghettos; nor is it just that significantly different conditions of life separate workers along these dimensions in the context of patriarchy, residential segregation, relations to the agencies of social and state control, marginality on the labour market and so on. Nor even is it that the bourgeoisie has played on these differences to ensure that the competition among workers essential to capitalism's existence persists. Nor even again that working class organizations, industrial, political and cultural, have institutionalized these differences. It is rather that the identities that exist and are reproduced along each of these dimensions cannot be, *and should not be*, effaced in so far as they also require organization and autonomy if the groups in question (even if the majority of them are also workers) are to be able to prosecute struggles against discrimination and oppression.

All of this pertains directly to the problem that has been exercising the minds of a good many socialists of late, namely the view that the root of the inability to develop a sustained and creative socialist practice lies in false assumptions about the revolutionary potential of the working class. Having been for so long seen as the fount of the realization of socialism, a political practice that grounds itself centrally in the working class is now seen by many as the obstacle to fundamental social transformation. There are really two versions to this by now quite common theme. The first focuses on the sociological decomposition of the old industrial working class in occupational, residential and cultural terms, and discerns in this the roots of 'the forward march of labour halted'. Out of this analysis comes a renewed call, in the face of bourgeois revolution from above in the 1980s, to revive something akin to the popular front strategy of the 1930s, targetting an electoral alliance between the elites of now weakened traditional political and industrial institutions of the working class with whatever bourgeois elites can be weaned away from the barbarism of Thatcherism or Reaganism towards a renewal of the politics of compromise. The second version goes beyond the first by challenging the notion of a distinct working class 'interest' in socialism, or indeed in anything else. Strategically, it is less concerned with alliances among elites, but, taking its cue from the relative vitality of new social movements, looks to an 'articulation' of diverse social groups, with the emphasis placed less on traditionally socialist solutions and more on completing the unfinished business of the liberal democratic revolution begun in 1789. Although the two consistently intertwine, the first version inflects back towards social democratic state interventionism and tripartite corporatism; the second version inflects towards strengthening a rather loosely defined 'civil society' against the state and capital.

Yet there is another way of looking at the problem. What becomes clear from a rereading of the *Manifesto* is not just how wrong Marx and Engels were to let their revolutionary aspirations carry them away to the point that they allowed their great insights on the historical development of capital and labour to lead them to the conclusion that '[the bourgeoisie's] fall and the victory of the proletariat are equally inevitable'. What also becomes clear is that such a claim *only* makes sense in light of the very next dimension of revolution that the *Manifesto* addresses. That dimension is the critical role played by political parties in '*the formation of the proletariat into a class.*' Only once this dimension is introduced can Marx and Engels' understanding of the bourgeoisie's continuing revolutionary role as a condition of that class's continued existence, and their sharp awareness of the vagaries that attend workers' struggles within the bounds of competition, be squared with their confidence in the revolutionary potential of the working class.

Little actual analysis of this followed in the *Manifesto*, however. Rather what followed was a brilliant polemic directed against the bourgeoisie. But once we accept the idea that capitalism does not of itself self-destruct, and that a homogeneous working class identity is neither possible, nor even desirable, then the work that parties do in the formation of the identity of the working class becomes the critical variable in the realization of socialism. The question becomes whether such parties, as they emerge out of the limited degree and form of working class identity and solidarity that develops spontaneously and through trade union organization within capitalism, can transform that identity and solidarity into a force that can realize the possibility of socialist revolution. To say this is certainly not to say they actually or inevitably do it, of course. On the contrary, what we need to analyze, at the end of the twentieth century, is what they have done and why, and what else they might have done or could do to realize socialist possibilities.

The failure to address the question of the party's role in class formation and identity at all seriously has been the most surprising aspect of that vast literature that has been produced in the 1980s on the strategic lessons that must be gleaned from how and why the working class has failed to be the fount of socialist change. The classic texts of Marxist politics at the turn of the century, in particular, have been pilloried for assuming that the working class was innately revolutionary; but the actual work that socialist parties did (or did not do) in relation to *forming* the political and ideological identities of the working class has hardly been examined. One might think that those who put an emphasis on the importance of 'discursive practices' in the formation of social and political subjects would want to undertake such enquiry, but their work has usually been highly theoretically abstract rather than what Gramsci called 'empirico-historical'. The result, of course, is that despite their disdain for 'impressionist and sociologistic descriptivism'[8], the writings of the 'discourse' school has been particularly laden with *exactly* such impressionistic descriptivism in their discussion of the actual practice of working class parties (as opposed to the 'texts' of socialist intellectuals). This is also true of their discussion of the new social movements. For all of their emphasis on the importance of 'articulation' among a plurality of social forces themselves formed through discursive practice, the actual relation between leaders and led in social movements has been substantively ignored. So has been the way in which bourgeois hegemony operates to reinfuse with bourgeois norms and values even those people who happen to construct their identity in terms of 'struggles against oppression', so that these movements often limit their struggle to securing for their supporters the mode and extent of opportunity, independence and consumption afforded to the bourgeoisie itself.

If our objective is a socialist strategy that pertains to the overcoming of capitalism and the building of a new house in which freedom and equality might dwell, then we cannot leave substantively undiscussed the role that 'the articulators of the articulation' would have to play – nor can we ignore what organizational forms this would have to take – in order to develop out of the experiences of black and white, female and male, young and old people *who also have their labour for sale* a modicum of common understanding of the way capitalism works as a system; and a modicum of a common sense of class identity and of common fundamental divergence of interests from the bourgeoisie. For in addition to the need for respect and tolerance for the experiences that make people's identities so rich in their differences, there is also needed a sense of their common exploitation (when they are able to sell their labour) or their common marginalization (when they cannot). The link between socialism, class consciousness and class struggle lies not in the reductionist mind of the Marxist, as so many would have it today: it lies in the nature of capitalism, the system that socialists are committed to try to transcend. For two central conditions of the bourgeoisie's existence – and continuing revolutionary part – are competition, including competition among workers, on the one hand; and, on the other, the exploitation of people who must sell their capacity to labour. The role parties or movements play in forming common class identities and perceptions of interest is an important (although not sufficient) determinant of realizing socialist possibilities precisely because it pertains to undermining these conditions of the bourgeoisie's continued existence.

It is, of course, possible to read the revolutionary classic texts of the turn of the century, given the idiom they were wont to use, in a manner that sees them as portraying political practice in terms of parties playing out nothing but pure Jacobin-style vanguardism; or, at the other extreme, as being nothing but the bearers of innate revolutionary aspirations of working class people. But such readings miss that dimension of socialist thought and practice which understood political organization neither in terms of the formation of a self-contained crack-troop of revolutionaries, nor in terms of the merely passive representation of pre-formed class consciousness, but rather as the very arena in which hegemonically-oriented class identity and consciousness were formed. In any case, precisely because they were traversing such virgin terrain, those who were the embattled leaders of the mass working class parties, which were, after all, an entirely new phenomenon in history, should hardly have been taken – on the basis of pamphlets and speeches wherein polemic and analysis were inevitably very much admixed – as providing the last word on the subject. Much less should they so be taken today either by those who pillory them for their faults or by those who treasure them for their insights.

Writing in 1922, Lukács appropriately began his essay, 'Towards a Methodology of the Problem of Organization', with the following words:

> Although there have been times when problems of organisation stood at the forefront of debate (e.g. when conditions of amalgamation were under discussion), it nevertheless remains true that theorists have paid less attention to such questions than to any others. The idea of the Communist Party. . . has yet often been seen purely in *technical* terms rather than one of the most important *intellectual* questions of the revolution. . . [N]o really vital theoretical energy seemed to be left over for the task of anchoring the problem of organization in communist theory. If much activity in this sphere is correct, this is due more to correct revolutionary instincts than to any clear theoretical insight. On the other hand, there are many false tactical attitudes, e.g. in the debates on a united front, which derive from a mistaken view of the problems of organization.'9

This essay by Lukács, now much ignored, still bears careful reading today. In many ways what he had to say in this essay is not very far different from another great revolutionary theorist of the 1920s who carried much further still the analysis of the role of party in revolutionary change, Antonio Gramsci. Attention has been properly paid to the 'war of position' versus 'war of manoeuvre' in the West, to the problem of ideology, to the concept of hegemony and to the question of 'alliances'. But the issue that concerned him most, the issue that pervaded his whole work, i.e. the determining role (and proper organizational form) of the mass party, of the 'Modern Prince', not only in the formation of appropriate strategy for socialist change, but in the creation of the collective will to change, above all in the working class itself, has gotten much less attention in this decade of socialist confusion and hesitation. If we paid more attention to the stress he laid on 'the importance and significance which, in the modern world, political parties have in the elaboration and diffusion of conceptions of the world'; and if we addressed the limits and failures of the predominant working class parties in this respect; then we would probably learn far more about 'what is to be done' than from dwelling on the sociological decline of the industrial working class or the proliferation of 'identities'.

In Gramsci's conception, the main role of the mass party, was not that of putting forward a team of political leaders, as broadly representative as possible of public opinion in an electoral contest. Nor was it that of forging a small band of revolutionaries. Nor was it that of coordinating a 'network' of alliances. Its main role – and its organizational form and political philosophy had to be forged in relation to this role – was that of

> . . . elaborating its own component parts – those elements of a social group that have been born and developed as an 'economic' group – and turning them into qualified political intellectuals, leaders and organizers of all the activities and functions inherent in the organic development of an integral society, both civil and political. . . That all members of a political party should be regarded as intellectuals is an affirmation that can easily lend itself to mockery and caricature. But if one thinks about it nothing could be more exact. There are of course distinctions to be made. A party might have a greater or lesser proportion of its members in the higher grades or in the lower, but this is not the point. What matters is the function, which is directive and organisational, i.e. educative, i.e. intellectual.[10]

Only with such a conception of what it means for parties to aim at 'the formation of the proletariat into a class' can we conceive of realizing socialist aspirations. It may, of course, not be possible. But we need to ask, as a priority, whether socialist parties have been oriented this way and, if not, whether it is now possible to create parties and movements that are. It is symptomatic of the current crisis of the Left, of the retreat from the creative role that socialist intellectuals can play, not only that this question has been so little addressed, but that on the few occasions it has been addressed, the tendency has been to substitute a mechanistic and pessimistic 'inevitability of failure' for the earlier mechanistically optimistic 'inevitability of revolution'. For instance, this decade's single major comparative historical study of the interrelationship between party and class formation, Przeworski and Sprague's *Paper Stones*[11], sets out to prove that there is an insurmountable barrier to realizing socialist aspirations in the West. The role of socialist parties in organizing workers into the political and ideological force called the working class is appropriately stressed; and it is recognized that this in turn generates the possibility of structuring social and political conflict along lines that go to the core of a challenge to capitalist hegemony, since this hegemony is founded on the denial of the salience of class. But there is a catch, a trick of capitalist social structure, which when combined with political democracy, determines that the work that socialist parties do in relation to the formation of class identity and organization is inevitably frustrated. And this determines a miserable outcome for the aspiration to achieve socialism in the West.

What is this 'catch'? As for choosing democratic means, there was, in the West, no real choice for socialist parties. They had to participate in elections since votes offered a welcome and viable substitute ('paper stones') for the fraught and bloody confrontations of the barricades. But since elections are decided by numbers, the fate of socialism was sealed, since workers, according to the narrow definition adopted by Przeworski and Sprague, have always been a numerical minority. (Workers allegedly are only 'manual' employees in 'productive' industries; nonmanual employees in these industries, all employees in 'non-productive' industries, as well as the agricultural petite bourgeoisie are all defined as 'middle class'.) Consequently, to win elections socialist parties had to broaden their appeal to potential allies in the 'middle class' to achieve electoral success. They were therefore forced to cast their appeal in such a way that it undermined their ability to define politics, even for the workers they organized, in consistent class terms.

It is probably correct that the political practice of electoral socialist parties increasingly tended towards diminishing the salience of class identity among workers. But the question that needs to be asked is whether this occurred *because* of socialist parties electoral appeal to the broadly defined 'middle class'. Despite the transformation of white collar work amidst the passage of the vast majority of the population to the status of those who had to sell their labour to gain a livelihood, Przeworski and Sprague are able to cite attitudal surveys to show that even lower level and unionized salaried workers tend not to think of themselves as working class and that manual workers do not recognize them as such. But is it in fact objectively impossible for this to be otherwise? Przeworski and Sprague undertake no detailed analysis of the nature of the appeal made by socialist parties to salaried or non-productive workers, or how it coincided with or differed from the appeal they made to allegedly 'real' workers. In fact, they do not undertake any systematic examination of the actual ideological and organizational transformations of the parties in question. The strategies they ascribe to parties are largely intuited from the distribution of votes, as embellished only by the odd reference to this or that phrase in a party programme. Other factors that might account for the attenuation of the parties' role in the formation of class identity, apart from the alleged minority status of ('productive') workers, are not systematically treated. Perhaps the parties diluted their class appeal (with appeals to nationalism, to local particularism, to deference to 'expertise', to moderation and consensus) because they sought to gain (the easy way, i.e. on the terrain of a hegemonic bourgeois discourse) the votes of those many *manual industrial workers* who resisted or were at least unmoved by earlier 'pure' class appeals? Perhaps they diluted their class appeal because the leaders themselves came to adopt some of these values themselves? Perhaps their decision not only to engage in electoral competition, but to accept the very structure of *parliamentary* decision-making, embodying the Burkean notions of a sharp separation between decision-makers within the state and the class 'without', itself had the effect of disorganizing the class they organized electorally in terms of a class appeal? Perhaps these parties diluted their class appeal because they sought to strike a compromise with capitalists, or to rationalize such a compromise entered into pragmatically by their leaders while in state office?

In other words, among the constraints socialist parties faced in respect to the formation of the proletariat into a class, not only the limited votes of industrial manual workers need to be counted; or at least such electoral constraints can only be counted in the context of other and ultimately more daunting ones, above all the power of capital and its ability to disorganise workers through competition as well as through its material and ideological reach *among workers and among socialist party leaders*. In the face of this constraint, such class identity as these parties continued to develop even among manual industrial workers was based on a notion of class interest increasingly conceived within the framework of capitalism, Burkean parliamentarism and trade union identity. Some parties could for a considerable time retain electoral loyalties from many workers on this basis, especially where a strong trade union movement itself fostered continued working class identity. But it became disconnected from any attempt to identify class interest with socialism, or at the very least it involved a redefinition of socialism so that it effectively meant corporatist-style state planning for capitalist economic growth.

The last paragraph of Przeworski and Sprague's book is cast in broad enough terms to fit this interpretation: 'Leaders became representatives and the struggle for socialism was delegated to representatives. . . They succeeded in making the very possibility of socialist transformation seem so distant from our daily lives. . .' Nevertheless, they still give the impression that it would all have been different if industrial workers were a numerical majority; that it might yet be different if socialist parties could only drop their ties to the working class; or that elections should now be simply ignored by socialists. Such either/or options are not the stuff of effective strategy. The first requirement for such must surely be that the parties become once again committed to socialism as a goal, and that they recognize clearly the salience of class for effecting a challenge to capitalist hegemony. This means actively engaging once again in fostering working class identity (among 'productive' and 'non-productive' workers) in the face of a capitalism which constantly deconstructs and reconstructs industry, occupation and locale. But it means above all (here we must learn well what Gramsci taught) developing the capacity among their members and supporters to offer socialist leadership in their communities in relation to multifarious forms of subordination, deprivation and struggle. This is not a matter of imposing a rigid set of socialist maxims on every struggle; it is a matter of developing the capacity to organize in a manner that relates socialist understanding and commitment to the problems and struggles of everyday life; and to engage in political discourse in a manner that is educative and that recasts and challenges the terms of capitalist hegemony.

VII

We turn, finally, from questions pertaining to whether constituencies for socialism can be fashioned by appropriate socialist agencies, to the question of socialist goals today. Here too, as we observed at the outset, hesitation and even pessimism are usually the order of the day. A recognition that social democratic reforms were inadequate to stay the 'revolutionary part' played by the bourgeoisie, forms some grounds, even among those who cling to the politics of compromise, for this hesitation and pessimism. If the answer to this is offered by socialists that these reforms had to be structured in a manner that led to popular support for taking capital away from the bourgeoisie, however, this answer then confronts another problem. For there is a widespread sense, in the context of the internationalization and globalization of production and finance which has advanced with extreme speed in recent years, that 'nationalization' – the word itself is significant – is no longer capable of laying hold of such integrated means of production as would lay the basis for coherent production or socialist planning. In other words, in so far as the locus of political power and democratic participation remains at the level of the nation state, the question is posed of whether, even if a socialist party were strongly legitimated at the polls, a socialist government could proceed very far to install a socialist programme in a world of international capitalism, where production itself, let alone finance and commerce, is increasingly and ever more tightly intermeshed. On top of all this, the turn to markets in the countries of 'actually existing socialism' seems to many in the West to proclaim once and for all that socialism, as a viable alternate economic system to capitalism, is a non-starter. We argued above that today's bourgeois revolution ought to reinforce on both ethical and logical grounds the basis for a commitment to socialism. Many would grant the ethical grounds; far fewer would grant the logical ones.

There are no easy answers to these problems, any more than there are to the problems of constituency and agency. What must first of all be said, however, is that in so far that these problems lead socialists straight back to the politics of compromise, then this is obviously no answer at all. It is not that reforms were not worthy. Who could say this about *social citizenship* reforms, which established rights in civil society such as education, health care, freedom of association? Or *redistributive reforms* such as old age pensions, social security, progressive taxation? Or *regulatory reforms* such as occupational health and safety standards, pollution controls, hours of work and minimum wage regulations? And who could say this about *public ownership* reforms, whether of utilities or transportation, or coal mines or steel mills, or indeed of housing and land? The only problem with these reforms was that they did not go far enough. They could not go far enough without fomenting a political break with capital, which, for all the reasons we already identified, the politics of compromise could not sustain. It could not sustain this increasingly by the inclination of social democratic leaders themselves, but also by the fact, which was of course related to the question of leaders' inclinations, that the parties that conceived and introduced such reforms failed to prepare their constituencies for such a break. They therefore could not count on their support, much less on their 'intellectual' capacities (in Gramsci's sense) to take over the organizational and administrative functions which seeing through such a confrontation would have demanded.

In saying these reforms did not go far enough, this does not just mean in a *quantitative* sense: more universal rights; more progressive taxation and social benefits; more regulation of capital, of its products, of the labour process and of labour markets; more public ownership. We mean that the reforms that were introduced always *qualitatively* fell short of their promise. The rights to education were always compromised by a hierarchy in education, by restricted access to quality education and by the content of education that reflected the class society in which education was embedded. The laws which granted and sustained freedom of association for workers also always policed trade union behaviour and limited the range and scope of industrial struggle. What was given in the form of progressive taxation was taken away in incomes policies, sales taxes, and the absence of price controls even on basic necessities. The social benefits were administered in such a bureaucratic fashion that even those most dependent on them could hardly feel that the 'welfare state' was theirs to influence, let alone control. Unemployment insurance was usually just that: insurance which reproduced the labour market even as it regulated and subsidized its vagaries. (That is, to get it, in most cases, you needed to have been employed; you then needed to be fired or laid off; you then needed to be actively looking for work; and you then lasted on it only as long as your previous payment of 'stamps' allowed.) The regulation of capital and of production and of products was always compromised by the close intermeshing of the regulators and the regulated when it came to the bourgeoisie – and by the distance from the regulators when it came to workers or consumers. The public ownership was state ownership, with economic democracy being outlawed (or, in a few instances, trivialized) to such an extent that few workers or consumers could feel they were losing something that belonged to them even when privatisation threatened their livelihood or quality of service. There were many variations in the reforms introduced in the advanced capitalist states. Yes, Sweden was (and remains, mercifully) very different from the United States. That said, the picture we have drawn is more or less recognizable in all of them.

The reason for this was inscribed in the politics of compromise. Partly this was because the reforms had to be structured and to operate in a manner that sustained capital accumulation and business confidence. But partly it was also because a dimension of reform, which would have radically transformed every one of the others mentioned, *the democratic reform of the machinery of government itself*, was absent. A reform in the state's own *modus operandi*, which would have meant the integration of popular representation and administration, and the control of the representative through recall and regular turnover, was very rarely conceived within the social democratic project. Whether this was because of a lack of imagination, or a sincere belief that parliamentary democracy was the end point of democracy, or the oligarchy that developed in social democratic parties, remains an old but still interesting question. Or did it, perhaps, above all reflect an *anticipation*, conceived subconsciously in the politics of social democratic gradualism and compromise, that capital would at all costs insist on the separation between decision makers and the people (short of the election of a political 'Board of Directors' every four or five years) lest the state set an example for the 'private sector' of a new form of decision making and administration which, if also struggled for and adopted in the 'private sector', would divest the bourgeoisie of its control over capital. After all, at least under 'nationalisation', it got compensated and could employ this liquid capital for accumulation elsewhere!

Was it then surprising that capitalist competition continued to underpin the whole structure of the society? And as the bourgeoisie adopted new directions and patterns of competition in, through, and around the 'interventionist' state, and as it entered new crises in the course of this competition, the 'interventionist' state found itself condemned to managing these crises in a manner that usually quantitatively as well as qualitatively retrenched on the earlier reforms. Was it then surprising that some of those who still nevertheless really benefited from the reforms could recognise in the bourgeoisie's new 'revolutionary' assault on the state some symbols that appeared to speak to their own alienation from it, although that alienation was very differently situated from that of the bourgeoisie? What is actually surprising is that so many people kept their heads, and saw through that aspect of the revolutionary rhetoric of Reagan and Thatcher that was indeed mendacious nonsense. This not only kept their vote at the absolute (if not relative) low level we spoke of, but it also restrained the inroads they could make against the old reforms.

Yet from the perspective of socialist goals, no matter how necessary it still is to defend the old reforms for what was always positive and humane about them, the project of restarting the motor of the old politics of compromise, even if the bourgeoisie could again find it in its interest to cooperate, is no

answer at all to the problems we identified. We must admit, however, that to
those other problems, we can offer no definitive answers. This is because any
attempt at socialist transition, once we conceive it as something other than the
inevitable outcome of implacable historical laws, *is* inherently risk-laden. It is
beset, as Rosa Luxemburg once famously put it, by 'a thousand problems'.
And that is why, as she insisted, the democratic freedoms of expression,
assembly and association are so necessary to finding 'the thousand solutions'
she hoped would also emerge. The main grounds for her optimism were not
different from Gramsci's (or, indeed, Marx's): they lay in the reliance on the
creativity of human beings (the same creativity that distinguished the architect
from the bee) and in the knowledge and experience that people might acquire
from organizing sufficiently well (not only *technically* but *intellectually*) to
make a revolution possible in the first place. To quote that famous passage:

> . . . we know more or less what we must eliminate at the outset in order to free the road
> for a socialist economy. But when it comes to the nature of the thousand concrete, practical
> measures, large and small, necessary to introduce socialist principles into economy, law and
> all social relationships, there is no key in any textbook. That is not a shortcoming but rather
> the thing that makes scientific socialism superior to the utopian variants. The socialist system
> of society should only be, and can only be, an historical product, born out of the school of its
> own experiences, born in the course of its realization, as a result of the developments of living
> history. . . The negative, the tearing down can be decreed; the building up, the positive cannot.
> New territory. A thousand problems. Only experience is capable of correcting and opening new
> ways. Only unobstructed, effervescent life falls into a thousand new forms and improvisations,
> brings to light creative force, itself corrects all mistaken attempts. The public life of all coun-
> tries with limited freedom is so poverty-stricken, so miserable, so rigid, so unfruitful, precisely
> because, through the exclusion of democracy, it cuts off the living sources of all spiritual riches
> and progress. . . The whole mass of the people must take part in it. Otherwise it will be decreed
> from behind a few official desks by a dozen intellectuals.[12]

Luxemburg was, of course, speaking to the Russian Revolution, as she
wrote these words. And these words are still germane in relation to the
pessimism on socialist possibilities induced by the turn to markets today in
'actually existing socialism'. If this is to be taken by socialists in the West
as the paradoxical proof that the Western bourgeoisie's almost century-long
aspiration to reverse the Russian Revolution is finally being realized, we
need at least to ask whether this is really because the horrendous problems
experienced by socialism in the USSR over the last 70 years was due to the
absence of market freedoms – or whether, as Luxemburg warned, it was due
to the absence of democratic freedoms. It is still far too soon to say whether
the salvation of that society, if there will be one at all, will lie in the 'icy calculations' of cost-accounting introduced through an economic *perestroika* from
above or in the democratic creativity induced by a political and intellectual
glasnost that takes root from below.

Is logic then really on the side of a commitment to socialism, after all? We
should probably not go so far as to claim this. We said earlier that socialists
cannot achieve their ends without the means, i.e. without taking capital away
from the bourgeoisie. The experience with the politics of compromise has

indeed proved this to be more and more logical, in the sense we have described. But the experience of 'actually existing socialism' as well as the limited range of even a democratic state to plan in today's international capitalist order suggests that taking capital away from the domestic bourgeoisie is no answer in itself. This end can, in fact, really only be a means, as Luxemburg understood, to the realization of socialism, the 'tearing down' that but opens up the *possibility* of the 'building up'. Robin Murray, who seems to have thought through most clearly, among socialists today, the limits of 'nationalization' in the face of capitalism's global integration of production, finance and commerce, has nevertheless also explained why '[t]he case for public ownership is as strong as it ever was.'[13] The restructuring taking place today reveals the limits of the bourgeois revolution. 'In the economy as a whole there are great barriers between sectors, which the market only makes worse. I am thinking of the relations between finance and industry, of military technology and civilian diffusion, or of branch plants and the wider economy. These are arguments for industrial restructuring and macro-economic planning which formed the core of the case for nationalization fifty years ago.' But there is even 'an even stronger argument', as Murray affirms, in so far as socialists have come to recognise, out of the experience with state ownership in this century, the priority that needs to be given not just to changes in ownership but to changing the social relations of production.

> One has only to read a few pages by socialist economists in the 1930s – Marxist or Fabian – to sense the extent of change that has taken place in socialist thinking today. The experience of the guerrilla movements, of a variety of post-revolutionary experiments, of the women's movement, the black movement, and a multitude of progressive community campaigns, all have contributed to a shift of focus towards the social relations of socialism. . . [T]his has meant a concern with the nature of work, with the division between mental and manual labour, with the question of working time and conflict between capital's time and labour's time (to have children, to collect them from school, to have time for meetings and classes, to control one's own working time rather than being paced on the line, and so on). It means a concern for different segments of the working class, unskilled as well as skilled, women and black people as well as the white male and white-collared workers. It also involves a concern for the use values of production and the diversity of need – with the saving of energy rather than nuclear production, for example, or with cultural variety and self-production rather than standardized mass consumption. . . [I]t is now realized that the forces of production are not neutral but that technology has been developed in such a way as to increase capital's control over labour. Nor are commodities neutral. They reflect in their content, and even their design, the particular production relations of capital.

This catalogue of contemporary socialist 'common sense', as Murray calls it, would not have sounded as foreign to the ears of the authors of the *Communist Manifesto* as many presume today. If much of this was ignored by socialists fifty years ago it reflected both the limits of the politics of compromise and the limits of a revolutionary socialism 'decreed behind a few officials desks'. Even then, such 'socialisms' were not accomplished without considerable repression or marginalization of those socialists who did not forget that, above all, capital, as the *Manifesto* put it, 'is a social power'; and that whereas in 'bourgeois society living labour is but a means to increase accumulated labour', the point of the whole socialist project was to build a 'society in which accumulated labour is but a means to widen, to enrich, to promote the existence of the labourer.' But if it is now more widely accepted amongst socialists that this cannot be achieved if we just try to revive the old, now unpopular, state ownership, so it must nevertheless also be made clear again, not least to the confused and dispirited socialist intellectuals of our time, that, as Murray puts it:

> If the aim of socialist economics goes beyond restructuring industry and improving productivity, if its aim is to change the social relations of production in production, then expanding social ownership becomes a necessity. For in spite of the fact that social enterprises are hedged round by monopolies and the market, in spite of the fact that they have to rely on capitalist managers to run them, these difficulties are only compounded if private property gets in the way. The reason why nationalization and social ownership should still be at the centre of any socialist strategy is that only in this way can we make progress in. . . 'the politics of production'. . . It must match capital in productive performance, yet change the social character of production in such a way that it regains popular support. It must show that it can work in practice, since nothing is as strong as the propaganda of practice. That alone will put nationalization back on the political agenda, not as a socialist solution but as a midwife to the socialist problem.

We must be clear, as well, that social ownership today, if it can be revived as an aspiration among socialists, and if political agencies can win the popular support to try to effect fundamental change through its introduction, can itself only lead at present to a new politics of compromise. Socialism will still not happen at one go. Certain sectors – whether they will be commanding heights or more modest fortresses of capital will depend on the locus and extent of popular support may be taken away from capital and transformed in their social purpose and administration. But they would still have to negotiate between the rocky shoals of powerful bourgeois hostility and market competition. Less metaphorically speaking, they would have to negotiate a degree of autonomy amidst their dependence on domestic and international bourgeois forces sufficient to allow them to act in a manner that liberated the human creativity that is in the end the sole basis of solving the socialist problem. But to look at public ownership as a necessary means to socialist ends is to see things in a very different way from the old politics of compromise. It would, indeed, be more akin to the politics of compromise that post-revolutionary regimes have always had to follow to survive in a world still in the bourgeois epoch. Our hope must be that we can gradually build out of a new 'spirit of revolution' – and on the basis of the limited autonomy that spheres liberated from bourgeois control could furnish – the grounds upon which that epoch would really be, gradually but fundamentally, challenged. This would then be a very different politics of compromise, a very different gradualism, precisely because it would be based on developing the intellectual capacities in the mass of the people, to organise and administer, to plan and create, wherein lies the true meaning of socialist revolution.

But this must take us back once more to the question of agency. The first goal of all socialist parties and movements, on the basis of whatever organizational resources they can muster today, and eventually with the resources they can liberate from capital and the capitalist state, must be to help form a new working class identity and intellectual capacity so that the members and supporters of these parties and movements actually do become, as Gramsci put it, 'leaders and organisers of all the activities and functions inherent in the organic development of an integral society, both civil and political.' They will need to be able to replace the capitalist managers on which even public ownership is now dependent. But they will need, first of all, to be able to learn and explain clearly how capitalism works as a system in the process of the organisational work they do, and to try to prefigure the kind of practice that will contribute to learning how to 'build up' even while people become committed to 'tearing down'. Programmes will be needed, but socialist intellectuals – partly because they are still too oriented to trying to educate the ruling class to socialism – are mistaken to give the priority they do to this today. The reforms they advance must rather be oriented to reviving, indeed building anew, the 'spirit of revolution' against the existing structures of power and privilege. The socialist purpose even today does involve 'building up', but this must mean building up whatever prefigurative changes can be achieved within the framework of actually existing capitalism, whether the sphere is health, education, housing, transport, the environment, or day care, or whether it is trade unions, parties or social movements themselves, since their organizational structures and political and ideological practices are far from being conducive enough to the task.

Popular support, in the form of votes for parties committed to socialist change, is essential; but such expression of support at the polls can never be enough. What is required is the penetration of socialist ideas and creative organisational and intellectual capacities throughout society. Revolutionary socialist change, in other words, requires the implantation and development throughout society of a socialist presence, at the moral, ideological, political and economic levels in the broadest possible range of institutions in society: in the parties, unions and movements long identified as composing the 'Left', but also in factories, offices, schools, universities, churches, community centres, and even in that contemporary centre of working class life – the shopping mall. This implantation forms part of what Gramsci called the 'war of position'. But there is today no single 'Modern Prince'. The task cannot only devolve today on socialist parties – although such parties must be built, or transformed into something very different from what they have been. But the task must also be undertaken by other organisations and agencies – feminist and ecological movements, anti-racist and peace movements, the movements of the physically and developmentally handicapped and the movements of those handicapped by poverty. In all of these and other movements, and in building alliances among them, those committed to fundamental social change must also pay careful attention to ensuring that the relationship between leaders and led is productive of popular capacities for organisational and intellectual development. Only in this way – and obviously, after all we have said, nothing is inevitable – will socialists be able to find 'once more the spirit of revolution'. And only in this way will that socialist spirit of revolution really make itself felt against a bourgeoisie that will certainly continue to struggle with the working class over who will play, historically, the most revolutionary part.

NOTES

1. Raymond Williams, *Politics and Letters* (London: Verso, 1979), pp. 383, 411.
2. Hannah Arendt, *On Revolution* (New York: Viking, 1965), p. 28.
3. Karl Marx, *The Eighteenth Brumaire of Louis Bonaparte* (New York: International Publishers, 1963), p. 17.
4. *Manifesto of the Communist Party*, in Karl Marx, *Political Writings Volume I: The Revolutions of 1848*, D. Fernbach, ed. (New York: Vintage, 1974), p. 70. All ensuing quotations from the *Manifesto* are drawn from this edition, pp. 69–81.
5. Fred Halliday, 'The Sources of the New Cold War' in *Exterminism and Cold War* (London: Verso, 1982), pp. 298–9.
6. See Roger Burbach and Orlando Nuñéz, *Fire in the Americas: Forging a Revolutionary Agenda* (London and New York: Verso, 1987).
7. Quoted in Kenneth McNaught, *A Prophet in Politics: A Biography of J.S. Woodsworth* (Toronto: University of Toronto Press, 1959), pp. 134, 96.
8. Ernesto Laclau and Chantal Mouffe, *Hegemony and Socialist Strategy* (London: Verso, 1985), p. 2.
9. Georg Lukács, 'Towards a Methodology of the Problem of Organization' in *History and Class Consciousness: Studies in Marxist Dialectics* (London: Merlin, 1971), p. 295.
10. *Selections from the Prison Notebooks of Antonio Gramsci*, Q. Hoare and G. Nowell Smith, eds. (London: Lawrence and Wishart, 1971), pp. 14–15. Cf. p. 335 for the quotation in the previous paragraph.
11. Adam Przeworski and John Sprague, *Paper Stones: A History of Electoral Socialism*, (Chicago and London: University of Chicago Press: 1986).
12. Rosa Luxemburg, *Selected Political Writings*, R. Looker, ed. (London: Jonathan Cape, 1972), p. 246.
13. Robin Murray, 'Ownership, Control and Markets', *New Left Review*, 164, July/August 1987, pp. 101–3.

REVOLUTION AND DEMOCRACY IN LATIN AMERICA

Carlos M. Vilas*

1989 marks the 200th anniversary of the French Revolution and the 30th year of the Cuban Revolution; it is also 10 years since the Sandinista Popular Revolution. The coincidence of these three anniversaries is a propitious opportunity to reflect on the perspectives and significance of a social revolution today in Latin America and the Caribbean. Furthermore, this multiple commemoration occurs in the moment of glasnost and perestroika, of an advancing process of 'rectification of errors and negative tendencies' in the Cuban Revolution, and of a return to market mechanisms in China. The implication in every case has been a profound self-criticism – albeit with different consequences – concerning the ways in which the construction of those different versions of socialism has been carried through.

In the social revolutions of the Third World, three basic issues are fused: democracy, national self-determination and development. The way in which each issue is posed, and their reciprocal articulation, is determined in the final analysis by what classes and social groups give impetus and leadership to the revolution[1]. In this essay, I shall consider the question of democracy from the perspective of social revolution, paying particular attention to aspects of the relationship between institutionalised political systems and the revolutionary struggle as it has arisen in Latin America. But is there any point in discussing social revolution in Latin America and the Caribbean, when it would seem self-evident that social revolution is not on the political agenda in the great majority of societies in the region, and when the revolution in Central America is facing such enormous difficulties in its attempts to transform socio-economic structures in Nicaragua, or to achieve power in El Salvador and Guatemala? Although the question will be answered directly at the end of this essay, it is hoped that the following discussion will lay the basis for a response.

I

What is generally meant by revolution is above all the violent overthrow of the institutional political order and the rapid transformation of socio-political structures.[2] Since the Cuban Revolution, that rupture has tended to be associated in Latin America with the successful outcome of a process of guerrilla

30

struggle, the constitution of popular politico-military organisations and their victory over the coercive mechanisms of the state. It is obvious that, in these terms, the Latin American scene today is desolate compared with a couple of decades ago. With the outstanding exceptions of El Salvador and Guatemala, and to a lesser extent Colombia, there is a general absence of armed revolutionary organisations. Even in the three cases cited, the revolutionary struggle is relatively stagnant. In Guatemala and El Salvador, the movement has had to face the strategies of institutional democratisation promoted by the U.S. government in alliance with sectors of the local ruling groups; in Colombia, the guerrillas have been contained within reduced territories; and none of these movements has escaped the deterioration that is the inevitable cost of any struggle that continues over a period of decades. The cycle that opened in the 1950s with the Cuban Revolution seems now to be reaching its close, as the 1980s draw to an end, with the revolutions in Central America.

To reduce the extremely complex problem of the viability of revolutionary alternatives for social transformation to the question of the existence or otherwise of politico-military organisations would be much closer to the crudest voluntarist explanations offered by the proponents of guerrilla politics (*foquismo*), than to an objective analysis of the question. The small number of revolutionary successes in Latin America and the Caribbean have to do not only with the existence of politico-military organisations, but with their articulation with the mass mobilisations of popular classes. The triumph of the Cuban Revolution was not just a military victory over an army trained by the United States; the military victory was built on the political capacity of the 26th July Movement guerrillas to articulate the 'mountain' (*la sierra*) and the 'plain' (*el llano*), the guerrilla struggle and the struggle of workers, students and urban masses.[3] It is well established how decisive was the role played by the mass insurrections in Nicaragua in 1978 and 1979 in the final victory of the Sandinista struggle, as is the combination within them of elements of spontaneity and organisation. In the final analysis, it was the insurrectionary urban masses who advanced against the Somoza regime *with guerrilla support*, and not vice versa.[4] The conditions for these mobilisations were many and varied, and owed as much to internal and international political factors as to economic causes. Without the masses, the guerrilla struggle can become endemic, isolated from the people; without a vanguard, the protests of the masses can prove fruitless, and be either integrated into the dominant system or simply repressed.[5]

Above all, social revolutions have to do with the transformation of the socio-economic structures and the political system of a country. In this sense, revolutions are broad and deep processes of political and socio-economic transformation, affecting directly the economic and social structures: the transformation of the relations of power between the classes; the development of socialised forms of property, of access to resources and of the administration of the means of production; the consolidation of sovereignty

and national self-determination; the development of political and social institutions with extensive and effective participation by the classes and groups
that are subordinated under capitalism; the elimination of forms of racial and
gender discrimination; and the development of values, attitudes and forms of
individual and collective behaviour based on solidarity and cooperation.

A revolutionary transformation is also, therefore, a much longer process
than it is generally thought to be. The image of a revolution as an instanta-
neous break with everything that has gone before and a rapid construction
of the new is infantile. The establishment of new economic structures, of a
new political system, and of new attitudes, values and forms of behaviour, is
a long process. The violence, the accelerated transformation, are at any event
aspects of the 'destructive' political dimension of revolutions, of the transfer
of political power from one class to another, or from one class to organisations
that assume the representation of other previously subordinated classes, a
transfer that is carried out by non-institutional means. The old material
regime – the political and economic institutions etc – is quickly destroyed;
but the construction of the new, and particularly the transformation of mental
structures, is a long and complex process.[6]

Nevertheless this distinction between the means and the content cannot be
taken too far. The possibility of carrying through socio-economic changes
that produce a society whose class configuration is different from that which
has hitherto existed in peripheral capitalism, has been associated historically
with the collapse of the prevailing political order – even if, as we shall discuss
below, this has basically been the result of attempts to oppose the advance of
the popular movement. Both revolutions as such and some populist processes
which modified the power relations of their respective societies, have either
rested on or had as their context a break with the previously existing institutional order. Even the Cárdenas period in Mexico (1934 – 1940) – which
altered the relations of power in the countryside, (as well as the relationship
to North American interests in the country) through a far-reaching agrarian
reform and the nationalisation of the oil and railway industries – occurred in
the context of a political system which had not yet achieved stable institutional
form, and which in any event was part of an agrarian revolution that shook
Mexican society to its very foundations.

II

The Latin American political scene today offers no perspectives for revolutionary change in the sense of a break in the class politico-institutional order,
even though the factors that traditionally create the substantive or objective
conditions for the unfolding of revolutionary processes are present: namely,
growing poverty, a general deterioration in the standard of living, a lack of
socio-economic perspectives, insufficient access to basic resources for large
sections of the Latin American population, both rural and urban. But a

revolution requires something more than socio-economic detonators, and this 'something else' is fundamentally related to the political configuration of a society, and to a shared perception among broad sectors of the dominated groups and classes of the impossibility of successfully articulating their demands within the prevailing institutional order. It is obvious that as long as the economically and socially dominated groups do not feel themselves to be politically oppressed, the possibilities of a revolutionary break remain remote. Consciousness of political oppression is undoubtedly related to the existence of popular organisations (political parties, trade unions, peasant organizations, student movement etc); but it also has to do with the capacity of the existing political institutions to channel effectively the discontent of the people.

These two factors are not independent of one another. Experience shows that the call for a revolutionary alternative will not arise as long as the masses are integrated in one way or another into the existing political system, and thus as long as there exists a possibility of a positive institutional response on the part of the political system to the demands and dissatisfactions of the people. Thus the factor that ultimately explains why there are revolutionary processes under way in Nicaragua, Guatemala, and El Salvador (each with their own particular characteristics), but not in Honduras or Costa Rica, is not fundamentally economic (for the five societies of Central America are substantially alike in their socio-economic structures) but political. In Nicaragua, Guatemala and El Salvador, the capitalist modernisation that created the socio-economic conditions for the development of revolutionary alternatives occurred under intensely repressive and dictatorial political systems which had closed off any possibility of institutional articulation of popular demands, and thus removed any possibility of legitimation.[7] In Honduras, and above all in Costa Rica, the political institutions demonstrated a greater receptivity and provided more space for the popular organisations – by giving legal recognition to peasant organisations and a measure of agrarian reform in Honduras, for example, or through broad institutional democratisation and the abolition of the army in 1951, in Costa Rica – and a more positive response to the demands of those social groups and classes most affected by agro-exporting capitalist modernisation.[8]

The option of revolution by violent means has always been a popular response to the violation of the law by the dominant classes. In contrast to what is suggested in the discourse of the ruling classes and the repressive apparatus – which has certainly found acceptance among some sectors of the population – there is no preference in principle for a violent revolutionary alternative. Traditionally, the popular revolutionary organisations have approached the question of the use of violence in terms of the collective exercise of legitimate self-defence in the face of ruling classes who violate their own legality or systematically turn to the repression of protest and of popular demands for better living conditions, effective democracy, and national independence. This is the consistent position expressed in Marxist and Leninist thinking,[9] and in revolutionary practice, up to the present.

Practically all the Latin American political organisations that at one moment or another have opted for the revolutionary road, have done so in response to dictatorial regimes, to violations of the legality of the regime itself, to the absence of institutional alternatives through which to press for social and political transformations. In Mexico, Emiliano Zapata rose up in arms after years of fruitless efforts to obtain by peaceful means the return of illegally appropriated communal lands.[10] The FSLN emerged and developed in response to the absence of institutional means of removing the Somoza family from power and improving the conditions of life of the popular classes. The formation and growth of the revolutionary organisations of El Salvador were responses to the fraudulent elections or their cancellation whereby the army and the dominant groups opposed any advance by the democratic opposition. In Guatemala the revolutionary struggle began early in the 1960s as a means of confronting the counterrevolutionary state established in the country after the U.S. government-sponsored invasion that overthrew the popularly elected government of President Arbenz.[11] The electoral proscription of Peronism from 1955 onwards, and the military coups of 1955, 1963 and 1966, were the framework for the emergence of the guerrilla organizations in Argentina. The same coincidence of a reactionary coup d'etat, the closure of the institutional political system and the emergence of guerrilla organisations can be seen in Brazil after 1964. In Grenada the New Jewel Movement directed its struggle against the dictatorship of Eric Gairy and the repression of all legal instruments of change. But in every case the success of revolutionary initiatives has depended fundamentally on the emergence of conditions that allowed these organisations to insert themselves in the masses, give expression to their conflicts with the system of domination and advance together with them.

The armed insurrection launched in April 1952 by the Nationalist Revolutionary Movement (MNR) in Bolivia followed the same lines. After the bloody overthrow of the nationalist government of Colonel Villarroel in 1946, the MNR was systematically persecuted by subsequent governments, each of them expressing the interests of the tin mining oligarchy known as the *rosca*. The great majority of the leaders of the MNR and their middle political and trade union cadres were forced into exile, and their press was banned. Although the MNR presented candidates in elections, and despite the considerable support they enjoyed, they were prevented from taking up their posts, which often meant that they were driven into exile. The trade union movement was brutally repressed and its leaders deported. The Presidential elections of 1951 were won by the MNR candidate. The government and the armed forces refused to recognise the result and formed a military junta, which then assumed control of government. In these conditions, the MNR called for an armed insurrection and, with the decisive support of the mining proletariat, overthrew the military junta and took power.[12]

Much the same can be said of the Cuban Revolution; the assault on the Moncada barracks, the subsequent formation of the 26th of July Movement and the development of the guerrilla struggle were all in their origins responses to Fulgencio Batista's military coup of March 10th 1952, and the closure that this implied of any type of political struggle within the framework of legal institutions. Those institutions were, of course, very limited in their application. Between 1946 and 1952, during the governments of Grau San Martín and Prío Socarrás, the struggles for working class demands were severely repressed, and the main leader of the sugar cane workers union was brutally murdered. The student movement, which had a long democratic tradition, maintained its existence through tolerance and repression. Corruption and graft were rife at all levels of the state apparatus; the subordination to United States economic interests – above all, in sugar – was almost total. Nonetheless this corrupt and limited system still made it possible for the Authentic Revolutionary Party (known as the *Ortodoxos*) to win the elections, given that it represented the most progressive forces in Cuban society: the working class, the democratic petit bourgeoisie, the non-sugar industrial bourgeoisie. Batista's coup d'etat took place in order to prevent the electoral victory of a political party that was certainly progressive, but which was not a revolutionary party.[13]

III

There are powerful reasons for this recurrent articulation of political democracy, the rupture of legality by the ruling classes, and revolutionary struggle. Obviously, different groups and social classes see democracy from different points of view and with different horizons. Initially, the popular classes and their political expressions accept the democratic institutions as a framework and a means for carrying through their programmes for political and socio-economic transformation; in principle there is no contradiction between a democratic institutional order and structural transformations. The contradiction between them is the result of resistance on the part of the ruling groups and classes, and of imperialism, to accepting the consequences of an established democracy when this implies significant alterations in the relations of power. Democracy ceases to work as soon as the dominant classes see that its continuing existence can lead to a questioning of the reproduction of their own domination. As they did in the old film 'Rollerball', the ruling classes establish the rules of the game, and reserve the right to change them whenever things begin to go wrong.

From the point of view of those people who in the end join the revolutionary struggle, especially in the mass insurrectionary phase, there are equally important considerations to be borne in mind concerning the seriousness of this option, its difficulties and the enormous burden it places upon the popular classes. For a distant observer, or from a romantic or even a naive point of view, revolutions can be beautiful moments in the history of a society; for their collective protagonists, however, they are usually a tremendously difficult, painful and costly experience. A revolution is something that people enter into when they see no other means of improving their lives or of defending the little which has as yet not been illegally taken from them. Fidel Castro recently put it very clearly:

That's why it is my conviction, and I believe it should be the conviction of every real revolutionary, that violence is the last resort, when no other road is open, when there is no other means of effecting change. And I hope that the men who have the responsibility in our hemisphere will be able to take the steps and carry through the measures that will resolve these problems, that will make it possible to avoid the trauma of a great social explosion; if they don't, then the ruling classes of today will play the same role that was played in their times by the last king and queen of France or the last czars of the old Russian empire. . . . And hopefully the political leaders are aware, and are wise enough first to resolve the objective problems faced by the economy of our countries, and secondly to carry through measures that achieve justice, equality, the redistribution of wealth, that is, the social changes that are inescapably necessary if social justice is to be achieved, without the terrible traumatic experiences that the classic revolutions of the past or indeed all revolutions have been.[14]

The option of revolutionary struggle, as far as the popular classes are concerned, is a matter of life or death. This is not literature. Almost all the accounts of those who participated in the Sandinista insurrection, for example, show that the decision to join the insurrectionary struggle against the Somoza dictatorship was taken only when there was no alternative, other than to resign oneself to being a victim of certain repression. People go out to fight, or to work with those are fighting, because they face repression in any case; and this feeling that it is a matter of life or death tends to become stronger and more decisive the more limited has been the level of previous participation in politics.[15] This contributes to giving mass revolutionary struggle the defensive character that has been identified by Barrington Moore in his study of the reasons why people rebel or fail to rebel against injustice.[16] But it is also testimony to a belief in the real political possibility of changing things, over and above the collective and personal cost.

IV

The fact that violence appears in revolutionary thought and revolutionary practice only as a last resort helps to explain the connections initially existing in many cases, between revolutionary organisations and previously existing legal 'reformist' social and political organisations. The revolutionary alternative usually emerges out of organisations that have operated legally until that moment, either because they have become the targets of repression, or have been forced underground, or as is more often the case, when internal factions or tendencies turn to direct action in the face of what they see as a compromise on the part of the official leadership of the party; at any event

whenever legal, institutional political struggle is judged to have become ineffective. That was the case of the FSLN in Nicaragua in its relations with some
elements of the Socialist Party; of the MIR in Venezuela in relation to the
Acción Democrática party; of the Colombian M-19 with respect to ANAPO;
of the Montoneros in Argentina with regard to Peronism; of the BPR (the
Popular Revolutionary Bloc) of El Salvador in relation to the Christian agrarian cooperative movement. The same can be said of many of the best known
revolutionary leaders, whose first weapons were forged in the very bosom of
institutional political democracy: Fidel Castro in the Ortodoxo Party, Carlos
Fonseca and Tomas Borge in Nicaraguan Socialist Party. That is, there is
a line of both continuity and rupture between revolutionary organisations
and their leaderships, and the previously existing political culture. In the
peripheral capitalist societies of Latin America you are not *born* to revolutionary positions in political life – you *arrive* at them.

   This also has important practical implications as far as the effectiveness of
the political struggle is concerned. The transition from the initial pursuit of
reform by legal means to the revolutionary alternative implies that, when
the moment comes for the latter, there is already a body of experience of
mass political work, of organisation, and that there is contact and mutual
recognition between the vanguard and the real or potential social base. This
was extremely clear in the Bolivian Revolution of 1952, which had a decisive
basis in the mobilisation of the working class movement, a mobilisation
made possible by a history of close relations between the MNR and the
mining proletariat. In Cuba, Fidel Castro was already a figure of national
significance when he disembarked from the *Granma* in December 1956; his
active participation in the student movement and later in the left wing of the
Ortodoxo Party facilitated his contacts with sectors of the bourgeois opposition and with the workers and peasant movements, which provided a broader
base of support for the guerrillas.[17] The same was true of the Montoneros in
Argentina in the early seventies, and of M-19 in Colombia.

   In fact this line of connection with previous political struggles goes far
beyond its immediate precedents. All Latin American revolutionary organisations with roots in the masses, assume themselves to be and present themselves to others as the contemporary expression of a popular secular struggle
against imperialism, political oppression and social exploitation. In this sense,
the development of a revolutionary organisation can also be seen as a reading
of national history whose key is the popular struggles against external domination of the nation, and at the same time, against internal domination by
ruling groups allied to colonialism and imperialism. The clearest example is
undoubtedly the Cuban Revolution, with its explicit connection between the
struggle against the Batista dictatorship in the first place, and later against the
Cuban bourgeoisie and North American imperialism in order to build socialism, and the independence struggle and political thought of Jose Martí. The
same can be said of the Sandinista National Liberation Front in Nicaragua, the

Tupamaros in Uruguay, the Montoneros of Argentina and the Cinchoneros of
Honduras, the 'Farabundo Martí' National Liberation Front in El Salvador
and the 'Manuel Rodríguez' Patriotic Front in Chile, and so on.

Each of these cases represents an attempt (with differing degrees of success)
to link present to past struggles, to rediscover a historical dimension denied in
the official history of the ruling classes and of external domination, a dimension in which contemporary revolutionary ruptures are set in the framework
of a popular anti-imperialist continuity which links national sovereignty to the
effective conquest of popular self-determination. In Latin America, and in
fact in the whole of the Third World, the national (ultimately anti-imperialist)
dimension of the revolutionary struggle emerges out of the respective history
of each country insofar as that history is subjected to a class reading and
interpretation. Democracy and national liberation are linked in a popular
political perspective directed towards far-reaching social transformations.

                                    V

All the social revolutions of the 20th century in Latin America and the Caribbean – irrespective of their later development – had as their detonator the
issue of democracy: Mexico, Bolivia, Grenada, Nicaragua. In Mexico, it was
the slogan 'effective suffrage and no re-election' that set in motion the revolution against the dictatorship of Porfirio Diaz; the other cases have already
been referred to earlier. But in all these instances the question of democracy
took on implications that carried it beyond the merely institutional sphere,
posing the question of changes in the relations of power between classes,
in their access to economic resources; of the nature of the state; of modifications in the structure of the relations of production; of an extension of
the levels, instances and range of popular participation; of changes in the
external articulation of the economy; of the reformulation of international
relations. In the final analysis it is precisely this broadening of the content
and extent of democracy in these processes (though they differ widely from
one to another), that makes them true social revolutions.

The experience of the Cuban Revolution is a particularly illustrative example of the way in which the revolutionary process can transform the issue
of democracy and national liberation into the context of the transition to
socialism. In fact the advance of Cuba towards socialism began in the 1959
– 61 period, in the framework of a remarkably consistent democratic and
anti-imperialist struggle with an increasing popular content (both in terms of
the participation of people and of the content of policies), conducted in the
face of an increasingly compromised Cuban bourgeoisie and a permanently
aggressive United States government.[18] The phase of the construction of
socialism came as the culmination of a struggle that began by fighting a
dictatorship, but which did not limit its objectives to the restoration of a
lost institutional order; for it identified the bases of that dictatorship in

Cuba's capitalist socio-economic structure and its subordination to North American imperialism. Faced with a bourgeoisie that saw the overthrow of the dictatorship as opening a space for a more democratic capitalism, the Cuban Revolution made democratisation one of the foundations of socialism.

The processes of democratisation unfold unevenly in social revolutions; in the socio-economic arena such processes – for example, the nationalisation of the fundamental means of production, social participation, improvements in the living conditions of the popular classes, broadening of social services etc. – are set in motion sooner than the corresponding changes in the institutional arena, where what is involved is a political (in the conventional sense) and electoral process. As yet, Latin American revolutionary thought has not confronted the problem of how to integrate institutional political democracy with the problematics of socio-economic transformation and non-electoral forms of popular participation.

This failure has to do with the contradiction, specific to the capitalist state, between the abstract principle of political citizenship and the formal equality of all individuals, on the one hand, and the reality of socio-economic – and hence political – inequality between social classes on the other. On the one hand, the subordination of the popular classes is first socio-economic, and then political. Democracy is reduced in the practice and ideological discourse of the ruling classes, to the institutional and electoral sphere; and in the last analysis even this already restricted democracy is obstructed by the ruling classes whenever, in spite of everything, it threatens to allow a greater participation and presence of the popular classes in the political system. The result in these conditions – conditions which the revolutionary movement *does not choose* – is an attitude of scorn or indifference towards the institutional and electoral aspects of democracy, whenever the popular classes conquer state power by revolutionary means and are able to set in motion the process of socio-economic transformation and national liberation.

Insofar as political democracy in the past has been limited to the participation of the ruling classes now removed from power and hardest hit by economic transformation, concern for the issue is doubly discredited. Democracy becomes a closed question within the popular revolutionary camp, especially as the previous ruling classes progressively move on to the terrain of counterrevolution where imperialism is increasingly the dominant force. Finally, the counterrevolutionary war, from which no social revolution has so far been able to free itself, places still more obstacles in the way of any early development of democracy in its institutional and electoral aspects. Wars are always the least propitious environment for the full exercise of democratic institutions, and this is doubly true when we are dealing with societies that have no effective democratic traditions, that are economically weak, and that are obliged to concentrate all their resources on a struggle for survival in the face of the greatest economic and military power the world has known.

The degree of emphasis placed directly on the political and socio-economic dimension, or on traditional electoral considerations, also has to do with the particular social profile of each revolutionary process. Generally, it is the petit bourgeoisie and those fractions of the bourgeoisie who in one sense or another throw in their lot with the Latin American revolutionary movements, who put the greatest emphasis on the question of democracy understood in the electoral sense. There is a logic to that. The contradictions on the basis of which these sectors join some revolutionary processes are fundamentally political or ideological, rather than economic in the strict sense. Socio-economic transformations and new forms of social and labour participation etc are less important to them than the continuing existence of representative institutions.

The Sandinista Revolution offers an interesting case of an attempt to articulate from the first moments of revolutionary transformation the principle of electoral representation and party-political pluralism, with the principle of broad and direct popular participation, and the recognition in the workings of democracy at both levels of the problematics of ethnic minorities. The process is still in its earliest stages, and is unfolding amid tensions and limitations of every kind; it would be premature to make any definitive judgment on it.[19]

VI

Today in Latin America the relationship between political democracy and social revolutions is linked to the extent and content of the so-called *democratic transition* in the region, i.e. those non-revolutionary processes whereby some military dictatorships in South America have given ground on the question of political regimes based on the principle of universal suffrage.

From the perspective of the necessity of introducing profound political and socio-economic changes in order to improve the material and cultural conditions of life of the majority of the population of Latin America, these processes of democratic transition exhibit a number of common features over and above their particular characteristics. Briefly, the following are the principal elements:

1) These processes are restricted to the institutional political sphere in its strictest sense. They do not project into the economic sphere, nor do they provide a framework for any substantial changes in the level of access of subordinate groups to socio-economic resources – by income redistribution, creating employment, improving living conditions etc.
2) In general, the areas in which the power bases of the dominant groups are concentrated, and the apparatuses of the state to which these groups traditionally turn to defend their own interests, are left untouched. There is no restructuring of the military, for example, nor is there any discussion about the need to establish a new matrix of relations between society and the armed forces in a democratic regime. Limits are placed on the identification

and punishment of military personnel involved in brutal and mass forms of repressions; those responsible are pardoned etc.

3)The economic policies developed in respect to some strategic questions – the external debt for example – show clear elements of continuity with the previous military regimes.

4)In general they are the product of negotiations between dictatorial regimes and political organisations which become possible when, for various reasons – military defeats, international pressures, internal divisions, economic crises – the direct control of the state exercised by the armed forces threatens to lead them into a blind alley and a consequent internal deterioration.

Let us be clear that these limited democracies represent objectively a step forward from the dictatorial regimes out of which they emerged. Anyone travelling from Chile or Paraguay to Argentina or from Haiti to the Dominican Republic, can see it clearly, particularly as far as improvements in the human rights situation (always the most traumatic issue in a dictatorship) are concerned. But what we want to emphasise here is the ambiguous character of these processes, and their instrumentalisation by the ruling groups and their political and military representatives. The turn to democracy is a means of reducing the levels of open or latent social conflict, not proof of a desire to encourage popular participation or set in motion a process of social transformation. In the case of Central America, it is part of the U.S. government's regional policy, whose aim is to destabilise the Sandinista Revolution and isolate it internationally. Once again different social groups and classes, and different political projects, see democracy in a very different light.

On the other hand, it seems clear that the popular movement is not in any position to impose more advanced alternatives. It serves little purpose to generalise in these matters, but it is certainly undeniable that one of the features of South American military dictatorships has been their intense, prolonged and general repression of social protest and popular opposition. The fact that they were not able to totally eliminate that opposition does not mean that the repression did not have a powerful impact on the capacity for action and organisation of the popular classes and the democratic forces. There is obviously a sharp difference in the capacity for popular mass mobilisation before and after the imposition of dictatorships, and the levels of organisation are equally severely reduced, as many leaders and cadres fall victim to repression or are forced into exile. There can be little doubt, therefore, that these processes of transition to democracy represent less than the popular movement might have demanded under other circumstances; but *under these conditions* it would not be realistic to expect very much more.

It is equally true that what the armed forces and the ruling groups see as a means of preventing more serious political breakdown, the popular movement may see as an opportunity for rebuilding the movement. There is thus an obvious tension between the content and achievements of a transition to democracy seen as a means of restraining the popular movement from developing higher levels of organisation and autonomy, and the content and achievements that the popular classes expect from it. In general it is the political organisations and intellectual representatives of the urban middle classes who find themselves most trapped by these tensions – and in some societies in the region that embraces a significant proportion of the total population.

Much of the recent literature concerning the transition to democracy has expressed the discomfort of these middle classes in the face of the express intention of the workers movement, the radicalised petit bourgeois groups, some political organisations, and others, to approach democratisation as an opportunity to consolidate a popular movement oriented towards achieving social and economic transformations in a number of areas: income redistribution, reduction of the political power of the armed forces and of some sectors of the ruling groups, national self-determination. From their point of view, popular demands and the mass mobilisations in support of them, the criticism of previous dictatorships – for example, in the demand that those responsible for torture, disappearances, and general violations of human rights should be punished – the demand for a nationalist response to the foreign debt, the demand that part of the profits appropriated by the traditional ruling classes be redirected towards the kinds of investment required by less exclusive forms of development etc, are so many threats to the process of democratisation, insofar as they *provoke* the hardliners within the armed forces or induce reprisals from the affected groups or institutions.[20] In other words, the fear is that the effective and pluralist exercise of democracy might lead to the weakening of democracy itself, rather than to its consolidation, precisely because it might reduce the power base of those very groups that have traditionally conspired against democracy. In the final analysis, such a view rests on an implicit or explicit assumption that it will still be these groups that will oversee the exercise of democracy, and set its limits.

The transition to democracy inevitably becomes an arena of political tensions, and ultimately of class conflict, between the extension of the process that the popular organisations seek to achieve, and the limitations that the traditional power groups try to set upon it. It is undeniable that the Latin American revolutionary movements have had difficulties in adapting to these processes of democratisation, for reasons which we can only briefly touch on here. First, the prevailing view of the question of democracy places the initial emphasis on socio-economic transformations, as was discussed earlier. Secondly, the replacement of dictatorial regimes by forms of restricted democracy that are a product both of popular pressures and also of the needs of the ruling groups, the armed forces and in certain cases of the United States government, substantially changes the political space in which the revolutionary struggle had been unfolding until then. The revolutionary organisations often find themselves pushed to one side, as the population are offered obviously less extreme institutional alternatives. Many sectors which had thrown in their lot with the revolutionary struggle begin to demobilise, to reduce their levels of commitment, to accept other forms of confrontation, and even to desist from confrontation with a regime that now seems to be more open. The result is a real possibility that the vanguard will become alienated from its mass support.

In the third place, experience shows that it is impossible for the revolutionary organisations to totally reimplant themselves under legal conditions, not because the organisations themselves resist the change, but because of the resistance that comes from those groups and sectors that had perceived the transition to democracy as a means of demobilising the popular movement. The negotiations between the Colombian revolutionary organisations and the then President Romulo Betancur produced an extremely enlightening outcome; the Colombian revolutionary movement lost more of its leaders and middle cadre as a result of the repressive measures taken against it, once it had accepted reintegration into the legal political system, than it had in more than a decade of armed struggle. The basic principle of every modern state is the monopoly over the means of legitimate coercion – a single army; for the revolutionary organisations, therefore, their reentry into the legal system implies by definition that they must disarm. The Latin American experience has been that sooner or later the coercive state apparatuses try, and generally succeed in making that monopoly effective at the expense of a disarmed enemy.

It is clear that these *transitions to democracy* enjoy greater support among the middle classes and the modernising segments of the bourgeoisie than among the working classes, the peasantry or the impoverished petit bourgeoisie; that they have more credibility among social scientists influenced by the work of their colleagues in the United States than among the Latin American popular masses. Over and above the theoretical discussions about their extent and their limitations, their merits or disadvantages, some results of these processes can already be seen in South America after several years of operation. It is the government of President Alfonsin in Argentina that offers perhaps the most pathetic testimony in this sense; an external debt almost 50% higher than it was at the beginning of his six-year Presidency, despite the fact that throughout this period the debt has been systematically repaid; successive concessions to the armed forces whose effect was to severely limit any real possibility of punishing those responsible for the massive violations of human rights, the murder, torture, abduction and rape of tens of thousands of people; the most regressive distribution of income the country has seen in four decades. The transition to democracy in Argentina has not to date produced any improvement in the living conditions of workers, any reduction in the external debt, or any justice. The situation in Brazil does not look very much more promising.

The failure of these restricted democracies to resolve the most pressing problems of their societies, and the declining living standards of the Latin American popular masses, seems in some societies – Mexico, Argentina,

Brazil, Peru, Venezuela – to be creating the conditions for an advance, within the existing institutional framework, of political projects with broad mass appeal, and ranging from populist to social democratic in character, which set out to reach government by electoral means. While they are the product of specific local conditions in each case, these proposals do share certain common features; an appeal to broad sectors of the popular and middle classes on the basis of the articulation of demands for broad democratisation, economic development, social justice, an opening up of the internal market, greater autonomy in the development of international relations and substantial changes in the ways of responding to the foreign debt.

To what extent it is possible to use the democratic spaces that have begun to open in Latin America to create the conditions for an advance in a socialist direction, is a matter that depends on a number of factors specific to each country – and which in many of the options which are now emerging are not even posed as a possibility. The tragic experience of the Popular Unity government of President Allende in Chile, and the current tribulations of the APRA government of Alan García in Peru, offer little room for optimism about the possibilities of institutional strategies for socio-economic and political transformation leading in a socialist direction, or indeed for an extension of democracy. At the same time the real configuration of the Latin American political map, and the impact that the strategies for restricted democratisation have had in any event on broad sectors of the population, have removed from the agenda the more radical strategies for political action.

This should not be seen as a pessimistic conclusion. All rhetoric aside, it must be acknowledged that revolutions are rare events in history. Their development, especially their degree of mass involvement, responds to an extremely complex set of causes in which accidental factors can act as detonators. There is nothing in the structure of a society that makes a revolution inevitable; but neither is there anything in the armoury of the ruling classes which ensures that revolutions will always by definition be defeated.

After two hundred years, many of the propositions of the French Revolution remain a dead letter in Latin America. In one way or another, a large part of the Declaration of the Rights of Man, not to speak of the Universal Declaration of Human Rights of 1948, form part of the present list of demands put forward today by the popular and working classes of region. In fact, the reverse is the case; the dependent insertion of Latin America into the international capitalist market, and the close alliance between the local ruling classes and first English and German and later U.S. imperialism, have meant that the progressive demands of the 18th century have become so many slogans justifying the pillaging of natural resources, the degradation of the standards of living of vast masses of the population, growing indebtedness, and the establishment of repressive political regimes. Free trade and un-free people: capitalism brought freedom of commerce but not fraternity or equality.

To return to the initial question: yes, there is still a great deal of point in discussing social revolution in Latin America.

Translated by Mike Gonzalez

NOTES

1. Cf. C.M. Vilas: *The Sandinista Revolution*; (Monthly Review Press, New York, 1986); Chap. 1.
2. For example: 'A rapid, fundamental and violent domestic change in the dominant values and myths of a society, in its political institutions, social structure, leadership and government activities and policies'. Samuel Huntington; *Political order in changing societies*; (Yale University Press, New Haven, Conn., 1968) p. 264
3. An articulation that was neither easy nor free from tensions; cf: Ramon Bonaechea & Marta San Martin: *The Cuban Insurrection 1952–1959*; (Transaction Books, New Brunswick, N.J., 1970).
4. 'The truth is that the masses were always considered, but they were viewed more as a support for the guerrilla, so that the guerrilla as such would break the National Guard, and not as happened in practice; it was the guerrillas that served as support for the masses, so that they, through the insurrection, could demolish the enemy'. Comandante Humberto Ortega, quoted in Vilas; *op. cit.*; note 1, page 124.
5. Cf: C.M. Vilas: 'Popular insurgency and social revolution in Central America' in *Latin American Perspectives*, 56, Winter 1988, pp. 55–77.
6. One of the central aspects of the current process of rectification in Cuba is a critique of the reproduction of individualistic, mercantilist attitudes, of gender discrimination, of consumerism in Cuban society thirty years after the revolution, when 55% of the Cuban population is under 30 years of age. Cf. Fidel Castro, *Por el camino correcto*; (Editora Politíca, Havana, 1988).
7. Cf: M. McClintock: *The American Connection*; (Zed Books, London, 1985).
8. Cf. C.M. Vilas: 'On the uneven development of revolutionary conditions in Central America' in *New Left Review*, forthcoming.
9. Cf: the discussion of the issue in the classic writings of the Marxism-Leninism, in A. Emanuel: 'The state in the transitional period', *New Left Review*, 113/114 (1979), pp. 111–131; cf: a comparative perspective on Africa, Asia and Latin America in J. Walton; *Reluctant rebels. Comparative studies in revolution and underdevelopment*; (Columbia University Press, New York, 1984).
10. Cf. J. Womack jr.; *Zapata and the Mexican Revolution*; (Vintage Books, New York, 1968); chap. III.
11. Cf. On Central America in general, James Dunkerley: *Power in the isthmus*; (Verso, London, 1988).
12. Cf. Robert J. Alexander: *The Bolivian national revolution*; (Rutgers University press, New Brunswick N.J.; 1958): pp. 38 ss; Herbert S. Klein: 'Prelude to the revolution' in James Malloy and Richard S. Thorn (eds); *Beyond the revolution, Bolivia since 1952* (Pittsburgh University Press, Pittsburgh, 1971); pp. 25–51.
13. Cf. Antonio Annino; *Dall'Insurrezione al regime. Politiche di massa a strategie instituzionali a Cuba 1953–1965*; Franco Anegli Editore, Milan, 1984; pp. 69 ss; A. Silva Leon; 'El 'Moncada': la respuesta al 10 de marzo', in *Cuba Socialista*, 34, July 1988, pp. 67–87.
14. Press conference in Quito, quoted in *Granma*, 16 August 1988, p. 4.
15. Cf. Vilas; *op. cit.*; note 1, chap III.

press, New Brunswick N.J.; 1958): pp. 38 ss; Herbert S. Klein: 'Prelude to the revolution' in James Malloy and Richard S. Thorn (eds); *Beyond the revolution, Bolivia since 1952* (Pittsburgh University Press, Pittsburgh, 1971); pp. 25–51.

13. Cf. Antonio Annino; *Dall'Insurrezione al regime. Politiche di massa a strategie istituzionali a Cuba 1953–1965*; Franco Anegli Editore, Milan, 1984; pp. 69 ss; A. Silva Leon; 'El 'Moncada': la respuesta al 10 de marzo', in *Cuba Socialista,* 34, July 1988, pp. 67–87.

14. Press conference in Quito, quoted in *Granma,* 16 August 1988, p. 4.

15. Cf. Vilas; *op. cit.*; note 1, chap III.

16. Barrington Moore jr; *Injustice; the social bases of obedience and revolt*; (M.E. Sharpe, White Plains, N.Y.; 1978).

17. Cf. for example: M. Winocur; *Las clases olvidadas en la revolución cubana*; (Grijalbo, Barcelona, 1980).

18. Cf. for example: Jose L. Rodríguez, 'Política económica de la revolución cubana (1959–1960)' in *Economía y desarrollo,* 54, July–October 1979, pp. 129–153.

19. On the ethnic question see for example C.M. Vilas: 'Democratización y autonomía en la Costa Atlántica' in *Revista Nicaragüense de Ciencias Sociales*; 4; April 1988, pp. 50–64.

20. Possibly the most developed academic expression of this literature is in G. O'Donnell, P. Schmitter and L. Whitehead; *Transitions from authoritarian rule*; (Johns Hopkins University Press, Baltimore, 1986).

THE SOUTHERN AFRICAN REVOLUTION

JOHN S. SAUL

Writing twenty years ago in *The Socialist Register 1969*[1] Giovanni Arrighi and I painted a bleak picture of independent Africa's prospects, suggesting the likely 'stability of existing neo-colonial structures' for the foreseeable future and arguing that 'the "Latin Americanization" of independent Africa is well underway'. This has proven to be an accurate prophesy, although, to be honest, we could not have predicted, even in our wildest imaginings, just how catastrophic for Africa this denouement to the continent's march towards independence would prove to be. Was there a bright side to the picture in 1969? 'Hope,' we argued, 'must instead be focused upon the liberation struggle in southern Africa, the implications of which are bound to have truly continental dimensions'

> In the 'centres' of southern Africa the peasantry has been effectively proletarianized and the social structure produced by the pattern of development in which the white settlers play the hegemonic role leaves little if any, room for a neo-colonial solution. Moreover, in the periphery of this region (the Portuguese territories) the neo-colonial solution has been blocked by the 'ultra-colonialism' of Portugal and the peasant revolution which has ensued is creating subjective conditions for socialist transformation which are generally absent elsewhere in independent black Africa.

We did counsel against 'any illusions concerning the nature and short-term prospects of the struggle in southern Africa' but concluded that, 'at the present historical moment, this (struggle) provides the main, if not the only, leverage for revolutionary change in Sub-Saharan Africa'.

The point stands. Of course, the conventional wisdom of imperial planners of the time was very different. 1969 was also the year of the notorious *National Security Study Memorandum 39*[2], a National Security Council report which apparently induced Henry Kissinger to conclude, in the words of one of the Memorandum's scenarios, that 'the whites are here to stay (in southern Africa) and the only way that constructive change can come about is through them. There is no hope for the blacks to gain the political rights they seek through violence. . .' Unfortunately for the likes of Kissinger history, in southern Africa, was already moving forward with seven league boots. Contrary to NSSM 39 'the outlook for the rebellions' in the 'Portuguese territories' of Mozambique and Angola was *not* 'one of continued stalemate'. Nor could the 'white regime' of Rhodesia 'hold out indefinitely', its internal security system able to 'meet foreseeable threats'. Indeed not even South Africa could, 'for the foreseeable future,. . . maintain internal security', even if it has been able, on balance, to 'effectively counter insurgent activity'.

A mere five years later the comfortable assumptions of NSSM 39 lay in tatters, the military victories of liberation movements in Africa having been the major precipitant of 1974's Portuguese coup; it was this coup, in turn, that paved the way for the installation of radical governments in Angola and Mozambique and for the escalation of armed struggled in Rhodesia. Nor was the mood of challenge borne by such changes to stop at the South African border. Victories elsewhere in the region were a source of inspiration there but, in any case, stirrings in South Africa had their own dynamic. The dramatic signs of renewed working class militancy visible in 1973's wave of strikes and the youth-centred militancy in the townships soon to come to a head in the Soweto events of 1976 announced that the long, dark night of the 1960s – when 'internal stability', imposed at bayonet point by Emergency regulation, had indeed been the order of the day in South Africa – was over.

In short, a revolutionary process was now afoot in the region and has continued to do so, bearing, among other things, considerable promise of a socialist future for southern Africa. This essay will attempt to evaluate that promise here, perhaps on firmer ground than was available in 1969 at the very outset of the revolutionary revival Arrighi and I sought to divine. However, it will be necessary, first, to trace in more detail the ebbs and flows of the process in question. Unfortunately, this essay will also have to specify the nature of the counter-revolution to which revolution in southern Africa has given rise. For the counter-revolutionary project mounted by Pretoria and its allies has been savage, setting new precedents of cruelty and cynicism. And it has determined that, whatever the achievements of the past two decades, the struggle for southern Africa is still very far from being resolved.

I. Liberation Struggle and the Radicalization of Nationalism

The launching of liberation struggles in the Portuguese colonies (Mozambique, Angola and, outside the southern Africa region but important to outcomes there, Guinea-Bissau) and in white minority-dominated Rhodesia transpired in a continental context of 'successful' nationalisms. As is well known the skilled machinations of such departing colonial powers as Britain and France meant that, in general, the decolonization effected with the granting of independence in the 1950s and 1960s would only be a 'false' one, a prelude to neo-colonialism and class collaboration with the rising elites of tropical Africa. For various good reasons of their own, Portugal and the Smith regime that seized power in Rhodesia by means of 1965's 'unilateral declaration of independence' refused to risk the ploy of attempting to coopt the emergent nationalist leadership into formal positions of authority. Nationalists in southern Africa would have to stand and fight, a requirement that was to make some difference to the terms of the decolonization bargain ultimately struck.

Not that all such nationalists could be considered immune to temptation, if, as and when a 'neo-colonialism' were to be placed on offer. Struggles would continue within the movements in Lusophone Africa and Rhodesia/Zimbabwe until very late in the day as to what the class content of liberation should actually be, once the relevant minority regime was forced to the bargaining table. Nonetheless, there was a radicalizing logic to guerilla warfare that began to imprint itself on movements like FRELIMO in Mozambique, the MPLA in Angola and even ZANU in Zimbabwe in discernible ways. Mozambique provided, perhaps, the classic case. It became apparent to many within the FRELIMO leadership that a guerilla struggle like the one launched in northern Mozambique in 1964 required a level of genuine popular participation in and identification with the emancipatory process very different from that evidenced in prior nationalist mobilizations. After all, the potential risks of throwing in their lot with the guerillas in a war zone were great for the peasantry. And the liberation movement needed not merely the peasantry's passive acceptance of its presence, but its active support – in scouting, in provisioning, in the carriage of materiel. Rejecting the *foco* approach – once in heated direct exchange with Che Guevara himself during the latter's African excursion – FRELIMO opted instead for its own version of 'people's war'.[3]

This meant beginning to construct rudimentary democratic structures in the expanding liberated areas, beginning to exemplify popularly based programmes in the health and education spheres, beginning to raise promising questions about such issues as the emancipation of women and even beginning to experiment with certain forms of collective production. This was a radicalization of practice on the ground that also fed back into the movement's theorization of this undertakings, giving rise to a remarkably indigenous process of discovery of the strengths of Marxism as a framework for revolutionary endeavour. This was not, of course, a level of insight that was automatically won. A fierce struggle broke out within the movement in the late 1960s, between those who were willing to accompany this kind of radicalization process and those, hankering for a 'false decolonization' of their own, who resisted it. At best, these latter pined for quick military victories in order to bring the Portuguese 'to their senses' even as they also sought to advance their own interests within the movement by politicking along tribal and racial lines or by conceiving self-aggrandizing economic schemes.

In the event the latter wing of the movement lost out and the proponents of an increasingly radicalized nationalism carried the day. Perhaps, as some observers have argued, there is a danger of romanticizing this achievement. The FRELIMO-inspired political structures were still cast in a discernibly military mould, with, they would argue, a degree of centralization of authority that could translate all too readily into a dangerous kind of 'vanguardism' in the post-liberation phase – especially when the model had to be generalized to that considerable proportion of the country which had not been directly touched by the experience of the liberated areas. Nonetheless, principles of democratic empowerment were being established as well as the beginnings of a left perspective very different from the obscurantist banalities of the 'African Socialism' school that had been so prominent heretofore on the continent. Even though still primarily the possession of the revolutionary vanguard itself, this new perspective manifested a much clearer and more forthright understanding both of the workings of capitalist imperialism and of the dynamics of class formation *within* African societies. Most importantly, it was to provide the springboard for the attempt to implement socialist development strategies in such countries as Mozambique and Angola after the military defeat of Portugal – and the fall of that country's fascist government – paved the way for independence.

The growing success of the armed struggle in Mozambique also gave a firm leg up to the Zimbabwean liberation movement. Although there were some signs, in the early 1960s, that Britain might be prepared to countenance a 'false decolonization' in Rhodesia the seizure of power by the Smith regime soon put paid to that idea while (at best) neutralizing Britain's notional responsibility for the fate of its quasi-colony. Military confrontation would prove necessary there as well in order to force the pace of change. However, it took some time for the popular movement in Zimbabwe to bring this necessity into focus. For it was riven with divisions of the most wasting kind, framed not in terms of genuine ideological differences but by the kind of jockeying for position between petty bourgeois politicians that so often in Africa has activated debilitating organizational rivalries (ZANU vs. ZAPU, in the Zimbabwe case) and even ethnic rivalries (Ndebele vs. Shona, for starters). Yet ZANU was ultimately – in the early 1970s – to avail itself of FRELIMO's offer to open up a more effective military front in Zimbabwe via the newly liberated areas of Mozambique's Tete Province and thereby work (especially after Mozambique's own independence provided an even more secure base) to undermine, slowly but surely, the viability of the settlers' UDI project.

Yet the escalation of armed struggle did not serve to radicalize the movement there as profoundly as had been true of Mozambique, this despite the fact that in Zimbabwe, too, the ideological discourses of the movement were increasingly cast in Marxist terms. For internecine politicking remained very much the order of the day both between ZANU and ZAPU as rival claimants to nationalist primacy and within the two movements themselves. Various attempts to transcend these limitations on a new, more ideologically progressive basis (the ZIPA initiative of the mid-70s, designed to displace the old guard leadership and initially viewed with some favour by the host FRELIMO government in Mozambique, provides a case in point) collapsed. Guerilla advances, arguably not as deeply rooted in popular assertions on the ground as had been FRELIMO's also seemed, in their impact, to be less integrated into the circuits of the exile leadership's politics. This, plus the fact that end-game in Zimbabwe saw the reassertion of the imperial factor (via Britain's orchestrating of the Lancaster House decolonization talks), narrowed considerably the further revolutionary potential of the popular movement's victory – though many felt, nonetheless, that the saliency of the land question in Zimbabwe and the existence of a relatively large African working class might serve to keep pressure on the leadership to deliver on the radical promise implicit in much of its rhetoric.[4]

If, however, the promise of radicalization ultimately appeared in somewhat muted form in Zimbabwe, the nationalists' victory there became an important piece in the regional pattern of advance against the redoubts of white minority rule, bringing the front-line of struggle ever closer to the region's core, South Africa. Moreover, South Africa was itself stirring during this period, the 1970s witnessing the dramatic revival of the popular movement there. As we shall see, the presence of a vast and remarkably creative working class in the latter country promises, perhaps more firmly than elsewhere in the region, that liberation there will take on an increasingly socialist edge. Yet the intricate interpenetration of racial oppression and class exploitation – and of both nationalist and socialist responses to such domination – have lent a note of unpredictability to this process. Look, for example, at the very terms of the revival we have mentioned.

Bear in mind that the 1960s represented a trough in the history of popular resistance in South Africa. That resistance had peaked in the 1950s with various dramatic campaigns of mass action, but the apartheid state all too soon had managed to regain the upper hand, using the post-Sharpville Emergency regulations to ban popular organizations like the African National Congress (ANC) and the Pan-Africanist Congress (PAC), to jail, ban or drive into exile large numbers of activists, to crush, in short, all open opposition. In fact the state had dealt the popular movement not merely a crushing physical blow but also a psychological one of deeply demobilizing proportions. As the banned organizations (most importantly, the ANC) struggled to reestablish a political – and now, of necessity, military – presence relevant to the new terrain, a vacuum was created that would only slowly be filled.

But filled it was, in the first instance by the emergence of the Black Consciousness movement. An ideological project that paralleled other cultural nationalist expressions of the time (like 'Black Power' in North America) it was largely the creation of petty-bourgeois intellectuals (albeit many of them of impressive stature like Steve Biko), with separatist overtones, limited strategic sense and a minimal grasp of the possible role of the popular classes in effecting social change. However, as a reaffirmation of racial pride and of the sentiment of resistance to the apartheid dispensation Black Consciousness was significant. Perhaps, as its themes began to permeate the ambience within which new generations were growing up, its immediate importance was more psychological than political. But not for long. For it was a fresh generation of youth who, as students, would soon rock the apartheid system to its foundations. Thus, in 1976, in Soweto and elsewhere, they squared off not merely against 'Bantu education' and the imposition of Afrikaans as a medium of instruction but against the entire system of oppression that they despised and now chose not to fear.

Of at least equal centrality to the rebirth of resistance was the stirring of the black working class, prefigured in various ways in the late sixties and early seventies and finding its most dramatic early expression in the strikes of Durban (in particular) in 1972–4. But perhaps dramatic confrontation was less crucial, at this point, than the more mundane process that also marked the seventies, that of laying the organizational foundations of what were to become a wide range of vigorously independent trade unions. True, in the Soweto events, the fit between students and workers was often less than smooth, even producing some conflict and tension. Moreover, the most solidly grounded of the new unions (those that would soon come together under the banner of FOSATU, for example) were often loath to move quickly and assertively onto the terrain of politics *per se*. In part this reflected a particular reading by some union activists of the history of the 1950s when, they felt, SACTU, the trade union wing of the Congress Alliance, had all too uncritically subordinated the consolidation of its presence on the shop-floor to the demands of nationalist mobilization. There was also some suspicion that the vanguardist pretensions of the ANC (and, perhaps even more to the point, those of the ANC's close ally, the South African Communist Party) might ultimately be pursued at the expense of the working classes' own interests.

Despite such tensions it bears emphasizing that what was being created in the 1970s was the context for creative interaction between a revived popular democratic politics and an increasingly radical working-class project. In the next section we will examine in more detail how these two strands have come together to create a particularly promising and South Africa-specific version of radicalized nationalism. First, however, something further must be said about the peculiarly regional nature of the radicalization process we have begun to trace. Self-evidently, the region's political economy is tied together by the omnipresence of the long arm of South Africa, the latter's hegemony forged by long years of southern African history. Small wonder, then, that the process of liberation should itself spring across national frontiers.

Thus, the 1975 victory over Portugal of nationalist forces in Mozambique and Angola, as well as the Angolan repelling of a South African invasion force in 1975 had great and visible resonance, being, without doubt, one of the inspirations that produced Soweto. Nor is it entirely accidental that the next dramatic popular outburst in South Africa – the school boycotts in Cape Town and beyond in 1980 – came hard on the heels of ZANU's victory and the realization of Zimbabwean independence. Of course, the unfortunate fact is that these kinds of linkage also fuelled the fires of counter-revolution in South Africa, making such 'front-line states' prime targets for South African 'destabilization' tactics in the next round. If victories on the 'front-line' had helped the South African movement rebuild its self-confidence it soon became apparent that the fate of such states was even more dependant on the pace with which the South African movement could build its own revolution in the region's heartland – and thus remove, from within, the chief source of their destabilization. Phrased in such terms the regional nature of the revolutionary process we are discussing has never been clearer than it is at the present moment.

II. The Socialist Promise

In the first flush of independence, however, and in the former Portuguese colony of Mozambique in particular, the prospect of consolidating the revolutionary promise of the liberation struggle seemed strong. True, the colonial inheritance from the Portuguese was a grim one, Portugal's status as the most backward country in Europe having left its grotesque mark on its colonies. Thus Mozambique was relatively undeveloped even by African standards, while much of such development as the Portuguese had facilitated was designed to service the South African economy – via the movement of migrant labour, the provision of transport outlets to the sea, the planned marketing of power from the Cabora Bassa dam project. The precipitant flight of the Portuguese settler community at independence merely brought further into crisis an already distorted system, now undermining the network of commercialization and key agricultural and industrial sectors in ways that the new FRELIMO government would have had trouble adjusting to even under the most favourable of circumstances.

But the circumstances were to prove far from favourable. Mozambique set itself to support the struggles of its Zimbabwean allies for freedom, providing a crucial rear base for the ZANU guerillas and immediately implementing sanctions against the Smith regime at very great cost (the Mozambican town of Beira, one of Rhodesia's chief outlets to the sea, becoming almost immediately a ghost port, for example). There were other costs to this act of solidarity, the most expensive, in retrospect, being Rhodesia's invention of the National Resistance Movement (the MNR or Renamo), conjured up from the dregs of Portugal's former colonial security apparatus to raise the costs of FRELIMO support for ZANU by creating havoc inside Mozambique. A pin-prick at first, the Renamo tactic was to become a major instrument of destabilization once taken over by the South Africans in the wake of Zimbabwean independence. Economic dependence on South Africa also gave FRELIMO's enemies leverage. Yet despite problems inside the country and without, the new government did seek to concretize its socialist aspirations.

It attempted, for example, to generalize the politically empowering experience of the liberated areas to all other parts of the country via the mechanism of the 'dynamizing groups', structures of democratic participation established in rural settings, neighbourhoods and workplaces. Truly stirring developments began to occur in the social services sphere, in education, health and the like, and significant changes were projected in the area of women's emancipation, for example. The economy, too, began to be brought under state control and planning – if at a pace, dictated by the vacuum created in many sectors by Portuguese abandonment of various economic enterprises, that sometimes ran ahead of FRELIMO's own better judgement. Within two years of achieving independence FRELIMO had become a 'vanguard party' of 'Marxist-Leninist' provenance and was conceiving large, even grandiose, plans of national economic development centred on state ownership and planning and peasant-based cooperatization.

The catastrophic forestalling of such plans is a long and painful story.[5] Certainly weaknesses in FRELIMO's own project provide part of the explanation. Was its vanguardism a little too closed and self-righteous, its 'Marxism – Leninism' too frozen and inflexible, its economic planning too preoccupied with high-tech, large-scale solutions and too little preoccupied with peasant need and incentives? Probably, but even as FRELIMO moved at its 1983 Fourth Congress to profit from the lessons of its mistakes its space for further manoeuvre had already narrowed disastrously, narrowed by dint of the regional war waged by South Africa that was fast enveloping the country. Soon FRELIMO found itself sueing for peace with South Africa (at Nkomati in early 1984), backing away as it did so from even that minimal level of concrete assistance it had felt able to give the ANC.

And it also found itself forced to treat much more solicitously than would have been its preference with the minions of international capitalism (the global aid network and the IMF for example), forced, concomitantly, to allow a much wider space for 'the logic of the market' to determine its choices both domestically and internationally. It seems fair to say that FRELIMO's earlier errors had been primarily those of a genuinely left leadership become too triumphalist and too self-confident of its ability to force the pace of advance. Yet many observers now feared that new strata were emerging around the state apparatus and in the private sector that might begin to have a vested interest in moving the country ever more definitively away from the vestiges of its socialist project. This will not happen easily. Certainly FRELIMO's Fifth Congress, set for July of this year, seems likely to be a forum within which tough debate will take place as to how best to safeguard something of the essence of the project first developed in Mozambique's liberated areas. But as with somewhat parallel developments in Angola – albeit developments produced in the latter country in the context of an even more direct and aggressive intervention by South Africa and the United States – the results in Mozambique are a sobering reminder of the limits on what can be achieved on the periphery of an untransformed region.

Developments in Zimbabwe are also sobering, as earlier comments in this essay have already anticipated. South Africa has sought to create trouble for an independent Zimbabwe certainly, even if in much more modest ways than has been the case in either Mozambique or Angola. But the main barrier to a Zimbabwean revolution has been largely self-generated, in ways anticipated during the process of liberation itself. For, as noted, the victorious movement remained less transformed by the practice of armed struggle than might have been hoped. Moreover, profiting (they argued) from the negative lessons of Mozambique's experience and, no doubt, cognizant of the hostile regional terrain, the ZANU leadership chose to approach the existing settler/capitalist economic structure very gingerly indeed. Yet it soon appeared that the leadership had come to make such a virtue of this apparent necessity that their revolutionary credentials were rendered increasingly suspect. Ibbo Mandaza has summarized the process in the following terms: 'as the African petty bourgeoisie began gradually to find access to the same economic and social status as their white counterparts so, too, did it become increasingly unable to respond to the aspirations of the workers and peasants. . . . It became imperative, as an act of survival for the new state, to put a rein on its mass base. . . . Political principles and ideological commitments appeared mortgaged on the altar of private property!'[6]

To be sure, advances were made via this route in terms of 'substantial levels of food production, the growth of a layer of medium to small peasant producers, a maintenance of infrastructure, improved educational and agricultural services for much of the population and an absence of racial polarization'. Yet even the commentator who makes these points confesses himself uneasy with Mugabe's 'commandist style of leadership' and his 'demobilizing (of) democratic forms of organization after independence'.[7] And other observers emphasize Zimbabwe's extensive, often quite supine, accomodations with international capitalism, the state's self-interested muzzling of the working class and its stalling of any very meaningful programme of rural transformation (cooperativization, the beginnings of land reform and the like). And they note the fact that the Zimbabwean polity – despite the running start towards a more fundamental transformation ostensibly provided it by the experience of armed struggle – has nonetheless come to be marked by additional negative features all too familiar from developments in African states elsewhere on the continent. Thus, what has transpired is less the mobilization of the mass of population along class lines (as 'workers and peasants') and more the instrumentalization of that population as ethnic constituencies (whether as 'Shona' vs. 'Ndebele' or in terms of intra-Shona distinctions) for regional political barons jockeying for power and privilege at the centre of the system. Nor has quasi-capitalist accomodation been altogether successful even in strictly economic terms, as Zimbabwe, too, finds itself increasingly in a mendicant posture towards the IMF and its attendants.

We must be cautious here. Sobering facts about the presently visible denouements to liberation from white-minority rule in the countries we have been discussing should not blind us to the importance of what has been achieved. This is especially clear once we have grasped the fact that – given the centrality of South Africa – revolution in the countries in southern Africa cannot be fully realized until that revolution encompasses the entire region. How much more clearly exposed is South Africa than it was a decade and a half ago, then, and how much further south has the front line of struggle in the sub-continent been pushed? Isn't Zimbabwe, in spite of its contradictions still on that front-line, still rock solid, for example, in its military support for a besieged Mozambique? And hasn't that front-line itself been pushed further south in recent months, when, as a direct result of a substantial military set-back suffered at the hands of the Angolans and their Cuban allies, South Africa has had to accept the prospect of a democratic political future for its own colony of South-West Africa/Namibia?

Once again, the answer to this latter question must be 'yes'-and 'no'. Unfortunately, as this essay is being completed (in February, 1989) it is still too early to be confident of the precise outcome of the United Nations' entry upon the scene in Namibia to supervise the transition to majority rule, although that entry is indeed something to celebrate. Yet there are also disturbing signs that South Africa will still manage to snatch a smattering of victory from the jaws of this defeat, working as it now is (with some western connivance) to warp the political process of Namibia's transition to independence more in its favour. Its goal: to undermine the U.N.'s ability to counterbalance structures of social control that Pretoria has spent decades implanting on the ground in Namibia.[8] Moreover, even if the process of transition is kept reasonably honest and open (thereby, undoubtedly, ensuring a SWAPO victory), the fact remains that South Africa's economic and military power will continue to hover over a post-independence SWAPO government in ways that may prove preemptive of any very great revolutionary content to the latter's project. In short, liberatory advance in Namibia could prove to be at least as flawed and as contradictory as it has been elsewhere in the region. We thus return to the heart of the matter, to the prospect for revolution in South Africa itself.

There, the key revolutionary 'moment' to date has proven to be the insurrection of 1984 – 1986, an insurrection that displayed graphically both the strengths and weaknesses of the South African movement, broadly defined. Towards that moment the seeds of resistance planted in the 1970s continued to grow.[9] Now, however, the two broad strands of above-ground resistance earlier identified began to interpenetrate even more markedly than had hitherto been the case. Certainly working-class activism as focussed around trade union initiatives became increasingly important. So much so that the dominant classes, caught off balance, sought (following the terms of the Wiehann Commission) to coopt this fledgling movement through recognition of black trade union rights within the framework of existing and quite restrictive labour relations structures. Although a heated debate ensued within trade union circles as to whether to run the risks of registration under these terms, ultimately the process of legalization was turned back against the regime, seized upon from below to carve out further space for working class assertion. The organizational drive continued, notably in the mines (where the National Union of Mineworkers gained increasing prominence), with the formation of the Congress of South African Trade Unions (COSATU) in November, 1985, ultimately defining a high water mark in this union sphere. Thus, by 1987, it was estimated that this union centre had as many as one million signed-up members.

Community-based activism also grew apace. Students/youth continued to be important; the 1980 boycott movement which fanned out from the Cape demonstrated this as has the prominence of school boycott and youth militancy in the insurrectionary moment of 1984–6. But community activism was now much more broadly based, the general ambience of defiance giving rise to a range of community-centred resistances running well beyond the classroom. These surfaced in every area where the impact of the regime's deepening economic crisis and its authoritarian practices could be felt, in rent strikes and consumer and transportation boycotts for example, and gave rise to a rich array of community organizations throughout South Africa. These organizations activated workers where they lived and reinforced their growing radicalization, while also providing a particularly important nexus for the entry of women into the struggle. It was this kind of ferment, too, that was to press (some) churches more firmly into the ranks of militancy. As a result, when the initiative was taken in 1983 to organize nationally to resist the government's imposition of a new tri-cameral parliamentary system (involving token chambers for Indians and 'Coloureds' and continued exclusion of Africans) the building blocks for the resultant umbrella organization, the United Democratic Front, were already in place. In the UDF, it has been estimated, were two million people represented by some 600 constituent bodies. They were successful, in the first instance, in undermining the legitimacy of the tri-cameral elections but were now also girded for further confrontation with the apartheid system.

This essay earlier alluded to the interpenetration of the two strands of resistance. This became very marked, full of promise for the increasing efficacy and increasing radicalization of the resistance movement, although also problematic in certain particulars. As suggested above, the trade unions harboured some (notably within the FOSATU camp) who approached the broader political arena gingerly, concerned to root the workers' struggle as firmly as possible on the shop-floor and suspicious of the merely 'populist' intentions of certain political leaders. As a result, it was often the best organized of trade unions that chose to keep at arm's distance from the UDF. At the same time the community activism of their own membership was a force drawing such unions into a more overt role in the political arena, making them, before long, active partners in many of the boycotts and stayaways that became such a prominent part of the struggle that fanned out from the Vaal Triangle after September, 1984. Moreover, there were also unions emerging (SAAWU and GAWU for example) that actually placed primary emphasis upon community organization and nationalist politics. As pressure for greater trade union unity developed these two elements (increasingly distinguished as 'workerist' and 'populist' tendencies) found themselves linked together in a relationship, sometimes debilitating and sometimes creative, that produced the aforementioned COSATU.

Particularly germane to the way in which these different emphases now began to play themselves out was the reemergence of the African National Congress to a position of centrality within the broad resistance movement. As I have argued elsewhere[10], the ANC's resurgence sprang from a combination of its historical legitimacy, its ability (unlike the rival Pan-Africanist Congress) to retain unity and coherence in exile and its unique promise, exemplified by an escalating level of sabotage actions ('armed propaganda' in the ANC's lexicon), to lend military muscle to any confrontation with the state. Moreover, as the struggle escalated, the ANC showed itself particularly skilled politically in bringing the broad array of popular resistance into focus around its own slogans and programmatic demands, even in periods when popular actions seemed to have been running, spontaneously, well ahead of any direct ANC mobilization. Examples to be mentioned include the anti-SAIC and anti-Republic Day campaigns, the Free Mandela initiative, the widely-publicized emphases upon, first, 'ungovernability' and then 'from ungovernability to people's power' and the successful attempt to bring the Freedom Charter back into prominence as a crucial touchstone of the movement's demands. In addition, in organizational terms, the ANC proved successful in linking itself to the most important new initiatives being mounted above ground inside the country – with the UDF, for example, and, more indirectly but equally importantly, with a rapidly crystallizing COSATU.

This trend was not uncontested, of course. There were rivals to this ANC – UDF – COSATU alliance that was slowly but surely emerging centre-stage in resistance circles in South Africa, notably those who continued to define their politics quite self-consciously with reference to a relatively unalloyed version of the black consciousness tradition (AZAPO, the National Forum, the National Council of Trade Unions/NACTU). Such resistance to ANC – UDF – COSATU hegemony sometimes presented itself in leftist terms, attempting to rationalize its racially exclusivist preoccupations as radicalism by highlighting the centrality of the *black* working class' to its project. Not particularly convincing in many of its protestations, this tendency has remained, in any case, a comparatively minor one within resistance circles. In practice, the real debate over the probable definition of the revolutionary

content of the South African movement has tended to take place *within* the
major alliance identified above[11].

Not that identifying the dynamics of the struggle over the emerging content
of liberation is a straightforward exercise. To begin with, there is the question
of the precise degree of radicalism represented by the nationalist project of
the ANC itself. Certainly the most prominent ANC ideological formulae have
tended to emphasize, over the years, the advisability of a two-stage process of
liberation (national liberation-cum-democratization first and socialism later)
– even if, more often than not, the working class is presented as being the
single most crucial element to the liberatory alliance and therefore, the ANC
line hints, some kind of guarantor of socialism in the next round. No doubt
there are tactical considerations at play here. Racial oppression is a particularly prominent reality in South Africa, needless to say, and it is tempting
to develop a politics that centres on mass sensitivity to that fact. Not only
might this be expected to broaden the class alliance of blacks pushing for
change, it can even speak, it has been argued, to workers in a genuinely
radicalizing manner. For with the state's repressive role etched in colour,
workers might be more inclined to broaden the 'trade union consciousness'
generated at the workplace into a potentially hegemonic project that implies
the actual overthrow of that state. Moreover, presenting the struggle as being,
first and foremost, a struggle for 'deracializaton' and democratization can be
expected both to add to the coalition of international supporters committed
to the overthrow of apartheid and even, possibly, to help to split the white
community inside South Africa itself in more promising ways than might be
the case were the emancipatory project defined, first and foremost, in even
more radical terms.

Yet there are also dangers to such an approach. If working-class power and
socialist priorities are not established absolutely firmly from the outset, how
is the pull towards mere petty bourgeois nationalism to be countered? For,
as the period of insurrection was to demonstrate, the nearer the movement
comes to power, the more actively will merely liberal forces in the white
business community and in the black petty bourgeoisie (including within the
ANC itself!) seek to narrow the nationalist agenda; moreover, the complex-
ities of dealing with South Africa's sophisticated economy will, in and of
itself, exert a formidably deradicalizing pressure upon any post-liberation
government for whom, at best, some form of 'social democracy' may seem
the most 'reasonable' course.

Set against this, however, is the ANC's own discernibly radical tradition
(this in part associated with the South African Communist Party, and therefore something of a mixed blessing – given the difficulties that party has had
in freeing itself from its long-term Stalinist incubus). Important, too, is the
continuing pattern of radicalization of the township youth, ever more inclined
(accurately enough) to underscore the links between capitalist exploitation
and racial oppression in South Africa. And, finally, there are the trade

unions, some of the most important of which (the Metalworkers are a good example) are very far from manifesting mere 'trade union consciousness' in their increasingly socialist claims upon the future. In part the ANC has had to go to school to such unions in reestablishing its preeminent position within the South African movement, and this is yet another promising portent. Moreover, as noted above, 'Charterist' elements have had to jockey with the so-called 'workerists' within COSATU in ways that have not split the union or the broader movement and may even have strengthened them – by foreshadowing the manner in which the issues of the future can be openly debated. In short, the imperatives thrown up by South Africa's class structure seem an important innoculation against the tailing off of successful struggle there into the mere Africanization of capitalism (even if this were to be presented, with some good reason, as a tactically necessary short-term bow in the direction of 'social democracy').

Needless to say, rendering permanent the South African revolution will be a source of on-going struggle even in a post-apartheid South Africa. Yet it is one thing to speculate about the post-apartheid future, another to reach that future by, in the first instance, actually overthrowing the apartheid state. In the 1984–86 period, when the pace of change in South Africa seemed to be accelerating geometrically, 'futurology' was the vogue. True, questions of class alliance germane to determining the likely long-term socialist content of liberation in South Africa are also relevant to defining the most appropriate line-up of class agents for change in the present phase of struggle. Yet, as the failure of insurrection was to demonstrate, there are also quite specific questions that arise regarding the modalities of insurrectionary practice itself. In fact, these are questions that the movement inside South Africa is only just beginning to wrestle with in the context of the set-back that South Africa's repressive Emergency regulations have meant for it. This essay will return to the consequent debate in its next section. Here, however, a brief look at some of the strengths and weaknesses of the revolutionary challenge exemplified in the 1984–86 confrontation is in order.

The range of incident that comprised the insurrection was significant, certainly, and so, cumulatively, was the number of South Africans involved. And it did shake the dominant classes, especially when domestic unrest also began to trigger off more dramatic sanctions activity from abroad (including, not least importantly, those 'market-induced sanctions' that saw the international banking community reconsidering the viability of South Africa's investment climate!) Yet just how deep did the organization of insurrection cut? Certainly there were those who felt, even at the time, that the UDF as a national body was top heavy, in too much of a hurry, and, in not grasping the necessity to further consolidate local organization, more merely parasitic of popular energies boiling away at that level than it should have been. At the same time it is true that, as events wore on, more emphasis was given to the genesis of streets committees, peoples' courts and the like, institutions that promised to provide greater resilience and an even greater sense of purpose and accomplishment at the base. And in some spheres remarkable examples of novel kinds of creativity appeared. Thus in education, in part at ANC urging, the tactic of mere boycott of the schools was scrutinized critically and, with the linking of parents groups to those of students in such organizations as the National Education Crisis Committee, exciting programmes began to be devised that sought to reclaim the schools as, in effect, quasi-liberated territory upon which to build new social relations and devise new syllabi; it was in such a context that the slogan 'Peoples's Education for People's Power' replaced that of 'No Education Before Liberation'! Perhaps, in the end, it was merely a matter of timing: the insurrection as learning experience was nipped too quickly in the bud by state repression to permit the movement to profit promptly from its mistakes and deepen its project sufficiently.

All the more disappointing, then, that the movement could not defend itself better from the state when the crunch came. This was especially so in light of the fact that a promise had been made by the ANC, both in the year or two immediately proceeding the insurrection and in 1985, in the heat of battle, at the movement's Kabwe Consultative Conference. The promise was that the ANC would be able to shift its military presence from mere 'armed propaganda' (however important that might be) to actively arming and defending the resistance on the ground in the townships. What actually transpired along these lines was very much less than this. And what of the goals of insurrection? Certainly the strategic focus of the dramatic events of the time was less than clear, in part because, almost inevitably, no one centre had real control over such events, in part because there often seemed operative the implicit premise that mere revolt, as widespread as possible, would produce relevant 'negotiations'. The ANC, at the centre of events in many important ways, did position itself deftly for such negotiations, as a string of visitors, including a weighty group of senior businesspeople, trooped dutifully to Lusaka. Yet this was not to prove adequate as a road to power.

III Counterrevolution and Future Prospects

The nature of the South African state's response to the growth of revolutionary challenge, both domestically and in the region at large, has already been anticipated at several points in this essay. We have noted, in particular, the key role played by South African destabilization in undermining much of the promise of socialism in such countries as Mozambique and Angola. In Angola this has involved direct military intervention from the very dawn of Angolan independence (November 11, 1975) when, with American encouragement, South African troops drove for Luanda. Only the eleventh hour military assistance of Cuba saved the MPLA government. But this was merely the first phase of the long and wasting war South Africa (and its American ally) was to inflict upon Angola, both directly and by essential support provided to its local cat's-paw in the fray, the UNITA movement of Jonas Savimbi. As noted, South Africa was defeated in southern Angola in 1988, but at great cost to Angola: left behind was a country in tatters, seeking economic succour from the IMF and forced to request the departure of the ANC, with its military bases, from its soil as part of 1988's peace accords.

This latter was no insignificant concession, especially given the fact that one of the key goals of South African destabilization has been a quarantining of ANC presence in the front-line states. A second goal has been to undermine the possibility of the front-line establishing an alternative grid of regional economic activity (under the auspices of the Southern African Development Coordination Conference, for example) outside the historically established economic overlordship of South Africa. Of course, this has been even more apparent in Mozambique where Zimbabwe's possible alternative links of transportation to the sea have been a chief target of Renamo activities, than in Angola. But there has been a third, quite self-conscious goal: to turn the promise of nationalist victory and, in particular, of socialist assertion in the region to mud, in order to undermine the resonance of such advances inside South Africa itself and to facilitate the broader counter-revolutionary goals of South Africa's western allies.

True, opinions have differed from time to time within the imperial camp as to when the process of military destabilization and consequent concessions made by the target regime could be said to have gone far enough. With Nkomati, for example, most western actors, including, somewhat surprisingly, the Reagan White House, chose to remove Mozambique from the top of their international hit-list, looking, increasingly, to the IMF and tied aid to finish the job of reabsorbing that weakened country into the global circuits of capital. Yet South Africa itself has preferred to drive on with its project of cruel destruction in Mozambique, seeking further to neutralize that country by, in effect, destroying the very fabric of its social life-targeting, through Renamo, essential economic linkages, murdering trained personnel and, literally, terrorizing the population. (In Angola, in contrast, as South Africa prepares to retire from the fray, the United States, at least momentarily, promises to pick up the slack in support for UNITA and works to block Angola's entry into the IMF!) Somewhat less dramatically, elsewhere in the region, South Africa has been prepared to use economic leverage (the sanctions that helped topple an awkward Lesotho government in 1986 or the economic whip that is constantly being cracked over the head of Zimbabwe, for example) and destabilization in a lower key (lightning raids into Botswana and Zimbabwe or the stirring of the pot of disunity in the latter country by sponsorship of the so-called 'super-ZAPU') to gain tactical advantage.

No less crucial has been the use of the iron fist where the threat to Pretoria's interests is even more acute – inside South Africa itself. Some measure of preemptive accomodation to be struck with black forces pressing for change has been, from time to time, part of the apartheid regime's domestic strategy, the attempted cooptation of the black trade union movement mentioned earlier being a case in point. But, in fact, this was merely one component of the broader 'reform' package of the late 1970s that was designed to peel away a significant stratum of urbanized, relatively better-off blacks into acceptance of the legitimacy of an only marginally altered system. As we have seen, mass mobilization around an emerging programme of far more meaningful liberation quickly put paid to such a tactic. Voices could still be heard, from some sections of the business community for example (and particularly in the context of subsequent insurrection), suggesting that more substance be given to the reform initiative. Yet only the most bold were prepared to suggest that anything even approximating to a complete deracialization (and colour-blind bourgeois democratization) of South Africa might be the best means to insulate South African capitalism from going down with the country's structure of racial oppression (cf. Zac de Beer's well known comment that 'we dare not allow the baby of free enterprise to be thrown out with the bath-water of apartheid'). For most in the white community any such changes were either absolutely unthinkable on first principles or (at best) judged to be far too risky. On the other hand, half measures of 'reform' seemed not to work either. In consequence, the state's response to insurrection was to be, almost exclusively, a repressive one. When, in turn, this repression seemed to 'work' – producing, at least in the short run, a measure of social stability – most nay-sayers in the business community and elsewhere lapsed into relatively comfortable passivity once again.

The modalities of repression utilized inside South Africa in the past several years have been no less ruthless than those developed by Pretoria in its regional counterrevolutionary activities. Indeed, one senses lessons learned in Mozambique and Angola have actually been carried back into South Africa for application in the black townships. Thus, in the late 1970s, the regime seemed momentarily to convince itself that it could find black intermediaries who might actually help sell 'reform' and cooptation to the broader mass of urbanized blacks and thereby legitimate the neo-apartheid system. Now, however, any black allies were much more obviously cast for the role of fellow policemen, junior partners in the repressive apparatus. True, the cutting edge of repression is still the police force and, increasingly, the army, the latter now also involved, within the framework of an innovative and remarkably comprehensive 'National Security Management System', in what is, for it, the relatively unconventional task of scourging the townships. The toll of death, arbitrary arrest and torture, crackdown on the media and banning of individuals and organizations that followed with the imposition of the partial Emergency of 1985 and the nation-wide, far more draconian Emergency of 1986 (and subsequent years) is well known. But enter, in addition, the vigilantes, black gangs with foot-soldiers drawn from *lumpen* elements but focussed around the initiatives of urban councillors and businessmen, of Bantustan politicians and warlords, who have chosen to profit from the existing system. These are killers to whom the police either have turned a blind eye or else actively trained and they have been encouraged to stalk the democratic movement with lethal intent, as seen in the debacle of Crossroads in 1985–86 or in the depradations carried out by Buthelezi and his Inkatha minions in Pietermaritzburg in 1987–8. Here is a 'scorched earth' approach to the project of neutralizing dissent fully worthy of Renamo.

More could be written about the barbarities of repression. Though less visible to the outside world because of severe restrictions on media coverage of developments in South Africa, 1988 actually witnessed an intensification of the crackdown. That this should still be necessary after several years of the Emergency is indicative of just how deep the resistance runs. Nonetheless, the costs should not be underestimated. As the Weekly Mail recently put the point, 'dealing with opponents on the left (is) one of the few areas where the government showed no hesitation and a clear-cut, imaginative policy. They produced a constant supply of new methods of repression, the best example of which was the Emergency restriction order. . . Individuals, organizations, even funerals, were subjected to the most extraordinary list of incomprehensible restrictions, dished out so fast that nobody could keep track. . . The government started the process by restricting 17 organizations in February, including the United Democratic Front and Azapo, with a partial restriction on COSATU. This dealt with the major and best known organizations. Gradually, as new bodies began to reveal themselves or old bodies took up the cudgels, they were dealt similar blows. . . It was a new form of prison without bars'[12]

Of course, there were plenty of bars as well, and other equally merciless tactics. Thus 'some of the major resistance leaders of the 1980s, the people who pioneered the UDF-style of non-violent opposition, were dubbed violent terrorists and sentenced to long terms of imprisonment in the "Delmas" treason trial'. Or take those churches that tried to step into the partial vacuum left by the February restrictions. 'Government response: the clergy were water-cannoned by the police in Cape Town, the headquarters of the SACC (South African Council of Churches) and the Southern African Catholic Bishops Conference were mysteriously bombed and the Reverend Frank Chikane's mother received a hand grenade in the post.' When 143 (white) conscripts announced that they would not honour their call-up for military service it looked, momentarily, as if the state might discuss seriously the possibility of alternative service with the End Conscription Campaign (ECC). Colder heads prevailed, however, and the ECC merely joined the list of restricted organizations. Assassination continued to be a favourite tactic of the powers that be, both at home (where the list of victims grew) and abroad, where a pattern of physical removal of ANC activists (about 50 since 1981) peaked with the murder of the ANC's Paris representative, Dulcie September, in

March. When, as the year progressed, more and more student and youth organizations became a particular target for state attack, the implications were sobering. If the apartheid government was not even marginally interested in finding real intermediaries for dialogue about a different kind of future, what alternatives were open. As youth representatives put the point: 'underground is not a healthy terrain for struggle for an organization that wants to reach the masses, make statements and operate above-board. But conditions of near-illegality have been forced on us'![13]

Clearly, the Emergency had narrowed the terrain for above ground activity, but had that terrain disappeared altogether? What could be done, for example, to follow through on the insight, produced by failed insurrection, that a firmer base would have to be built at the grass roots level both to keep the struggle alive in the short-run and to prepare a base for any future dramatic confrontation? There were those who argued that, given the strength of the state, a politics of bargaining and negotiation with the state, was the only kind of viable politics in any case. Here an analogy with the trade union's entry into the industrial relations system (the better to find space for further manoeuvre and demand) has been suggested – *ad nauseam* by Steven Friedman of the South African Institute of Race Relations, for example.[14] Could not township organizations also group around concrete local demands, analogous to the wage demand, in order both to make gains, build strength and gradually transform the South African situation.

Of course, this was already being done in some ways (with rent strikes in many townships) and plotted in others (the aforementioned NECC programme for the schools, for example). Nor need an extension of this approach collapse, by definition, into reformism. Perhaps a revival of Andre Gorz's concept of 'structural reform' (which he distinguishes, precisely, from 'reformism') would be illuminating here, in part because it leads to a far more revolutionary understanding of the kind of activities being identified here than does Friedman's studied 'pragmatism'.[15] For Gorz suggests that in periods when revolution is not immediately on the agenda organization for reform can be a revolutionary act – provided the gains demanded and won are self-consciously understood by the political movement in question as implicating, systematically, a series of further demands and provided, as well, that the mobilization of people around such demands leads to the crystallization of organizational forms that mark a process of cumulative empowerment and developing revolutionary potential. In a situation like that of South Africa this approach could mean visible advance on specific fronts (thereby giving people a necessarily *concrete* sense of the ongoing struggle in the short-run) while also building the popularly-based organizational infrastructure crucial to another, more successful round of insurrection sometime in the future. Might more of this kind of strategic thinking have given a greater sense of focus to the insurrection just past? More importantly, do possibilities for such a 'structural reform' approach still exist in the South Africa of the Emergency?

It was by thinking about similar questions, as I wrote after a recent clan-destine visit to South Africa, that 'some UDF activists even briefly floated, for discussion, the idea of participating in the local blacks-only elections, and thereby seizing hold of state-structured township councils as one possible way of giving fresh focus to popular resistance to the state. Ultimately the idea was rejected, since the councils are, in fact, so tightly controlled by the apartheid administrative apparatus that they grant the democratic forces little real room for manoeuvre. In fact, only the most obvious of collaborators concluded otherwise, while Bishop Tutu and others, at some risk to themselves, called for a renewed boycott of such structures in the October elections. For its part, the state used its powers (and considerable manipulation of the electoral procedures) to neutralize the boycott and to attempt – with no great success, as things turned out – to manufacture the appearance of support for those few blacks prepared to help make its system work. Continued boycott of the councils made sense, I think, but some further discussion of the merits of the boycott made sense too. In any case, this was merely one example among the many I found of the readiness of South African democrats to scrutinize past practice in their effort to devise new and more relevant tactics.'[16]

The unions must operate in the short-run, too, and have, in fact, a little more space within which to do so. After all, a scorched earth tactic is scarcely viable for the state in the factories or the mines where the unions' constitu-ents, the workers, are vital to the production process. Yet the unions also find themselves on the defensive under the Emergency since the state and capital have both seized on the opportunity to roll back gains that have been made. Most dramatic has been the state's harsh new Labour Relations Amendment Bill, designed to reverse the gains unions have made for themselves in recent years. But one also finds a much more pugnacious attitude on the part of employers in their wage bargaining (typified in 1987 by the reaction of so rhetorically liberal an employer as Anglo-American to the mineworkers strike and by the actions of any number of corporations since). Unions have fought back with continuing industrial action to be sure, and even stayed in the pol-itical arena despite the restrictions on their so doing. The dramatic three day stayaway in June, 1988 (jointly coordinated with popular political structures) which saw as many as three million workers off the job demonstrated this, as did COSATU's attempt (aborted by the state) to have an all-in anti-apartheid conference in September of the same year. This is still a long way from the prospect of mobilizing the working-class at the point of production to, say, occupy the factories as part of a coordinated general strike, although one could hope that another insurrectionary moment would find action along such lines playing a more prominent part. But it is significant, nonetheless.

The planned September conference was significant for another reason – even though it did not occur. For its structuring envisaged a broadening of the alliance of resistance in very suggestive ways. Certainly those on the socialist left of COSATU felt it positive that Black Consciousness – related organizations were to be invited, less because of any objective weight in the struggle these organizations might have, however, than because of the principle of inclusiveness such an invitation established over and against the intolerance towards dissenting voices sometimes manifested by UDF-cum-Charterist cadres within and without the unions. Perhaps, it was hoped, failed insurrection had taught such cadres some greater humility than they had displayed during that insurrection or even in its immediate aftermath. If so, the democratic movement may be all the more open to the kind of self-critical learning experience it will need to undergo in order to regroup effectively – as well as more open, now and in the future, to voices of the left that continue to raise uncomfortable questions about the precise substance of the liberation that is being fought for. Indeed, some such questions might already have been relevant regarding the September meeting, given the amount of effort put into incorporating novel expressions of white liberalism (exemplified by the various sophisticated initiatives of Van Zyl Slabbert and others) into the proposed proceedings. Not that attempting this kind of outreach can be deemed to be, by definition, some kind of mistake. Merely something for wary revolutionaries to keep an eye on!

Unfortunately, the fact that the state ultimately banned such a meeting may be the most important thing about it. If it is significant that fresh attempts continue to be made to regroup the struggle aboveground, the difficulties of doing so underscore, as noted above, the importance of also having an underground. Insofar as this latter must also be conceived as being a *military* underground there is another possible dilemma, however. How is it possible to seek to split the white community by entering (however circumspectly) into dialogue with such credible liberal forces as exist there, while simultaneously attempting to raise the costs of apartheid for its beneficiaries by means of armed action? This is not an academic question. It has surfaced, apparently within the ANC itself, around the question of 'hard' and 'soft' targets. The ANC had already made it clear that, in pursuing military targets on the terrain now offered by the apartheid regime, there could be fewer guarantees than previously that civilian casualties could be avoided. Then, in mid-1988, statements by certain ANC personnel were taken in the South African press to imply that direct attacks on (white) civilians could not be ruled out, a controversy that coincided with a spate of such attacks inside South Africa. As it turned out, some of these attacks were of uncertain provenance (quite possibly provocations) and others the ANC disowned as mistakes, eschewing publicly – and not for the first time – the use of such tactics (just as it had on an earlier occasion been moved to condemn the wave of 'necklacing' that momentarily swept the townships). Not that the issue is undebatable. Would a collapse into 'mere terrorism' actually harden white attitudes as is often claimed, or might it, in the longer run, wear down white intransigence while further mobilizing black support? The case of Northern Ireland, to go no farther afield, tends to suggest the latter scenario to be an unlikely one, something the ANC, at the end of the day, is itself well aware of. At the same time, it is not difficult to imagine a certain desperation entering, from time to time, into the calculations of some armed liberators when faced with so gross and unyielding an enemy as the South African state.

Fortunately, the ANC is chiefly active on the military front in other, more promising, ways. Indeed, it 'carried out an unprecedented number of guerilla attacks (in 1988), despite security force claims that the movement's momentum had been broken. According to South African Police statistics, a total of 238 guerilla attacks took place in the first ten months of 1988, compared with 234 during the whole of last year, 230 in 1986, 136 in 1985 and 44 in 1984.'[17] In addition to the familiar brand of exemplary sabotage, many of these actions seem to have directly targeted army and police personnel (something promised, in June of 1988, by ANC military leader Chris Hani and quite welcome). Moreover, it seems likely that, more than previously, much of the back-up for these actions – the training and logistics – is grounded within structures internal to the country. This is just as well since South African destabilization in the region probably has had a negative impact on ANC's military capacity (lengthening supply lines and raising costs, for example); indeed, this may have been one important factor in making the ANC's armed presence less evident during the 1984–86 insurrection than might have been expected. As is true generally of the popular movement, then, there are lessons to be learned by the ANC from failed insurrection. Yet there is a clear indication that questions regarding both underground work and broader political strategy are being taken very seriously indeed within the ANC as it attempts to lay the ground-work for future advance.

One thing is clear, in any case: there is unlikely to be any purely military solution to the struggle in South Africa. Unfortunately there will be no negotiated settlement of the apartheid question (let alone of the capitalism question!) either – not until the existing regime is weakened very much more than it has been to date. Make no mistake: the apartheid regime is not all-powerful even now. Underlying its repressive bluster are very real economic weaknesses and vulnerabilities, these being signalled by continuing problems of slow growth, chronic unemployment, on-going balance of payment difficulties and vulnerability to sanctions (whenever, in international response to a renewed visibility of dramatic popular resistance, these may become a serious threat once again).[18] Nor is the political ground on which the government walks altogether solid. Certainly dissent exists on the centre-left of the white political spectrum. More important is the well-publicized 'rise of the right' (the Conservative Party, the neo-Nazi AWB), although this is less of a threat – and certainly less of a brake on 'reform' – than is sometimes claimed. For most problematic of all, in fact, is the lack of direction within the Nationalist Party camp itself, 'hard-liners' and 'soft-liners' (insofar as they can be meaningfully distinguished) more often than not merely neutralizing each other while also producing a mishmash of contradictory state policy. The passing from the scene of P.W. Botha, very much 'the leader' as the last surviving member of apartheid's parliamentary class of 1948, will not ease matters in this regard – even if intensified repression can serve for some time as a policy refuge for his immediate successors.

Yet, in the last analysis, one is drawn back to the fact that the regime can find no way to legitimate its rule politically vis-a-vis the black population. This is its real weakness. True, that black population is not an unproblematic category for the resistance movement either. The creative energy of the emergent South African movement has been formidable, a point to which this essay will return. But what is ultimately so tragic about the intransigence of South Africa's apartheid regime is how it has moved to choke off and denature such energy. Baulked of fulfillment, however temporarily, some of this energy can turn sour. Recall Gramsci's aphorism: 'The crisis consists precisely in the fact that the old is dying and the new cannot be born; in this interregnum a great variety of morbid symptoms appears.'[19] The pathology apparently attendant upon Winnie Mandela's recent role in Soweto is merely one example of such a morbid symptom. So, too, are those former militants amongst the township youth who have turned vigilante or informer, as the police rally to rebuild their own brand of township network. So, too, are those who permit themselves to be mobilized by ruthless warlords, along patron – client lines, against progressive trends in Natal or Crossroads.

As noted, the state will continue with attempts to shore up its own strata of black intermediaries – new urban partners for the Bantustan elites already in place. How much space can it hope to buy in this way? And how much by diverting some financial resources, especially to townships that have proven to be revolutionary flashpoints in the past, in order to complement its harassment of local militants with a modicum of economic betterment? (Housing is a particularly popular sphere for current experimentation in such up-grading of the living conditions of some of the more stabilized of black urban dwellers, for example.) Nor can one rule out other kinds of 'formative action', designed by capital and the state further to divide, rule and coopt. Indeed, even progressive trade union leaders worry aloud about a possible stratification of the working class itself that might prove counterproductive to revolution. What, they ask, are the implications of a gap that is emerging between workers in full-time, often skilled or semi-skilled, employment, workers who are organized and even relatively better off, and others, the marginalized, the unemployed or underemployed, who are piling up in the sprawling peri-urban shanty towns?[20] Specifically, the unions have attempted to counter the perils of a split between such strata with programmes for organizing the unemployed and such innovations as the 'Living Wage Campaign' (albeit, to date, with only modest success). Yet this is just one of the many challenges attendant upon uniting and mobilizing a black population whose profile is constantly being reshaped by the vagaries of an increasingly complex South African economy.

Indeed, it is the growing political capacity of the popular movement, faced with these and other challenges, that will determine just how fatal is the fact that neither state nor capital can legitimate themselves in South Africa. Certainly, the Emergency of the 1980s is not the Emergency of the 1960s. 'Morbid symptoms' to the contrary notwithstanding, the psychology of resistance now runs very deep. Inevitably, because of this, there will be dramatic flash-points of national significance; the regime itself has nightmares about the likely mass reaction if Nelson Mandela were to die on its hands in prison (although it equally fears to release him). But flash-points are not a revolution, even if they can prove to be privileged moments for focussing revolutionary energies. How will that energy, undoubtedly present in South Africa, find more effective focus? There can be no doubt that lessons have been learned. The latest *Weekly Mail* provides the mundane but instructive example of recent actions by the Western Cape Students' Congress: 'The burning barricades, the demonstrations violently broken up by police recalled the turmoil of 1985. But a new discipline and maturity underlay student action. Instead of adhoc reactions, protests formed part of a co-ordinated programme marked by thorough canvassing of student opinion for properly mandated change.' Moreover, the action's 'major significance. . . lay beyond the (large) numbers involved: it resulted in police reversing a decision to enter schools and ensure teaching took place'.[21]

'Discipline and maturity'. 'A coordinated programme'. Too often the image of South African protest in the western media, even when that coverage has been reasonably well-intentioned, has been that of the rock-throwing black mob, angry with good reason perhaps, but a mob nonetheless. A more accurate image of the history of the last ten or fifteen years of resistance (as sketched in the above account of it) would be that of profound political creativity and an ever higher level of organizational achievement on the part of the South African resister. As seen, the considerable revolutionary energy this essay has often alluded to as distinguishing the South African scene has already found powerful expression in an impressive array of organizations – in organizations like COSATU, like the UDF, like the ANC, like a hundred others, in organizations that focus the commitment of tens of thousands of individuals, in organizations bent but not broken by repression. This, and the renewal of a psychology of resistance, are the key facts about contemporary South Africa to be noted by those who would wish to see it transformed. It is these organizations that will not give the regime peace, these that carry the promise of ultimately finding the key to liberation. As I have hinted, within and between them struggle will occur (and often it will be class struggle) not only about the modalities of the current struggle but also about the precise content of liberation, about just how profoundly revolutionary that liberation will be. But already these organizations have served to empower the workers of South Africa, to empower the black population of South Africa, in significant ways. And they continue to do so.

In the end, it is the promise represented by the trajectory of such organizations that gives resonance to Magdoff and Sweezy's characterization of South Africa, penned several years ago: 'Its system of racial segregation and repression is a veritable paradigm of capitalist superexploitation. It has a white monopoly capitalist ruling class and an advanced black proletariat. It is so far the only country with a well developed, modern capitalist structure which is not only 'objectively' ripe for revolution but has actually entered a stage of overt and seemingly irreversible revolutionary struggle.'[22] Irreversible? In fact, Magdoff and Sweezy do themselves contemplate other possibilities, warning that 'a victory for counter-revolution – the stabilization of capitalist relations in South Africa, even if in somewhat altered form – would. . . be (a) stunning defeat for the world revolution'.

And some such 'stabilization' there has certainly been. It would be wise not to be triumphalist about South Africa. No matter how often it is said that fundamental change is – must be! – inevitable there, it is still something that will have to be won. The apartheid state will have to be overthrown, the logic of capitalism ('racial' or otherwise) that has been so integral to the repressive South African state will have to be qualified and, ultimately, reversed. This essay has reflected on some of the difficulties of so doing. But if triumphalism is no answer it would be equally unwise to despair. Reflect back upon the National Security Study Memorandum with which this essay began. As stated at the outset, things have come a long way since 1969 – in what has been, measured as 'historical time',· a relatively short span. Moreover, to repeat, this essay has been able to affirm that the crystallization – psychological, organizational – of advances already achieved provides a formidable legacy upon which the southern African movement, broadly defined, can mount the next round of challenge. Recall the story (perhaps apocryphal, although one hopes not) about Mao Zedong and the events of 1789. How did he evaluate the outcome of the French Revolution, he was asked. 'Its too soon to tell', he replied.

True, as well, of the southern African revolution. Yet the prospect of victory – for South Africa, for southern Africa – remains a good one. Later rather than sooner perhaps, undoubtedly at much greater cost than could be wished, likely to be a bit murkier in its outcome than one might have predicted a few short years ago – but a good chance nonetheless. Is there a possibility that Magdoff and Sweezy's hopes for the world-wide resonance of developments in South Africa will also then be realized? 'A victory for revolution, i.e. a genuine and lasting change in basic power relations in South Africa,' they write, 'could have an impact on the balance of global forces comparable to that of the revolutionary wave that followed World War II'! For such a global outcome, too, the struggle continues.

NOTES

1. Giovanni Arrighi and John S. Saul, 'Nationalism and Revolution in Sub-Saharan Africa', *The Socialist Register 1969* (London: Merlin Press, 1969).
2. 'National Security Study Memorandum 39' of 1969 was published, with a useful introduction by Barry Cohen and Mohamed A. El-Khawas, as *The Kissinger Study of Southern Africa* (Nottingham: Spokesman Books, 1975).
3. On Mozambique see, *inter alia*, John S. Saul (ed.), *A Difficult Road: The Transition to Socialism in Mozambique* (New York: Monthly Review Press, 1985).
4. See my 'Zimbabwe: The Next Round' in *The Socialist Register 1980* (London: Merlin Press, 1980); this appears, in up-dated form, in John S. Saul, *Socialist Ideology and the Struggle for Southern Africa* (Trenton, N.J. and Toronto: Africa World Press and Between the Lines, 1989).
5. See my 'Development and Counterdevelopment Strategies in Mozambique' in John S. Saul, *Socialist Ideology. . .* (ibid.). as well as the various articles on Mozambique (notably by Judith Marshall, Otto Roesch and John Loxley) in recent issues of *Southern Africa Report* (available, by subscription, from TCLSAC, 427 Bloor St. W., Toronto M5S 1X7, Toronto).
6. In Ibbo Mandaza (ed.), *Zimbabwe: The Political Economy of Transition, 1980–1986* (Dakar: CODESRIA, 1986), p. 51.
7. J. Hyslop, reviewing A. Astrow, Zimbabwe: A revolution that lost its way? in *South Africa Labour Bulletin* (Johannesburg) 12, 6/7 (August/September, 1987); see also, in this special issue of *SALB* on 'Labour in Post-Independence Zimbabwe', the debate feature, anonymously authored, entitled 'The Political Economy of Zimbabwe: Is Zimbabwe in Transition to Socialism?' and Ian Phimister, 'Zimbabwe: The inheritance of the anti-colonial struggle' in *Transformation* (Durban), 5 (1987).
8. Victoria Britain, 'Stacking the Deck in Namibia', *Southern Africa Report*, 4, 4 (March, 1989).
9. John S. Saul and Stephen Gelb, *The Crisis in South Africa*, revised edition (New York: Monthly Review Press, 1986); see also, *inter alia*, Rob Davies, Dan O'Meara and Sipho Dlamini, *The Struggle for South Africa*, new edition (London: Zed Press, 1988). There is a wealth of sources on the various phases of the evolution of events in South Africa, most importantly such regularly published South African journals as *The Weekly Mail, Work in Progress, South African Labour Bulletin, Transformation* and *South African Review*.
10. John S. Saul, 'South Africa: the Question of Strategy', *New Left Review*, 160 (November–December, 1987).
11. See *ibid.*
12. Anton Harber, 'On the Move. To Nowhere', *The Weekly Mail* (Johannesburg), 4, 46 (December 23, 1988 to January 12, 1989); this issue contains a number of articles usefully reviewing South African developments in 1988.
13. Quoted in Shaun Johnson and Vusi Gunene, 'Under siege. Slogan-chanting students retreat underground', *The Weekly Mail (ibid.)*.
14. See Friedman's regular column in *The Weekly Mail*, as well his suggestive pamphlet *Reform Revisited* (Braamfontein: South African Institute of Race Relations, 1988).
15. The reference is to Andre Gorz, 'Reform and Revolution', *The Socialist Register 1968* (London, Merlin Press, 1968).
16. John S. Saul, 'Without Proper Papers: Inside South Africa', *Monthly Review*, 40, 8 (January, 1989), pp. 9–10.

17. Gavin Evans, 'The figures show ANC's alive and bombing', *Weekly Mail*, (op. cit.).
18. See the special issue of *Southern Africa Report* on 'Apartheid Economics', 4, 4 (March, 1989) as well as various papers prepared in 1988 under the auspices of the Johannesburg-based Labour and Economic Research Centre; these papers, the product of a collective effort coordinated by Stephen Gelb, are shortly to be published in book form.
19. Quoted in Carl Boggs, *Gramsci's Marxism* (London: Pluto, 1976).
20. On this and other related issues see 'COSATU: The Year in Retrospect' in *Southern Africa Report*, 4, 3 (December, 1988).
21. Gaye Davis, 'Tough DET clamps "throw down gauntlet to students"', *Weekly Mail* (*op. cit.*).
22. Harry Magdoff and Paul Sweezy, 'The Stakes in South Africa', introducing a special issue of *Monthly Review*, 37, 11 (April, 1986), on 'South Africa in Struggle'.

ONE REVOLUTION OR TWO?
THE IRANIAN REVOLUTION AND THE ISLAMIC REPUBLIC

By Val Moghadam

Introduction

The bicentennial of the French Revolution happens to coincide with the tenth anniversary of the Iranian Revolution. While the first has been widely regarded as the quintessential social and transformative revolution, the second is problematical both theoretically and politically. Whereas the October Revolution was in many ways the vanguard revolution par excellence, the Iranian Revolution appears retrograde. In the Marxist view, revolution is an essential part of the forward march of history, a progressive step creating new social-productive relations as well as a new political system, consciousness and values. In this context, how might events in Iran be termed 'revolutionary'? Precisely what kind of a revolution transpired between 1977 and 1979 (and afterward)? Surely clerical rule cannot be regarded as progressive? In what sense, then, can we regard the Iranian Revolution as a step forward in the struggle for emancipation of the Iranian working classes? Clearly the Iranian Revolution presents itself as an anomaly.

The major revolutions that have been observed and theorized are categorized by Marxists as bourgeois or socialist revolutions.[1] This is determined by the revolution's ideology, leadership, programme, class base and orientation, and by changes in the social structure following the change of regime. Further, there is a relationship between modernity and revolution, as discussed by Marx and Engels in *The Communist Manifesto*, suggested by Marshall Berman in his engaging *All That Is Solid Melts Into Air*, and elaborated by Perry Anderson in a recent essay.[2] Some academic theorists of revolution and social change (Barrington Moore, Theda Skocpol, Charles Tilly, Ellen Kay Trimberger, Susan Eckstein, taking their cue from Marx) have stressed the *modernizing* role played by revolutions. But in these respects, too, the Iranian case presents difficulties: a) during much of the anti-Shah uprising there was neither a definitive leadership nor a coherent programme; b) the social structural outcome of the Revolution was neither bourgeois nor socialist; c) the whole experiment is regarded as anti-modern and anti-western. How, then, to approach the Iranian Revolution?

This essay implicitly takes issue with the perception of the Iranian Revolution as *sui generis* and unlike any other 'great' or Third World revolution. This is not to deny its original features and its specificities (to be described below), including its emergence in the context of contemporary 'political Islam' in the region, but rather to contest the prevailing ('orientalist') perspective of the Middle East as the unpredictable and incomprehensible 'Other'. The specific features of the Iranian Revolution and its outcome (indeed, the phenomenon of political Islam in the Middle East) must be understood in terms of the absence of a thorough-going bourgeois revolution in the region. I also dispute the characterization of the Revolution as reactionary.[3] My argument is that what transpired in 1977–79 was a political revolution against the Shah, the salient features of which were populist, anti-imperialist, and anti-monarchical, with strong Third Worldist underpinnings. Beginning spontaneously and containing diverse strands, it lacked a clear programme for modernization or democratization but had an overall emancipatory character. It was populist by virtue of its multi- and cross-class composition, petty-bourgeois outlook, and discursive framework (elevation of 'the people'; demands for independence [esteqlal], freedom [azadi], and republic [jomhouri]). The language and organizational resources of the Islamic establishment eventually dominated the anti-Shah movement, and Ayatollah Khomeini became the charismatic leader of the Revolution in its final stages, but the question of class/state/political power was by no means settled; indeed multiple sovereignty and power contention continued until 1981. It was then that Islamization, a process which had begun at least as early as April 1980 (the advent of the 'Islamic cultural revolution'), was carried out systematically. Islamization was meant to transform existing social structures – the political system, values and property relations – to conform to an ill-defined and contested (amongst Islamicists) Islamic norm. This is the sense in which the question of one revolution (the populist revolution against the Shah, a 'punctual' even, to draw again from Perry Anderson)[4] or two (the second being the attempt to transform society by means of Islamization) becomes salient in the Iranian case.

I shall also argue, however, that while an analytical (and political) distinction is called for between the Iranian Revolution and the Islamic Republic, the latter is in some measure an extension of the Revolution and therefore contains the *modern* features demanded by the Revolution (Parliament, constitutional separation of powers, universal suffrage, elections, etc.). This essay will demonstrate that due to its populist nature and the outcome of the power struggle (themselves rooted in pre-revolutionary developments), the Iranian Revolution was followed by a contradictory new social order which is best described as Islamic populism.[5] Furthermore, and despite itself, the Islamic Republic is not, and cannot be, anti-modern.

The Roots of the Revolution
The character of the Iranian Revolution, the clerical access to resources and organizational facilities, the outcome of the power struggle between clerics,

liberals and leftists, and the Islamic Republic's intractable hostility toward superpowers were shaped and conditioned by events in Iran since the beginning of the century. The overview of recent Iranian political history which follows suggests the salience of what Moore has called 'suppressed historical alternatives.'[6]

Domestic class and political struggles unfolded within the context of uneven socio-economic development and a consistent pattern of foreign domination. The Constitutional Revolution (1906–11) was a watershed in modern Iranian political history, and was carried out and supported by Iran's intelligentsia, bazaaris, and some clerics. One cleric, however, Sheikh Fazlollah Nouri, was hanged by the constitutionalists for his opposition to constitutional rule and insistence on an Islamic state. (Not surprisingly, he is considered a hero and martyr by today's Islamicist rulers.) Constitutional monarchy and Iranian sovereignty were violated and undermined by British and Czarist Russian intervention and opposed by the Qajar monarchs. Soviet Russia's renunciation in 1917 of Czarist imperialist policies offered some relief, but British intrigue continued apace, mainly to guarantee control over Iran's oil industry. A brief experiment in parliamentarism and republicanism was terminated by the assumption to power of Reza Khan, commander of the British-controlled Cossack Brigade, who crowned himself Shah in 1928. Socialist and communist parties, ethnic-based movements for autonomy, and the incipient trade union movement were repressed as Reza Shah built a centralized state with a modern military, a growing bureaucracy, Iran's first university, and infrastructural projects including roads, railroads and light industries. This process of modernization from above was neither deep nor extensive, and feudal relations remained pervasive. Moreover, Reza Shah appropriated estates, villages, and forests for his personal use, and the Pahlavi family emerged as major landowners.[7]

Iranian sovereignty was once again violated in 1941, when the Allied powers rejected Iranian claims of neutrality in the Second World War. Iran was occupied by British forces in the south, Soviet forces in the north, and American forces in the centre. Nonetheless, the interregnum (1941–53) afforded yet another experiment in parliamentarism, and the respite from dictatorship encouraged the revival of socialist and communist parties, nationalist politics, militant trade unions, and ethnic-based autonomy movements. The period 1941–46 saw the rise and rapid expansion of the Tudeh ('masses') Party, Iran's pro-Soviet communist party. It also witnessed the rise and fall (1945–46) of the Mahabad Republic (in Kurdestan) and of the Azarbaijan Autonomous Republic, both remarkable experiments in ethnic self-rule.

Following the withdrawal of Red Army forces in 1946, domestic politics became more contentious. The young Shah (Mohammad Reza Pahlavi) sought to strengthen his position; various prime ministers came and went (and one was assassinated); the Tudeh Party agitated for oil concession rights for the Soviet Union; the nationalists, led by Mohammad Mossadegh of the

National Front, sought to legislate Iranian ownership and control of the oil industry. The 16th Majlis (Iran's Parliament) voted to nationalize oil and take over the Anglo-Iranian Oil Company, and Mossadegh became prime minister in 1951. A Western boycott of Iranian oil, British and American subterfuge, tensions between nationalists, communists, and clerics, intrigue by the Shah and his twin sister Ashraf Pahlavi, and finally, a CIA-sponsored coup d'etat in August 1953, combined to end the interregnum, terminated the process of parliamentarism and democratization, and ushered in the second dictatorship. Had the coup not been engineered, a very different kind of Iran would have emerged from the process.

It is important to appreciate the impact on later developments of the nature and principal features of the second Pahlavi regime: highly centralized, anti-democratic, autocratic and personalist, dependent capitalist, pro-American, extremely inegalitarian and violently opposed to political participation by liberals or the Left. The National Front and the Tudeh Party were all but destroyed; subsequently they operated clandestinely and in exile. The Tudeh-leaning Confederation of Trade Unions was dismantled and yellow syndicates organized in its stead. Nationalization was not repealed, but effective control was transferred to a consortium of major international oil companies, which bought, refined and distributed the crude oil extracted from the southern oilfields. (The Abadan refinery was for domestic consumption.) A large and ferocious secret police, SAVAK, was organized in the mid-1950s, and formerly militant factories and workplaces were regulated by semi-retired military men and SAVAK agents. This prohibited the rise of autonomous class organizations.

The new Kennedy Administration urged the reluctant Shah to institute social-economic reforms, and the U.S.-approved Amini cabinet sponsored an agrarian reform law that was the brainchild of the populist Agriculture Minister, Hassan Arsanjani. Five other reforms – the vote for women, profit-sharing for factory workers, nationalization of forests, literacy corps, and sale of public sector factories to pay compensation to landlords affected by land redistribution – came to be called the White Revolution; this was put to a referendum in January 1963. The White Revolution was strongly opposed by a major cleric, Rouhollah Khomeini, and other clergy; they disliked the land reform (because it would take some property belonging to the religious establishment), votes for women, and the Shah's high-handedness. The National Front, now nominally revived, favoured the reforms but opposed the unconstitutionality of their implementation. Nonetheless, the citizenry approved the reform by an overwhelming majority.

That Spring, tensions mounted as clerics demonstrated against the reforms and the Shah's regime. Khomeini became increasingly vocal and vehement in his criticism of the regime, calling it 'tyrannical'. The protests and demonstrations were joined by other opponents of the 'coup d'etat regime', and an uprising took place in June 1963 involving teachers, students, writers, bazaaris and clerics that has since been called a dress rehearsal for the 1977–79 revolution. It was brutally put down but, like the 1953 coup d'etat, never forgotten.

In 1964 the issue of granting diplomatic immunity to American citizens, military or civilian, engaged in military projects in Iran caught the popular imagination. Public opinion was so strong against this that the otherwise docile Majlis deputies were unwilling to pass the appropriate bill. Once again protests arose, and Khomeini was vocal and visible. As a result, he was exiled from Iran. He spent a year in Turkey before moving on to Najaf, Iraq, where he stayed until 1978. Thereafter the American presence in Iran increased, and the benefits enjoyed by the United States in its 'special relationship' with Iran included an intelligence listening post on the border with the Soviet Union. In return, the Shah could acquire whatever military hardwares his heart desired, paid for by Iranian oil revenues.[8]

Notwithstanding Khomeini's exile, the clergy in Iran did not wane but on the contrary enjoyed rights, benefits, and privileges beyond the wildest dreams of liberal and left-wing dissidents. In the first instance, the clerical establishment had a nation-wide network of mosques which actually expanded during the second Pahlavi rule.[9] Moreover, there was the array of theological seminaries, religious charities, endowments, lecture halls, religious journals, periodicals and publications, and access to official and government-controlled print and electronic media. For example, Ayatollah Morteza Motahhari, later a leading ideologue of Islamic revolution, appeared on radio and television, and was interviewed by magazines and newspapers. His views on Islamic marriage and his criticism of gender relations in the 'godless societies' of the West and East were well known as they had been serialized in the popular women's magazine, *Zan-e Rouz* (Today's Woman). The Hosseinieh Ershad, a religious forum in northern Tehran, was frequented by many of the later leaders of the Islamic Republic, including Ayatollah Beheshti (leader of the Islamic Republican Party after the Revolution) and Hojatoleslam Ali Khamene'i (currently Iran's President). It was here that Dr. Ali Shariati, the Paris-educated Islamic sociologist, lectured prior to his imprisonment and exile from Iran.[10]

In their publications and public speeches, the clerics and their lay associates – many of whom were Western-educated and inspired by Third World anti-imperialism – crafted a radical-populist Islamic discourse which condemned oppression, privileged the poor, called for a 'government of God', sympathized with national liberation movements in the Third World (and Black struggles in the U.S.), and denounced secularism, materialism, communism and westernization. These themes struck a responsive chord among the urban poor, the traditional petty bourgeoisie suffering from anomie, alienated workers, and passive-aggressive members of the educated middle class. Contributors to this discourse included Ali Shariati, Abolhassan Bani-Sadr (a Paris-educated economist), and the Narodnik-like Iranian writer,

Jalal Al-e Ahmad.[11] The latter penned an enormously popular tract entitled *Gharbzadegi* (variously translated as Occidentosis, Euromania, West-
struckness) which was an extended attack on Iran's westernized intellectuals
and bureaucrats. As a concept and as an idea, *gharbzadegi* permanently
entered the Iranian lexicon. After the Revolution, this term was used as a
pejorative toward certain individuals, organizations and ideas deemed un-
Islamic and/or 'alien'.

In contrast to the activities, resources and legal status of the Islamicists, the
Tudeh Party remained banned, and the guerrilla organizations (Fedayee and
Mojahedin), formed in the early 1970s, were hounded and nearly decimated
by 1975. Without access to the type of vast organizational resources at the
clergy's disposal, the Left was at a decided disadvantage when the revolution
erupted. That the Left organizations (particularly the new guerrilla groups)
managed to attract followers at all and mobilize public opinion as well as
organize workers and peasants is all the more remarkable. It should be
noted that this is attributable not only to the tireless organizing efforts of
party cadres, the moral example set by the left organizations and expected
of a membership that was self-sacrificing, serious, puritanical, and utterly
devoted to the people's cause, the positive popular image of the Fedayee
and the Mojahedin created by their years of armed struggle against the
vastly superior army, gendarmerie and police, and the many 'martyrs' that
died under torture or in battles with the authorities. It is also testimony to the
tenacity and rootedness of the socialist tradition in Iran (and its inevitability,
given the development of capitalism and the advent of some modernity) – a
fact that the Islamicists would deny.[12]

By the mid-1970s, a number of factors converged to create what has
been called the structural origins of the Revolution, a series of events,
incidents, and developments that set the scene for revolutionary uprising and
socio-political change. Mismanaged agrarian reform had resulted in massive
rural-urban migration and the creation of a vast pool of urban poor in the
outskirts of Tehran and other major cities. An overheated economy, rife with
inflation and speculation, was oppressing the salaried middle class. A shortfall
in oil revenues and a recession halted development projects and construction sites, rendering many workers redundant, unemployed, and angry. To
fight inflation, the Government launched an anti-profiteering campaign that
targeted Bazaar merchants. Government credit policies favouring large capitalists and discriminating against small producers and the Bazaar had already
antagonized bazaari merchants. Now there were plans to raze the Bazaar,
Tehran's traditional urban market, and replace it with supermarkets. In a
spectacularly stupid move, the paranoid and megalomaniacal Shah dissolved
the (ineffectual) two-party system and created the single-party Rastakhiz ('renaissance'), declaring that all patriots must join, and that the Bazaar (among
others) must contribute financially to the new party. To add insult to injury,
he also introduced the royalist calendar in April 1976, creating widespread

confusion and anger. In the midst of all this, the new American president, Jimmy Carter, announced his human rights policy, and cited Iran as one of the problem countries. Feeling secure, and still wanting American weapons, the Shah agreed to some liberalization, and in February 1977 released several hundred political prisoners. This was the beginning of the end of the Pahlavi state.

The Course of the Revolution

The anti-shah revolution went through several distinct stages, each marked by a particular mode of mobilization, dominated by a particular coalition of opposition groups, and distinguished by the use of a particular set of confrontational strategies.[13] The release of political prisoners in February 1977 encouraged intellectuals to express themselves, and a number of open letters on political repression, speeches criticizing human rights violations, and poetry reading sessions by dissident writers were followed by non-violent protests and gatherings in which the intelligentsia played the dominant role. In January 1978 the second stage was precipitated by a newspaper article defaming Ayatollah Khomeini, leading to clashes between theology students and police in the religious city of Qom. Forty days later, the city of Tabriz commemorated the Qom tragedy with a major demonstration in which banks, cinemas and liquor stores were attacked. During this period, the Amouzegar Government's recessionary measures of the past 10 months had created favourable conditions for the rise of protest on economic grounds. This drew the industrial and non-industrial working classes into the anti-Shah agitation, and a revolution was in the making.

The third stage (July–Sept. 1978) is characterized by the cycle of mass demonstrations, prompted in part by a tragic fire in a cinema in the city of Abadan, killing hundreds of working class men, women and children, followed by inflammatory speeches by clerics. 'Black Friday', in which helicopter gunships were used to attack demonstrators on 8 September, ushers in the fourth stage, marked by disruptive and ever-widening cycles of strikes (Oct.–Nov. 1978) enveloping factories, banks, and government offices. Here the most impressive development is the strike by oilworkers, steelworkers, railroad workers, and workers in other major productive units. Rosa Luxemburg's famous essay on the characteristics and significance of the mass strike as a mechanism and means of self-education and self-organization of workers remains most pertinent in the Iranian case, as strike committees evolved into workers' councils, which later encountered the centralizing and monopolizing tendency of the new Islamic regime.[14] In the final stage of the Revolution (Dec. 1978–Feb. 1979), dual sovereignty emerged with the parallel governments of Shahpour Bakhtiar, named by the Shah before his departure from Iran, and the provisional government of Mehdi Bazargan, named by Ayatollah Khomeini. (In fact, this was tripartite sovereignty, for Khomeini had also organized the secret and clergy-dominated Islamic Revolutionary council, which later overshadowed the Bazargan cabinet.) For two days (9–11 February) an armed battle pitted dissident airmen, Fedayee and Mojahedin guerrillas against the Shah's personal guard, the so-called 'Immortals' (*Javidan*). Following this, the Military Supreme Council announced its decision to step aside, maintain 'neutrality in the present political crisis', and ordered troops to return to their garrisons. Here the U.S. decision to withhold support for a military coup, following discussions between General Huyser (President Carter's special envoy) and Khomeini associates, was instrumental.[15]

Thus ended the Pahlavi state, bulwark of American imperialism in the region, always the coup d'etat regime to its citizens, a developing capitalist economy with an outdated and outrageous political system, whose corruption, conspicuous consumption, and secret police reflected and furthered its lack of legitimacy.

It is important to appreciate the multi-class character of the Revolution. This was by no means 'the rising of the Muslim People', as some misguided and popular accounts would have it. (And here Islamicist and orientalist perspectives converge.) A populist revolt does not necessarily represent the absence of class struggle and/or class consciousness; these were clearly present in the workers' strikes and demands. However, Pahlavi rule had resulted in a diminished role for the Left and the absence of autonomous working class organizations, while the traditional petty bourgeoisie and the traditional bourgeoisie (mercantile) enjoyed independent organization (in the bazaar and the mosque). The Left's role in the two-day armed insurrection was paradoxical. While it advanced its own cause, the insurrection also paved the way for the assumption of power by the clerics. (This historical irony worked to the Left's disadvantage. Had the armed struggle taken two years rather than two days, the clerics would not have emerged as the predominant group following the collapse of the Pahlavi state.) Nonetheless, anti-communist obsession led outside observers to exaggerate the challenge represented by the Left and minimize the significance of the Islamicists. There was a widespread perception that 'Islamic revolution' was a lesser evil than 'communism'.

Another important point is that despite its efficacy as a mobilizing ideology in the later stages of the revolution, the Islamic discourse was not a single, monolithic and politically coherent ideology. Various Iran scholars have identified at least four versions of Islamic discourse: the 'radical Islam' of the young intelligentsia, Khomeini's 'militant Islam', 'liberal Islam' of people like Bazargan, and the 'traditionalist Islam' of the ulama.[16] It is also necessary to note that despite its central importance, the clerical estate under Khomeini's leadership was only one of the social groups in the original revolutionary coalition. The revolutionary coalition of 1978–79 included also the leftist guerrillas, the Westernized bourgeoisie as represented by the National Front, the Bar Association, and the Writers Association, and the traditional bourgeoisie of the Bazaar.

Much has been made of the presumed centrality of ideology (Shi'a Islam) in the Iranian Revolution. On the contrary, Shia ideology did not cause the Shah's fall. Instead, it was used as a tool for popular mobilization by groups already in conflict with he Shah over an economic policy that discriminated against the bazaar merchants and traditional manufacture, and over state corruption and centralization that excluded the professional and middle classes from effective participation in governance. The chronic inability of the Pahlavi state to establish legitimation, and the repression of liberal and socialist thought and organizations meant that the more effective mobilizing ideology would be the one with the longest tradition, established institutions and organizational resources: Shiism, especially the radical-populist variant that had been developing since the 1960s. While socialist and secular thought in Iran can be traced back to the turn of the century, it has been too discontinuous and constantly under siege to have been able to have widespread impact. By contrast, Islamic thought in Iran has enjoyed continuity, institutions, and long-standing legitimacy (though clerics have not always been so well regarded, and there is also a popular tradition of anti-clericalism). Still, to reiterate, ideology is not what caused the Revolution. Rather, a number of social, economic, and political factors converged to create a revolutionary situation in which the dominated classes were unwilling to go on as before and the ruling class was unable to rule as before. A populist collectivity emerged which sought to end the Shah's autocracy and Iran's ties to the U.S., and to establish republican and constitutional rule. As noted by Marx and Engels, revolutions and social processes are above all carried out by people: *'Ideas* can never lead beyond an old world system but only beyond the ideas of the old world system. Ideas cannot carry anything out at all. In order to carry out ideas men [sic] are needed who dispose of a certain practical force.'[17]

The political revolution that overthrew the Shah was an enormously liberating and rejuvenating phenomenon, and exhilaration was universal – at least in the first year. A feature of the immediate post-Pahlavi period was the explosion of freedom that occurred. For the first time since the 1940s, there was space for socialists and communists. The revolution provided the Left with the opportunity to strengthen itself and expand its forces; headquarters were established by all the large left organizations, and a number of smaller left groups were created. The left-wing press proliferated; the sidewalks were cluttered with books and posters; meetings, rallies and cultural events took place daily; *Kayhan* and *Etelaat,* the official newspapers, operating since the end of 1978 by a left-dominated council, ran features about and interviews with left activists and with relatives of dead guerrillas. A host of new structures were also created during the Revolution, most of which operated autonomously: neighbourhood committees, strike committees, factory councils, student councils, Revolutionary Guards. The anti-Shah movement thus eventuated the phenomenon of 'multiple sovereignty'. This period can be dated from the appointment of Bakhtiar in the last days of December 1978 to the ouster of President Bani-Sadr in June 1981. The 'dawn of freedom', as it was called in Spring 1979, was short-lived, however. Multiple power centres and the collapse of the revolutionary populist collectivity led to intense power struggles, and to fierce battles over political, ideological and economic issues.

After the Revolution: Contestation and Islamization
It may be helpful to periodize the twists and turns of post-revolutionary events, so that the discussion below of the most salient developments may be understood within a chronological framework. Thus the period from February to November 1979 constitutes one stage, beginning with the victory of the revolutionary forces and establishment of the Islamic Republic, and ending with the takeover of the American Embassy and the resignation of Prime Minister Mehdi Bazargan. November 1979 to September 1980 is another period, when the embassy issue is at centre-stage; Abdolhassan Bani-Sadr is elected Iran's first president; the Iraqis invade Iran. The period dating from September 1980 to June 1981 is dominated by the increasing conflict between the Islamicists and Bani-Sadr and his associates; it ends with Bani-Sadr's impeachment. From June 1981 to September 1982 a mini civil war takes place between the Mojahedin and the regime; the latter unleashes its terror also on the communist organizations; Iranian forces make major gains on the war front. Following this period (roughly early 1983 to the present), state power rests firmly with the Islamicists, who intensify the programme of Islamization, especially in the areas of culture, ideology, education, law, morality and lifestyle. At the same time, the war with Iraq continues, and the state of the economy worsens.

After the Revolution, the Left organizations, principally the Fedayee, Mojahedin, Tudeh, and Paykar, became major political forces on the campuses, especially after the new government quickly re-asserted control in the oilfields and some major factories. These organizations included substantial groups of people who had gained valuable political experience and insights in exile, while underground, or in prison. Their ranks were swollen by the many dissident students who returned to Iran en masse in the Spring of 1979, as well as by daily recruits to the Left cause.[18] The Left presence was keenly felt all that year, and very quickly a principal tension arose between the Islamicists and the array of Marxist, socialist, and communist organizations and parties.

Things were not easy for the Left. In addition to the sense that they were newcomers or marginals, overshadowed and somewhat overwhelmed by the Islamic rhetoric and the political power and organizational advantages of clerics, the Left had to come to grips with the nature of the new regime, a difficult task. Was the regime progressive or reactionary? It will be recalled that in early 1979, paradoxically (or perversely), world-wide left-wing support was extended to the new, revolutionary, anti-imperialist regime in Iran, but not to the Marxist government of neighbouring Afghanistan. Illustrious European, North American and Arab intellectuals waxed eloquent over the putative post-modern, anti-systemic, spiritual, cultural manifestations of Iran's revolution, and of the fierce independence and anti-imperialism of the ayatollahs. The revolution and the regime were conflated, and both were regarded as 'Islamic'. Meanwhile, elements within the Left worried that the Islamicists were about to kidnap the revolution and alter its direction. The Left press of that period is replete with articles expressing the concern that the revolution needed to continue and that freedoms had to be extended. An open letter to Khomeini from the Fedayee organisation praised his personal stance but complained about harassment from Islamic zealots and noted that the Revolution belonged to all those who had taken part in it, including the guerrilla organizations which had consistently fought the Shah since the early 70's and lost hundreds of worthy comrades.[19]

For this reason, appeals by Khomeini and Bazargan to armed citizens, air force personnel, and the guerrilla organizations to surrender their weapons yielded poor results. The Fedayee openly rejected the call, saying it was their duty to safeguard the Revolution. In response, Khomeini said, '[Le pays] ne supportera pas ces gens sans culture et [le peuple] va les ecraser comme il a ecrase la force diabolique du Shah' (quoted in *Le Figaro*, 23.2.79). While respectful of Khomeini, the Fedayee criticized the repressive ways of the local committees, the *pasdaran*, or revolutionary guards, and the *hezbollahi*, fascistic, self-styled partisans of God. At a huge rally held at Tehran University the Fedayee speakers called on Khomeini to reveal the names of the Islamic Revolutionary Council (IRC) members, and to replace secret trials by the revolutionary courts with open trials by people's courts in order to inform and educate the masses. They also called for a social order based on workers' control and councils.[20] Along with the Mojahedin, the National Democratic Front, and other left and liberal organizations and individuals, the Fedayee stressed (though admittedly not forcefully enough, and without the requisite unity) the people's right to a democratic form of rule. In response, Khomeini declared, 'Democracy is another word for usurpation of God's authority to rule.' When protests were voiced at home and abroad about the secret trials and summary executions, Hojatoleslam Mohammad Reza Mahdavi-Kani, the IRC member in charge of the revolutionary committees, said, 'We must purify society in order to renew it.' In its use of moral and religious language, egalitarian and anti-monarchical message, and emphasis on purification, the IRC brings to mind England's revolutionary Puritans and the French Revolution's 'Twelve who ruled'. Iran's Islamicists, however, turned increasingly intolerant and theocratic.

The post-revolutionary regime sought quickly to institutionalize itself, even while in the process the clerical and liberal wings of the new regime clashed over the meaning of 'Islamic Republic.'[21] A series of steps were taken to obtain legitimation and power. First came the referendum on changing the political system of the country. The question on the ballot read 'Should Iran be an Islamic Republic?' There was considerable protest over the wording, and the Fedayee, National Democratic Front (led by a grandson of the late

Premier Mossadegh), and several regional parties boycotted the referendum. On 1 April 1979, however, an overwhelming majority of voters answered in the affirmative. But the question of what the Islamic Republic should look like was still open.

Second, the Islamic Republican Party (IRP) was formed by leading clerics and at least two lay individuals. It was to become the official Islamicist party, and increasingly intolerant of other parties in and around the political elite, notably the Azarbaijan-based Muslim People's Republican Party, led by Ayatollah Shariatmadari, a liberal Muslim cleric opposed to direct rule by the clergy, Prime Minister Mehdi Bazargan's Movement for Liberation, and the National Front, the party of several cabinet members. The IRP was of course violently opposed to any of the Marxist parties and organizations, although it tolerated the Tudeh Party (which had become totally supportive of Khomeini's 'anti-imperialist' positions and contemptuous of the 'bourgeois liberals'), until 1982.

Third, revolutionary courts were set up that functioned outside the jurisdiction of the Justice Ministry. At first they concentrated on trying royalists and members of SAVAK. Later they evolved into religious courts guided by the Sharia (Islamic/Koranic law) which co-existed uneasily with civil law and courts of appeal until the latter were abolished in early 1983.

Fourth, a draft constitution was written in April and elections were held in August to select a small Assembly of Experts to study it. The original idea had been that a large, representative and elected constituent assembly would draft the constitution. As a result of the change, and due to the clerical bias of the screening of candidates for the Assembly, there was, again, much left-wing protest. But by now, each time such a protest took place, armed *hezbollahi* or *pasdaran* would harass and break up the gatherings. In the course of their deliberations, the Assembly of Experts, now dominated by the IRP, introduced and adopted the controversial concept of *velayat-e faghih,* or rule by the supreme interpreter of the law – in this case, Khomeini. This met with the opposition of the left, of Shariatmadari, and of the National Democratic Party (but not of the liberals in government). Nonetheless, the Constitution, much of which was a quintessential radical-populist document on economic issues and matters of foreign policy, while also establishing Iran as an Islamic state, was overwhelmingly approved in another referendum in December. The Constitution (of which more below) adopted the system of parliamentary elections, which were held on schedule with large voter turnouts even in the midst of crisis.

Throughout this period, the Left organizations struggled to come to grips with the nature of the Revolution, the character of the new political order, class structure and consciousness, and their own tasks and responsibilities at the stage in question. Was it a democratic revolution (the Tudeh Party)? Was it a national, anti-imperialist revolution that had to be furthered (Fedayee)? Should socialists focus on defeating imperialism and its domestic base, concentrating on preventing royalist sabotage (Mojahedin, Tudeh, Fedayee)? Or was their task to organize and mobilize the working class toward a socialist transition (Peykar, Rah-e Kargar, Organization of Communist Unity)? There were also debates in the left press and in meetings about the clergy and the petty-bourgeoisie: did the clergy constitute a caste, or was it a part of the petty-bourgeoisie? Everyone on the Left welcomed (indeed, took part in) the revolution against the Shah, the expropriation of comprador/monopoly capital, the relinquishing of power by the big bourgeoisie. But was the petty-bourgeoisie up to the task of transforming socio-economic relations, and extending democratic rights? When clerics assumed political power, some socialists argued that what had transpired was not a revolution (*enghelab*) but a revolt, or uprising (*ghiyam*). Others opined that the clergy were inexperienced at state craft and could not possibly run a dependent capitalist state and economy; the clergy's days were numbered and they were bound to defer to their liberal partners. Still others averred that the clergy (like the petty-bourgeoisie) was 'close to the working class', opposed to imperialism and big capital, and therefore progressive, unlike the liberal bourgeoisie. Another, very different, left theory was that clerical fascism was in the offing, and a counterrevolution in the making (Rah-e Kargar). The Tudeh Party and the Mojahedin had similar views: the regime was petty-bourgeois and therefore fundamentally contradictory, with both progressive and reactionary elements within it. *Their* role was to support and strengthen the progressive wing, and vigilantly watch and contest the reactionary elements. But the two organizations differed over who was progressive and who reactionary. The Tudeh Party (keen to be Iran's 'legal Marxists') tended always to side with the Islamicists (Khomeini and the IRP), while the Mojahedin gradually defined the IRP as 'internal reaction'. As for the other Left organizations, they determined early on that the Islamic state in its totality was neither benign nor progressive. The regime's increasing repression confirmed this view. But their preoccupation with fighting imperialism and dependent capitalism, as well as their chronic disunity, precluded the construction of an alternative movement and agenda.

The first challenge to creeping Islamization and repression came on March 8, 1979, when thousands of women protested against the new sexual politics and in particular Khomeini's decree that women appear in public in *hejab*, or Islamic dress. As a result of their protests, he backed down – but only temporarily.[22] The next major challenge to the new centre was from Iran's periphery, in particular the national and ethnic minorities of Kurdestan and Turkaman Sahra, who were demanding autonomy. There and elsewhere peasants were expropriating large landlords, and in the cities the Left was agitating for a land reform based on the concept of land to the tiller. Meanwhile, the workers' councils were proliferating, in large part due to Left organizing efforts, and were encountering harassment from the IRP-controlled revolutionary guards. The rise of class and ethnic struggles, competition between various political parties, and the challenge of the Left during that first year (which the regime sought to end by sending *pasdaran* in September 1979 to close down the offices and headquarters of the Left parties and organizations) was dealt with by the Islamicists in a novel fashion – by deliberately antagonizing the international facet of the populist contradiction.[23] With the takeover of the American Embassy in November 1979, the Islamicists hoped to undermine their rivals, discover (or manufacture) incriminating evidence against them, and impress the populace with their own anti-imperialist credentials.

The seizure of the embassy and of hostages was a drama staged by the Islamicists with the intention of creating a situation of permanent revolution and mass mobilization controlled by the IRP. Its architects must have studied Mao Tse-tung's ideological mobilizations and especially the Cultural Revolution. (The 'students' who occupied the Embassy may be likened to the Red Guard.) This action allowed the Islamicists to practise considerable ideological manipulation as well as violence – in the name of their supreme anti-imperialism. Conspiracies against the revolution were seen everywhere, and the 'students' who had seized shredded embassy records diligently put them together to discover an array of information that could be used against the opponents of the IRP and of Islamization.[24] Ayatollah Shariatmadari, President Bani-Sadr (elected in January 1980), members of the National Front and a number of secular government officials were tarnished by this evidence.

In April 1980 the increasingly powerful IRP initiated an 'Islamic cultural revolution' aimed at the universities, which had a pronounced Left presence and were governed by councils. As Khomeini had said: 'Our universities have changed into propaganda battlefields. Many university teachers are at the service of the West. What frightens us is cultural dependence. We fear. . . universities which train our youth to serve the West or serve communism.'[25] Bani-Sadr endorsed the scheme – which entailed pitched battles with students and closing down the universities for two years – so he could stay on the bandwagon. But his days were numbered, for in the absence of a liberal-left alliance the Islamicists steadily increased their influence and power.

The Left camp too, was by now rather badly divided. The Fedayee organization split in early 1980 into a 'Majority' wing that endorsed the regime as anti-imperialist and progressive, and a 'Minority' wing which regarded it as reactionary and as having fundamentally altered the character and direction of the Revolution. The Tudeh Party was for all practical purposes the party of Khomeini, endorsing his every move and statement, and taking the side of the Islamicists (on the basis of their presumed anti-imperialism and non-alignment) in the intensifying battle with Bani-Sadr in 1981. Peykar had consistently opposed the Islamic regime and was at odds with the organizations that it felt had compromised or wavered on this issue. One of these was the Mojahedin, which had extended qualified support for the Islamic regime (its

meeting halls were always adorned with the portraits of Khomeini and Ayatollah Taleghani, a more tolerant and liberal cleric who died in 1980), but in 1981
cast its lot with the beleaguered Bani-Sadr. Thus with some left organizations
(Fedayee, Peykar), ideological purity was paramount and prevented compromise and alliances, while with others (Mojahedin, Tudeh), opportunism and
the overriding concern for the expansion of their own organizations precluded
a broad left-wing alliance and a united movement against the Islamicists. The
entire left was preoccupied more with fighting imperialism and excoriating
the U.S. than with building socialism and a united left front. Had there been
unity in the left ranks, and a left-liberal alliance for a democratic and secular
republic (rather than liberal collaboration with clerics in government), the
trajectory of the Revolution would arguably have been much different.

As it happened, the ideological manipulation and mass mobilization
afforded by the U.S. Embassy takeover heightened following the Iraqi
invasion of Iran in September 1980. Far from undermining the new regime
(the reason behind the Iraqi invasion), the war increased patriotic sentiment,
rallied the population around the regime, and allowed the regime, and especially the IRP, to bolster and strengthen its political position and increase
its institutional supports. Bani-Sadr's position meanwhile weakened. When
the Mojahedin decided to support the beleaguered president, and protest
demonstrations were staged against the IRP, an angry Khomeini repudiated
Bani-Sadr and the government moved to impeach him. What followed for
roughly a year after Bani-Sadr and Mojahedin leader Massoud Rajavi fled
to Paris (assisted by supporters within the Air Force), was a cycle of violence marked by spectacular Mojahedin assassinations and bombings and
exceedingly brutal regime reprisals. This implosion suggested that the Iranian
Revolution, like the French Revolution before it, had devoured its young.

In the end the IRP won its domestic war. But its battles continued: the
IRP was unified only in its opposition to liberals and Marxists. On issues
of economic restructuring, government expenditure, and foreign policy, the
Islamicists were deeply divided. These divisions continue to this day; perhaps
as a result of the ineffectual and contingent nature of the IRP, the party was
dismantled in early 1988. Thus the IRP was fundamentally unlike other revolutionary parties. Guided by a vague philosophy of Islamic populism, it lacked
ideological rigour and coherence and held together groups of people who
differed from each other more than just temperamentally. Among the issues
over which serious differences arose: land reform; labour law; urban tenants' rights; industry-first or agriculture-first economic development; heavy
industrialization or appropriate technology; private ownership rights; the
direction and composition of trade; to export the revolution or to concentrate
on 'building the Islamic revolution in one country', as it were. The differences
over economic issues have prevented the implementation of a comprehensive
national development plan; planning has been at best ad-hoc.[26] Thus, unlike
other revolutionary states (for example, Russia, China, Cuba), the Islamic

Republic is notable for its inability to transform socio-productive relations. At the same time, it is unlike non-revolutionary, reformist governments (the so-called democratizing regimes of Argentina, Uruguay, the Philippines), which have not altered the political system, the military, and economic relations. In Iran, social structural changes have occurred, to which we now turn our attention.

Social Structural Changes in the Islamic Republic

The Constitution of the Islamic Republic is an eclectic mix of theocratic, modern, and Third Worldist elements. Its radical populism is expressed in its assertion that 'the Iranian Revolution. . . has been a movement aimed at the triumph of all oppressed and deprived persons over the oppressor.' It then goes on to reject both capitalism and socialism: 'Government does not derive from the interests of a certain class,' and asserts that 'the economy is a means, not an end. This principle contrasts with other economic systems where the aim is concentration and accumulation of wealth and maximization of profit. In materialist schools of thought, the economy represents an end in itself.' The Constitution also declares 'economic independence' from foreign domination and elimination of 'poverty and deprivation' to be among the basic goals of the Islamic republic.[27]

The two most important and controversial aspects of the constitution are the principle of *velayat-e faghih* (the government of the jurist) and the pre-scribed economic model. It is worth noting, as Behdad has pointed out, that whereas the former generated heated debates in the Assembly of Experts, the latter was passed without much discussion or disagreement but became con-troversial in the years that followed. The economic aspects will be discussed presently, but for the moment it is worth pondering the eclectic philosophical content of the Constitution. It ironically included features associated with the West, which is otherwise excoriated by the Islamicists. There is thus a dualism discernible in the Constitution (and in the Islamic Republic itself – as well as in its very name).[28] On the one hand the Constitution establishes theocratic structures, such as the rule of the *faghih*, a cross between the head of state and the chief justice; a 12-member Council of Guardians overseeing the Majlis (Parliament) to ensure that legislation is in accordance with both the constitution and Islamic law; the Supreme Judicial Council, which must be dominated by *mujtahids* (Islamic jurists). The Constitution also establishes Twelver Shi'a Islam as the official religion, describes the Islamic Republic as 'a system based on the belief in religious leadership and continuous guid-ance', maintains that sovereignty derives from God, and mandates efforts towards 'unifying the world of Islam.' On the other hand, the constitution describes Iran as an independent state with a foreign policy predicated upon non-alignment. It also firmly establishes Iran as a *republic*; after the *faghih*, the president is the most powerful figure, and his role is described as 'implementing the constitution and organizing the relationship between the three powers.' Elected directly for a four-year term by an absolute majority of the votes cast, the president is the chief executive who signs and executes the laws passed by the Majlis. In parliamentary style, he nominates a Majlis deputy as the prime minister; and once his nominee has won the endorsement of the Majlis, he administers the oath of office. He approves cabinet ministers proposed by the premier before they are presented to the Majlis for a vote of confidence. Over the past eight years, the president, prime minister, and Majlis speaker have emerged as the key political figures after Khomeini.

The Constitution also describes the Islamic Republic as based on 'sovereignty of the people.' One of the principles states that 'the affairs of the country must be administered on the basis of public opinion expressed by means of elections, including the election of the president, the representatives of the [parliament], and the members of councils, or by means of referendums in [certain] matters'. In theory and in practice, the Majlis is an autonomous organ; since 1980 it has often clashed with the Council of Guardians over bills vetoed by the latter. Gone is the rubber-stamp parliament of the Pahlavi days. Gone too is the obsequious press of the Pahlavi era. For the first time, newspaper editorials question and criticize government policies or the juridical vetoing of bills. The Islamic-populist discursive universe, while limited and intolerant of explicitly Marxist or liberal-democratic perspectives, is larger than the official ideological framework of the Pahlavi era.[29]

The Constitution also provides for 'the rights of the people', all of which have been violated, mainly because these rights are circumscribed by the explicit qualification that they accord with the laws of Islam. For example, the rights of women are guaranteed, but 'in all areas according to Islamic standards' (Principle 21). And: 'Publications and the press are free to present all matters except those that are detrimental to fundamental principles of Islam or the rights of the public' (Principle 24). What this has meant in practice, apart from the banning of publications deemed un-Islamic, is that a well-known journal can carry on a debate on the merits or failures of the Stalin era, but articles on historical materialism or critiques of religious intolerance are prohibited. And any discussion of sexuality, apart from what the ayatollahs have already written about the essential natures (and therefore different needs, rights, limitations) of males and females, is strictly *verboten*.

Nonetheless, the Islamic Republic is striking for the interaction of modern and traditional elements. Charles Tilly has distinguished 'reactive' and 'proactive' forms of collective action. But surely all revolutions have had both 'reactive' and 'proactive', forward-looking and conservative, features? In Iran's case, however, its historical development, pre-revolutionary political features, and Islamic institutions have lent greater weight to conservative and reactionary forces. Yet even clerics are not totally opposed to modern, western forms. They are not opposed to western technology (or instruments of torture), to parliamentarism, or to modernization per se. For example, in criticizing the Shah's 'false modernization', Khomeini said in November

1978: 'Etendre les industries de montage dépendantes [par la création] de quelques centaines d'usines, est-ce cela moderniser?'[30] In 1964 he had argued: 'Comment voulez-vous moderniser l'Iran si vous faites emprisonner et tuer les intellectuels?. . . Vous voulez faire des Iraniens des instruments dociles et passifs au service du pouvoir et de vos maitres étrangers, alors que la véritable modernisation consiste a former des hommes qui aient le droit de choisir et de critiquer, des combattants qui sachent résister á la domination exterieure, a l'injustice et au pillage.'[31] Spoken like a true Third Worldist – though his concern for the rights of intellectuals was a sentiment he largely ignored after 1979. Which goes to show, yet again, that modernization and repression are not incompatible.[32]

A major change effected by the new Islamic regime which greatly bolstered itself was one which was ironically encouraged by the Left – the transformation of the Shah's military. It will be recalled that in the course of the revolution against the Shah, groups of people armed themselves: among them, the guerrilla organizations, Kurdish parties, and local, neighbourhood committees. The latter came to be controlled by the local mosques. The Left groups retained their weapons; the Mojahedin in particular formed an impressive militia which would hold public exercises. The Left agitated for the dismantling of the Shah's military and the establishment of a people's army; the Bazargan government, however, was against this idea. Meanwhile, the Islamicists were organizing their own fighting force: the revolutionary guard.[33] Its core consisted of several hundred militants who had received military training in PLO camps in south Lebanon. Fresh recruits came from youths (urban lower middle class) who had been active in the anti-Shah demonstrations. In its discipline, ideological motivation and organization, this was similar to other revolutionary armies. By June 1979 the Islamic Revolutionary Guard (*pasdaran*) constituted a parallel force to that of the military and to the guerrillas. Soon controlled by the IRP, the *pasdaran* monitored the activities of the leftists and liberals, broke up demonstrations and strikes, kept a watch on army barracks and police stations, and suppressed ethnic revolts in Kurdestan and Turkaman Sahra. This wasn't quite what the Left had in mind by a people's army.

After the dissolution of Bazargan's original cabinet and his own resignation following the U.S. Embassy takeover, the Islamicists undertook a major purge of the military in the summer of 1980. Presumed royalists were targeted, as were those suspected of sympathizing or collaborating with an attempted coup led by former prime minister Shahpour Bakhtiar and General Oveissi, formerly of the Shah's military. Executions and purges continued until the Iraqi invasion in September. The Iraqis no doubt thought they would encounter an extremely weakened, demoralized and ill-organized fighting force, as indeed the military was. They did not consider the Pasdaran, one of the major institutional supports of the new regime, and a formidable fighting force, as the Mojahedin were also to discover when they decided to take on the Islamicists in June 1981. In time, the paramilitary Pasdaran became a full-fledged fighting force, complete with its own government agency. And the military, in the course of the war with Iraq, has been revived and relegitimized.[34]

In the economic sphere, many changes have occurred, though not the deep and permanent changes in a democratic and socialist direction that had been aspired to by Iran's Marxists. In the first instance, the dominant class under Pahlavi rule was dispossessed of its industrial, financial and commercial holdings. The leaders of the Islamic Republic were not from the dominant economic (landed, commercial or industrial) classes. Political and economic power shifted from the Pahlavi family and the big bourgeoisie (industrialists, financiers, large capitalist landowners) to the petty bourgeoisie: its traditional stratum is favoured economically, while the new/modern wing occupies the bureaucracy and military. The mosque remains a powerful institution while the economic independence of the Bazaar is checked by state controls (especially over prices and foreign trade) and the existence of a large public sector. Thus the big bazaaris have clashed often with the government, while small producers and distributors have been favoured by the state managers. Constitutional limitations on private property ('private ownership, legitimately acquired, is to be respected. The relevant criteria are determined by law') have been a consistent source of tension between the state and the private sector, and between the pro- and anti-capitalist factions within the regime.

The Constitution of the Islamic Republic provides for an economic system consisting of (in order of importance) a state sector, a cooperative sector, and a private sector. A popular revolutionary demand, which was incorporated into the Constitution and implemented by the first government, was sweeping nationalization. According to the Constitution, the state sector includes 'all the large-scale and major industries, foreign trade, major mineral resources, banking, insurance, energy, dams and large irrigation networks, radio and television, post, telegraphic and telephone services, aviation, shipping, roads, railroads, and the like.' In 1979, all banks were put under government ownership; contracts with multinational corporations were nullified and all major industries taken over by the state; foreign trade was under *de facto* if not *de jure* control of the government. (The Council of Guardians has rejected parliamentary bills to establish formal state ownership as contrary to Islamic respect for private property and entrepreneurship.) Economic sovereignty was to be achieved by means of a self-reliant strategy (*khodmokhtari*). Attempts focused on reviving agriculture and promoting small-scale productive units by means of various credit and price support policies. A parallel policy of import-substitution industrialization and protectionism was also followed in the hope of stimulating domestic production of certain durable and non-durable consumer products. Most new industrial investments went to production units which used more local inputs.[35] The nationalization of banks was meant to support the new changes. The mass media was used to convince the people that national independence could not be achieved without accepting hardship in the short run and making sacrifices in both levels and quality of living standards. The 'Western pattern of consumption' was also denounced as non-Islamic and harmful to the goal of self-sufficiency.

Two crucial institutions created to alter economic relations and effect social justice were the Housing Foundation (created to provide housing for the poor, particularly in urban areas) and the Reconstruction Crusade (established to provide rural areas with electricity, water, feeder roads, schools, health clinics, housing, and other social and infrastructural services). Legislation was passed to reduce the gap among wage rates as a result of which the workers' wages were raised by 60 percent. A policy of price support in the form of subsidies for basic needs items were instituted to protect the poorer groups from the rampant inflation that had followed the economic decline during the revolution. Modifications were proposed in the tax system to make it more progressive and prevent excessive concentration of wealth. Nationalization of major industries, banks, insurance companies, and foreign trade were meant to weaken further possibilities of emerging large-scale private accumulation.[36]

Most of these policies, which were attempted at different points in the postrevolutionary period up to the end of 1982, had to be subsequently suspended, reversed or modified under enormous domestic and international pressures, and due to the exigencies of the war economy.[37] The First Social, Economic, and Cultural Development Plan of the Islamic Republic (1983–88, with a 20-year horizon) had to be shelved because of the factional politics within the state. Support for agriculture, rural and regional development, small-scale productive units, labour-intensive techniques, major economic reforms, and social services were reduced. Wages and employment were frozen in the state sector but price subsidies for basic consumption items continued. Taxes were increased in an attempt to reduce dependency on oil but also to boost the public budget. Under the new policy, deficit spending became acceptable to the government and a more active role was given to the private sector and market mechanisms. A number of nationalized industries were sold to the public or returned to their original owners and the cooperative sector was left to its ambiguous and weak position in the economy.[38] Modern technology again became acceptable to planners and policy makers. The money saved was not, however, put into building new industrial capacities. Rather, much of it went to the war effort.[39]

The policy of diversifying the sources of dependency for exports and imports was only marginally successful. The price of oil continues to be determined within the capitalist world market.[40] The trade with socialist and Third World countries, except for Turkey and Pakistan, did not expand to any significant degree despite frequent policy pronouncements to the contrary. With the failure of the new policy and worsening economic problems the state turned to an Emergency Plan in 1986.

The nationalization of foreign trade is mandated by the Constitution but bitterly opposed by Bazaari interests and has been contested by the conservative and clergy-dominated council of Guardians; the latter argues that it violates Islamic respect for private ownership and freedom of commerce. However, the war economy and declining oil revenues made state control over foreign trade imperative; the government reduced the imports of luxury items and concentrated on importing foodstuff, spare parts, raw materials, and other basic goods, in addition to weapons supplied principally by China and North Korea. Revolutionary ideology – and the Constitution – required that Iran reduce its dependence on oil exports, diversify the economy, engage in balanced growth, and favour Third World and Islamic countries in its trade policy. But by 1982 the Islamic Republic was trading mainly with Western countries and capitalist Third World countries (West Germany, Italy, Japan, Turkey, Brazil), while also increasing economic ties with East Europe (but not the USSR). Moreover, its foreign exchange receipts were still derived almost exclusively from oil exports – which the government increasingly sold for cash on the spot market at discounted prices.

Small-scale enterprise remains favoured. By all accounts and indications, domestic craftwork – small-scale and privately-owned enterprises producing Iran's famous gold- and silver-work, as well as its carpets and handicrafts – has prospered. (Unfortunately, it is now prohibited to export these items, or even carry them out of the country as gifts.) The largest sector by far is the state sector, which spans industry and services (education, health, welfare, public utilities, rail and air transportation, communications, major media). Because of the war and the cleavages within the ruling elite, however, the regime has had uneven and limited success in redirecting the course of economic development in various sectors.

Thus since the Revolution, there have been changes in property relations, ownership rights, and class relations. These have not been *transformed*; rather, Pahlavi-style capitalist relations have been suspended while political power has shifted to the petty bourgeoisie, and the spheres of politics and culture/ideology have predominated over economic development/accumulation. In the Islamic Republic populist and redistributive economic measures (widespread distribution of food, allocation of some housing, cheap utilities and oil, which have favoured the urban poor and war veterans and families of war 'martyrs'), has substituted for rational planning and production investment. Whatever else the Islamic regime is, it is not properly speaking a capitalist state: capital accumulation is not (as yet) its raison d'etre or defining feature. Nor can it be said that the bourgeoisie is the dominant political and economic class, and that its ideas hold sway. What can be said is that the Islamic Republic is following a Third Worldist pattern in which the petty-bourgeoisie (military or civilian) comes to power and evolves into a state or bureaucratic bourgeoisie. Nowhere has a clerical caste played as dominant a role in politics and in state power as in Iran (although Israel's rabbinate has an important, though arguably not dominant, role). However, Iran's clerics do appear to be part of the petty-bourgeoisie. The regime's statist and nationalist ideological orientation also follows a Third Worldist pattern. In July 1988, the Government of the Islamic Republic of Iran finally accepted UN Resolution 598 and a ceasefire with Iraq. What direction might the Islamic Republic take? It is not at all unlikely that clerical power will wane after Khomeini's death; direct clerical rule has been discredited, and no-one can truly succeed a charismatic leader. Islam might continue to figure prominently in state ideology and policy, while a mixed economy is reconstructed and a non-aligned foreign policy continued. As such, a likely scenario for Iran after the death of Khomeini and the cessation of hostilities with Iraq is a period of normalization and stabilization ('the routinization of the revolution', or its Thermidor) in which a social formation similar to Algeria may evolve.[41] What programme might be advanced in a situation of budgetary pressures, where the role of state enterprise is now considered to be circumscribed? Two roads seem to be open to Iran. One is to continue and strengthen the statist strategy currently in place. The alternative is to follow a now familiar Third World pattern, where restrictions on domestic private sector activities could be relaxed, especially if private entrepreneurs can be coaxed into becoming more export oriented. Further, the leadership might re-examine previous restrictions on transnational corporations and other sources of private direct investment. In a word, they could effect a re-linking with the world market or world capital. In such a situation, transnationals can be particularly seduc-tive; they can bring in capital that does not add to the foreign debt burden, they provide employment, and they can plug the developing country into an already existing international marketing network, boosting exports. This may yet be tried out in the Islamic Republic.

A conservative period will likely emerge, as well. By all accounts the popu-lation is not only war-weary but politically fatigued, and tired of constant ideological exhortation, much like the Chinese were by the time Mao died. As a result, what will emerge following the succession is a programme for reconstruction and development – and a return to the capitalist orbit, albeit under different terms than with the Pahlavi state. Thus 'modernization' will resume, but at a different pace and rhythm than under the *ancien regime*.

Conclusions

The expansion of the state apparatus, the superstructural institutionalization of Islam, changes in the political structure and economic restructuring all represent a qualitative break from the past. Is it a progressive or reactionary break? In this essay I have tried to show the importance of distinguishing between the Revolution and the regime. The first was a popular, populist, political rupture; the second is proof positive that an anti-imperialist, non-aligned petty-bourgeoisie can be profoundly reactionary and wildly at odds with the socialist project. I have focused on the class and political struggles following the Revolution to underscore the difference and to demonstrate that the outcome of the revolution against the Shah was not predetermined, even though the clerics came to the political scene with considerable advantages over the left and secular forces.[42]

Was Iran's revolution premature? Perhaps, if one is fixated on the French Revolution (or the Russian Revolution) as the epitome of progressive transformation. But of what utility is the idea of an historic norm, a standard, against which all subsequent revolutions are measured?[43] The political trajectory of the 'East' has been very different from that of the 'West'. We must therefore expect revolutions to be in the first instance specific phenomena, motivated by internal and external forces, structural and socio-psychological, that will necessarily differ with each historical epoch as well as in concrete social formations. Beyond this, we must also recognize that the failure of social revolution in the West has placed an enormous burden on progressive forces in the Third World. The bourgeoisie of Third World countries have proven incapable of genuine social modernity (Pahlavi Iran is a good example), while the few attempts at initiating social democratic change have been thwarted by the United States. Political repression and economic brutality, as well as the nationalist impulse, have resulted in numerous political revolts throughout the Third World. But the absence of socialism in the West, the peculiar nature of socialism in Eastern Europe, and the Soviet Union's overriding concern for its own interests have not provided a climate conducive to social transformation in the Third World. Consequently, political revolution has been 'easier' to accomplish than social revolution. In this sense, all Third World revolutions might in fact be 'premature'.

In theory and in real life, there has always been a tension between determinacy (or 'lawfulness') and human agency, between inexorable structural determinants and conscious class action, between the idea of inevitability and the need for deliberate intervention. Revolutions will come about because people will determine that oppressive political or economic conditions must change. These 'people', however, are divided along class and ideological lines; within the class structure and among the political organizations there is a definite hierarchy and differential weights. The outcome is determined as much by historical and international forces as by conscious political struggle. As Marx reminds us in his dialectical formulation, we make history within certain limits. These limits include historical legacies (for example, the absence of a long-standing democratic tradition), international or world-systemic constraints, and the differential resources of contending classes, social groups and political parties. In this essay I have tried to show that the Iranian Revolution was a contradictory phenomenon containing progressive and repressive features which constituted a necessary and positive step forward.[44] The outcome of the Revolution was not predetermined but was the result of protracted class and political conflict which was won by the Islamicists.

Because of the violent repression and religious dogmatism of the Islamic regime, Marxists will perhaps continue to regard the Iranian revolution with considerable ambivalence. It was indeed a project that went awry.

NOTES

Acknowledgements: This essay is the product of years of discussion with a number of close friends and colleagues, with whom I share a preoccupation with the meaning of the Iranian Revolution, the role of the Left within it, and the prospects of socialism in the Middle East. I am especially indebted to Ali Ashtiani, Mohammad Razavi and Mohammad Tavakoli-Targhi, though they might not agree with all of my views and interpretations; Ahmad Ashraf and Hooshang Amirahmadi have been very helpful as well. Bogdan Denitch has also been a sounding board for some of the ideas on populism and revolution.

1. Academic theories of revolution have sought to attribute the causes/origins and outcomes of revolution to specific determinants: strains in the social system caused by modernization, leading to socio-psychological tensions (expressed in such propositions as relative deprivation, rising expectations, status inconsistency, downward mobility) that turn frustrations into aggression; structural factors (agrarian crisis, war, military breakdown) leading the state to lose control over the means of coercion and therefore to the successful overthrow of the ancien regime; political conflict and multiple sovereignty, in which access to resources, organization and mobilization are key factors in determining the outcome; the nature of the state and/or elite structure, which effects states' vulnerability to revolutions and their ability to coopt or to repress uprisings. Some of these factors were present, and the variables valid, in the Iranian case. For a survey of academic theories of revolution see Stan Taylor, *Social Science and Revolution* (NY: St. Martin's, 1984) and J. Goldstone, ed., *Revolutions: Theoretical, Comparative and Historical Studies* (San Diego: Harcourt Brace Jovanovich, 1986). Also pertinent is the symposium on the Iranian Revolution in *Theory and Society*, May 1982, organized around Theda Skocpol's 'Rentier State and Shi'a Islam in the Iranian Revolution.'
2. Perry Anderson, 'Modernity and Revolution', in *Marxism and the Interpretation of Culture*, edited by Cary Nelson and Lawrence Grossberg (University of Illinois Press, 1988).
3. For a discussion of the Revolution as reactionary, refer to Said Amir Arjomand, 'Iran's Islamic Revolution in Comparative Perspective', *World Politics*, April 1986; and Fred Halliday, 'The Iranian Revolution: Uneven Development and Religious Populism', in Fred Halliday and Hamza Alavi, eds., *State and Ideology in the Middle East and Pakistan* (NY: Monthly Review, 1988).
4. Anderson, *op. cit.*, especially the discussion that follows his essay.
5. A number of Iranian academics and activists have been theorizing the populism of the Revolution and the Islamic populism of the regime in doctoral dissertations or in Persian-language articles. The dissertations include Manoucher Dorraj (Univ. of Texas, Austin, 1984), Kaveh Afrasiabi (Boston University, 1987), Mohammad Tavakoli-Targhi (University of Chicago, 1988). The journals *Nazm-e Novin* and *Kankash* have carried several articles on the social and intellectual bases of Iranian populism.
6. Barrington Moore, *Injustice: The Social Bases of Obedience and Revolt* (White Plains, NY: M.E. Sharpe, 1978), esp. ch. 11.
7. Recommended sources for modern Iranian political and social history include

Ervand Abrahamian, *Iran Between Two Revolutions* (Princeton, NJ: Princeton Univ. Press, 1982); Said Amir Arjomand, *The Turban for the Crown: Iran's Islamic Revolution* (Oxford Univ. Press, 1988); Nikki Keddie, *Roots of Revolution* (New Haven, CT: Yale Univ. Press, 1981); Nikki Keddie, *Iran: Religion, Politics and Society* (London: Croom Helm, 1980); Fred Halliday, *Iran: Dictatorship and Development* (Harmondsworth: Penguin 1979); Homa Katouzian, *The Political Economy of Modern Iran 1926–77* (NY: NYU Press, 1982); Habib Ladjevardi, *Labour Unions and Autocracy in Iran* (Albany, NY: SUNY Press, 1985).

8. See Robert Graham, *Iran: The Illusion of Power* (NY: St. Martin's Press, 1979), for a discussion of the Shah's economic policy and military expenditures as factors in the political crisis and revolutionary uprising.

9. For an extended discussion of clergy-state relations see Shahrough Akhavi, *Religion and Politics in Contemporary Iran* (Albany, NY: SUNY Press, 1980); refer also to Michael Fisher, *Iran: From Religious Dispute to Revolution* (Cambridge, MA: Harvard Univ. Press, 1980).

10. Roy Mottahedeh, *The Mantle of the Prophet* (Princeton, NJ: Princeton Univ. Press, 1986) discusses the role of the various *hosseinieh,* and of the impact of the writings of Shariati and Ale-e Ahmad.

11. For an interesting discussion of the formulation and impact of these ideas, see Hossein Bashiriyyeh, *The State and Revolution in Iran* (NY: St. Martin's Press, 1984). See also Ali Ashtiani, 'The Sociology of Three Periods in the Intellectual History of Contemporary Iran,' *Kankash,* 2–3, Spring 1988 (in Persian).

12. I have discussed the strengths and weaknesses of the Left in 'Socialism or Anti-Imperialism? The Left and Revolution in Iran', *New Left Review,* no. 166, Nov.–Dec. 1987. Ali Ashtiani and I have further analyzed their role, significance, social bases and prospects in 'Islam and the Left: The Tragedy of the Iranian Revolution', (mimeo, 1988).

13. For a detailed and descriptive account of the unfolding of the anti-Shah movement, see Dilip Hiro, *Iran Under the Ayatollahs* (London: Routledge & Kegan Paul 1987). Also very useful is Ahmad Ashraf and Ali Banuazizi, 'The State, Classes, and Modes of Mobilization in the Iranian Revolution', *State, Culture and Society,* Spring 1985.

14. I have discussed the role of Iranian industrial labour in the following essays: 'Workers' and Peasants' Councils in Iran', *Monthly Review* Oct. 1980 [by Shahzad Azad]; 'Industrialization Strategy and Workers' Response: The Case of the Workers' Councils in Iran', in Roger Southall, ed., *Trade Unions and the New Industrialization of the Third World* (London: Zed, 1988); 'Industrial Policy, Culture, and Working Class Politics: A Case Study of Tabriz Industrial Workers in the Iranian Revolution', *International Sociology,* June 1987. See also Assef Bayat, *Workers and Revolution in Iran* (London: Zed, 1986) for a discussion of the councils and of workers' control after the Revolution, based on the author's extensive fieldwork.

15. Following the neutralisation of the military and the assumption of power by the new revolutionary regime, several top generals were executed (and others removed). General Rabii, head of the Air Force, and General Moghaddam, SAVAK chief, were among those executed. Generals Hossein Fardoust and Abbas Gharabaghi were retained, however, apparently because of their critical part in paving the way for the disintegration of the the Armed Forces. As for why the Shah's vaunted military proved so ineffectual, see General Abbas Gharabaghi, *Verites sur la crise iranienne* (Paris: la pensee universelle, 1985), especially pages 69–94, where he explains: 'Le mecontentement et les points de faiblesse resident essentiellement dans la corruption financiere et la mauvaise administration des lois relatives au status des personnels de Forces Armees Imperieles.' The issue of low

morale and ill-treatment of soldiers (including the *ressentiment* of the *homafar,* the non-commissioned air force personnel who were trained as technicians and could not aspire to officer grades; these were the airmen who rebelled at Lavisan Air Force Base) was also echoed by former Navy Admiral M. Arianpour, in a talk delivered in New York, February 1988. (Arianpour 'was retired' before the Revolution for his criticism of kickbacks, and re-instated by the revolutionary government in 1979 until his own resignation and departure from Iran.) See also Shaul Bakhash, *The Reign of the Ayatollahs* (NY 1984) for a further discussion of the military.

16. See Ashraf and Banuazizi (op. cit.); see also William Shepard, 'Islam and Ideology: Toward A Typology,' *International Journal of Middle East Studies*, 19(3), Aug. 1987, pp. 307–336.
17. K. Marx and F. Engels, *The Holy Family*, quoted in Bogdan Denitch, *The Legitimation of a Revolution: The Yugoslav Case* (Yale, 1976), pp. 205–6.
18. I have referred to the significance of the Confederation(s) of Iranian Students, the student movement abroad, in my essay 'Socialism or Anti-Imperialism. . .' (see note 12 above).
19. One translation of the Fedayee (or Fedaii, or OIPFG) organization's Open Letter to Khomeini was printed in *MERIP Reports* [? 1979].
20. See my 'Workers' and Peasants' Councils in Iran' (note 14). Fedayee concerns were recorded in leaflets, pamphlets, and their weekly paper, *Kar* (Labour). These were translated and distributed by Fedayee supporters, including the present author, in the United States.
21. A good account of post-revolutionary developments is Shaul Bakhash, *The Reign of the Ayatollahs* (NY 1984). See also Hiro, *Iran Under the Ayatollahs* (London 1987).
22. It must be said that the women's movement was bifurcated: there were pro-Khomeini and anti-Khomeini women's organizations. For documentation of the women's movement(s) of that period, see Azar Tabari and Nahid Yeganeh, eds., *In the Shadow of Islam: The Women's Movement in Iran* (London: Zed, 1982). For a discussion of women's current legal and economic status, see my essay 'Women, Work and Ideology in the Islamic Republic', *International Journal of Middle East Studies*, May 1988.
23. This point has also been made by Kaveh Afrasiabi, in his unpublished dissertation *Populism and the State in Iran* (Boston University 1987).
24. These were subsequently published in 40 volumes under the quaint title *Documents from the Den of Spies*, Tehran. Notwithstanding the motivations of the Islamicists, the shredded documents meticulously put together constitute a veritable goldmine of information, including the role of the late Shah in precipitating the Afghan coup.
25. *The Guardian* 23 April 1988.
26. In 1983 the government introduced a 5-year plan with a 20-year horizon. It was eminently unrealistic and unworkable, as it had something in it for everyone, with wildly ambitious and optimistic goals. It was withdrawn after a year. As recently as September 1988 the Minister of Heavy Industries, Behzad Nabavi, reiterated the absence of a development strategy guiding economic policy. See *Iran Times* Sept. 16, 1988, p. 4. For economic analyses, see H. Razavi and F. Vakil, *The Political Environment of Economic Planning in Iran 1971–1983* (Boulder, CO: Westview Press, 1984); Sh. Bakhash (op. cit.); Sohrab Behdad, 'The Political Economy of Islamic Planning in Iran,' ch. 7 of *Post-Revolutionary Iran*, Hooshang Amirahmadi and Manoucher Parvin, editors (Boulder, CO: Westview, 1988).
27. Sohrab Behdad, 'The Political Economy of Islamic Planning in Iran' (*ibid.*), p.

113. Behdad, among others, has noted the eclectic nature of the Constitution and the various influences, including Marxian, that the document reflects. Refer to *The Constitution of the Islamic Republic of Iran*, Hamid Algar, translator (Berkeley: Mizan Press, 1980).

28. This point is also made by Sami Zubaida, 'An Islamic State? The Case of Iran', *Middle East Report*, no. 153, July/Aug. 1988, pp. 3–7.

29. Several years ago, a view entertained by certain Iranian leftists and published in Persian-language journals was that 'totalitarianism' was being established in the Islamic Republic. Apart from the fact that the totalitarian thesis is conceptually slippery as well as associated with cold warriorism, this view occluded the tensions, contradictions, and countervailing tendencies in post-revolutionary Iran. The book by Cheryl Benard and Zalmay Khalilzad, *The Government of God: Iran's Islamic Republic* (Westview, 1983), also advances the totalitarian thesis quite inappropriately in my view. See my review of their book in *Middle East Studies Bulletin* 19(1), July 1985, pp. 82–84. It should be noted that a number of decidedly non-Islamic journals are published in Iran, notably the literary and cultural magazines *Mofid* and *Adineh*.

30. Y.A. Henry (editor and translator), *Pensees Politiques de l'Ayatollah Khomeyni* (Paris: Editions ADPF, 1985), p. 47. This quote comes from the periodical *Majmu'e*, 7 Nov. 1978.

31. *Ibid.*, p. 47. Ayatollah Khomeini's statements and declarations have also been translated into English and annotated by Hamid Algar in *Islam and Revolution* (Berkeley, CA: Mizan Press, 1981). For other examples of Islamicist writings that mix modern and theocratic themes, see Ayatollah Morteza Motahhari, *Discourse on the Islamic Republic* (Tehran: Islamic Propagation Organization, 1985), and Ayatollah Yahya Nouri, *Islamic Government and Revolution in Iran* (Glasgow: Royston, 1985).

32. Because the Islamicists are not fundamentally anti-development, and technocrats exist among them (notably the Minister of Heavy Industries, Behzad Nabavi), the modern industrial sector was not dismantled after the Revolution. (Also, the workers' councils–and even the Islamic associations that supplanted them–would not have allowed this.) However, the state of permanent revolution, political conflicts, and ideological mobilization subordinated economic development and productive investment. Thus the (now nationalized) modern firms remained intact, but were ill-managed and under-utilized.

33. According to Admiral Arianpour (see note 15 above), the new revolutionary government had no plans to re-organize the military or reconstitute a new fighting force and basically got the idea from the Left. Oral communication, New York, February 1988.

34. At this writing (October 1988), the Government has announced plans to combine the Ministry of the Pasdaran and the Defence Ministry. This is part of the post-war reorganization of the state apparatus.

35. Hooshang Amirahmadi, 'Middle Class Revolutions in the Third World, and Iran,' in *Post-Revolutionary Iran*, H. Amirahmadi and M. Parvin, eds. (Boulder, CO: Westview, 1988).

36. Ibid. See also Sh. Bakhash, 1984, op. cit.

37. Amirahmadi, 1988; Bakhash, 1984; Behdad 1988.

38. Amirahmadi, 1988 (op. cit.).

39. V. Moghadam, 'Oil, the State, and Limits of Autonomy: The Iranian Case,' *Arab Studies Quarterly*, Spring 1988.

40. Ibid. See also Michael Renner, 'Determinants of the Islamic Republic's Oil Policy: Iranian Revenue Needs, the Gulf War, and the Transformation of the World Oil Market,' in *Post-Revolutionary Iran*, H. Amirahmadi and M. Parvin, eds. (op.

cit.), and Cyrus Bina, *The Economics of the Oil Crisis* (NY: St. Martin's Press, 1985).

41. Recently, a number of steps have been taken in the direction of post-war normalization. Parliamentary elections were held in April 1988, and the Third (Islamic) Majlis convened in May, with a more homogenous composition than previously. Earlier, in January, Ayatollah Khomeini had clipped the wings of the Council of Guardians (dominated by clerics who abide by the more conservative texts in Islamic jurisprudence which respect private property, the Council had blocked economically radical bills) by creating a new body to settle disputes between the reform-oriented Parliament and the conservative Council. He also declared in a *fatva* (religious decree) that 'the interests of the community' has precedence over 'even Islamic law'–this has been interpreted to mean that Khomeini has prioritized the government over the clergy. Hojatoleslam Hashemi Rafsanjani, Speaker of the Parliament and leader of the pragmatic/moderate wing, was made commander of Iran's armed forces; the dual ministries of the Revolutionary Guard (Pasdaran) and Defence are being merged. In the summer of 1988, Iran took steps to revive diplomatic and economic ties with the West, naming an Ambassador to France and welcoming a group of British legislators for talks in Tehran (see *New York Times* 24 June 1988, p. A3). At the same time, a wave of executions of political prisoners took place, which by late October had reached 350, according to Amnesty International. Presidential elections are scheduled for 1989.

42. In this connection, mention should be made of the persistent pattern of Western (U.K., U.S.) subterfuge. By undermining nationalist, socialist, and democratic movements and governments (whether motivated by economic interest or anti-communism), Western imperialism has contributed to the diminution of secular discourse and movements and the rise of political Islam. Examples are the UK–and US-sponsored coup against Mohammad Mossadegh in Iran in 1953; US support for Maronite hegemony in Lebanon and the entry of US troops in 1958; the hysteria over the nationalization of the Suez canal by the late President Nasser; hostility toward the democratic-secular Palestinian nationalist movement; subversion of the Marxist government of Afghanistan and military support for the fundamentalist Mujahideen. This is the sense in which Western powers are complicitous in the rise of anti-democratic religious movements in the Middle East.

43. See Perry Anderson, *Passages from Antiquity to Feudalism* and *Lineages of the Absolutist State* (London: New Left Books, 1974). While these books are extremely learned and have had an immensely positive impact, Anderson's idea of the French Revolution as the model of a pure bourgeois revolution, and his discussion of the 'paradoxes', 'impurities', 'prematurities', and 'singularities' of British political history (earlier criticized by E.P. Thompson and most recently by Michael Barratt Brown in *New Left Review*), have been problematized and critiqued by Mary Fulbrook and Theda Skocpol, 'Destined Pathways: The Historical Sociology of Perry Anderson', in *Vision and Method in Historical Sociology*, ed. by Th. Skocpol (Cambridge Univ. Press, 1984).

44. Paul Valery once remarked that all theory is autobiography. Alvin Gouldner put it thus: 'Much of theory-work begins with an effort to make sense of one's experience. Much of it is initiated by an effort to resolve unresolved experience; here the problem is not to validate what has been observed or to produce new observations, but rather to locate and to interpret the meaning of what one has lived' (from *The Coming Crisis of Sociology*, NY: Avon Books, 1970). This paper may be read as one such endeavour.

'REVOLUTIONARY REFORM' IN SOVIET FACTORIES: RESTRUCTURING RELATIONS BETWEEN WORKERS AND MANAGEMENT

David Mandel

On June 2 1962, on the second day of their strike, the workers of the giant Novocherkassk Electric Locomotive Factory, joined by the rest of the worker population of this southern Russian town, set off for the city centre some 10 kilometers away. Peter Siuda, then a worker at the locomotive factory and one of the strike leaders who had been arrested early that morning, gives the following account of what followed, based on eye-witness reports. 'Red flags and portraits of Lenin appeared in the columns. The demonstrators sang revolutionary songs. As they approached the bridge over the railway and the Tuzlov River, the demonstrators saw on the bridge a cordon of armed soldiers and two tanks. The column halted and fell silent. The revolutionary songs ceased. Then shouts rang out: "Make way for the working class!" These shouts grew into a mass chant. With precision and tremendous force, they repeated: "Make way for the working class!" The soldiers and tankmen did not try to stop the column but began to help the workers over the tanks. The massive current of humanity flowed around the cordon and over the tanks on the bridge. Spirits soared and the demonstrators again took up the revolutionary songs, louder that before, more forcefully, and in unison.'[1]

'This wasn't the programmed celebration of people going to our May First demonstrations,' comments Siuda. 'These were free, unchained workers on the march. They were convinced of the justice of their cause. They were going to defend their rights. And, in the last analysis, they were going to their own Soviet government. I'm speaking of revolutionary songs, banners, portraits of Lenin. This was no game, no holiday spectacle directed from above. They believed. They were going to their Soviet government, to their party, in search of truth. They wanted to be heard and to discuss. And when they arrived, the city party committee was cordoned off by troops. No one came out. No one wanted to speak to them.' In the chain of events that followed, the workers stormed and seized the party committee. When they learnt that there had been arrests, some headed down the street to the police station (adjoining the political police) and stormed it. The order to open fire was given here and at the party committee. To this day, the state has not revealed the number of workers, their family members and bystanders, all unarmed, killed in this massacre. Their grave-sites also remain a state secret.

In Siuda's account, several elements form the background to these events, which were a part of a larger wave of worker protest that swept the Soviet Union in this period.[2] 'The Novocherkassk events were preceded in the 1950s by the processes of public revelation [bringing to "glasnost"] of the crimes of Stalinism, of debunking of the "cult of the personality", of attempted humanization of socialism. The people believed in the genuineness of these processes [. . .] This democratization announced in the 1950s once again took in the people, gave the toilers hope that they could successfully conduct a dialogue with the authorities [. . .] But the party "chiefs" and state leaders, while condemning the "personality cult", left intact stalinism itself, the criminal party-state system, [. . .] the voluntarism of the "chiefs", of the leaders and bureaucrats, the arbitrary rule of the élite and the absence of rights of the masses, the organs of repression, the KGB and MVD [Ministry of Internal Affairs], that remained outside of society's control.'

At the same time, 'in those years, wage rates were being arbitrarily lowered virtually every year. This allowed the bureaucrats to attain the high indications of labour productivity and lowered production costs demanded by the central authorities, without the corresponding capital investments, increased mechanization and automation of production, or organizational changes and qualitative improvement of technological processes. [. . .] Beginning from January 1, 1962, at the locomotive factory, the campaign began anew to lower wage rates in all the shops. They were reduced by 30–35%. The last shop to have its rates lowered was the steel foundry, in May. [. . .] Then on June 1, the central radio announced a sharp, "temporary" rise in the prices of meat, milk, eggs, and other food products.'

The housing and food supply situation in Novocherkassk were particularly bad, 'but even these circumstances would probably not have led to a strike, if a presumptuous bureaucrat bastard had not thrown into the "powder keg" of popular indignation and dissatisfaction the spark of insult, of lordly impudence.' On the morning of June 1, the workers were discussing the news of the price rise in their shops. They were especially angry in the steel foundry. Still, no one was talking about a strike. The director and party committee secretary came to talk to the workers. As they spoke, a woman went by carrying meat pies. Seeing this, the director turned to the workers: 'If you don't have money for meat and sausage, then eat liver pies.' This was the spark that set off the strike: 'And the bastards are even laughing at us!' In a few minutes, the whole factory was shut down by a spontaneous movement that ended in the city centre with the seizure of the party committee building and the massacre of demonstrators and bystanders. Early on in the strike, the workers had tried to notify other towns of their action – to this end, they stopped a passenger train on the

Moscow-Rostov mainline – but the town was sealed off by the authorities with amazing speed.

This article analyzes, not the events of the early 1960s, but the changes that are occurring in the relations between labour and management in Soviet industry today. One can certainly question the appropriateness of beginning an analysis of the current restructuring in the factories with an account of events that took place 27 years ago under Khrushchev. On both the levels of discourse and practice, the 'perestroika' makes the Khrushchev era seem a timid affair. The present Soviet leadership has repeatedly declared its intention to carry through a deep, structural reform of the economy and has explicitly recognized that there can be no such reform without democratization of the state. And although what has been achieved until now falls far short of these declared aims, even if the 'perestroika' were to end today, it would still have been an incomparably more radical episode than the Khrushchev years.

In many ways, the official conception of the 'perestroika' appears aimed not only at improving economic performance but also at eliminating the very basis for Novocherkassk-type confrontations. 'Probably the most serious social consequence of the period of stagnation in our country,' write two Soviet economists, 'is the alienation of the bulk of the working masses from the management of production and the life of society, the split of society as a whole, of territorial communities, and labour collectives into managers and subordinates, rank and file and bosses, that has taken form and consolidated itself in the consciousness of all social groups. A direct consequence of this is the indifference, not only of the bureaucratic apparatus, but of many workers, toward concrete actions of restructuring [perestroika] on their jobs, in their shops, enterprises, micro-districts, etc. Overcoming this division, the transformation of the worker into a real owner of the socialist property, is the goal both of the restructuring of the economic mechanism now occurring and of the growing democratization of management'.[3]

Yet this passage typically directs its criticism at the 'period of stagnation' i.e. the Brezhnev era. By contrast, favourable parallels are being drawn between the 'perestroika' and the Khrushchev period. Indeed, Khrushchev, with official approval, has become something of a hero in the Soviet media. He had shortcomings, we are told, but he was moving in the generally correct direction, only to be cut short by the 'forces of stagnation'. The following examination of the 'perestroika' from the perspective of the shop floor (at least as it has manifested itself until now) does, in fact, give one a certain sense of déjà vu. And it leaves one wondering about the significance of the fact that, despite the current preoccupation of Soviet writers and journalists with the past, Siuda has so far been unsuccessful in his attempts to draw the Novocherkassk events into the realm of 'glasnost'.

WORKER-MANAGEMENT RELATIONS UNDER THE 'COMMAND ECONOMY'

In the past, under the 'command economy', workers enjoyed de facto job security.[4] In addition, although wages might vary from month to month, a worker's average wage was virtually guaranteed, as long as he or she observed basic discipline. Bonuses, premiums, participation coefficients and other supplementary payments – up to 50% of the takehome pay – that in theory depended on quality and intensity of work, were to a significant degree automatic. Instead of wages depending upon norms, as measures of labour, norms were often adapted to ensure a specific wage level, itself only loosely, if at all, related to productivity. Notices on Soviet factory gates commonly promised a takehome pay that already included bonuses and premiums.

This arrangement was necessary in order to attract and keep a large enough work force to meet plan targets in conditions of chronic labour shortage and the uneven supply to the enterprise of raw materials and semi-manufactured goods. The 'command system' by creating and maintaining this labour shortage thus afforded the workers a certain bargaining power (they could 'vote with their feet'), even in the absence of trade unions to defend their interests. At the same time, management had little countervailing incentive to economize on labour costs. The enterprise's wage fund came from the state budget and was calculated largely on the basis of past performance in such a way as to discourage too-significant rises in productivity (that would penalize the enterprise the next year) and to encourage managers to maintain the average wage and number of workers at relatively higher levels.[5]

An additional consequence of this situation was a pronounced levelling tendency in wages within enterprises and sectors. Although the spread in basic pay rates (tarifnye stavki) of different skill levels was quite broad, the effect of these differentials was undermined by the various supplementary payments, which, as noted, were to a significant degree automatic and which made up a large, and increasing, part of the takehome pay. This levelling tendency was further reinforced by the practice of assigning workers to the higher skill levels, regardless of actual qualification, as a means of attracting scarce labour.

The worker's wage thus bore a rather a loose relationship, not only to the intensity and quality of his or her individual labour, but also to the performance of the enterprise. Even if in principle a part of a worker's total annual wage and social benefits depended on enterprise performance – mainly, meeting and surpassing (though only slightly – to avoid an overly difficult plan the next year) gross output indicators – in practice the ministry would often intervene to lower the targets of failing enterprises. After all, it was also interested in the 'success' of its enterprises.

The motivating role of the individual wage was further undermined by the relative importance of the social wage – free or subsidized goods and services – that, by the definition, bears no direct relationship to the individual labour furnished. The significant growth of the part of the social wage in incomes over the past few decades was a goal of the party programme adopted under Khrushchev, who saw this as a measure bringing Soviet society closer to communism.[6]

Under the 'command system' relations between workers and enterprise management were fundamentally conflictual. Labour under this system, as under capitalism, remained alienated i.e. essentially coerced. And so workers saw their interest in withholding effort; management's task was to intensify it. But this antagonism was tempered by an element of shared interest and collusion. For, to a very large extent, management too was interested in concealing productive potential in order to avoid too-difficult plans imposed from above and to be able to deal with the irregular supply system. Neither side, for example, wanted 'hard' norms. Workers – for reasons common to all alienated labour; management – because 'soft' norms gave it the reserves needed to meet plan targets, especially by the inevitable 'storming' at the end of the month and quarter, in conditions of chronic supply problems and frequent outside demands on its labour force (so-called 'patronage tasks'). Management generally did its best, through legal and often illegal means, and in the face of contrary pressures from central authorities, to give the workers a relatively higher and stable wage. (It is now admitted, however, that because of price rises, 'although the nominal wage in the national economy rose regularly over the past 18 years from [an average of] 122 to over 200 rubles [a month], real incomes remained at the same level and in certain groups of the population even declined.')[7] It also looked the other way at certain infractions of discipline. In return, the workers helped management meet plan objectives by tolerating violations of labour legislation and bad work conditions.[8]

While these characteristics of Soviet labour relations had existed in some degree since the 1930s, this system attained its fullest expression under Brezhnev. For this reason, some workers, only half-ironically, refer to the last half of the Brezhnev era as their 'golden age' – because it was relatively easy then to reach a working agreement with management. But it is important to emphasize that the extreme development of this system was the direct consequence of the regime's refusal to reform the economy, a refusal dictated by the corporate interests of its bureaucratic base as well as by a more general fear of the popular forces a structural reform of the economy might unleash. (The 'Prague Spring' strongly reinforced these fears.) Brezhnev's regime was the bureaucratic regime par excellence. Brezhnev came to power declaring that he, unlike Khrushchev, would 'respect cadres'. Under his rule, the Politburo was eventually reduced to little more than the arbiter of particular bureaucratic interests.

It has been argued, especially by some members of the Soviet intelligentsia, that the workers were privileged under this system and corrupted by it. And yet, this system, in whose development the workers had had no say, was really directed against their fundamental interest in an efficient economy, responsive to popular needs. It did provide certain social guarantees, but they remained at a medicore, inadequate level, and the price exacted for them was a heavy one: intensifying political repression, tremendous economic waste, widespread corruption, and the moral and cultural, and even physical degradation of society. The workers merely adapted as best they could, and the régime was forced to tolerate the situation in the enterprises as the cost of maintaining power. In theory, of course, the workers had an alternative: they could have sought collective, political solutions to their situation. But the failed wave of worker protest at the end of the Khrushchev period (several years before the appearance of the 'dissident movement') had shown that conditions were not then ripe for a successful popular mobilization. As for their being corrupted, as we shall see, dissatisfaction with the existing economic system is today no less strong among workers than in the rest of the population. If workers have so far shown no particular enthusiasm for the economic reform, it is not because they oppose change. It is rather that they have doubts about the nature of the change that is being offered them.

REFORM MEASURES

The logic (if not necessarily, so far, the practice) of the 'market reform' is to place enterprises under a 'cost-accounting régime' (khozraschet), doing away for the most part with obligatory plan targets, and giving them broad autonomy to pursue profit within a regulated market context. The (central) state will continue to plan and regulate the economy, but through indirect methods, i.e. through control and manipulation of such economic (as opposed to administrative) levers as prices, credit, taxation and competitive state contracts.

This reform would end job security, since layoffs and bankruptcies become possible and, in fact, are already beginning to occur, though so far on a limited scale. It would also put an end to wage guarantees, since wages are to depend such more than before on the actual performance of the enterprise, as measured by profit, i.e. what is left from sales after various payments have been made. The reform provides for two methods of calculating wages, one more 'radical' than the other (the more radical one being officially preferred but so far rarely applied):

> a) Basic wages are paid as part of fixed costs according to state norms and so are guaranteed. But bonuses and premiums are paid out of profits, after other financial obligations have been acquitted, and so depend upon enterprise performance.
> b) No part of the wage is guaranteed. Wages are paid from what is left after meeting other financial obligations. In this case, the entire wage depends upon enterprise performance, as measured by profits.[9]

The wage reform also includes a review of skill classifications and norms, with a view to encouraging workers to raise their skills and to release hidden productive reserves. Accordingly, the part of the basic wage in takehome pay is to rise to 70–75%, and bonuses are to be made more difficult to achieve. To compensate this, basic wage rates are to rise on the average 20–25% (more for specialists and white-collar workers) over the course of the current five-year plan 1986–90. This rise, however, will not be financed by the state budget but must come from savings realized by the enterprise. That is why the specific timing of the reform's introduction is left up to the enterprise.[10]

An avowed goal of the reform is to increase wage differentiation in order to enhance the incentive role of wages. To the same end, there has been much discussion about the need to reduce the part of the social wage in incomes. This will be achieved through price reform, the reduction or elimination of subsidies, and the establishment of user fees for services that are presently free. 'Levelling' stands officially condemned (as it has since Stalin's time, though perhaps now more insistently than ever) as economically inefficient as well as socially unjust, since, it is claimed, such egalitarianism contradicts the 'socialist principle of distribution according to labour'.[11]

The reform thus aims to tighten things up on the shopfloor. But another goal is to link the workers' well-being more closely to the performance of the enterprise, while the enterprise, on its part, enjoys significant autonomy in the pursuit of profit in a market context. The goal is to create a common motivation among managers and workers to discover and to release productive reserves, to increase individual and enterprise efficiency, and to produce quality goods that meet the needs of clients and consumers.

Those aspects of the reform aimed at democratizing enterprise management follow logically from this goal. In Gorbachev's words: 'The well-being of the worker will depend upon the abilities of the managers. The workers should, therefore, have real means of influencing the choice of director and controlling his activity.'[12] This is a politically necessary corollary of enterprise autonomy. Otherwise, the Soviet enterprise director, freed from control from above in his or her disposition of the enterprise's resources and in setting prices, and newly armed with the means (the 'stick' of dismissal and 'carrot' of the reformed wage system) to extract an intensified labour effort, would resemble all too closely his or her capitalist counterpart. This would mean a unilateral abrogation of the old system of labour relations, which had allowed the regime to 'buy' the workers political quiescence by affording them certain social guarantees and means of defence, at the same time as it fostered a collusive relationship with a paternalistic enterprise management. A 'market reform' without enterprise democratization would be perceived by workers as a drastic and unjust undermining of their position vis-à-vis management, and it is not difficult to imagine them responding with massive unrest and/or the formation of independent economic (and almost by definition in the Soviet context) political organizations. Thus, for political and related ideological reasons, this is not a real option for the Soviet leaders.

Of course, the thinking behind enterprise democratization is not only political. It also has a more directly economic objective: together with the wage reform and cost-accounting, it is an attempt to overcome the workers' alienation, their indifference to the fate of the enterprise, and to foster a sense of responsibility toward this public property. Such an attitude has been woefully lacking (though not only among the workers, but also in management at all levels). According to the director of research institute of the U.S.R.R. State Committee on Labour, 'self-management today is designed to [. . .] awaken people, force them to feel themselves masters of production and of the country [. . .] Self-management is a way of uniting the interests of rank-and-file toilers, social groups and collectives with the interests of society.'[13]

There are two main measures of enterprise democracy provided for by the 'U.S.S.R. Law on the State Enterprise (Association)': the election of managerial personnel, and the empowering of the worker collective and its elected labour-collective council to participate in management decisions and in the monitoring of their execution.

> Management of the enterprise is realized in conditions of broad openness (glasnost') through the participation of the entire collective and its social organizations in reaching highly important decisions and monitoring their fulfillment, the election of managers, and one-man management (edinachalie) in the administration of the enterprise. The pooling of the working people's efforts and the development of their initiative in achieving work results, the instilling of good work organization and discipline in personnel and the raising of their political consciousness are ensured on the basis of self-management.[14]

Before examining the present state of labour relations, it is worth pointing out the fuzziness and ambiguity of the law itself. The elected management 'expresses the interests of the state and the labour collective', but the law does not explain what happens when the interests of the state and the labour collective come into conflict. Similarly, the director is elected by the collective but must be confirmed by the higher level agency, which can force a new election if it does not like the winner, although it must explain why. This veto power from above has been variously explained by possible 'excesses' that can occur in the early stages of democracy and by the fact that the enterprise is state property, and the state must ensure its interests.

The law is equally unclear on the powers of the labour collective and its council in relation to management. The appearance, without commentary, of the terms 'democratic centralism' and 'one-man management', notorious since the late 1920s for their authoritarian interpretation by the régime, is in itself worrying. The law also repeatedly uses the vague term 'participation' to describe the role of the labour collective and its council in the decision-making process. And it does not really clarify matters when the law finally states that 'decisions of the labour-collective council that are adopted within the bounds of its authority and in accordance with legislation are binding for management and the members of the collective.' It is clear neither about the bounds of the council's authority nor about the other legislation that constrains its power. This absence of clarity cannot but raise doubts, since under Brezhnev labour collectives also enjoyed broad powers on paper; yet it was the rare worker indeed who was even aware of their formal existence, let alone had ever seen them put into practice.[15]

In a similar vein, the call to revive trade-union democracy and to restore the unions' functions as defenders of the workers' interests appears as a strikingly incongruous element.[16] The provision for self-management and elected managers, whose aim is to overcome alienation and foster a real sense of ownership, would seem to obviate the need for trade unions. Even if conflict arose between labour and management, certainly the trade unions could be no more effective in resolving them than the labour-collective councils, which after all, are elected by the same people but possess broader powers.

THE IMPACT OF REFORM IN THE FACTORIES

How have worker-management relations in industry changed so far under the perestroika? First of all, it seems that the initial enthusiasm for the election of managerial personnel has waned. The authors of an article on the subject note that significantly fewer articles are being published on the subject, and their tone has become more sober, sometimes even pessimistic. 'Such a shift in mood is the result of the fact that all those who especially wanted to have already tasted this "dish".'[17] It seems that not all the workers (not to speak of managerial personnel!) were excited by the opportunity to hold elections and that those that were enthusiastic often found the 'dish' less tasty than expected. Where workers did embrace elections as a means of changing things, of 'putting affairs in order', they only too often had their hopes dashed.[18] This leads the authors of the above article to appeal 'not to allow this important democratic principle to be "buried"'.

The new organs of 'self-management', specifically the labour-collective councils, have not fared much better. The head of the Department of Ideological Work of the party's Institute of Social Sciences concluded in mid-1988 that 'the participation of the workers in management still remains a wish, a goal, rather than a reality.' In a survey conducted by his school, only 14% of the respondents said they felt themselves the masters (khozyaeva) at work. (39% felt there was no owner, in the sense of someone concerned with, and responsible for, the fate of the enterprise.)[19] In another survey of ll,180 workers and white-collar employees of 120 large industrial enterprises from mid-1988, only 2.7% considered the councils to be 'very active'. 52.8% replied that they 'have not yet fully shown themselves,' and 18.3% said they were inactive. 11.1% replied that their enterprise had no council, and 15.3% were unable to give any opinion. V. Ivanov, the director of the Institute of Sociological Research interpreted this to mean that the attitude was one of 'wait and see'.[20] Another assessment made in the same period found that 'the

Law on the Enterprise is not functioning as it should. Collectives often refuse to take up the broad powers that have been given them. Democratization of management is clearing itself a path through outdated views and indifference only with great difficulty.'[21]

As for the trade unions, by virtually all accounts, they have not responded to the calls for change: in conflicts between workers and management (not to speak of conflicts between workers' interest and those of the state at higher levels), they remain solidly with the latter.[22] A survey conducted by the research institute of the Central Trade-union Council found that only one or two workers out of every hundred would turn to their trade unions in disputes involving wages. Meanwhile, although 80% of trade-union activists consider that the introduction of the wage reform in their enterprise is not in full accord with the law, the unions nevertheless remain silent.[23] In a letter to the trade-union paper *Trud*, a worker from Kharkhov province wrote:

> It is no secret to anyone that trade unions don't always take the side of workers. That may not be tragic if it's a minor issue and not one of principle. But when management takes revenge against a worker for criticism, and the trade union is either silent, or worse, supports the administration? I'll soon be 64 and I've often come up against such a situation.[24]

A trade-union activist from Novosibirsk asks:

> Why is it that our trade-union leaders, elected by the workers, again and again find themselves taking the side of the administration? [. . .] Earlier, I would not even have entertained the idea of going to management and demanding that it change this or that decision. But now we have democracy. Why are we not in a rush to use it?[25]

Of course, if self-management were becoming a reality, if the workers were acquiring a real voice in management and were adopting an attitude of solidarity with the administration in the common aim of improving the performance of the enterprise, the absence of trade-union combativity would not be an important issue. But not only is this is not happening – the opposite is occurring. According to published reports from different Soviet sources, the number of conflicts between workers and management has risen sharply, this as a direct reaction to the perestroika as experienced in the factories.[26] So far, at least, the perestroika has failed to create in the workers a sense of ownership. Not only has it not reduced their alienation from enterprise management (let alone from the higher levels), but it appears to be intensifying their attitude of opposition, the sense of 'us against them'. It has done this by breaking down the old bases of collusion under the 'command economy' without creating new bases for economically healthy worker-management co-operation.

This surely explains why the calls for the transformation of trade unions into militant organizations for the defence of the workers' interests have not yielded results: in circumstances of intensifying opposition and conflict between workers and management, neither the political leadership nor certainly enterprise management can really be interested in facilitating independent worker organization. Such organization could sabotage the reform (at least as presently conceived), and perhaps even threaten political stability. In private, and not so private, conversation, Soviet social scientists often advocate a firm hand, if not a 'Cavaignac', to push through the reform. Or else they emphasize the need for a 'responsible democracy' – as opposed to what the people, 'unfortunately' want – a 'democracy of desires'.[27] At the June 1988 Party Conference, convened to discuss democratic reforms, the only speaker to even mention the trade unions was the chairman of the Central Trade-Union Council. And the theses published in preparation for the conference said nothing of the labour-collective councils, which, after all, are officially intended as a form of democracy on the enterprise level.

LABOUR UNREST UNDER THE REFORM

An examination of the types of conflict occurring offers a more concrete picture of the situation in the factories. A major source of conflict is the arbitrary and illegal application of the wage reform. A group of electricians from the Simsk Assembly Factory in Chelyabinsk province complained to *Trud* about the manner in which management had recently introduced the reform. The director called a meeting of the workers, but 'not to discuss ways of raising productivity, economizing on labour, etc. but to get formal approval for the change that had already been decided without our participation.' In fact, the director announced an across-the-board 20% reduction of bonuses and the demotion of all workers to lower skill grades.[28]

The wage reform is supposed to be carried out in close consultation with the workers. The review of skill classifications, according to government instructions, takes place in two stages. In the first, a commission of worker and management representatives is established. It looks at each case separately, considering the opinions of those who work with the individual – the other brigade members, the brigade leader, department head – and makes a preliminary evluation. In stage two, the worker is invited before the commission and informed of his or her proposed classification in accordance with the new Unified Skill-Rate Handbook. If the proposal is a demotion, there must be an explanation, and the worker is provided with the opportunity to defend, through testing, his or her skill level. Only after that, on the basis of all the material, does the director make the final assignation.[29] The wage reform is also to be introduced gradually, as the enterprise assembles the conditions and means necessary, in particular those required for raising the basic wage rates, which are to constitute the major part of the total wage, the share of bonuses and other supplementary payments declining significantly.

But managers, in a hurry to show results, often resort to old trusted methods. The Vice-Director of the Department of Industrial Production and Wages of the Central Trade-Union Council has admitted that 'in many cases the procedures of the reclassification are brutally violated. The first stage [. . .] is often totally omitted, and the affair [. . .] begins with an order that the worker is told to sign. And an order, as we know, is not open to discussion. [. . .] This is in total contradiction with the process of democratization of the entire life of our society.'[30] The arbitrary, across-the-board reduction of workers' skill classifications is an easy way of conforming on paper to the wage reform: management indeed raises basic wages rates, but the worker is, in fact, left with the same basic wage as before, while facing new, harder norms and so lower bonuses, or none at all.

To make matters worse, this arbitrary and authoritarian approach is often accompanied by unconcealed discrimination against women. At a Chelyabinsk factory making construction materials, all men in the steel-fittings department were assigned to the fifth skill grade and all the women to the third. 'This was openly explained by the fact that we are women and that men's skill classification should be two grades higher than women's.' In other cases, women on maternity leave were illegally demoted in their absence.[31]

Despite all the talk about democratization, management, at least in the confines of the enterprise, still has the means to impose its will. (Even the official instructions appear to leave the last word with the director). At some factories, the workers were told to look for work elsewhere if they did not agree with the demotion.[32] At the Gidromontazh Assembly Factory in Tadzhikistan, the director gave the workers a choice: vote to reduce your-selves by one skill grade or else, as a result of the formal review of skill grades, you will be reduced two or three.[33] At another factory, 'in the morning, as we came off the night shift, without forewarning, they organized a biased test for us. We were so tired, we couldn't make any sense of it.' At the Biisk Garment Factory, 'recently the management has begun to lower skill classifications for insufficient knowledge of the political situation. If a sewing-machine operator cannot answer how many delegates there were at the Nineteenth Party Con-ference, she can be demoted. Does this mean we should hire journalists who are experts in world politics to work at the machines?'[34]

In the workers' letters, the dominant sentiments are anger but especially deeply wounded human dignity. In the above-cited letter, the workers noted the 'malicious joy' of the managerial personnel, as they administered the test. 'Why such humiliation?' they asked. 'They insulted us,' wrote another group of workers, 'reducing our skill grades, without explaining or asking anything. Do we deserve such a lack of respect for our twenty years of honest labour?' And the workers see this as a test of the perestroika: 'Does the administra-tion really think,' concludes the letter, 'that it can pass off this farce as a restructuring?' 'Is this what perestroika consists of?' 'The whole factory is buzzing: "So this is the perestroika!".'[35]

In the absence of trade unions that defend them or even inform them of their rights, and given the prevalent authoritarian attitudes and practices of management, the workers' recourse is to the newspapers (which by law have to investigate complaints that are sent to them), to higher authorities (the joint commission of the State Committee on Labour and the Central

Trade-Union Council charged with overseeing the reform is swamped with complaints) and/or the strike (increasingly frequent). The published reports of such conflicts usually end with their successful resolution, through a careful and differentiated review of skill classifications.

We do not know how often such appeals occur and how often they end satisfactorily for the workers. But we do know that many workers remain dissatisfied. For even in the course of a differentiated and careful review of skill classifications, a significant proportion of workers will find themselves demoted, since the reform is attempting to put an end to the common practice of assigning workers to higher skill grades than merited (a practice designed to attract scarce labour). Similarly, it is admitted that the introduction of a 'cost-accounting regime', designed to restore the 'socially just principle' of 'payment according to labour', can, at least in the short run, lead to a decline in wages for 'workers not possessing high skills and diligence'.[36]

To the workers affected, these reforms really create injustice by making them pay for practices for which they bear no responsibility. As they constantly repeat in their letters, no one ever asked them their opinion about anything. Indeed, in the final analysis, these practices existed so that the régime would not have to ask the workers' their opinion about anything. More generally, these 'past injustices' are a consequence of a planning and management system that was first established in the late 1920s in accordance with the interests of the bureaucracy. Much later, when it became clear that the system had become a major obstacle to further economic progress, the régime, guided by the interests of this same bureaucratic base, rejected structural reform. (It is, of course, an open question to what degree the system will be reformed even now.) The workers' sense of justice demands that if they are being asked to make sacrifices, the same should be asked of the real author of the 'past injustices'. Anyone familiar with the Soviet scene, knows the depth of popular anger at bureaucratic privilege and the workers' sense that they are being made to work for the upkeep of an unjustifiably bloated mass of parasitic 'chinovniki'. But despite the intermittent exposés in the media, there is little sign of this privilege being eliminated or even seriously diminished. True, there is to be a major reduction of staff in the various apparatuses, but at present it seems unlikely that the higher or even upper middle circles of the bureaucracy will suffer.

Typical of this type of conflict was the strike at Ryazsel 'mash, an agricultural machinery factory in Ryzan', in the early fall of 1988. The coverage in *Sotsialisticheskaya industriya* reflects the official attitude (and that of most social scientists) to the issue of 'past-injustices'. The conflict was between a brigade of about 50 electric welders and the new department head. According to the paper, things had been pretty lax here. Former department heads came and went, concerned primarily with meeting gross output targets (the main success indicator under the old system). They bothered little with such matters as economy of labour and materials. As for the workers, their attitude was 'grasping' and 'selfish', and they behaved according to the slogan: 'After us – the deluge, as long as we get our wages.' (We are not told why they should have cared about anything else, when the department heads and higher management themselves did not look past their bonuses and personal career interests, and when the workers had no say in how the enterprise was run nor virtually any material interest in the enterprise's real contribution to the economy.) Discipline was weak, continues the report, and wages did not correspond to the work done: norms were easy.

This situation had its origins several years back, when the department was being set up and it was hard to find workers. The easy norms were also a way of compensating workers for inevitable losses caused by difficulties in installing and mastering new technology. These circumstances no longer existed. Yet, because of the continued arhythmic character of production in the department, large sums have to be paid for overtime and other 'incentive payments.' 'These are basically young workers,' sadly noted a 'labour veteran', 'but look how they have been corrupted by easy money.' Even stragglers here made more than experienced welders elsewhere. Such were the sad consequences of the 'agreement' between workers and management. This, continues the report, became unacceptable under a cost-accounting régime.

The new department head set out to 'introduce order with a firm hand.' For failure to fulfill certain plan indicators in June and July, the welders were twice deprived of bonuses, even though they had overfulfilled output norms by a large percentage. 'Having grown accustomed to "indulgence", the welders reacted 'oversensitively' to these sanctions and warned the department head not to be so strict or he could expect a strong reaction. In all this, the trade union played no role – the workers acted through their own informal leaders. The department head had expected the support at least of the eight Communists among the workers. But, alas! 'For them, too, charity apparently begins at home'. As the department head stepped up his pressure, the workers retaliated with a slowdown strike, twice turning off the machinery to hold meetings. This is when the department head issued a 'draconian' order that included many harsh punishments (we are not given the specifics), in response to which the workers put down their tools.

The reaction in the rest of the factory was mixed. 'Some unconditionally condemned the brigade. Others, on the contrary, supported it. Yet another group simply could not believe such a thing could be taking place. A fourth group [the managerial personnel?] openly gloated: now they'll see what playing with democracy brings.' The labour-collective and the trade-union councils condemned the strike and threatened to disband the brigade if the strike was repeated. The two most active worker leaders were excluded from the trade union for one year. This means, among other things, a loss of important social benefits. Management was instructed to finally bring labour norms into line with the labour expenditures actually demanded by technology. The article concludes philosophically with the thought that the real losers are the 'perestroika' and democracy. 'The brigade still feels that it was punished for trying to resist arbitrary rule. And the department head is certain that this is how order has to be introduced today. The victims are mistrust and a lack of faith.'[37]

In the sixth sheet-rolling department of the giant Magnitogorsk Metallurgical Factory, an experiment, which subsequently became permanent, was introduced to fight levelling. Previous forms of 'socialist competition' had had a mainly exhortatory, formal character, with little practical incidence on production. Under the experiment, the bonus is attributed not to each brigade, but to the department as a whole, on the basis of the final results. However, it is distributed in a very differentiated manner among the workers, according to the place their 'coefficient of effectiveness of labour' (based on quality and quantity of output) takes in the competition. The difference between a winner and a loser can be 50–60 rubles. (The average industrial wage in the Soviet Union is 220 rubles).

According to *Trud,* under the new system, 'no one holds back reserves, hides potential. Now it is not profitable. . .' Nevertheless, a large part of the workers have demanded an end to this form of competition. One problem is that in calculating results, conditions beyond the workers' control are not considered, such as the illness of a partner or failure of another department to supply the necessary parts on time. But the chairman of the trade-union committee feels that fundamentally the workers 'fear the loss of the "benefits" of levelling [. . .] Frankly, many of us have forgotten how to work intensely, thoughtfully, creatively. And it hurts now to have to pay for that with the ruble.'[38] The report does not explain what the 'benefits' of levelling are. But one can ask if it is fair to describe these workers as 'corrupted' by the old system? Withholding of effort, while not a trait of human nature, is certainly inherent to alienated labour, which necessarily perceives any intensification of work as an intensification of exploitation, particularly when there is no control over the size and permanence of the reward. And so far under the reform, the immediate experience has often been an intensification of labour without a significant rise in wages. In conditions where 'democratization' and 'self-management' have yet to be translated into reality, 'levelling' is still perceived by workers as an important means of defence against attempts at 'speed-up'. (How much income inequality they would choose even under completely democratic conditions is, of course, another question. Defence mechanisms aside, there are indications of strongly held egalitarian values in the Soviet population.)[39]

What political leaders, managers, economists and journalists portray as legitimate attempts to eradicate the injustices of the preceding era, workers tend to see as a unilateral abrogation by management of longstanding arrangements regulating their mutual relations. The new arrangements often amount to a deterioration of their immediate situation, and workers have little confidence that they might benefit from them at some later stage. In any case, it appears to them that they are being asked to bear all the sacrifices. Faced with this, workers, in their turn, are abandoning their tolerant attitude towards managerial shortcomings and the widespread failure to observe legal norms. They are encouraged in this by the political liberalization and the official policy (if not yet the practice) of democratization, which are creating a new sense of what it possible in a contest with management. As a result, conditions and practices which workers once grudgingly accepted are now also becoming objects of open conflict.

In March 1988, several dozen bus drivers at a Saratov transport enterprise struck when their wages for February, following the introduction of the wage reform and cost accounting, turned out to be well below normal. When they complained, they were told to earn the difference. According to the newspaper report, these workers had grown accustomed to levelling and to management's toleration of slack discipline. Typically, the workers had not been consulted about the changes. 'What can you expect,' said one driver, 'if they speak with us mainly from top down? No one gives a damn about our opinion, and management does whatever it likes. Meanwhile, the administrative apparatus is impossibly bloated.' But the wage dispute was only the spark that ignited the strike. Management's unilateral action over wages allowed the release of years of pent-up dissatisfaction over the drawn-out construction of a new building, overcrowding, poor ventilation and lighting, failure to modernize the repair base, the shortage of spare parts and the poor quality of repairs. A party meeting placed the blame with management, the trade union and the party organization, who in the past reconciled themselves to indiscipline and poor work and now failed to prepare the workers for the shift to cost accounting. It was decided to organize elections to management at all levels, to prepare more carefully the shift to new conditions and to work off the lost time outside of regular hours, the wages to be paid to the Children's Fund (a national charity).[40]

Overtime and its major cause – the arhythmic character of production, with long bouts of idle time followed by mad storming – have always been an important source of worker dissatisfaction under the 'command system', unable to assure regular supply of materials to the enterprises. Overtime in the Soviet Union is by no means always paid at higher rates, as the law prescribes (enterprises would greatly exceed their wage bills), and even when it is, it does not always make up for wages lost during periods of enforced idleness. More important, the irregular work hours wreak havoc with workers' lives. The overtime (regulated by law) is often illegal to boot. Nevertheless, overtime was usually begrudgingly accepted by workers under the old system of labour relations and only now is it becoming a major source of open conflict.

In December 1987, the workers of the Yaroslavl' Motor Factory struck for seven days. Management had compiled a work schedule calling for workdays of seven hours and 50 minutes and fifteen 'black Satudays' over the course of 1988. In past years, despite some grumbling, the workers had accepted similar schedules. This time it was different. They held 60 local meetings that yielded 60 resolutions, all calling for an eight-hour day and only eight Saturdays. (The ten minute difference in the workday over the course of a year equalled the seven extra Saturdays in the administration's schedule). Nevertheless, the labour-collective council – chaired by the director himself! – ratified management's schedule, with only one opposing vote. So did the trade-union committee – without comment.

It was after this that the strike broke out. The next day the director met with the workers assembled in the yard. He explained why supply problems made fifteen 'black Saturdays' necessary. From the crowd came shouts: 'That's your concern!' He explained that the cafeteria would not to be able to manage. From the crowd: 'That's your concern!' He explained that public transport could not cope and that the enterprise would have to pay 100,000 rubles in additional transportation costs. 'That's your concern!' Workers who took the floor told the director that he had had a whole year to prepare conditions for a normal work schedule but had done nothing. As for the transport question, the factory had buses that stood idle in the evenings. Even the intervention of the vice-minister did not sway the workers. 'When are we supposed to rest?' asked one. 'And what about our families?' 'You say you are defending our interests?' interjected another worker. 'You are thinking more about the motors [. . .] And we are there working day and night at the end of the month. That's illegal!' 'But you get paid more for that,' replied the director. To this a worker retorted: 'We're idle at the beginning of the month and then [to make up for lost earnings] we get bonuses.'

The meeting voted unanimously for the workers' '8–8' schedule. 'A clean split has occurred,' concluded the district party secretary. 'The workers versus the general director, and there is no intermediate link.' The trade union continued to side with management and applied pressure on the workers' informal leader, Makarov. But he explained: 'It isn't just a question of rest. When we say an eight-hour day, we mean a real shift, with no idle time. Now, idle time makes up 9% of the shift. An eight-hour day would give management an incentive to intensify labour. As things stand now, it doesn't care, since the lost time can be made up on days when we aren't supposed to work.'

The labour-collective council decided to call a meeting of worker delegates. The hall was packed. Management explained that the plan targets could not be met with the '8–8' schedule. But according to one worker, less worked Saturdays would leave more time for regular maintenance of the equipment, which is old and tended to only after it breaks down and stops production. But there was also the social aspect: 'Many tie the demand for the eight-hour day with faith in perestroika'. It was a question of new methods of work, discipline, renewed technology.

The meeting lasted five hours, and the vote was finally 359 vs. 296 for management's schedule. Applause was thin and it came mainly from the front rows (where management's people were seated). It is possible, noted the *Izvestiya* reporter, that management and the trade-union committee had applied pressure before the meeting. But more likely factory patriotism won out. After the vote, Makarov took the floor and proposed that in 1989 there would be a shift to the eight-hour day. Someone else called to put a total end to illegal Saturdays. Both resolutions passed unanimously.[41]

In a poll conducted by *Izvestiya* after the publication of this report, 69% of the worker respondents approved of the Yaroslavl' workers' refusal to work 'black Saturdays', though half of these said they would have yielded in order to save the plan. All felt that the cause of the strike was dissatisfaction with the organization of labour – the irregular character of production, the poor quality of materials and of the goods produced as a result of this.[42]

This strike shows forcefully that workers hold management (at all levels) responsible for the poor state of the economy. This is quite a different understanding of the situation from that which one usually hears from social scientists, managers and journalists, who tend to lay a good share, if not all, of the blame on the workers' indolence, indiscipline and corruption. Some of this undoubtedly exists. But most workers sincerely wonder how they could work better in the given circumstances and they see the criticism directed at them as a way for managers to cover up for themselves. For example, a foreman at the diesel factory explained that 'a regular pace of production determines everything else. But it does not exist. You work Saturday and Sunday. And then there is no work on Monday. In such circumstances it makes no sense to punish workers for lateness or absences, since idle time can last days.' [43]

The strike at the Yaroslavl' factory illustrates how the 'perestroika' has not only not fostered beneficial work-management solidarity but has actually deepened the gulf between the two to an unprecedented degree. In the director's words: 'The essence of the perestroika is that there should not be "we" and "they", as is the case here now, but that the collective be united.' The problem at the Yaroslavl' factory, and at most others, is that the organs of self-management, provided for by the Law on the State Enterprise, are not functioning as prescribed. At the diesel factory, neither the labour-collective council nor the trade-union represented the workers. The council, chaired by the director himself, was clearly a tool of management, which thought it could continue to run things in the old authoritarian way. The workers had other ideas. However, they did not demand that genuine self-management be introduced, so that they could directly implement the changes they wanted. Rather they united behind an informal leader against management in defence of their interests, refusing responsibility for the administration of the factory.

This refusal is, in part, due to the workers' perception – generally a valid one – that management is not prepared to give them any real say in running things. They, therefore, see 'self management' as a trap to get them to take responsibility for failures of management and of the economic system as a whole. The leader of a brigade of mechanics, chairman of the labour-collective council of the Kamaz Auto Factory, wrote to *Trud* in June that,

> although all managerial personnel in the factory are elected, so far this democratization is more external than deep. In its relations with the labour-collective council, management, as before, adheres to the military code: an order from a higher rank is not open to discussion. For example, the administration orders the workers to appear on their days off, and neither the labour-collective council nor the trade union even try to protest, even though we have passed the limit of [legally] allowed overtime.[44]

At the Perm' Motor-Repair Factory, the director was also chairman of the labour-collective council, which had met only once in its nine months of existence. Workers here struck over delayed payment of wages. Asked why they would act thus against their own interests, when the new cost-accounting régime means that the losses from the strike come out of their own pockets and when they now had their own organ of self-management, a turner replied simply that the 'workers don't believe in that council'.[45] As the letter from Kamaz indicates, elections have not given the workers real power. In the case of lower managerial personel, at least, the elections are often 'organized' by the director to make sure his or her candidates get through, and, in any case, the director retains the final say.[46]

Political leaders and the press often lament the workers' passivity in face of the 'perestroika', attributing this to the corrupting effects of the old system. But the workers' apparent indifference to self-management is based much more on their disbelief in the possibility of making it a reality under the present régime. When they have decided to give it a try, the results have been disappointing. In 1987, at an electoral meeting of the trade-union council of the jewellery department of the Moscow Jewellery Factory, in the spirit of the 'perestroika', the workers let it be known that they 'were sick of working in the old way', in conditions of disorganization and arhythmic production, requiring massive overtime and storming that were turning them into nervous wrecks. So they elected a new trade-union committee with the mandate: 'Put the place in order'.

The committee began by holding elections for department head. The workers saw this measure as real. It 'gave them confidence in their own forces, showed them that they can, all the same, influence matters in the department.' But at a union meeting a year later, the gulf between workers and management was deeper than ever, as the workers complained about norms, wages, skill classifications. What happened? According to the author of the report, 'the workers demanded changes and were ready to actively participate in them [. . .] But their insistence apparently irritated the managers. The latter still did not have answers to many of the production problems. Instead of calming the workers and explaining the situation, they used the old trusted methods of command: your business is to do what you are told.' 'You know,' one of the workers explained,

after the election of the department head, when we saw that we can run things in our department, out spirits rose and the desire to work better appeared. But when we understood: the
administration had been playing at democracy with us. It turns out that we are the masters
more in theory. They listen to our opinion when it coincides with the boss's, when its in
their interest.

And so at at the latest union election meeting, there was total indifference.
'People had lost interest in what was occurring in the hall; they kept glancing
at the exit, in a rush to get to the cafeteria.'[47]

Management's reluctance to give up or to share power is not surprising, given the constraints and pressures placed upon it by the still largely
unreformed 'command' system. Prejudices and other considerations aside, to
give the workers a real voice in these conditions is to make a manager's hard
life even more complicated, to deprive him or her of the flexibility (a familiar
theme to Western ears) needed to meet taut plan objectives in conditions of
irregular material supply (still administered from the centre).

But management's resistance is not the only reason self-management is
having trouble getting off the ground. For even where the labour-collective
councils are genuinely participating in enterprise decisions, the workers often
remain indifferent and mistrustful. In an interview to *Trud,* the chairman of
the labour-collective council of a Leningrad machine-construction factory,
himself a turner, painted a picture of genuine council involvement in enterprise management, including negotiations with the ministry over various plan
targets. Still he complained of indifference and lack of faith in democracy
among the workers. They take their complaints to the party, to the soviet or
to the press, rather than to the labour-collective council, a workers' organ.
This is because 'they do not know what we can achieve. They do not believe
that the labour-collective council is a real force.'[48]

The workers' continued mistrust of 'self-management' even in those rare
cases when management welcomes their genuine participation, has the same
source as the managers' general reluctance to give the workers a real say:
the continued power of the ministries and other external bureaucratic forces
that still largely determine the fate of the enterprise. In these circumstances,
even if management is prepared to share power, the workers still perceive a
trap to get them to accept responsibility for something they cannot effectively
control. This emerges clearly from an article in *Komsomol' skaya pravda* by
a young mechanic-assembler, a brigadier at the Kazan' Motor Factory. This
is one worker who is definitely enthusiastic about self-management. But he
finds himself constantly frustrated by the unreformed system:

The perestroika is for all without exception! But, all the same, let's look the truth in the
face. As long as the ministries, as is stated in the Law on the State Enterprise, bear full
responsibility for the branch, the most militant labour-collective council will inevitably find
itself against a brick wall. You can't bear responsibility without at the same time taking
rights away from the enterprises. And so too, our labour-collective council does not 'make
the weather' in the enterprise. Not because it doesn't want to – because it can't. . . How
can you ask me to feel myself the master, when practically nothing depends upon me?[49]

The article is appropriately entitled 'We're Sick of Being Pawns.'

At the Ural'mash Machine-Construction Factory, the labour-collective council, along with management, were successful after heroic efforts in resisting an attempt by the ministry to impose new, impossibly high plan targets (in the new form of a 'state contract'). At Ural'mash, with its liberal director, the labour-collective council appears to be genuinely participating in management. But, notes its chairman, a brigadier, of late the council has been receiving letters from the councils of client and supplier enterprises, asking for special favours, such as extra deliveries and special parts not specified in the contracts. In other words, the councils are becoming a 'democratic' variant of the old 'pushers' sent out by management. Instead of coming with complaints and proposals about production, they are acting as the errand boys of management in an unreformed management system.[50]

A roundtable discussion on the labour-collective councils in the coal-mining sector made clear that the major problem facing the councils is that the law itself is vague on the relative powers of the councils vis-à-vis the ministry and that, in practice, the ministry rules. 'The labour-collective council has no say in planning for the enterprise. It all comes from above.'[51] 'The ministries are violating right and left the rights of the enterprises,' states the director of the State Labour Committee's research institute.[52] Indeed, a new form of conflict has emerged recently: labour-collective council against ministry, over losses to the enterprise caused by apparently illegal ministerial actions.[53] Besides the imposition of new 'states contracts' in mid-stream, complaints include ministerial refusal to extract fines from its own enterprises for non-respect of contracts when the losses are incurring to another of its enterprises ('It's all in the same family'), and the attachment of indebted and failing enterprises to more 'profitable' ones.[54] Such 'levelling' practices by the ministries stand officially condemned, but they largely continue, despite reports of bankruptcies.[55]

One reaction to this situation, one that is reported most frequently by the press (that has been exhorted recently by Gorbachev to support the reform), is for the labour-collective councils to demand real enterprise autonomy: only thus can self-management become real. But one suspects that this reaction comes mainly from enterprises that would be favourably situated in a market reform, because of the type of goods manufactured, geographical location, technological level of equipment, etc. (Actually, given the fact that resources are still centrally allocated, most directors are not eager to be freed from 'state contracts'.)[56] Thus, the secretary of the party bureau of a Tallin machine-construction factory describes how the labour-collective council successfully beat back efforts by the ministry to shift the factory to a newly created trust. 'We were united and had rationality on our side. We were accused of worrying about our own profits. But we fought for the cost-accounting regime, for the flourishing of our enterprise that produce goods that are in demand – and thus for the interests of society.'[57]

This is clearly the attitude of a part of the skilled workers, especially the younger, well-educated ones who are brimming with energy and initiative and have been straining to put these to productive use. The young brigade leader from the Kazan' Motor Factory cited earlier suggests the leasing of the machinery to the workers. But despite the official and media support for these views, they do not seem to have the support of most workers, who have serious doubts about the market as an agent of rationality and social justice. The Kazan' brigadier, after calling for enterprise autonomy and the leasing of machinery, continued:

> But there are people today who are energetically pushing public opinion to condemn to worker-'graspers' (khapugi), who feel no embarassment in talking about high wages. They shout: mercenary interests, petty philistine passions! Come on! Who is it then that moves our economy, that is the main support of production, if not the 'grasper', the one who breaks all norms, who is keen-witted and full of initiative, taking care of his means of production – his lathe and instruments. Of course, today's transitional situation does not please the lazy yes-man, who always keeps one eye on management: 'At your service!' But it's a case of 'either – or'.[58]

WORKERS AND SOCIALIST DEMOCRACY

When there is no immediate prospect of democracy at the centre of power (and unfortunately, this is still the situation in the Soviet Union), this way of seeing the alternatives – either the market and the enterprise as guarantors of efficiency, or centralized bureaucratic management and continued waste – comes naturally to those who impatiently seek a creative outlet for their energies. But ultimately this is a dead end. Self-management and the market in a non-democratic political context are in fundamental contradiction. For when workers' power is limited to the enterprise level, they use it to guarantee their jobs and salaries. This means there can be no real labour or capital markets. This is one of the lessons of the Yugoslav experience.[59]

Most Soviet workers are wary of the market as the ultimate arbiter of rationality and justice.[60] V. Vishnyakov, a law professor at the Trade-Union institute, expressed these fears when he called recently for genuine democratization of trade unions and their real participation in state policy-making:

> The cost-accounting and self-financing régimes in the enterprises, the new labour legislation, have made more acute the problem of the social protection of the individual: *will not the humanism of socialist principles be sacrificed in practice on the altar of economic gain?*[61]

In the current Soviet political context, such concerns are usually condemned as reactionary advocacy of 'levelling' and 'social dependency'. But they are real fears and they are greatly exacerbated by the absence of genuine democratic control over the reform, either at the central or the enterprise levels. And a 'Cavaignac' at the helm, rather than facilitating structural reform, ultimately only makes its introduction more unlikely, because it deprives the reformers of the support of the working class, the only political base potentially strong enough to carry through the reform against the resistance from within the bureaucracy.

The concerns of Soviet workers do not mean structural reform of the economy and democracy are incompatible. All the evidence shows that Soviet workers want reform, they want to 'put the economy in order'. Nor do their concerns mean they would reject any application of the market mechanism in the economy. Rather, it is a question of whether the market will impose its criteria of efficiency and justice on society or whether society will subordinate the market mechanism to the type of development it collectively chooses. For the latter to be the case, the central state must retain key powers to plan and to regulate the economy. Despite past Soviet experience, this need not be a formula for continued economic waste and stagnation – if the state is democratic, i.e. freed from bureaucratic control. Only when national economic policy is decided in a democratic context can constraints placed upon enterprise autonomy cease to appear as external, to provoke resistance and the concealment of reserves.

The sincere proponents of self-management in the Soviet Union see it as a way to resolve the fundamental problem of the Soviet economy – the coherent linking of the interests of rank-and-file workers, managers, social strata and regions with each other and with the overall interests of society. The reform so far was patently failed to do this. It has deepened the divisions, and the level of conflict has risen sharply. The evidence analyzed here points to the undemocratic context in which the reform is being decided and promulgated as the underlying cause of this failure. The conclusion that presents itself from Soviet experience with reform to date (and from the experiences of other Soviet-type societies) is that for self-management to be effective, it must extend to all levels of economic decision making, including decisions about the character of the reform and the economic system it is designed to create.

What has been happening in Soviet factories can be seen as a qualitatively new, if still limited, stage of labour activism. So far the workers have organized only episodically around informal leaders and for essentially local ends. But before the 'perestroika', strikes involving entire enterprises (and the bulk of Soviet workers are concentrated in huge factories) and lasting several days were rare events. The main factors that have contributed to this change are the political liberalization, the absence of genuine democracy (the main reform measures to date all been dictated from above, albeit with public discussion of the details), and the introduction of a wage reform that is putting an end to the collusive ties with management and their corrupting influence on worker consciousness.

As – and if – the market reform progresses in its present fundamentally top-down manner and is more concretely felt by the workers, one might see developing more permanent, large-scale, independent working class organizations. There are some signs of this happening already. In Yaroslavl', a 'workers' group' composed of representatives of the major industrial enterprises has been formed as part of the city's 'Popular Front'. (This is an independent movement of citizens that arose at a mass meeting on June 8, 1988 to protest the 'election' of the unpopular Yaroslavl' provincial party committee first secretary to the 19th Party Conference in Moscow.) The moving force behind the formation of this group was the workers' club of the Yaroslavl' Motor Factory, formed (against the opposition of management and the party committee) following the seven-day strike over the 'black Saturdays'.[62] A similar 'workers' group' exists in the town of Andropov. Toward the end of 1988, in the Lithuanian city of Kaunas, 300 delegates from 70 enterprises founded the Kaunas Union of Workers. Its basic goals are defined as the 'struggle for restructuring of the trade-union committees in the enterprises, for the corresponding restructuring of the content of the local factory newspapers, and for the protection of the rights of workers against managerial arbitrariness.' Similar unions were being set up in Vilnius and Klaipeda.[63]

A price reform, without which there can be no market reform, might give a major push to such organization. Opposition to it is very widespread in the population, and the authorities are, accordingly, refusing to say anything precise about it, while they discuss the matter in secret. This could serve to unite workers on a larger scale in defence of their interests, since, unlike the wage reform, it would be a measure promulgated from the centre. Rather than mean an end to the perestroika, such a development would set the scene for a genuinely revolutionary restructuring in the Soviet Union, one in which the initiative comes from below, the only one that has a realistic chance of succeeding.

Are contemporary Soviet workers really capable of independent political activity? Needless to say many inside and outside the Soviet Union are sceptical about this and even doubt the workers' interest in socialist democracy. But the events of 28 years ago in Novocherkassk have something to tell on this score. Perhaps the most striking thing about them is the level of class consciousness displayed by the workers. This was a spontaneous movement of workers, with no participation of the intelligentsia. Despite provocations, it was a sober movement, without 'excesses' on the workers' part – they occurred only on the side of a régime that showed how much it feared the workers when they took soviet power seriously. There was none of the 'anarchism' supposedly inherent in the Russian 'masses'. These people identified themselves and their movement with the working class. They tried to establish contact with their comrades in other cities. They claimed the Soviet revolutionary tradition as their own.

And yet, Novocherkassk had no traditions of working class struggle. It was and remains a backwater provincial town that at the time of the revolution had no industrial workers. All of its large-scale industry dates from the 1930s and after. According to Siuda, the working class consciousness and traditions and even many aspects of the strike itself – so reminiscent of strikes in Tsarist Russia – came from the workers' schooling, from books and films and, of course, from their shared situation. Isaac Deutscher's discussion of this issue comes to mind:

> The fact that the rulers and leaders of the Soviet Union have never stopped evoking their revolutionary origins, has also had its logic and consequences. All of them, including Stalin, Khrushchev, and Khrushchev's successors, have had to cultivate in the minds of their people the sense of revolutionary continuity. They have had to reiterate the pledges of 1917, even while they themselves were breaking them; and they have had to restate, again and again, the Soviet Union's commitment to socialism. [. . .] The educational system has constantly reawakened in the mass of the people an awareness of their revolutionary heritage.[64]

Novocherkassk was only partly about prices and wages. On a deeper level, it was about socialist democracy, something the workers had never experienced but which they had no difficulty in understanding. Siuda describes the atmosphere in this way:

> The time – excuse me because this might sound blasphemous in view of the tragedy that followed–but the time was a happy one, a time of spiritual emancipation, a full emancipation of the protest that had surely been accumulating in everyone's hearts. It was short-lived, but it was still freedom, independence. You must understand that we were always living with the slavish feeling: careful, what will the authorities [nachal'niki] think, say?. . . If you ask any worker for a chronological account of the events, they couldn't tell you. Because we felt so strongly our freedom that we lost our sense of time. I never again felt such total emancipation. Personally, I don't feel it now either. Because I see the reality and not what is being said or written in the papers.

A group of workers from the Urals, after reading Siuda's essay on the Novocherkassk events, wrote him the following letter dated June 17, 1988:

> We have read your letter about the tragedy of June 1–3, 1962 in your town and we express our sympathy and solidarity. We want to send this information to some paper, to *Komsomol' skaya pravda*, for example. The workers, on the whole, believe the account of the facts in your article, but for the good of the cause, we would like to receive personally from you a confirmation with a brief account of the course of events. This will be a document of sorts against the local bureaucrats, opponents of the revolutionary renewal, in whose hands, unfortunately, the real political power rests. This is a treacherous class of exploiters of the toilers, that uses as a cover that which is most sacred to the working class–Marxism–and passes itself off as the true representatives of the party of the working class, of Soviet power, of the people, and against them one must fight skilfully, with their own arms. Of course, after this deception of the workers, unprecedented in the history of humanity, it will take a certain amount of time for the course of democracy and glasnost, to yield fruit: the dictatorship of the working class, its full power through its own institutions–the soviets, in their Leninist understanding. We are sending a letter to Gorbachev, N.S., signed by a group of workers of the metallurgical factory. In this connection, we would like to know your critical comments on this letter and your advice on the methods of struggle against the enemies of the working class–the bureaucratic bourgeoisie, or, as Lenin called them, the sovbours.
> We await your answer as soon as possible. It is needed for our struggle for the cause of the working class.

Notes

1. The following is from an interview I conducted with Siuda in the summer of 1988 as well as from his unpublished essay that has been circulating in the'informal' movement.
2. See. V. Belotserkovskii, 'Les soulèvements ouvriers des années soixante,' *L'Alternative*, no. 3. March 1980, pp. 28–31.
3. V.I. Gerchikov and B.G. Proshkin, 'Vybornost' rukovoditelei: pervyi opyt, pervye problemy,' *EKO*, no. 5, 1988. p. 90.
4. See my article 'Economic Reform and Democracy,' in *Socialist Register 1988*.
5. 'Norma truda v novykh usloviyakh khozyaistvovaniya,' *Sotsialisticheskii trud*, no. 5, 1988, p. 38; V.I. Shcherbakov, 'Kardinal'naya perestroika oplaty truda,' *EKO*, no. 1, 1987, p. 38; G. Konstantinov, 'Perestroika zarplaty–chto yei meshaet', *Agitator*, no. 13, 1988, p. 17.
6. W. Brus, 'Utopianism and Realism in the Evolution of the Soviet Economic System,' *Soviet Studies*, vol. XL, no. 3, July, 1988, p. 440.
7. S. Minaeva, Director of the Central Trade-Union Council's Department for Social Development, in *Trud*, Jan. 12, 1989.
8. See, for example, V. Dement'ev and Yu. Sukhotin, 'Sobstvennost' v sisteme proizvodstevennykh otnoshenii sotsializma,' *Kommunist*, no. 18, 1987, p. 71; 'Economic Reform and Democracy . . .' pp. 139–42.
9. *Sotsialisticheskii trud*, no. 2, 1987, pp. 57–96, and no. 3, 1987, pp. 54–66.
10. V.I. Shcherbakov, 'Kardinal'naya perestroika oplaty truda,' *EKO*, no. 1, 1987, p. 37–52.
11. See D. Mandel, 'La perestroika at la classe ouvrière,' *L'homme et la société*, winter 1988–9. There has been no serious debate about what this principle should mean in practice. It goes without saying that it is open to diverse and contradictory interpretations. For a discussion of this, see A. Zimine, *Le stalinisme et son 'socialisme réel'*, Paris: La breche, 1983.
12. *Pravda*, Jan. 28, 1987.
13. Interview with E.G. Antosenkov, *Nedelya*, no. 49 (1497), 1988, pp. 6–7.
14. *Pravda*, July 1, 1987.
15. On this, Antosenkov stated: 'If we are to be honest and not close our eyes to reality, before there were words about the participation of toilers in management rather than their real participation,' *Nedelya*, no. 19 (1497), 1988, p. 7
16. See, for example, the speech of Shalaev, chairman of the All-Union Council of Trade Unions, at the Trade-Union Congress, *Pravda*, Feb. 25, 1987. This has also become a constant, though not unambiguous, theme of the central trade-union paper *Trud*.
17. Gerchikov and Proshkin, 'Vybornost' rokovodiiclei . . .,' p. 17.
18. See, for example, A. Kozlov, 'Nachinal tsekhkom s zhelaniem', *Trud*, Sept. 29, 1988.
19. Zh. Toshchenko, 'Soznanie, nastroenie, deistvie,' *Agitator*, no. 12, 1988. p. 11.
20. 'Stimuly i tormoza,' *Sotsialisticheskaya industriya*, June 19, 1988.
21. G. Konstantinov, 'Perestroika zarplaty . . .', p. 18. Discussions at a conference on the labour-collective councils organized by the Leningrad 'Perestroika' club at the end of June 1988 similarly made clear that their impact so far has been small.
22. V. Vishnyakov, 'Prosit' ili trebovat'?', *Trud*, Oct. 6, 1988.
23. E. Terent'ev, 'Sotsial'naya sfera i profsoyuzy,' *Trud*, July 8, 1988.
24. *Trud*, July 8, 1988.
25. Ibid., June 1, 1988. An exceptional case of a trade union actively defending the collective interests of workers and even leading them in a strike is that of Khabarovsk Regional Committee of the Union of Workers of Local Industry

Khabarovsk Regional Committee of the Union of Workers of Local Industry
and Communal Services. In a remarkable letter published in *Trud*, the chairman
of the regional committee admitted that this was an extreme measure but he
recalled Lenin's justification of strikes as a legitimate means of defence against
'bureaucratic deformations' in the Soviet state and he warned that such means
would continue to be used. G. Tkachenko, 'Dlya raskachki vremeni net,' *Trud*,
Oct. 12, 1988. This case, written up in the central trade-union paper is, indeed,
significant and therefore deserves mention. If at the same time, I have relegated
it to a footnote, it is because it is an isolated case. It is also worth noting that it
involves a distant region and a politically marginal category of workers scattered
in a myriad of very small enterprises.

26. See, for example, I. Leshchevskii, 'Idti vmeste,' *Sotsialisticheskaya industriya*,
    June 26, 1988; E. Terent'ev, *Trud*, July 8, 1988; V. Kazachenko, 'Rodoslovnaya
    zhaloby,' *Trud*, Sept. 3, 1988; G. Konstantinov, 'Perestroika zarplaty . . .', pp:
    15–18.
27. See, for example, A. Ulyukaev, 'Perestroika–kto "za", kto "protiv"', *Nedelya*, no.
    18, 1988, pp. 11–12.
28. *Trud*, July 8, 1988.
29. A. Levina, 'Operatsiya "stupeni masterstva",' *Rabotnistsa*, no. 10, 1988, p. 17.
30. Ibid.
31. Ibid., and Konstantinov, 'Perestroika zarplaty . . .', p. 15.
32. *Trud*, July 8, 1988, and Levina, 'Operatsiya . . .' p. 17.
33. Konstantinov, 'Perestroika zarplaty . . .', p. 16.
34. Levina, 'Operatsiya . . .', p. 17; 0. Zhadan, 'Dekol'te na samosvale, *Trud*, Jan.
    17, 1989.
35. Levina, p. 16–18, and Konstantinov, p. 16.
36. A. Mineev, 'Evolyutsiya obshchestvennogo soznaniya,' *Moskovskie novosti*, Jan.
    15, 1989, p. 8.
37. V. Lifanov, 'Zhestskii pressing,' *Sotsialisticheskaya industriya*, Oct. 4, 1988.
38. A. Rostarchyk, 'Protiv uravnilovki', *Trud*, Nov. 24, 1988.
39. See Mandel, 'La perestroka . . .' V. Chervyakov of the Institute of Sociological
    Research states that research shows a widespread 'psychology of levelling', but
    he blames this on the effects of what he maintains was the past state policy and
    philosophy of levelling. 'Formula spravedlivosti', *Trud*, Jan. 18, 1989.
40. A. Vorotnikov, 'Konflikt nazrel,' *Pravda*, April 13, 1988.
41. 'Sem'dnei,' *Izvestiya*, Dec. 25, 1987.
42. 'Sem'dnei,' *Izvestiya*, Jan. 6, 1988
43. 'Sem'dnei,' *Izvestiya*, Dec. 25, 1987.
44. *Trud*, June 15, 1988.
45. V. Konstantinov, 'Profkom v prostoe, *Trud*, September 4, 1988.
46. See, for example, the letter form Izhstal' in ibid., July 8, 1988.
47. A. Kozlov, 'Nachinal tsekhkom s zhelaniem,' *Trud*, Sept. 29, 1988.
48. *Trud*, July 7, 1988.
49. C. Bulatov, 'Nadoelo byt' peshkamy', *Komsomol'skaya pravda*, Oct. 5, 1988.
50. *Sovetskaya Rossiya*, June 26, 1988. See also 'Uchitsya upravlyat' samim!',
    Nedelya, no. 49, Dec. 5–11, 1988, p. 7.
51. *Trud*, June 17, 1988.
52. 'Uchitsya upravlyat' samim!', p. 7.
53. V. Kazchenko, 'Rodoslovnaya zhaloby', *Trud*, Sept. 3, 1988.
54. Ibid., 16 June, 1988.
55. See, e.g., 'Bankroty,' ibid, Sept. 16, 1988.
56. P. Bunich, 'Goszakaz ili prikaz?' *Ogonek*, no. 44, Oct. 1988, pp. 14–16.
57. Ibid., July 16, 1988.

59. See, C. Samary, 'De la Yougoslavie a l'URSS', *L'homme et la société*, winter 1988-9.
60. See Mandel, 'La perestroika . . .'
61. V. Vishnyakov, 'Prosit' ili trebovat'?', *Trud*, Oct. 6, 1988.
62. A. Mineev, *Moskovskie novosti*, Jan. 15, 1989, p. 8
63. N. Belyaeva, 'Natsional'nyi ili nardonyi,' *Moskovskie novosti*, p. 10, Dec. 25, 1988.
64. I. Deutscher, *The Unfinished Revolution*, London: Oxford University Press, 1967, p. 36.

OBSTACLES TO REFORM IN BRITAIN*

Tony Benn

Introduction

The experience of societies that have undergone a revolutionary change under socialist leadership–as, for example, the Soviet Union, China, Yugoslavia and Cuba has been well documented to bring out the lessons which it may teach about the positive and negative forces that come into play to advance, or inhibit, the processes of social transformation. But less has been written about the attempts made to bring about social change in bourgeois democracies, when social democratic governments have been elected to office on radical political programmes, that might, if implemented, have actually changed the balance of power in a significant way. This may, in part, be because there are so few examples of social transformation even being seriously advocated, let alone attempted, or it may be because even when the idea of social trans-formation appears in the rhetoric of the social democratic left, few expect that anything will come of it, or the failures are attributed to the betrayal of individual leaders. But neither collective nor personal cynicism should be accepted as an excuse for failing to look at the actual situation which may develop where real progress has been promised, nor should the experience of the toppling of Allende in Chile or, say Grenada, which faced an American-led invasion, be taken to be the only way by which elected reformers can be frustrated in their work. For in some other countries, parties of the Left have been elected to a parliamentary majority on radical programmes and their intentions have been much more subtly frustrated over a long period.

This article deals with the actual experience of a socialist Minister in the 1974–9 Labour Government in Britain, and seeks to identify some of the obstacles placed in the way to prevent the policies on which that Govern-ment was elected from being carried out. Obviously the circumstances that existed then were different from those which exist today, and the political situation in Britain is very different from that which prevails in other com-parable countries, but even so, the lessons learned may have a more general application where a Government with a majority, in a bourgeois democracy, tries to carry through changes which would in any way alter the structure of power and wealth or reform the institutions which sustain them.

---

*This is a revised version of a talk given at the Graduate School of the City University of New York in December 1988.

1. The British Constitution

The British people are regularly told that they live in a democracy and that the Mother of Parliaments is respected all over the world as the model on which other democracies have based their own structures and practices. However, in reality, the institutions of Britain are far from democratic and the term democracy is almost always qualified by the adjective 'parliamentary' which may appear to be a minor change but, on close examination, turns out to be a major variation of the idea that the people are sovereign. For, when the text-books are consulted, our system of Government is described as a 'constitutional monarchy' by which is meant that, in law, Britain is governed by the 'Crown-in-Parliament', an idea that goes back three hundred years to the so-called Glorious Revolution of 1688 when the present constitutional settlement was accepted by Parliament. It was then agreed that the Crown would, in future, govern by and with the consent of Parliament–at that time composed of two Houses–the Lords made up primarily of major landowners, and the Commons representing only about 2% of the male population, all of them very wealthy too. By preserving this fiction that the Crown is still the source of authority, a number of institutional obstacles to change are embedded in our system. Although the Crown in the form of the current King or Queen has very limited discretion in practice, confined to the power to dissolve parliament and decide who to ask to form a government, and its role is completely overshadowed by the Royal Family with which the monarchy is associated, it remains true that the core of the British system of Government is still feudal in character and the extent to which democracy has been allowed to penetrate it is strictly limited. Moreover, when a government comes to office, through the ballot box, and is formed under its leader, who becomes Prime Minister, that prime minister acquires, personally, many of the real powers of the Crown, for the exercise of which they are not democratically accountable, and are thus able to control those whom they were elected to represent, so long as he, or she, retains that position and the support of a majority in the House of Commons. The residual powers of the monarch personally are important because if they are used, as in Australia by the Governor General to dismiss a prime minister, the judges will regard that dismissal as constitutional, and would uphold the Crown's right to do that against the claim of the dismissed prime minister that he or she had been removed even though enjoying the support of parliament. Thus if there were ever a coup in Britain in which the Crown participated and collaborated by dismissing the prime minister, that coup would be legal and not illegal. Therein lies the essential weakness of British democracy, for it is a democracy on sufferance and not by right, making it quite different from the provisions of the American Constitution where a president who sought to dissolve or disregard Congress would have his action ruled unconstitutional by the Supreme Court. When the Crown powers exercised by a prime minister in office are examined they are much more substantial, in that making war; signing treaties; appointing and dismissing Ministers; creating peers; appointing judges, archbishops and bishops; the chairmen of the BBC and other public authorities; together with a mass of other appointments, are all authorized under the Prerogative, not one of which legally requires the assent of parliament or even the cabinet.

Every constitution in the world has some provision for presidential or executive power to be exercised in an emergency but none approach the scale which is present in a British prime minister derived from the Crown which he or she is supposed to serve. Even a state of emergency permits full executive powers to be exercised, during that emergency, by a body called the Privy Council which normally has a purely formal function but can be called–on a small hand picked basis–to issue Orders-in-Council which have the force of law and derive from the prerogatives. All this needs to be stated in order to provide some background understanding to the nature of the state apparatus which an incoming Labour Government is elected to control, and every civil servant, military officer and judge and bishop is sworn on oath to bear allegiance to the Crown and not to the Prime Minister, the Government, or to the majority in Parliament or Parliament as a whole, let alone the citizens. It should be noted in passing all these institutions were originally developed by a class which was committed to the status quo, and to prevent any government from altering that status quo.

The economy of Britain is overwhelmingly capitalist in character, even more so than it was a decade ago since when the great state enterprises have been privatised and sold off piecemeal, to companies which now run them and which are entirely free of any constitutional responsibility to the people of the country. However, the problems do not end there because both the structures of the state and the structures of capital ownership each have their own international links which reinforce them in their capacity to prevent change. The two main institutional links between Britain and foreign governments are NATO led by the US and the EEC, which now very largely controls the freedom of action available to British Governments. For example the decisions to invite American forces to base themselves in Britain, and to build the British atomic bomb, were taken by the post-war Labour Prime Minister, Clement Attlee, without consulting the whole of the Cabinet or Parliament. Similarly when Mr Edward Heath, as Prime Minister, signed the Treaty of Accension of Britain to the EEC he did it using prerogative powers and the Treaty which he had signed on behalf of Britain was never published until he had signed it. One final example of prerogative powers used by the Prime Minister of the day occurred when Mrs Thatcher took armed action against the Argentine Government in the Falklands/Malvinas conflict.

2. The Labour Party Constitution

It is against this constitutional background that an incoming Labour Government is expected to take charge of the state apparatus and used it for its own purposes, which are to serve the interests of those it represents. In order to build the parliamentary majority necessary to secure an electoral victory, the Labour Party has, while in opposition, to represent those interests effectively, raise the issues that concern those whose support it is seeking, project an alternative policy and campaign for that policy against the Government it is seeking to defeat. The policy of the Labour Party, designed to do all that, is made by a variety of processes including resolutions from local parties, local trade unions, regional conferences, women's conferences, and then is carried on to the Annual Conference, which in theory has the final say, where the affiliated trade unions enjoy 92% of the vote and the constituencies 8%. Resolutions that get more than a two-thirds majority become part of the programme of the Party and are eligible for inclusion in the manifesto even though there is no certainty that they will feature in it. For the election manifesto itself is drawn up by the National Executive Committee, elected by Conference sitting with the Cabinet or 'Shadow' Cabinet, representing the leadership of the parliamentary Party which, in opposition, is elected but, when Labour is in Government, is appointed by the Prime Minister. Thus a new obstacle faces socialists in that the Leader of the Labour Party has often claimed that he has the right to veto items that come up for inclusion in that manifesto to which he objects, even if that policy has received the two thirds majority at Conference referred to above.

That veto was applied by Harold Wilson as Leader of the Labour Party in 1973 when he objected to the inclusion in the manifesto of a pledge that 25 major companies would be brought into public ownership by an incoming Labour Government. Since Wilson was the Leader of the Party, the manifesto committee accepted his veto because, if they had overruled him, they would have discredited the Leader under whom they hoped to win victory by showing him to be impotent in dealing with his own supporters. This means that however successful socialists may be in winning support for their policies in the party they may find it impossible to put those policies before the electorate because of this first and substantial obstacle–the use by the Leader of a vote of confidence to get his own way against the Party he leads.

3. The political image-makers

The next stage is the election campaign itself where the pressure on the Party leadership to water down the policy is very intense, mainly orchestrated by the mass media, which are owned or run by proprietors who are hostile to socialism and keep up an unremitting attack upon socialist policies in the hope of forcing the Labour Party to abandon them before polling day, in return for the generalised suggestion that, by doing so Labour will win more votes. This is all based upon the general theory of public relations politics that the way to win elections is to target the centre and persuade people in that centre to vote Labour rather than Conservative or Liberal. But in making that choice, there is an equally conscious decision to take socialist support for granted and to ignore the non-voters who may represent 20% or 30% of the total electorate and whose abstention may derive in part from the fact that they cannot see a difference between the two parties contending for office, an idea re-inforced by the absence of any vitality or substance in the political debate. Insofar as non-voters come from the poorer sections of the community whose interests would best be served by a Labour victory, the decision to concentrate on the centre is very ill-advised, because if those non-voters voted, it is reasonable to assume that a majority of them would, in self-interest, vote Labour and there are far more such people than there are hovering indecisively in the middle. But so powerful are the pollsters and image makers in modern parliamentary political campaigning that they carry the day on almost all occasions, and thus represent another major obstacle to the presentation of socialist policies. If despite all these handicaps a Labour Government is elected, as it was in 1974, a real opportunity for socialists to press ahead with the manifesto policies does appear, since election victories disorientate those opponents who have been defeated, raise the hopes and expectations on the part of supporters and this creates a general sense of excitement, and transfers the Labour Party from the role of critic to the role of responsible managers of the situation they have inherited.

There is no doubt that an election victory thus creates the conditions in which radical policies are more likely to be expected, and accepted, by the electorate. But one word of caution must be added and it is this: that when the Labour Party moves from Opposition to Government its leadership moves into ministerial offices and becomes primarily concerned with the task of man-agement and less involved, if involved at all, in the role of leading the Party which put them in power. Indeed, victory may decapitate a whole layer of Party leaders, leaving the Party feeling ignored and neglected and denying it many of its most experienced spokespersons who would continue to be advocating its social and political objectives, because they would be then be busy in the ministerial offices. In short, those leaders who may have been most articulate in pressing for social change, finding themselves absorbed in departmental work may honestly persuade themselves that socialism has arrived, whereas all that has really happened is that they have arrived person-ally. This is a very much neglected obstacle in the path of socialists because it is one that follows inevitably at the moment of victory. The effect of this may not be felt for a long time since the neglect of socialist propaganda and education on the morrow of a victory is cumulative, and after a long period of Labour Government, the absence of that education unquestionably offers to opponents on the right wing an opportunity to occupy the high ground of argument with propaganda of their own. This was very clear in 1979 when the Labour Party which had been in office for eleven of the previous fifteen years was defeated by Mrs Thatcher and it became obvious immediately that, as her parliamentary soldiers crossed the electoral boundaries to form a majority in the House of Commons, they discovered that hundreds of thousands of acres of ideological and moral territory ahead of them had been evacuated years before, and their ideas were able to fill the vacuum thus left.

4. The State Apparatus

Next we come to the problem facing Labour or socialist ministers as they enter their Departments and meet the civil servants with whom they have to work. It is one of the great myths of British parliamentary democracy that the British civil service is politically neutral, ready, anxious and willing to work with equal enthusiasm for any political party that may form a majority. This is a complete illusion largely spread by those who know perfectly well that the civil service is neither ready, anxious, nor willing to work for socialist policies but has to be presented in that way so that it can perform its task of obstruction without being accused of partiality. But any social analysis will reveal that most senior civil servants come from a very narrow class base and are broadly ignorant of, and unsympathetic to, the aspirations of socialism. In addition, these senior civil servants are the very ones who devised the policies which the incoming Labour Government has been elected to reverse, and they would not be normal if they did not feel some commitment to those policies. The general thrust of policy objectives will have come from the previous Conservative Government but the patient working out of them is always left to the administrators to do, and they are bound to want to defend their work.

The power that the senior civil servants have derives from their position as permanent officials with enormous administrative experience, an intricate pattern of inter-departmental connections at official level and with the knowledge they have of all the discussions that went on in the previous Government which are withheld from the incoming Government. The only papers passed from one Government to another relate to international negotiations and understandings, which carry on uninterrupted, despite a change of Government and, in those matters, the new ministers do have to know what their predecessors had done before their removal from office. Otherwise they know nothing about what has happened before, and this protection of one administration, from the inquisitive eyes of its successor, necessarily protects the status quo and denies an incoming Government information that it might be able to use to get across to the public precisely why it was setting a new course. Most of the international links that exist are maintained by permanent officials who are in very close daily contact with their opposite numbers in other countries, at NATO, in the Common Market, the IMF or GATT and the policies that have been agreed with those international organisations make them exceptionally difficult for an incoming Government to unscramble even if it wishes to do so. It is one of the theories of constitutional government in Britain that there should be a continuity of foreign and defence policy into which no party interests should be introduced–which is another way of saying that the choices open to the electors in a parliamentary democracy should not extend to foreign affairs or defence.

5. The Myth of Realism

These arguments are presented to departmental ministers in the form of 'ministerial briefs' which have been prepared by the civil service during the election campaign, one set for the Conservatives, if they were to win, and another set for Labour. The preparation of these briefs occupy most of the time of departments during an election campaign itself, when the outgoing ministers are drained of their political legitimacy because the election is in progress, and the civil servants are keeping the departments going on a care and maintenance basis, whilst reading the manifestes of the major parties and preparing these briefs. Thus when the ministerial appointments have been made and the new ministers arrive in their departments, they are handed these thick bundles of briefs by the Permanent Secretaries and are expected to read them. However, in the aftermath of an exhausting election campaign, most ministers are much too tired, and too busy, to absorb such a mass of material, particularly as a number of urgent questions will no doubt be on their desk for immediate decision. As a result, they probably do not realise the importance of the document that has been given to them, which is the only document in the whole electoral cycle in which senior civil servants indicate their own policies, drafted in the guise of suggesting how the manifesto policies of the Labour Party can best be implemented. But the framework of thinking is official and ministers will be told how civil servants see the task of manifesto implementation, and the changes the civil servants do not want to see made will be highlighted, and a more 'realistic' way will always be indicated, in line with the policies the senior civil servants want, which is to steer radical Ministers gently into the mainstream of coalition politics.

All ministers in effect receive an offer from their senior civil servants–unspoken but nonetheless real–which runs along the following lines:

> If you follow the policies we recommend, we will help you, in every way we can, to pretend that you are implementing the policy on which you were elected.

Ministers who accept that tempting offer will soon find themselves described in the right wing press as 'exceptionally able' and 'much admired in Whitehall' for their 'strong handling of departments' which will be accompanied by similar praise from commentators who are known to be violently opposed to the Labour Party and its policies. Those ministers who are not prepared to submit to this temptation will find themselves being described as 'difficult', 'indecisive' or 'divisive' and this briefing may come direct from the civil servants in the department which that Minister heads, or it may come from number 10, Downing Street where the Prime Minister's senior permanent advisers will have been fed a series of negative briefings from the Minister's own civil servants who are always quick to use their own Whitehall network to undermine a minister who will not do what they want. Of course none of this would be possible if the prime minister of the day was to make it clear to his own civil servants that he gives full support to a minister thus being systematically undermined, for officials would be much more nervous about criticising a minister they knew had the approval of the prime minister himself.

6. Civil Service Obstruction

This general account of how socialists within a Labour Government can be sidelined, marginalised and ultimately frustrated can easily be documented and one vivid example occurred in the winter of 1977/78 when a decision had to be reached about the nature of the next nuclear reactor system to be introduced into Britain. Britain had always used a gas cooled system designed in Britain, but for some time the Generating Board and the civil servants had wanted us to move over to the American PWR system. My careful reading of the brief for incoming ministers had alerted me to this and it was common knowledge that Prime Minister James Callaghan preferred the American system. I had conducted many consultations and decided to continue with the British system. However, my Permanent Secretary and all the relevant senior officials, came to my room and announced that they were united in supporting the American system and we had a very long and full discussion of the issues. At the end, I told them of my decision and asked them to prepare a paper for the Cabinet setting out my view as the responsible minister. The permanent officials then simply refused to prepare the paper that I had commissioned, on the grounds that they did not agree with the policy that I wished to put forward.

Though obstruction is common, I can never recall such a situation ever happening quite as crudely before or since and it left me with only one choice which was to ask the two political advisers in my Department to draft the paper, which they proceeded to do. My civil service private secretary whose specific task it was to work for me, as his minister, was shocked by what had happened, and he went to the Permanent Secretary to point out the constitutional issues involved, and he was able to get an assurance that my advisers could seek technical advice from more junior members of the Department who would be instructed to answer practical questions and make it possible for my paper to be prepared, which they did. However, my senior officials, unable to persuade me to take their view, then wrote the paper they had wanted me to submit and circulated it through official channels in Whitehall to mobilize other departmental ministers to frustrate my policy in favour of their own. The main vehicle for their plan was the Central Policy Review Staff–the so-called 'Think Tank' headed up by a former senior civil servant who was permitted to submit papers of his own direct to the Cabinet Committee which was going to be considering my paper.

At a social gathering just before Christmas 1977, I met one of the junior members of that 'Think Tank' who told me exactly what he was doing and he said, 'The CPRS is subversive'. When I asked him what he meant, he said, 'Oh, if a minister will not do what his civil servants want him to do, then we subvert that minister by putting in papers reflecting the view of the officials in the department in question and use the power of Whitehall against him.' It was a very naive and ill-advised comment for him to have made because it alerted me to exactly what was happening and that was how I discovered that this 'subversive briefing' was going round to other ministers on the official network. In order to frustrate this I decided to use the political advisers again, this time to ring the political advisers in the Departments circulated by the CPRS to inform them what was happening and the reasons for my own recommendation. Thus when the matter came to Cabinet my departmental colleagues had before them both the official briefing against my paper which had come from my officials through the CPRS to their private offices, and the political briefing in favour of my paper which my political advisers had circulated to their political advisers, and, in the event, the decision reached by Cabinet secured 99% of what I had wanted. The only point on which I was forced to concede was that, although the Cabinet agreed to choose the British reactor, they also agreed that some preliminary design study work was to be done on the American reactor.

I have set out this story in some detail because it shows how the Whitehall mechanism works, in this case to defend the nuclear lobby, and anyone who wants to understand the difficulties which face a minister who chooses to go against the advice of his officials must understand this. It is worth noting that, after the defeat of the Labour Government in 1979, the new Conservative Government decided to go ahead with the American PWR, the first one at Sizewell and others to follow in series.

7. Official Secrecy

But the problem of the loneliness of a socialist minister is one that requires a great deal more attention because life is so much easier for a minister who goes along with what his officials want and it is very difficult indeed to defeat them. This is, in part, because of the workings of the Official Secrets Act which constitutes a ring fence of information control situated along boundaries of government, locking ministers in with their officials and excluding their political supporters–or the general public–from access to the knowledge they will need to influence the decisions before they are made. The only way in which a minister can gain access to that outside knowledge and support, which he must have, if he is to win, is by making it public, from the outset what decisions are about to be reached, what the issues are, what official advice he is getting, and actively seek the views of those who may have as much, or more, expertise as his officials, but who could never make it available unless they knew what was being discussed inside the Whitehall. Here is where the enactment of a Freedom of Information Act would be so helpful,

not only to an electorate that is entitled to know what is being discussed, but
to a beleaguered Minister who wants support in order to implement the policy
on which he was elected.

8. Establishment Pressure Groups

In addition to civil service power it is necessary to identify some of the most
powerful pressure groups that exist within the ring fence of official secrecy,
and which are able to operate because no-one outside knows what they are
doing. The most powerful Whitehall pressure group exists amongst the military who have the professional responsibility for defending the country from
its enemies–an objective which naturally commands general popular support,
and who, as we know from the experience of other countries have the power
to take over the reins of government if they were ever to decide to do so.
Any Labour Government, and especially the socialists within it, inevitably
face serious opposition if they wish to do anything–as for example reduce
military expenditure or cancel a nuclear weapon–which the military would
oppose, and, since few ministers have much military knowledge, the capacity
of the military to mislead and deceive Ministers about the balance of forces
in the world is immense. The second internal pressure group operating within
Whitehall is the Bank of England, nationalised by the Labour Government
in 1946 as an instrument by which that Government could control the City of
London and the banking and financial sector in the interests of national planning. The 1946 Bank of England Act allows the Bank to give directives to any
other bank, and the Treasury has the statutory power to define what a bank
is, so that the role of the government is, in theory, complete. But in practice
the Bank has merely become a permanent voice, inside Government, for the
City of London and the Governor of the Bank who is a public appointee but
not a member of the administration, acts quite independently to try and force
any Labour Cabinet to meet the policy requirements desired by the City and
the international financial establishment. He has enormous power as a result,
because, if the Governor sees the Chancellor and warns him that cuts in public
expenditure, or some other change in economic policy are necessary to restore
'confidence in the pound sterling' the Cabinet finds that a pistol has been put
at its head, and on a number of important occasions–notably in 1976 when
the Governor and the IMF worked together to secure major cuts in public
expenditure–Labour Cabinets have capitulated.

This analysis highlights another informal understanding which Labour ministers are expected to accept, and it is offered by the banks, finance houses
and industry, internally and externally, that they will not organise a run on
the pound and undermine confidence to the point where it would bring down a
Labour Government provided that that the Labour Government itself will not
seriously challenge the power of capital. One of the most vivid examples of
this emerged from Harold Wilson's book 'The Governance of Britain' where
on page 75 he describes occasions when it was necessary for him to reassure

the City about policies that had been developed by the NEC of the Labour
Party and his account of how he did it is a follows:

> 'Quite often, therefore, I had to make this point clear, by answers to questions in Parliament
> or published replies to anxious letters from City based financial institutions such as the British
> Insurance Association, or the merchant banking community, *on more than one occasion drafting
> the letter to which I was at pains to reply myself.*'

In short here was a Labour prime minister actually volunteering a repudiation
of socialist policies by inviting the City to ask him to deny, personally, that
socialist policies were even being considered.

The third internal pressure group or groups, which are the most secret of
all, are the security services themselves–M15, M16, and the Police Special
Branch which operate under the loosest of ministerial control, hitherto on
a non-statutory basis, and are in effect, free to do what they like without
telling Ministers. The *Spycatcher* book, which Mrs Thatcher tried so hard to
suppress, was only the tip of the iceberg, and the problem goes much much
deeper than that. These security services operate on policies of their own,
maintaining surveillance over all individuals or groups that they themselves
have decided to be hostile to the status quo, or to constitute the 'enemy
within', and in this category may be included ministers in the Government
they are supposed to be serving, as happened in the case of the plot against
Harold Wilson. On the one occasion when this all came to light, the Labour
Prime Minister of Southern Australia, Don Dunstan, demanded access to the
files of the security services when he came to power, but was initially refused
it on the grounds that his head of security argued that his loyalty was not
to the prime minister or elected government of South Australia, but to the
Crown. Here we come up against the Crown in a new and sinister role, for the
Crown is the embodiment of the State and the oath of allegiance to the Crown
which are required of every military, civil and judicial official, is interpreted
by them as superseding any loyalty which they might be expected to have to
the elected Government. It should be added that when those Australian files
were subsequently examined they were shown to consist mainly of details of
the Labour and trade union movement in the state, which the security services
regarded as subversive.

This constitutional fiction of personal loyalty to the crown, overriding any
duty to ministers is therefore much more substantial than it may at first sight
appear and represents an obstacle that has never been properly discussed, let
alone dealt with, by any Labour Government. Ministers who have ever had
responsibility for the security services will almost certainly have been privy
to some, though by no means all, of the operations upon which they have
been engaged, and if they were to call for a greater public control, later,
the security services would be in a position to make it known, through the
press or Parliament, that they had been operating with ministerial approval,
thus undermining the credibility of their former chiefs. This suggests another

'understanding' which ministers are offered, namely that if they never challenge the independence of the security services, but limit themselves to marginal comments when they are seen to have behaved inefficiently, the security services will protect the minister and not deliberately destabilise or expose him, for put crudely the security services have got something on everybody, though they may only use it when it is their interests to do so.

9. The Media and its political strategy

The next source of power with which a socialist minister has to deal is the media itself. The nationalisation of the BBC which was undertaken by a Conservative Government in 1922 was done for much the same reason as Henry VIII nationalised the Church of England, in that any state power wants to be sure that it has control, as far as it can have, of the minds of those it governs, which is why the chairmen of the BBC and the IBA are appointed by the Prime Minister, and its responsible officials are vetted by the security services. The BBC thus has always been able to be relied upon to pump out information and analysis which broadly re-inforces the idea that Britain is a democracy, that the staus quo is fair to all, and that those who advocate radical socialist change are hostile to democracy. Any socialist minister who dares to question the myth that the BBC is politically independent inevitably finds himself subjected to a great deal of hostility by the BBC in its own political coverage.

The Press is, by contrast, free from any direct government control, but as 66% of all the newspapers are owned and controlled by three rich men, there does not need to be any but the lightest of censorship, and the only example of it is the system of D Notices which warn editors against publishing any matter which governments believe to raise security matters, together with the possibility of court actions as with the *Spycatcher* book. The establishment know that socialist ideas will never be allowed to be presented in an attractive way in a capitalist media, and those who advocate them are liable to experience abuse and harassment on a massive scale. This, in its turn, shapes public opinion in opposition to socialism, and such a hostile public opinion can be quickly harvested through the public opinion polls, which are then re-published (sometimes very selectively) as 'independent' evidence of the unpopularity of such views, in the confident knowledge that such polls can be relied on to discourage the leaders of the party from following lines of policy unacceptable to the proprietors. These proprietors buttress their power by offering another unofficial understanding to Labour leaders along these lines: 'If you, as leaders of the party, never challenge our right, as proprietors, to run the newspapers we own, according to our own interest, we, for our part, will support you in dealing with the socialists in your own party, and will accept your right to govern, even when we disagree with you.'

Historically this understanding has been tacitly accepted by every Labour leader and, in return for the limited press support which they have gained as a result, certain press proprietors have then been made into peers–hence the phrase Press Lords. But even such a discreet understanding has never protected even right-wing Labour leaders from experiencing bitter personal attacks that go far beyond what should be acceptable in a democracy, and this combination of press pressure, de-stabilization and harassment has always played a part in undermining public backing for Labour governments. In this connection it may be worth identifying the priorities which the British establishment media always have in the back of their minds when they organize their political campaigns. Their first preference is, and must always remain, the maintenance in power of a right-wing conservative government that they can rely on to defend their interests. If, for any reason, such a government seems unable to rely on public support, then they move to their second choice which is a 'liberal' Tory government that will be more sensitive to public opinion–in order to survive electorally–but which will keep the socialists out of office, for the nagging fear that exists in their minds is that the extreme right-wing might actually precipitate a real swing to the left. If even that sort of moderate Tory government cannot maintain its public backing, the third establishment choice would be a Tory and Centre coalition, also designed to keep Labour out, and in the hope that the policies followed by such a government would protect the status quo.

If all these options are ruled out then the establishment will go for a moderate Labour government, preferably controlled by some sort of a pact or electoral arrangement with the centre, along the lines of the Lib-Lab pact of 1977–8, when James Callaghan, as Prime Minister, gave instructions to all his ministers that they were not to bring any major proposals to cabinet until they had been cleared personally by the Liberal spokesperson, allowing the Liberal Party to know much more about the government's intentions than the Labour Party or Labour MPs whose support was taken for granted. If that moderating mechanism does not work, then a right-wing Labour government, with a working majority, may have to be accepted by the establishment as the last resort, and it will be hoped that the skilful use of the pressure groups, described above, can keep it from surrendering to its 'wilder' rank and file. The one situation that the British establishment will, under no circumstances accept–nor for that matter would the American government–would be a Labour government committed to the policies of its conference, or any attempt to carry through any sort of social or political transformation, and if one were elected the campaigns to undermine, destabilize or destroy it would be on a massive scale and would include attempts to organize sufficient external pressure to secure a retreat from the Manifesto policies upon which such a government was elected. If we are to understand what is happening at any one time, these priorities need to be borne in mind, for the establishment will move up and down the scale of options set out above, as circumstances require, sometimes appearing to be supporting the conservatives, sometimes the centre and sometimes backing the right-wing of the Labour if that is all that stands between their interests and political change.

10. International Institutions and Capital

So much for the internal pressures, now let us turn to those which emanate from abroad, all of which will have close links with the internal pressure groups. With the emergence, in the last generation, of an absolutely free international market for finance and for industry, through the multinationals, the scope for pressure from abroad is almost unlimited, and so is the readiness of those who have that power to use it to secure the acceptance of policies that will protect their interests. There were a number of occasions when I had direct experience of that pressure, as for example with Phillips of Eindhoven (who ran a balance of trade deficit on their UK operations, by transfer pricing); with IBM (who tried to cancel out the effects of a British devaluation by raising their own prices in the UK); and with the Oil companies (who did everything they could to frustrate our North Sea policy)–but the practice is so normal as hardly to need to be illustrated.

The greatest and most effective pressure can, and is, exerted by the bankers and the IMF to force Labour governments to adopt monetarist policies, as happened in 1976, and which ultimately brought Labour down in 1979, by securing such cuts in public expenditure as to lead to a confrontation with many working people, so that they withdrew their political support in the election of that year. In dealing with the international institutions, of which Britain is a member, we come up against their legal right to interfere in our own affairs, under the treaties which bind us to them. For example the NATO Council asserts its right to determine the level of our defence expenditure, and as a result has saddled Britain with a burden of weapons expenditure that has denied us the civil investment that would have contributed to our economic growth and recovery–a pressure that came primarily from the United States, which sees NATO as an arm of its own foreign and defence policy. Most effective of all has been the influence of the EEC, which now has the legal power to override domestic British legislation under the terms of the Act passed in 1972 which gave effect to the Treaty of Accession of Britain to the Common Market–a power that will be widened and deepened, after 1992, when the Single European Act comes into force and could, according to Jacques Delors, President of the E.E.C. Commission, 'federalize' as much as 80% of all British legislation under the control of the appointed Brussels Commission. This commission has interfered regularly in Britain, and amongst its interventions were some that would have removed our control of oil policy and cramped our capacity to create jobs in areas of high unemployment.

Conclusion

But the greatest constitutional obstacle in the way of reforming socialist ministers derives from the immense power which a British prime minister exercises under our constitution, controlling as he (or she) does the whole executive machine, setting the agenda for cabinet, establishing cabinet committees that other ministers may never hear of, and demanding collective responsibility from colleagues who have no knowledge of what has been agreed, by whom or when. This form of personal rule is backed up by the power of instant dismissal of ministers who may dissent, coupled with appeals to blind loyalty from the party, and buttressed by the capacity to take disciplinary action against individual members of the party, with the assistance of the National Executive Committee on which the trade union leaders have a large majority. These powers have proved to be singularly effective and it must also be added that they have hitherto been exercised by people who have shown few signs of seriously wanting to see fundamental socialist policies applied, though, in fairness, if any Labour Prime Minister were to attempt this task he, or she, would then have to run the gauntlet of all the external and internal pressures referred to above.

I have tried to identify some of the characteristics of the actual situation as it would confront any new Labour government and of the institutions it would have to change, and how they could be defeated if they attempted to block progress. The key to success would certainly lie in the extent to which popular support could be mobilized, and that, in its turn, would require a far greater deal of openness and serious political education than has ever been attempted. News management and manipulation are not going to be enough, for the truth must be allowed to come out in a very full way, and there would also be a chance of maintaining links with our own supporters, who are normally left out in the cold and do not know what is happening or why.

The failure of Labour governments in the past is that they have never told the people the truth, which is that Britain is not a democracy, that office and power are not the same, and in the absence of that knowledge people have never been encouraged to mount the counter-pressure that could shift the balance in favour of Labour and against capital, and persuade the establishment that they have no choice but to concede to that pressure because of the strength which it commanded. Historically all social progress has always come from below, yet, almost by definition, those Labour leaders who sit in parliament, in cabinets, or in the higher counsels of the trade union movement, have won their own positions by climbing up a ladder called the 'status quo' and in doing so have escaped from many of the pressures and difficulties which are experienced by those they were elected to represent. But if the demands for change are insistent enough then they cannot be ignored by those at the top and have to be addressed seriously. My experience suggests that such demands are, at first ignored, then denounced as mad or dangerous. But if they continue there is a pause while the top people come to terms with the inevitable, the changes are made, and a few years later you cannot find anyone who will admit ever to have been against them.

One way of bringing home to the establishment, and to the electors, the opposition of the Labour and Socialist movement to the status quo, would be for us to be far more explicit in our criticism of the institutions which sustain it.

We should back this up with a partial withdrawal from involvement in some of these institutions by, for example, refusing to continue with inter-party talks at the leadership level on what are known as 'Privy Councillor terms' (which are confidential and hence exclude the party and the public), by declining to nominate for the House of Lords or for the position of 'Labour' Commissioner in Brussels, and by persuading the TUC to stop nominating its members of the National Economic Development Council, all of which give legitimacy to the conservative state apparatus which prop up the present system.

We should also be spending much more time on the institutional and constitutional reforms which Labour would introduce, when it comes to power, campaigning actively, and publicly, for major changes that would extend democracy in our political, economic and industrial system.

It is sometimes argued, by those who fully understand everything described in this article, that all the evidence set out proves that reform is not enough and that revolution is the only answer, but, if the experience of earlier Labour governments is re-assessed, it is so obvious that no reforms in the structure of the state were ever attempted, and that, if they had been, they would have amounted to a revolution–carried through by consent obtained through the electoral system–and backed up by insistent pressure from those whose lives would be radically improved if they had occurred. That may be the main lesson for the future which we can learn from the past, and if we decline to learn it Labour will never be able to graduate beyond its past role of being an alternative management team for capitalism, only allowed to win when the rich and the powerful know that such a government is essential if working people are to be persuaded to accept cuts in their living standards, so that capitalism can, under intensive care, be able to recover–then to be handed back to its 'rightful owners'. Such a role can have no appeal to socialists, and were it to represent the limits of Labour's political aspirations it would not justify the effort, nor could such a strategy be guaranteed to produce electoral success, for many people have sensed what is going on and would not bother to work or vote for a party that had set its sights so low.

REFLECTIONS ON REVOLUTION IN AN AGE OF REACTION

V.G. Kiernan

There is not always, perhaps not often in history a clear demarcation between eras of progress and eras of regression; frequently the two things coincide. The 16th century in Europe was a time of technical, scientific, cultural advance, and also of scholastic hair-splitting and burning of heretics and witches. Its worse features marked the backward pull of the past, its better ones the magnetism of the future. Today capitalism as a system of production is flourishing, as science is, but the civilization it fostered in its earlier phases is rotting, while another is struggling to be born. A socialist economy cannot grow up within capitalism, as a capitalist economy did within feudal-absolutism, but something like a socialist outlook or mentality can. Positive and negative, wholesome and regressive thinking are contending in every country, every class or community, often within the same mind.

We are faced by a bewildering situation, made dangerous by the sorcerer's apprentices who rule us. Britain's economy is a precariously balanced pyramid of speculation on a dwindling productive base. In the country of the blind, as Thatcherite England (not Scotland) often seems to be, the trickster, the City slicker, is king; capitalism is degenerating into financial juggling, obsession with quick unearned gains. In old Germany there used to be jokes about a ladder of ten officials handing down instructions to one workman; in Britain now each workman seems to be expected to fill the pockets of ten money-grubbers. Modern England has experienced no political or social change except by imperceptible degrees, and this has made it hard to recognize a need for radical all-round change – other than Mrs Thatcher's cannibalizing version, the transfer of public wealth into private pockets. A fundamental inertia is masked by a perpetual barrage of novelties, household gadgets and dress styles and so on, which give the man in the street the illusion of rapid progress. We combine an avid taste for novelties with an underlying dread of genuine innovation, reminiscent of Mr Pooter's uneasiness at hearing an American say that without bold new thinking there would have been no discovery of America.

Visions of 'revolution', a mode of existence remote from what mankind has condemned itself to, have always been afloat. Through most of history

146

they have been no more than dreams of a lost Eden, a golden age in the far past; only in modern times has that shining past been transposed into a bright future. Christians have inherited with their book of Revelations one of the earliest glimpses of a new Heaven and a new earth, however fantastic their shape. Socialism is one of Christianity's heirs: its most prominent exponents, the Marxists, have been the most earnest porers over old revolutions and designers of new ones. Their early preoccupation, highly realistic in some senses but less so in others, was with the 'seizure of power'. Engels comprehended before his death a hundred years ago – looking at things as an old soldier – that insurrection cannot succeed in a modern country, unless there is a total breakdown of the State as in 1917. In later years Communist parties tacitly accepted this, but were slow to think about alternatives.

Obviously all socialists have much new thinking to do. With reaction so firmly in the saddle in so many parts of the Western world, and Britain in particular, it may among other things be proper for Marxist historians to ask what has enabled ruling classes to remain so tenaciously on top, in spite of all that popular forces have been able to achieve. History hitherto has been made far more from above than from below; it is this that we have to find ways of reversing. In general, Marxist thinking has brought a vital advance, but politically it has failed to keep up with the rapidity of world change, and its practitioners in this century have too often been playing billiards with twisted cues and elliptical balls. In the 1920s capitalism might well seem to have run down, exhausted its historical mission, and therefore to be ready for supersession. Instead, since then it has displayed an astonishing resilience and adaptability, under the stimulus of three principal factors: war, proliferation of technology, and the need to keep ahead of the USSR and meet the challenge of socialism. To uncritical voters with short memories, savouring their ration of the fleshpots, this acceleration of capitalist prosperity can appear impressively smooth, wonderfully bountiful. This is to forget the enormous calamities and crimes it has cost, and continues to cost, with two world wars at the head of the bill. But the dead are gone, and soon forgotten; the unemployed are forgotten nearly as easily; the exploited millions up and down the colonial world have scarcely been thought of at all.

All this must be saddening for everyone with hopes of the human capacity for meaningful, instead of *ersatz*, progress; but Marxists cannot very well complain, seeing that they have always expounded a materialist theory of history and bothered too little about adding to it any ethical conceptions. Party acolytes used to be admonished that the first of the cardinal virtues was 'faith in the working class'; but there was a perpetual confusion between belief in its innate progressive qualities, and a conviction that its interests, irreconcilable with those of its employers, would one day force it into rebellion. A touch of the 'pathetic fallacy' can be seen in the projection by socialists of their own feelings on to the working class, their assumption that it was by nature socialistic, or at least receptive to socialist teaching. Or it might be compared to the old theory of Phlogiston, that inflammable substances burn because they contain a property of combustibility. And there is some analogy between the Marxist reliance on the working class to overthrow capitalism, and Western Maoists some years ago, when Maoism was in fashion, pinning their hopes on the Third World.

In England (unlike Germany) socialist ideas never caught on at all with the workers; the story has been a continual one of the horse being led to the water and refusing to drink. Labour has struggled, with admirable resolution, to better its condition; and a recent writer has emphasized that this did not mean bread and butter alone, but was concerned also with *honour*, the 'dignity of labour', the workman's refusal to be treated like a serf.[1] The boss had to be taught to keep a civil tongue in his head, as well as to pay something better than a starvation wage. But this did not lead on to the idea of getting rid of him. Very grudgingly, capitalism consented to improvements that it could easily afford. Fifty years ago workers might still be consoling themselves with the old Methodist hymn–

> We shall have a new name in that land,
> In that bright, that sunny sunny land;

but their grandchildren have found the land of sunshine nearer home, on the Costa del Sol.

Lacking socialist ideas, the labour movement has been, outside its own trade-union sphere, directionless; partly because of this, even in its own sphere its energies have been wilting. A critical point came in the years after 1945, when ailing industries were being nationalized. It was labour's opportunity to get its foot in at the door, insist on a share in management, make those industries a success and transform them into models for socialism. No such attempt was made. Leaders were timid, trade unions hidebound, there was no push from the shop floor except for more money for less work: a very rational aim in itself, but self-defeating when pursued too one-sidedly. Taking a share of control would have meant sharing responsibility for necessary industrial changes, some of them unwelcome. Remaining independent, labour leadership could pillow itself comfortably on time-honoured routine, until the Thatcherite storm broke over its head.

Those looking for progress towards socialism must look round for every possible ally, but not expect to find them too easily. There are no readymade socialists, no socialist classes. Today when all problems are immensely more complicated than in the days of Karl Marx and Queen Victoria, the great divide cannot be crossed or even contemplated without elaborate preparation. This cannot be the task of any single class; it cannot be envisaged without the participation of the working class, but it calls for a far mcre alert and intelligent one than we have today. Communist parties everywhere have done their best to bridge the gulf between labour and socialist thinking, to bring workers and intellectuals closer together; but they relied too much on bread and butter struggles to kindle the sacred flame, and sparks cannot be struck from butter. In Britain success has been minimal, because of a prevalent 'labourism',[2] a long-standing alienation of the working class from nearly everything good in the national life. This did not make it immune from infection by what was bad, as the maniacal 'patriotism' of 1914 showed so tragically, or more recently and farcically the applause of part at least of the working class for adventures at Suez and in the Falkland Islands.

Political quiescence among the workers left the middle classes to enjoy a similar agreeable torpor, only disturbed by odd moments of panic. Such a state of mind has been an accompaniment of the modern, settled, well-policed style of life, surrounded by a bewilderingly vast world outside the citizen's parish that he prefers to shut his eyes to. J.G. Lockhart in 1819 was deploring the contracting circle within which men's minds moved, 'that barren spirit of lethargy into which the progress of civilisation is in all countries so apt to lull the feelings and imaginations of mankind.'[3] More succinctly, seventy years later Oscar Wilde wrote to his compatriot Bernard Shaw: 'England is the land of intellectual fogs'.[4] A good many later Victorians, oppressed by the senselessness of their daily lives, took to dabbling in spiritualism, the occult, 'Oriental wisdom', reincarnation. A typical dabbler was Rider Haggard.[5] Since then the more morbid sections of bourgeois society have been sliding further down the slippery slope into a muckheap of freak cults presided over by well-paid Swamis and Gurus.

Weakening of social and moral fibre on one side, affluence bestowed by technology on the other, have reduced us to Thatcherism. It is a logical enough climax to Britain's failure to get a grip on itself and its affairs; there is some truth in the adage that a country gets the government it deserves – even a Thatcherite government. There could not be a more extraordinary programme than it has been able to carry out, almost unresisted by flaccid opposition parties, with its privatizing, or privateering. It sells shares in national properties, at cheap rates, mostly to the rich; it then uses its receipts to reduce income tax, mostly for the rich, thus handing their money back to them. They are to be given a further large bonus at the public expense, by a new mode of local taxation, what the government calls its 'community charge', and others call a poll-tax. It will relieve the rich of having to pay in proportion to the value of their often palatial residences; duke and cottager will pay at the same flat rate. Everything this government can get hold of is turned by its Midas-touch into gold, and bestowed on profiteers. Whether or not property is theft, privatized property certainly is. It will not be very astonishing to hear of the army being privatized – it was once very much a private – enterprise affair – , or the Church of England; or the Royal Family, which could be made much more entertaining under up to date management by businessmen like Mr Packer. Meanwhile the masses, which today include the miscellaneous middle classes, have succumbed with incredible ease to

Tory demagogy, grunting contentedly over their crumbs from the City feast, and only afraid of being deprived of them by Labour party Reds. Tennyson summoned his church bells to

Ring out the feud of rich and poor;

Mrs Thatcher seems to have succeeded better than any bells, by making the rich richer and the rest more gullible.

What is most revolting about our capitalists is their monstrous egotism, their conviction of being entitled to prodigious salaries, boundless profits, wealth as fabulous as any in the Arabian Nights. It is a greed as mindlessly instinctual as the voracity of feudal lords or monarchs for more and more territory, or of eastern potentates for harems of hundreds of women and eunuchs. There must be a real sense in which obsolete ruling classes can be said to go out of their minds, to become sufficiently twisted in their reflexes as to be no longer sane. This is what might be said of the French aristocracy's behaviour in the two years before the Revolution, and still more of the future that our oligarchy is so blithely planning, with the atom bomb, a sharper sword of Damocles, hanging over all our heads. America's president, the most powerful man in the world as Americans like to boast, is led by the nose by his astrologers, we have been learning of late. Here is a relapse of two millennia, to the days when part of the duty of a Roman consul was to watch the flight of passing birds and draw omens from them to guide policies of State.

Unless reformers can find a way to bring sanity and a sense of direction into the bedlam that our society is fast becoming, what must be expected is not a revolutionary explosion, but creeping social disintegration. It was so in the late years of the feudal order, when there were indeed some mass outbreaks of social revolt, and many minor ones, but far more, across Europe, of elemental disorder: unemployment, vagabondage, sturdy beggars on every road, crime, and a prevalent spirit of indiscipline, old institutions in town and country in decay, the family at odds with itself, the individual frighteningly exposed and insecure. Profiteering and rat-race competition, preached as a healthy stimulus calculated to bring out the best in us all, lead more predictably to psychological wear and tear. Alcoholism and drug addiction are stages in social degeneration, part of the drying up of rational protest against the world we have made. Another effect of capitalism as we see it today, and its deteriorating social ethos, is to accumulate a latent store of unreasoning violence, that may break out anywhere. With high-life gangsters setting the tone, society indulges this bellicosity in fantasy with low-life gangsters films, in practice in drunken brawls. No doubt most of these are at any rate no sillier than the officially approved ones, between Mrs Thatcher and an Argentine dictator for instance, and far less harmful.

With opposition parties in Parliament that seldom oppose, and left-wing sects outside that are usually opposing each other, it is no wonder that reaction is triumphant. As Wordsworth said of his own time, bad men, united and unhesitating, have fairly carried off the palm from the vacillating, half-hearted good. Yet reaction looks far stronger than it really is. Its inordinately aggressive behaviour, its blatant greed and egotism, have left it vulnerable to attack on many fronts. Mrs Thatcher and her spongers-up of public money have been wildly indiscreet in their liaison with the Stock Exchange, so aptly described in the New Testament as a den of thieves, – their fiddling and diddling while Britain burns, or moulders. They are polluting sea and air, at home and abroad, while neglecting the hospitals, along with the roads, sewers, schools. They have squandered billions on an atavistic colonial war, to flatter national pride, while toadying abjectly to America. They are making Britain a dumping-ground for other countries' toxic wastes. They have been letting industry run down, and Britain drift towards the level of a tourist showplace for wealthy Americans, Germans, and Japanese, with Britons respectfully polishing their shoes in hope of tips. Open land is reserved for City brokers and foreigners to shoot over, while Britons are forbidden to walk over it. Our capitalists, more predatory and parasitic than their successful rivals abroad, are nibbling away at civilized life, much as the intelligent newts in Karel Capek's 1936 novel nibbled away at the earth's coastlines to make more room for themselves, lulling mankind the while with soothing tunes on the radio.

Toryism is not unaware of how damagingly it has been exposing itself; this shows in its growing resolve to suffocate criticism, by gagging the press and the BBC, by frantic spending of public money (which ought to have come out of Tory party funds) in an effort to prevent the public from reading a book that might give it some insight into how our oligarchy operates, – and by domestic espionage. We have been told that the Kremlin may be spying on us; we know that Downing Street is spying on us. In a long BBC television programme on 15 September 1987 on the secret services, Mr Callaghan reluctantly confessed to second thoughts about the charge against MI5 of trying to destabilize a Labour government; he also admitted that when in office he gave very little time or thought to what it was doing, whether legal or not. Even Mrs Thatcher's rhinoceros-skin has failed to keep out all sense of resentments she has provoked, that must break out sooner or later. When Scotland's national Church held its annual General Assembly of representatives of the clergy and laity in May 1988, she was, very reprehensibly, allowed by the presiding Moderator to deliver an address to it, in vote-beggingly sanctimonious language. Later in the year, she astonished the country by suddenly announcing an ardent belief – despite all appearances to the contrary – in conservation. Her wardrobe of disguises and pretences must be running out when she has to resort to masquerading as a Christian or an ecologist.

When we look round to try and estimate the forces that may be counted on for any progressive activity, the inventory may at first appear gloomy. It may indeed prove that Britain, like old India or China, has come to be so firmly locked into immobility as to be incapable of stirring, especially with conservatism now having such a range of tranquillizers, physical or ideological, at its disposal. Perhaps Britain will have to be dragged forward in the end by a changing Europe. Short of an atomic war, economic crisis may seem the likeliest banisher of slumber. A catastrophic breakdown is scarcely to be desired, however, until socialism is much stronger (and until Russia and China are economically stronger and politically more worthy of respect, and have stopped snarling at each other). As things are, a crash like that of 1929 would probably have consequences equally calamitous.

By and large the British working class has shown very little interest in or wish for more education; individuals with more aspiring minds have always been more or less obliged to migrate out of the class, a loss to it like the emigration abroad of so many of its most energetic members. Rising demand for skilled labour, rising unemployment for unskilled, must help in time to bring a change of attitude; but until this has gone fairly far the prospect is of more and more workers being educated away from the working class. Many of these are likely, for a longish spell, to feel satisfied with their promotion, and think Mrs Thatcher's world a passable one. Like the old aristocratic order before it, capitalism has always thriven by sucking up individuals from below. Often this had had the demoralizing effects of which Balzac's novels have so much to say. But by promoting mobility capitalism can also have an enlarging influence, liberating individuals as well as society from old inertias and making them capable of criticism and self-criticism.

Our middle classes are multiplying, growing more diverse; and it has always been the essence of middle-class thinking to be mixed and contradictory, far less homogeneous than the mentality of those either above or below. It has for instance been the main repository of a religion palpably at odds with the way the bourgeois lives and must live, and yet of real meaning to him. Among these miscellaneous strata, which have in common two very different attributes, property and education, there is here and there more interest in socialism and in Marxism than the working class has ever displayed. They include nearly all of those specifically reckoned intellectuals. Boundaries here are hazy, but at the two poles there is a category of spinners of conservative ideologies, ideas designed to perpetuate the status quo, and another of seekers of ideas to light the way towards a higher civilization. In broader terms we must think of an 'intelligentsia' of all men and women enlightened enough to know that our present civilization is in a mess, and quite likely heading for disaster, and to want a better world for themselves and their descendants to inhabit. A good many of these will be recruits from the working class, carrying with them its better qualities.

Socialism will have to cultivate a more Arminian spirit, a wider hope of human redemption than the Calvinistic exclusiveness that Marxism has suf-

fered from. After all, in late years we have seen one of the most conservative
of all forces, official Christianity – and particularly its most benighted branch,
Roman Catholicism – , beginning to turn over a new leaf. Conservatism in its
more respectable days used to be fond of denouncing socialist atheism and
materialism; Mrs Thatcher and her crew, with their gospel of undiluted greed
and self-seeking, are ruling that out, or making it sound ludicrous. The long
partnership between Church and Mammon is sagging, and whereas until not
long ago an archbishop of Canterbury was virtually the Tory party's domestic
chaplain, nowadays Anglicans dare to find fault with a Tory government –
much to its indignation, like Balaam's when reproved by his ass. The further the Churches move towards Christianity, the closer they will come to
socialism; the 'Christian Socialism' laughed at in the *Communist Manifesto*
will be turning into a reality. It was the long-immovable Catholic Church that
recognized the need for *aggiornamento,* in principle at least, years before Mr
Gorbachev began preaching it.

Labour party policy-forming has too often resembled the fight at the bridge
in Macaulay's *Lays*, when

those behind cried 'Forward',
And those in front cried 'Back'.

It is necessary that the electorate should be given a clear understanding
of both the immediate programme that a Labour government would carry
out, and its longer-term intentions; so that while denouncing Toryism the
party would also be advertising itself and mobilizing support. One great
stumbling-block is the term *socialism*. Traditionally it has meant, first and
foremost, public ownership of the means of production. Ultimately this must
come about all over the world, if civilization is to have more than a limited
future. In Britain in any near future it is unfortunately out of reach, simply
because there are not enough socialists. The Labour party is not really and
never has been a socialist party, but its use of the name has allowed its enemies
to profit by accusing it of intentions it has never had.

Much of the pressure for socialism in the sense of public ownership has
come from infiltrators into the Labour Party from Marxist splinter groups.
Some of it has come from trade-union diehards, little representative of
their rank and file. Ron Todd, head of the Transport and General Workers' Union, made a sensation at the party conference in October 1988 by
attacking Kinnock's reformism and insisting on the movement's 'commitment to public and social ownership'. Such declarations, along with Benn's
challenge to Kinnock's reelection as leader, heavily defeated though it was,
enable Tories to go on painting the party in Bolshevik colours, as the tool of
fire-raising trade unions.

Really, what left-wingers mean when they talk of 'socialism' is very often
no more than *social-welfare* measures for the benefit of the old, the sick, all

disadvantaged sections of society, along with improvements for the benefit
of all, in health, education, foreign policies conducive to peace. On all
these issues a vigorous reforming party could make great headway, without
arousing the phobias that have been implanted in the public by deafening
Tory propaganda. It could hope for support on many of them from a Liberal
party with a similarly active left wing. At the beginning of this century the
party contained an 'Advanced Liberal Association' (some of whose members
were among the opponents of the Boer War); there ought to be something of
the same kind now, with an insistence on a positive plan of reforms instead of
the present sterility.

But reform proposals can and must be pushed a great deal further than
any programme limited to 'welfare' in its narrower meaning. In the immediate future, the prime aim should be to make democracy, so loudly trum-
peted nowadays by anti-socialists, a reality instead of the sham it largely is
today. Proportional representation must be one step. Better have no government than another Thatcherite minority government. Devolution should
be another very early one; it may prove to be the only means of averting a
total breakaway of Scotland from England, something that Mrs Thatcher has
succeeded in making appear, for the first time, rational and even inevitable. A
third priority should be abolition of hereditary voting in the House of Lords,
and that body's transformation into a genuine Second Chamber. There have
been moments lately when it could seem – a change as amazing as that of any
Church – our last line of defence against the worst excesses of Toryism. The
vote of May 23, 1988, when droves of backwoods peers, political zombies,
were with brazen effrontery summoned to Westminster to push through the
poll-tax bill – and thereby put thousands of pounds in their own bulging
pockets – , was so scandalous that even Tories would now find it much harder
to object to a further drastic reform, a logical sequel to the introduction of
life peerages and the virtual abandonment of any new hereditary creations.
As long as hereditary legislators are tolerated, we are still in the penumbra of
feudalism. We shall not be completely out of it until we get rid of hereditary
control of our economy as well.

A mass of 'sensitive paper' lying in the archives should be opened to
inspection on terms at least as liberal as in the USA. It is imperative that
firm measures be taken to bring the secret services under control, and to
purge and prosecute all individuals responsible for misusing them. Finding
ways to destabilize MI5 will not be a simple matter. Members of the public
should be brought into an investigation of its sins.

In a longer-term programme, all former national industries, all public
utilities, all enterprises putting a strain on scarce natural resources, should
be brought under some degree of permanent scrutiny and direction by the
government, which should have representatives on their boards. There should
also be representation in their management (and eventually in that of all
industries) of the workers, and of consumers. A ceiling might well be fixed on

their dividends. It may be that in countries where industry is already in being, instead of having to be built from scratch as it was in Russia, what is required, for a fairly long time, is not so much national ownership as public supervision. This could include some degree of the *dirigisme* which did so much for French industry during its post-war recovery. But the British economy is in a very half-and-half condition, because of the collapse in recent years of so much of its older industrial base, inadequately replaced by investment in newer technology. Since the gnomes of the City have so little interest in rebuilding industry, there can be no rational objection to the task being undertaken by public enterprise, both centrally and locally.

In all new undertakings, there must from the start be far broader participation in management that there was in any of the industries formerly nationalised. To make way for this, as well as for many other reasons, all the organs of the State will have to be ventilated and overhauled. Such a spring-cleaning will be indispensable for opening the way to socialism, as well as in a nearer future to national well-being; but it is clearly justifiable on democratic principles, and if the electorate does not choose to go on from democracy to socialism it will only have to say so.

Many of these reforms are in line with what the 'Bennite wing' of the Labour Party has stood for. But few of them have much chance of being ventured on by the Labour Party until the climate of opinion in the party and the country has considerably altered. Its leaders' notion of how to win votes seems to be to keep so low a profile as to be virtually out of sight or hearing. Pressure from its left wing seems only to push them into further compromise with the enemy, in their anxiety to convince everybody that a Labour government would not hurt a fly, let alone a duke or a City racketeer. The merit of the next Labour government will be largely the negative, but very great one, of not being a Tory government. Preparation for any far-reaching measures will in any case require time, for the training for example of a new sort of civil servants for new duties; this will call for special seminaries, though progressive individuals will also have to be brought in from outside, just as the Tories have been making use of strong-arm men from big business.

Because the Labour party can only slowly be transformed into a socialist or even a truly progressive one, and because it cannot be radically changed from within, but only by a change in the atmosphere round it and in public expectations, there is urgent need of a separate Socialist party; not to heckle and abuse Labour, in the old Communist style, but to give it new life by refreshing the stale political air with the oxygen of ideas. The first business of socialists is to come together, as the founders of the Communist party did in 1920. To keep a straggling set of small ineffective left-wing groups going is mere waste of effort. They are all the prisoners of their past, and the perennial vendetta of Stalinist and Trotskyite is as totally irrelevant to British affairs today as the schism between Shia and Sunni, rooted in an Islamic succession quarrel of ages ago.

Restlessly militant activists in (or expelled from) the Labour party might find themselves more at home in a Socialist party which would be teaching and learning by participation in struggle as well as in debate. Some others after serving an apprenticeship in the Socialist party might settle down as loyal Labour party members. But the rapid turnover of membership, recruits quickly gained and quickly lost, that has been a feature of all our organizations of the far left, should be less excessive in a bigger, more loosely structured, less isolated body, with more varied tasks and a less frenetic tempo of activity than was felt proper when every trade-union dispute signalled a revolution round the corner. A united Socialist party could collect, or draw on, the ideas of, a larger array of public-spirited thinkers than any other; its opinions on many issues would come to be regarded as a national asset. Its prime duty will be the more exact working out and spreading of socialist and generally progressive ideas, and campaigning for them on issues that arise. It will not need to compete with Labour for parliamentary seats, or will only want a small number to make its voice heard at Westminster.

No direct highway leading to full socialism is in sight now, or any chance of a direct assault on fundamental problems still invisible or incomprehensible to the average voter. But many other unpleasantnesses of our present condition stand out more obviously, and in the next few years progress is likeliest to come from mobilization of feeling against them, translation of feeling into opinion and opinion into action. It is the defects and abuses of an old order, far more than the appeal of a new, untried one, that do most to undermine it. To take one instance, there is growing concern about what is happening to 'our heritage', as Tories are fond of calling it, though most of it belongs to *them*, and growing sympathy with movements endeavouring to check its erosion. It is one of the contradictions of capitalism that even conservatives may be conservationists as well, impelled to challenge some destructive features of modern industrialism. Conversely, it has to be acknowledged, with the experience of the USSR before us, that socialism narrowly understood as public ownership does not automatically put an end to them.

It is being realised, again, that civil liberties are at serious risk, though hitherto there has been far too little protest. There have been times in the past when the same could be said. 'You cannot think too meanly of our people', Henry St. John wrote to a friend in 1709; blinded by party spirit, they are in danger of losing their liberties to 'victorious tyranny. . . . Britons might be driven like a flock of turkeys: nay, we are tamer still, for by my soul we should not cackle.'[6] So one may be tempted to fear today; but a counter-current is visible, and may swell. Over a still wider field of life, the old 'Natural Rights' exploded by Bentham have come back as 'Human Rights': hitherto chiefly as convenient propaganda for 'Western democracy', but with spreading recognition of how arbitrarily, even atrociously, the individual may be treated by the modern State, capitalist as well as Stalinist. In many other fields too dissatisfaction is growing, and only needs a vigorous lead. All these

'good causes' are important partly because they depend on ethical as well as
practical considerations; and the human conscience has much more to do than
Marxists have commonly realised with steering mankind towards socialism.
We need a vision of society as Burke, in his best moments a socialist in spite
of himself, saw it, a partnership in all science and in every virtue.

Progressive movements and good causes cannot be managed and mani-
pulated into coming together on the right course, as the Communist party in
its brash youth imagined. They must find their own way. Groups confronting
any of our social evils or duties will find more common ground the further they
go, and along with it recognition that what they want to achieve will demand
changes that must make life harder for some capitalists, beginning with the
more villainous species such as arms dealers or investors in South Africa.
Socialism cannot be imposed on any country without being fatally denatured.
Equally, capitalism cannot be kept going indefinitely in a country where people have learned to want something better. A time must come when it will
be afraid to look at itself in the mirror of public opinion, much as the aging
Elizabeth was afraid to look in any mirror for fear of seeing her wrinkles.
We shall be stumbling forward rather than marching, as 'scientific socialism'
expected us to do. There will of course at every stage be fierce resistance from
the beneficiaries of today's system of what may be called organized anarchy.
Only the growth of progressive public opinion will be able to overbear it. But
a Socialist party will be needed, for one good reason, as a watchdog, ready to
give the alarm when conspiracy shows its teeth.

Russia's revolution like all earlier ones failed to fulfill all its promise, as
Paul Dukes writes, but today 'there is an overwhelming necessity for a new
revolution incorporating the best of the spirit of 1649, 1776, 1789 and 1917',
– 'a revision of our historical consciousness which will help to avert conflict
and promote progress.'[7] Marx was undeniably too optimistic in his hopes of
a world transformed, but he set mankind thinking anew of such a possibility.
It cannot be brought about overnight. Lenin himself knew that a revolution
might take decades for its completion. It is more likely to take generations.
To say this may seem a retreat to the 'inevitability of gradualness'; but there
is a great difference between accepting small concessions designed to keep a
bad social system intact, and pressing for limited reforms designed as stages in
a continuing advance. Today's world has lurking in it so many unpredictables
that the line of advance cannot be charted as seemed possible in simpler times
when an abacus could do duty for a computer. Socialists must be prepared for
any contingency, in the spirit of Robert Bridges' maxim that

wisdom lies
In masterful administration of the unforeseen.

NOTES

1. W.M. Reddy, *Money and Liberty in Modern Europe* (Cambridge, 1987), chap. 5.
2. About the phenomenon of 'labourism' there is much to be learned from John Saville, *The Labour Movement in Britain* (London, 1988).
3. *Peter's Letters to his Kinsfolk*, Letter 55.
4. Letter of 23 February 1893.
5. See W.R. Katz, *Rider Haggard and the Fiction of Empire* (Cambridge, 1987), and P. Brantlinger, *Rule of Darkness. British Literature and Imperialism* Cornell Univ. Press, 1988), Part 3.
6. Letter to Lord Orrery, 1 Sep. 1709, in a correspondence edited by H.T. Dickinson, Camden Miscell., 1975, p. 147.
7. Paul Dukes, *October and the World. Perspectives on the Russian Revolution* (London, 1979), p. 189.

THE MARXIST CASE FOR REVOLUTION TODAY

Ernest Mandel

I. *What is A Revolution?*

Revolutions are historical facts of life. Almost all major states in today's world are born from revolutions. Whether one likes it or not, our century has seen something like three dozen revolutions – some victorious, others defeated – and there is no sign that we have come to the end of the revolutionary experience.

Revolutions have been, and will remain, facts of life because of the structural nature of prevailing relations of production and relations of political power. Precisely because such relations are *structural*, because they do not just 'fade away' – as well as because ruling classes resist the gradual elimination of these relations to the very end – revolutions emerge as the means whereby the overthrow of these relations is realized.

From the nature of a revolution as a sudden, radical overthrow of prevailing social and (or) political structures – leaps in the historical process – one should not draw the conclusion that an impenetrable Chinese wall separates evolution (or reforms) from revolution. Quantitative gradual social changes of course do occur in history, as do qualitative revolutionary ones. Very often the former prepare the latter especially in epochs of decay of a given mode of production. Prevailing economic and political power relations can be eroded, undermined, increasingly challenged or can even be slowly disintegrated, by new relations of production and the political strength of revolutionary classes (or major class fractions) rising in their midst. This is what generally characterises periods of pre-revolutionary crises. But erosion and decay of a given social and/or political order remains basically different from its overthrow. Evolution is not identical with revolution. One transforms dialectics into sophism when, from the fact that there is no rigid absolute distinction between evolution and revolution, one draws the conclusion that there is no basic difference between them at all.

The sudden overthrow of ruling structures is, however, only one key characteristic of that social phenomenon. The other one is their overthrow through huge popular mobilisation, through the sudden massive active intervention of large masses of ordinary people in political life and political struggle.[1]

One of the great mysteries of class society, based upon exploitation and oppression of the mass of direct producers by relatively small minorities, is why that mass in 'normal' times by and large tolerates these conditions, be it with all kinds of periodic but limited reactions. Historical materialism tries, not without success, to explain that mystery. The explanation is many-dimensional, drawing upon a combination of economic compulsion, ideological manipulation, cultural socialisation, political-juridical repression (including occasionally violence), psychological processes (interiorisation, identification), etc.

Generally, as one revolutionary newspaper wrote at the beginning of the French revolution of 1789, oppressed people feel weak before their oppressors in spite of their numerical superiority, because they are on their knees.[2] A revolution can occur precisely when that feeling of weakness and helplessness is overcome, when the mass of the people suddenly thinks 'We don't take it any longer', and acts accordingly. In his interesting book, *The Social Bases of Obedience and Revolt,* Barrington Moore has tried to prove that suffering and consciousness of injustice are not sufficient to induce large-scale revolts (revolutions) in broader masses. In his opinion, a decisive role is played by the conviction that suffered injustice is neither inevitable nor a 'lesser evil', i.e. that a better social set-up could be realized.[3] A concomitant brake upon direct challenges to a given social and/or political order, however, is the locally or regionally fragmented nature of revolts pure and simple. Revolts generally become revolutions when they are unified nation-wide.

Such challenges can be explained, among other things, by that basic truth about class societies formulated by Abraham Lincoln, empirically confirmed throughout history, and which is at least reason for historical optimism (belief in the possibility of human progress) when all is said and done: 'You can fool all of the people some of the time and some of the people all the time. But you can't fool all of the people all of the time'.

When the majority of the people refuse to be fooled and intimidated any longer; when they refuse to stay on their knees; when they recognise the fundamental weakness of their oppressors, they can become transformed overnight from seemingly meek, subdued and helpless cattle into mighty lions. They strike, congregate, organise and especially demonstrate in the streets in increasing numbers, even in the face of massive, gruesome, bloody repression by the rulers, who still have a powerful armed apparatus at their disposal. They often show unheard of forms of heroism, self-sacrifice, obstinate endurance.[4] This may end in their getting the better of the repressive apparatus which starts to disintegrate. The first victory of every revolution is precisely such a disintegration. Its final victory calls for the substitution of the armed power of the revolutionary class (or of a major class fraction) to that of the former rulers.[5]

Such a descriptive definition of revolutions has to be integrated into an analytical-causal one. *Social revolutions* occur when prevailing relations of production cannot contain any more the development of the productive

forces, when they increasingly act as fetters upon them, when they cause
a cancerous growth of destructiveness accompanying that development. *Pol-itical revolutions* occur when prevailing relations of political power (*forms* of
state power) have likewise become fetters upon a further development of the
productive forces within the framework of the prevailing relations of production, a development which is however still historically possible. That is why
they generally consolidate a given social order, instead of undermining it.

This materialist explanation of revolutions offered by marxism seems indispensable for answering the question: 'why, and why just at the moment?'
Revolutions have occurred in all types of class societies but not in a uniform
way. It appears clearly illogical to attribute them either to permanently operating psychological factors (humanity's allegedly inborn aggression, 'destructiveness', 'envy', 'greed' or 'stupidity') or to accidental quirks of the political
power structure: particularly inept, stupid, blind rulers, meeting increasingly
self-confident and active opponents. According to the particular school of
history concerned, one can see that blind ineptitude either in the excessive
recourse to repression, or in the excessive amplitude of suddenly introduced
reforms, or in a peculiar explosive combination of both.[6]

There are of course kernels of partial truth in such psychological and political analyses. But they cannot explain in a satisfying way the regular and
discontinuous occurrence of revolutions, their cyclical nature so to speak.
Why do 'inept' rulers at regular intervals succeed 'adequate' ones, so many
times in so many countries? This can surely not be caused by some mysterious
genetical mutation cycle. The big advantage of the materialist interpretation
of history is to explain that occurrence by deeper socio-economic causes. It
is not the ineptness of the rulers which produces the pre-revolutionary crisis.
It is the paralysis engendered by an underlying social-structural crisis which
makes rulers increasingly inept. In that sense Trotsky was absolutely right
when he stressed that 'revolutions are nothing but the final blow and *coup
de grace* given to a paralytic'.

Lenin summarized the underlying analysis in a classical way by stating that
revolutions occur when those below do not accept any longer to be ruled as
before and those above cannot rule any longer as before. The inability of
a ruling class or major fraction to continue to rule has basically objective
causes. These reflect themselves in increasingly paralysing internal divisions
among the rulers, especially around the question about how to get out of
the mess visible to the naked eye. It intertwines with growing self-doubt,
a loss of faith in its own future, an irrational search for peculiar culprits
('conspiracy theories') substituting for a realistic objective analysis of social
contradictions. It is this combination which precisely produces political ineptitude and counterproductive actions and reactions, if not sheer passivity. The
basic cause always remains the rotting away of the system, not the peculiar
psychology of a group of rulers.

One has obviously to distinguish the basic historical causes of revolutions from the factors (events) triggering them off. The first ones are structural, the second ones conjunctural.[7] But it is important to emphasize that even as regards the structural causes, the marxist explication of revolutions is by no means monocausally 'economistic'. The conflict between the productive forces and the prevailing relations of production and/or political power relations isn't all purely economic. It is basically socio-economic. It involves all main spheres of social relations. It even eventually finds its concentrated expression in the political and not in the economic sphere. The refusal of soldiers to shoot at demonstrators is a political-moral and not an economic act. It is only by digging farther below the surface of that refusal that one discovers its material roots. These roots don't transform the political-moral decision into a pure 'appearance', or a manifestation of mere shadow boxing. It has a clear reality of its own. But that substantial reality in its turn doesn't make the digging for the deeper material roots irrelevant, an exercise in 'dogmatism' or an 'abstract' analysis of only secondary interest.[8]

In any case, the inability of the rulers to continue to rule is not only a socio-political fact, with its inevitable concomitant of an ideological moral-crisis (a crisis of the prevailing 'social values system'). It has also a precise technical-material aspect. To rule also means to control a material network of communications and a centralised repressive apparatus. When that network breaks down, the rule collapses in the immediate sense of the word.[9] We must never, therefore, underestimate the technical aspect of successful revolutions. But the marxist theory of revolution also supersedes a peculiar variant of the conspiracy theory of history, which tends to substitute for an explanation of victorious revolutions an exclusive reference to the technical mechanism of successful insurrections or *coups d'état*.[10] Instead, it is the material interests of key social forces and their self-perception which provide the basic explanation of turning points of history.

II. *Revolutions and Counter-revolutions*

While revolutions are historical facts of life, counter-revolutions are likewise undeniable realities. Indeed, counter-revolutions seem regularly to follow revolutions as night follows day. Etymology confirms this paradox. The very concept of 'revolution' originates from the science of astronomy. The movements of planets evolve in an orbital manner, returning to the point of departure. Hence the suggested analogical conclusion: the role of revolutions as great accelerators, as locomotives of history, is just an optical illusion of short-sighted and superficial observers, not to say utopian day-dreamers. It is precisely such an interpretation (denigration) of revolutions which is compatible with the great Italian historian Vico's cyclical conception of world history.

Under the influence of the victorious counter-revolution in England in 1660, the great political philosophers of the 17th century, above all Hobbes and Spinoza, developed a basically pessimistic view of human destiny. Revolutions are doomed to fail: 'Plus ça change, plus ça reste la même chose'. Two thousand years earlier, Greek and Chinese political philosophers had arrived at similar conclusions. There is supposedly no way out for human destiny but the search for individual happiness under inevitably bad social conditions, be it happiness through self-discipline (Stoics, Confucians, Spinoza) or through hedonism (the Epicureans).[11]

In the 18th century, the Enlightenment questioned both the empirical and the theoretical roots of dogmatic sceptical pessimism.[12] The belief in the perfectability of humankind (only sophists or dishonest critics identify perfectability with actually attaining a final state of perfection, be it said in passing), in historical progress, and thus likewise in the progressive role of revolutions, re-emerged. Revolution indeed looked beautiful in times of reaction. But already before the outbreak of the revolution of 1789, the camp of the Enlightenment had split between the basically sceptical and socially cautious, if not outright conservative, bourgeois like Voltaire ('cultivez votre jardin')[13] and the more radical petty-bourgeois ideologues like J.J. Rousseau, who would inspire the Jacobin revolutionists. This split deepened in the course of the revolution itself. After the successive stages of counter-revolution (Thermidor, the Bonapartist Consulate, the Empire, the Bourbon restoration) the reversal to 17th century scepticism became general, including erstwhile enthusiasts for revolution, exemplified by the English poet Wordsworth (but not Shelley). Only a tiny minority continued to pin their hopes on future revolutions and to work for them.[14] The near-consensus was: the overhead of revolution is too large, especially given the fact that they achieve very little.[15]

The Russian revolution's Thermidor and its tragic aftermath, the horrors of Stalinism, reproduced the same revulsion towards revolutions, first in the late nineteen-thirties and the forties, then, after a temporary reprieve in the sixties and the early seventies, on a generalised scale from the middle seventies on. The Soviet military intervention in Czechoslovakia, and especially Cambodia and Afghanistan, but more generally the reflux of the revolutionary wave 1968–1975 in Europe, from France through Czechoslovakia, Italy, Portugal, strengthened this political retreat. The near-consensus can again be summarized in the formula: revolutions are both useless and harmful from every point of view, including that of progress towards a more humane society. Indeed, this is one of the key platitudes of today's prevailing neo-conservative, neo-liberal and neo-reformist ideologies.

It is, however, based upon obvious half-truths, if not outright mystifications. The idea that revolutions revert to these historical points of departure, if not to situations worse than the pre-revolutionary ones, is generally based upon a confusion between social and political counter-revolutions. While a few social counter-revolutions have indeed occurred, they are the exception, not the rule. Neither Napoleon nor Louis XVIII restored semi-feudal socio-economic conditions in the French countryside, nor the political rule of a semi-feudal nobility. Stalin did not restore capitalism in Russia, nor did Deng

Hsiao-ping in China.[16] The restoration in England was quickly followed by the Glorious Revolution. The compromise of the American constitution did not lead eventually to the generalisation of slave labour but to its suppression, after the civil war. The list can be extended *ad libitum*.

To this objective balance-sheet, the problems of subjective choice are closely related. They confront the sceptics and the pessimists with a real dilemma. Counter-revolutions are not simply 'natural' reactions to revolutions, the product of an inevitable mechanical yo-yo movement so to speak. They originate from the same exacerbation of a system's inner contradictions which give rise to the revolution, but with a specific shift in socio-political relations of forces. They reflect the relative decline of political mass activity and efficiency. There is indeed a 'natural law' operating here. As genuine popular revolutions generally imply a qualitatively increased level of political mass activity, this cannot be sustained indefinitely, for obvious material and psychological reasons. You have to produce in order to eat, and when you demonstrate and participate in mass meetings, you don't produce. Also, great masses of people cannot live permanently at a high level of excitement and expenditure of nervous energy.[17]

To this corresponds a relative rise of activity and efficiency of the old ruling classes or strata and their various supporters and hangers-on. The initiative shifts from the 'left' to the 'right', at least momentarily (and not necessarily with total success: there have been defeated counter-revolutions as there have been defeated revolutions.[18]) There are likewise preventive counter-revolutions: Indonesia 1965 and Chile 1973 may be taken as examples. But precisely these preventive counter-revolutions clearly reveal the pessimistic sceptic's dilemma. They are generally very costly in terms of human lives and human happiness – much more costly than revolutions. It stands to reason that much more repression, much more bloodletting, much more cruelty, including torture, is needed to suppress a highly active, broad mass of ordinary people than to neutralize a small group of rulers. So by abstaining from active intervention against a rising counter-revolution – on the pretext that revolution itself is useless and bad – one actually becomes a passive if not active accomplice of bloody counter-revolution and large-scale mass suffering.

This is morally revolting, as it means tolerating, aiding and abetting the violence and exploitation of the oppressors, while finding all kinds of rationalisations for refusing to assist the oppressed in their self-defence and attempted emancipation. And it is politically counter-productive as well as obnoxious. In the end, it often proves to be suicidal from the point of view of the sceptics' alleged devotion to the defence of democratic institutions and reforms.

The most tragic example in that respect was that of German social-democracy at the end of World War One. Under the alleged motive of 'saving democracy', Ebert and Noske kept the Imperial army's hierarchy and the Prussian officers' corps intact. They conspired with it against the workers – first in Berlin itself, then in the whole country. They made the generals of the *Reichswehr* into the political arbiters of the Weimar Republic. They permitted them to create and consolidate the *Freikorps* from which a good part of the later SA and SS *cadres* were recruited. They thereby paved the way of the rise and eventual conquest of power by the Nazis, which in turn led to the social-democrats' destruction. They thought they could contain regression and reaction in the framework of a democratic counter-revolution.[19] History taught the bitter lesson that democratic counter-revolutions in the end often lead to much more authoritarian and violent ones, when the sharpening of the socio-economic contradictions makes a total instead of a partial suppression of the mass movement into an immediate goal of the ruling class.

This again is not accidental but corresponds to a deeper historical logic. The essence of revolution is often identified with a widespread explosion of violence and mass killings. This is of course not true. The essence of revolution is not the use of violence in politics but a radical, qualitative challenge – and eventually the overthrow – of prevailing economic or political power structures. The larger the number of people involved in mass actions targeting these structures, the more favourable the relationship of forces between revolutions and reaction, the greater the self-confidence of the first and the moral-ideological paralysis of the second, and the less the masses are inclined to use violence. Indeed, widespread use of violence is counter-productive for the revolution at that precise phase of the historical process.

But what does occur most often, if not always, at some point of the revolutionary process, is the desperate recourse to violence by the most radical and the most resolute sectors of the rulers' camp, intent on risking everything before it is too late, because they still have human and material resources left to act in that way. At some culminating point, the confrontation between revolution and counter-revolution thus generally *does* assume a violent character, although the degree of violence largely depends upon the overall relationship of forces. In answer to reaction's violence, the masses will tend towards armed self-defence. Disintegration, paralysis and disarming of the counter-revolution paves the way towards revolutionary victory. Victory of counter-revolution depends upon disarming of the mass.[20]

When the chips are down, when power relations are stripped of all mediations and are nakedly reduced to bare essentials, Friedrich Engels' formula is then borne out by empirical evidence: in the final analysis, the state *is* indeed a gang of armed people. The class or layer which has the monopoly of armed force possesses (either keeps or conquers) state power. And that again is what revolution, and counter-revolution, are all about. Sitting on the sidelines cannot prevent this confrontation. Nor can it contribute to delaying for ever the day of reckoning. In the last analysis the sceptics' and reformists' revulsion from revolution covers an implicit choice: the conservation of the *status quo* is a lesser evil compared to the costs and consequences of its revolutionary overthrow. This choice reflects social conservatism, not a rational judgment of the empirically verifiable balance-sheets of 'costs' of historical, i.e. real, revolutions and counter-revolutions.

No normal human being prefers to achieve social goals through the use of violence. To reduce violence to the utmost in political life should be a common endeavour for all progressive and socialist currents. Only profoundly sick persons – totally unable to contribute to the building of a real classless society – can actually enjoy advocating and practising violence on a significant scale. Indeed, the increasing rejection of violence in a growing number of countries is a clear indicator that at least some moral-ideological progress has occurred in the last 70–75 years. One has just to compare the wild and brazen justification of war by nearly all the leading Western intellectuals and politicians in the 1914–1918 period to the near universal revulsion towards war today in the same milieu to note that progress.

Double moral standards still reign supreme in inter-class and inter-state relations, but the legitimacy of widespread use of violence by the rulers is at least increasingly questioned in a systematic and consistent way by a much greater number of people than in 1914–1918 or 1939–1945. The future, indeed the very physical survival of humankind, depends upon the outcome of this race between increasing consciousness about the necessary rejection of armed confrontation on the one hand, and increasing *de facto* destructiveness of existing and future weapons on the other. If the first does not eliminate the second through successful political action, the second will eventually destroy not only the first but all human life on earth.

But such a political action can only be revolutionary and thus implies the use of at least limited armed force. To believe otherwise is to believe that the rulers will let themselves be disarmed utterly peacefully, without using the arms they still control. This is to deny the threat of any violent counter-revolution, which is utterly utopian in the light of actual historical experience. It is to assume that ruling classes and strata are exclusively and always represented by mild well-meaning liberals. Go tell that to the prisoners of the Warsaw ghetto and of Auschwitz, to the million victims of Djakarta, to the oppressed non-white population of South Africa, to the Indochinese peoples, to the Chilean and Salvadorian workers and peasants, to the murdered participants of the *Intifada,* to the millions and millions of victims of reaction and counter-revolution throughout the world since the colonial wars of the 19th century and the Paris Commune. The elementary human-moral duty in face of that terrifying record is to refuse any retreat into (re) privatisation and to assist by any means necessary the oppressed, the exploited, the humiliated, the downtrodden, to struggle for their emancipation. In the long run, this makes also the individual participant a more human, i.e. happier person, provided he does not make any pseudo-*Realpolitical* concessions and observes unrestrictedly the rule: fight everywhere and always against any and every social and political condition which exploits and oppresses human beings.

III. *The Possibility of Revolution in the West*

Revolutions and counter-revolutions, being real historical processes, always occur in really existing social-economic formations which are always specific. No two countries in the world are exactly alike, if only because their basic social classes and the major fractions of these classes are products of the specific history of each of these countries. Hence the character of each revolution reflects a unique combination of the general and the specific. The first derives from the logic of revolutions as sketched before. The second derives from the specificity of each particular set of prevailing relations of production and relations of political power in a given country, at a given moment, with its specific inner contradictions and a specific dynamic of their exacerbation.

A revolutionary strategy[21] represents the conscious attempt by revolutionists to influence by their political actions the outcome of objectively revolutionary processes in favour of a victory of the exploited and the oppressed, in today's world essentially the wage-earning proletariat, its allies and the poor peasantry. It has therefore in turn to be specific to have a minimum chance of success. This means that it has to be attuned to the differentiated social reality which prevails in today's world. We can use the formula of the 'three sectors of world revolution' to designate significantly different strategic tasks, that is, roughly: the proletarian revolution in the imperialist countries; the combined national-democratic, anti-imperialist and socialist revolution in the so-called 'third world countries'; the political revolution in the post-capitalist social formations.[22] We shall consider each of these in turn.

Regarding the industrialized metropolises of capitalism, a formidable objection is raised with regard to the possible effectiveness of revolutionary strategy. Many sceptics and reformists do not limit themselves to allege that revolutions are useless and harmful. They add that revolutions are impossible in these countries, that they won't occur anyway, that to hope for them or expect them is utterly utopian; that to try to prepare for them or to further them is a total waste of time and energy.

This line of reasoning is based on two different – and basically contradictory – assumptions. The first one (which is still true) states that no *victorious* revolution has ever occured in a purely imperialist country up till now. The case of 1917 Russia is seen as an exceptional case, a unique combination of under-development and imperialism. But is is irrational, even childish, to recognize as revolutions only those that have been successful. Once one accepts that revolutionary processes did occur in 20th century imperialist countries, surely the logical conclusion for a revolutionist is to study them carefully so as to be able to map out a course which will make defeat unlikely when they occur again in the future.

The second assumption is that whatever in the past triggered revolutions[23]

(revolutionary crises and processes) will never happen again. Bourgeois society – the capitalist economy and parliamentary democracy – are supposed to
have achieved such a degree of stability and 'integrated' the mass of wage
earners to such an extent that they won't be seriously challenged in any
foreseeable future.[24] This assumption, which already prevailed during the
postwar boom (in obvious function of the undeniable increase in standard of
living and social security which was its by-product for the Western proletariat)
was seriously challenged in May 1968 and its immediate aftermath, at least in
Southern Europe (and partially in Britain in the early seventies). It regained
a powerful credibility in the wake of the retreat of the proletariat in the
metropolitan countries towards essentially defensive struggles after 1974–75.

We should understand the nub of the question. The seemingly a-prioristic
assumption is in reality a prediction which will be historically either verified
or falsified. It is in no way a final truth. It is nothing but a working hypothesis.
It assumes a given variant of the basic trends of development of capitalism in
the latter part of the 20th century: the variant of *declining contradictions,* of
the ability of the system to avoid explosive crises, not to say catastrophes.

In that sense, it is strikingly similar to the working hypothesis of the classical
version of reformism, i.e. of rejection of a revolutionary perspective and revolutionary strategy: that of Eduard Bernstein. In his book which launched the
famous 'revisionism debate', he clearly posited a growing objective decline
in acuity of inner contradictions of the system as premises for his reformist
conclusions: less and less capitalist crises; less and less tendencies towards
war; less and less authoritarian governments; less and less violent conflicts
in the world.[25] Rosa Luxemburg answered him succintly that precisely the
opposite would he the case. And when under the influence of the Russian
revolution of 1905, Kautsky came the nearest to revolutionary marxism and
was the undisputed mentor of Lenin, Rosa Luxemburg and Trotsky,[26] he
also explicitly identified the perspective of *inevitable catastrophes* to which
capitalism was leading as one of the main pillars of marxism's revolutionary
perspectives.[27] When he moved away from revolutionary marxism, he started
to consider these catastrophes as becoming more and more unlikely, i.e. he
started to share Bernstein's euphoric working hypothesis.[28]

What does the historical record reveal? Two world wars; the economic crisis
of 1929 and onwards; fascism; Hiroshima; innumerable colonial wars; hunger
and disease in the third world; the ongoing ecological catastrophe; the new
long economic depression. They leave out that it has been Rosa Luxemburg
who has been proven more right than Bernstein; and that it was the Kautsky
of 1907 who has been proven right by history and not the Kautsky of the 1914
'ultra-imperialism' theory. Today it seems truer than ever, to paraphrase a
famous formula of Jean Jaurès, that late capitalism carries within itself a
succession of grave crises and catastrophes like clouds carry storms.[29]

One transforms that obvious truth – obvious in the sense that is born out by
solid historical evidence for three-quarters of a century – into a meaningless

caricature when one insinuates that revolutionary marxists expect or predict *permanent* catastrophes, every year in every imperialist country, so to speak. Leaving aside the lunatic fringe, serious marxists have never taken that stand, which doesn't mean that they have never been guilty of false analysis and erroneous evaluations regarding particular countries. If one soberly analyses the ups and downs of economic, social and political crisis in the West and Japan since 1914, what emerges is a pattern of *periodic* upsurges of mass struggles in *some* metropolitan countries which have at times put revolutionary processes on the agenda. In our view, the mechanisms leading in that direction remain operative today as they were since the period of historical decline of the capitalist mode of production was first posited by marxists. The burden of proving that this is no longer the case is upon those who argue that today's bourgeois society is somehow *basically* different from that of 1936, not to say that of 1968. We haven't yet seen any persuasive argumentation of that nature.

The concept of *periodically and not permanently* possible revolutionary explosions in imperialist countries logically leads to a *typology of possible revolutions in the West*, which sees these revolutions essentially as a qualitative 'transcroissance' of mass struggles and mass experiences of non-revolutionary times. We have often sketched this process of 'overgrowing', based not upon speculation or wishful thinking but on the experience of pre-revolutionary and revolutionary explosions which have really occurred in the West.[30] We can therefore limit ourselves to summarizing the process in the following chain of events: mass strikes; political mass strikes; a general strike; a general sit-down strike; coordination and centralisation of democratically elected strike committees; transformation of the 'passive' into an 'active' general strike, in which strike committees assume a beginning of state functions, in the first place in the public and the financial sector. (Public transport regulation, access to telecommunications, access to saving and bank accounts limited to strikers, free hospital services under that same authority, 'parallel' teaching in schools by teachers under strikers' authority, are examples of such inroads into the realm of the exercise of quasi-state functions growing out of an 'active' general strike.) This leads to the emergence of a *de facto* generalized dual power situation with emerging self-defence of the masses.

Such a chain of events generalizes trends already visible at high points of mass struggles in the West: Northern Italy, 1920; July 1927 in Austria; June 1936 in France; July 1948 in Italy; May 1968 in France; the 'hot autumn' of 1969 in Italy; and the high points of the Portuguese revolution 1974–75. Other general strike experiences[31] involving a similar chain of events were those of Germany 1920 and Spain (especially Catalonia) 1936–37. (Albeit in a very different social context, the tendency of the industrial proletariat to operate in the same general sense in revolutionary situations can also be seen in Hungary 1956, Czechoslovakia, 1968–69, and Poland 1980–81.)

Such a view of proletarian revolutionary behaviour in the imperialist countries makes it easier to solve a problem which has haunted revolutionary
marxists since the beginning of the 20th century: the relation between the
struggle for reforms (economic as well as political-democratic-ones) and
the preparation for revolution. The answer given to that problem by Rosa
Luxemburg already in the beginning of the debate remains as valid today as
it was at that time.[32] The difference between reformists and revolutionists
does not at all lie in the rejection of reforms by the latter and the struggle
for reforms by the former. On the contrary: serious revolutionists will be the
most resolute and efficient fighters for all reforms which correspond to the
needs and the recognizable preoccupations of the masses. The real difference
between reformists and revolutionary marxists can be thus summarized:

1. Without rejecting or marginalizing legislative initiatives, revolutionary socialists prioritize
the struggle for reforms through broad, direct extra-parliamentary mass actions.
2. Without negating the need to take into consideration real social-political relations of forces,
revolutionary socialists refuse to limit the struggle for reforms to those which are acceptable
to the bourgeoisie or, worse, which don't upset the basic social and political relations of power. For that reason, reformists tend to fight less and less for serious reforms whenever the
system is in crisis because, like the capitalists, they understand the 'destabilizing' tendency
of these struggles. For the revolutionists, the priority is the struggle for the masses' needs
and interests, and not the defence of the system's needs or logic, nor the conservation of
any consensus with capitalists.
3. Reformists see the limitation or elimination of capitalism's ills as a process of gradual
progress. Revolutionists, on the contrary, educate the masses in the inevitability of crises
which will interrupt the gradual accumulation of reforms, and which will periodically lead
to a threat of suppression of conquests of the past, or to their actual suppression.
4. Reformists will tend to brake, oppose or even repress all forms of direct mass actions which
transcend or threaten bourgeois state institutions. Revolutionists, on the contrary, will systematically favour and try to develop self-activity and self-organisation of the masses, even
in daily struggles for immediate reforms, regardless of 'destabilizing' consequences, thereby
creating a tradition, an experience of broader and broader mass struggle, which facilitates
the emergence of a dual
power situation when generalized mass struggles – a general strike – actually occur. Thereby, proletarian revolutions of the type sketched above can be seen as an organic product –
or climax – of broader and broader mass struggles for reforms in pre-revolutionary or even
non-revolutionary times.
5. Reformists will generally limit themselves to propagating reform. Revolutionary marxists
will combine a struggle for reforms with constant and systematic anti-capitalist propaganda.
They will educate the masses in the system's ills, and advocate its revolutionary overthrow.
The formulation and struggle for transitional demands which, while corresponding to the
masses' needs, cannot be realized within the framework of the system, plays a key role
here.

Doesn't such a view of 'really feasible revolution' in the west seriously
underestimate the obstacle which the Western proletariat's obvious attachment to parliamentary democracy constitutes on the road towards the overthrow of bourgeois institutions, without which no victorious revolution is
possible? We don't think so.
In this first place, many aspects of the legitimate attachment of the masses
to democratic rights and freedom is not at all an attachment to bourgeois

state institutions. It expresses, to use a clarifying formula of Trotsky, the presence of nuclei of proletarian democracy inside the bourgeois state.[33] The larger the masses' self-activity, self-mobilization and self-organisation, the more the butterfly of democratic workers' power tends to appear out of its 'bourgeois' chrysalis. The fundamental issue will be one of growing confrontation between the 'naked core' of bourgeois state power (the central government, the repressive apparatus, etc.) and the masses' attachment to democratic institutions *which they themselves control*.

In the second place, there is no reason to counterpose in an absolute and dogmatic way organs of direct workers and popular power, and organs resulting from undifferentiated universal franchise. Workers and popular councils and their centralized coordination (local, regional, national, international council congresses) can be more efficient and democratic forms of making possible the direct exercise of political, economic and social power by millions of toilers. But if it is necessary to reject parliamentary cretinism, it is likewise necessary to reject anti-parliamentary cretinism. Whenever and wherever the masses clearly express their wish to have parliamentary-type power organs elected by universal franchise – the cases of Hungary, Poland and Nicaragua are clear in that sense – revolutionists should accept that verdict. These organs need not supercede the power of soviets insofar as the masses have learned through their own experiences that their councils can give them more democratic rights and more real power than the broadest parliamentary democracy alone; and insofar as the precise functional division of labour between soviet-type and parliamentary-type organs is elaborated into a constitution under conditions of workers power.

Of course, soviet institutions can and should also be elected on the basis of universal franchise. The fundamental difference between parliamentary and soviet democracy is not the mode of election but the mode of functioning. Parliamentary democracy is essentially representative, i.e. indirect democracy, and to a large extent limited to the legislative field. Soviet democracy contains much higher doses of direct democracy, including the instrument of 'binding mandates' of the electors for their representative and the right to instant recall of these by their electors. In addition, it implies a large-scale unification of legislative and executive functions which, combined with the principle of rotation, actually enables the majority of the citizens to exercise state functions. The multiplication of functional assemblies with a division of competence serves the same purpose. A key specificity of soviet democracy is also that it is producers' democracy, i.e. that it ties economic decision-taking to work places and federated work places (at local, regional and branch levels etc.), giving those who work the right to decide on their workload and the allocation of their products and services. Why should workers make sacrifices in spending time, nerves and physical strength for increasing output, when they generally feel that the results of these additional efforts don't benefit them, and they have no way of deciding about the distribution of its fruits?

Producers' democracy appears more and more as the only way to overcome the declining motivation (sense of responsibility) for production, not to say the economy in its totality, which characterises both the capitalist market economy and the bureaucratic command economy.

IV. *The Lessons of Third World Revolutions*

The revolutionary processes in the Third World since World War II have confirmed the validity of the strategy of permanent revolution. Wherever these processes have climaxed in a full break with the old ruling classes and with international capital the historical tasks of the national-democratic revolution (national unification, independence from imperialism) have been realized. This was the case of Yugoslavia, Indochina, China, Cuba, Nicaragua. Wherever the revolutionary process did not culminate in such a full break, key tasks of the national-democratic revolution remain unfulfilled. This was the case of Indonesia, Bolivia, Egypt, Algeria, Chile, Iran.

The theory (strategy) of permanent revolution is counterposed to the traditional Comintern/CP strategy since the middle nineteen twenties, to wit that of the 'revolution by stages', in which a first phase of 'bloc of four classes' (the so-called 'national' bourgeoisie; the peasantry; the urban petty-bourgeoisie and the proletariat) is supposed to eliminate by a common political struggle the semi-feudal and oligarchic power structures, including foreign imperialist ones. Only in a second phase is the proletarian struggle for power supposed to come to the forefront. This strategy first led to disaster in China in 1927. It has led to grave defeats ever since. It is increasingly challenged inside many CPs themselves.

It is of no avail to avoid making this fundamental choice by the use of abstract formulas. The formulas, 'workers and farmers government' or, worse, 'people's power' or 'broad popular alliance under the hegemony of the working class', just evade the issue. What revolutions are all about is state power. The class nature of state power -- and/or of the question which major fraction of a given class exercises state power – is decisive. Either the formulas just cited are synonymous with the overthrow of the bourgeois-oligarchic state, its army and its repressive apparatus, and with the establishment of a workers state; or the formulas imply that the existing state apparatus is not to be 'immediately' destroyed – in which case the class nature of the state remains bourgeois-oligarchic and the revolution will be defeated.

When it is said that without the conquest of power by the working class, without the overthrow of the state of the former ruling classes, the historical tasks of the national-democratic revolution will not be fully realized, this does not mean that *none* of these tasks can be initiated under bourgeois or petty-bourgeois governments. After World War II, most of the previously colonial countries did after all achieve political national independence without overthrowing the capitalist order. In some cases at least, India being the most striking one, this was not purely formal but also implied a degree of economic autonomy from imperialism which made at least initial industrialization under national bourgeois ownership possible. Starting with the late sixties, a series of semi-colonial countries succeeded in launching a process of semi-industrialization which went much farther (South Korea, Taiwan, Brazil, Mexico, Singapore, Hong Kong are the most important cases), often supported by substantial land reforms as indispensable launching pads for these take-offs. The famous controversy of the nineteen fifties and the nineteen sixties on the so-called 'dependencia' theory – the impossibility of any serious degree of industrialization without a total break with imperialism – has thus been settle by history.

It is likewise incorrect to interpret the theory of the permanent revolution as implying that the overthrow of the old state order and the radical agrarian revolution must perforce *coincide with* the complete destruction of capitalist private property in industry. It is true that the working class can hardly be supposed to tolerate its own exploitation at factory level while it is busy, or has already succeeded in, disarming the capitalists and eliminating their political power. But from this flows only that the victorious socialist revolution in underdeveloped countries will start making 'despotic inroads' into the realm of capitalist private property, to quote a famous sentence of the *Communist Manifesto*. The rhythm and the extent of these inroads will depend on the political and social correlation of forces and on the pressure of economic priorities. No general formula is applicable here for all countries at all moments.

The question of the rhythm and the extent of expropriation of the bourgeoisie is in turn tied to the question of the workers – peasants alliance, a key question of political strategy in most of the third world countries. Keeping capitalist property intact to the extent of not fulfilling the poor peasants' thirst for land is obviously counter-productive. Hitting private property to the extent of arousing fear among the middle peasants that they too will lose their property is counter-productive from an economic point of view (it could become also counter-productive politically).

On balance, however, experience confirms what the theory suggests. It is impossible to achieve genuine independence from imperialism and genuinely to motivate the working class for the task of socialist reconstruction of the nation without the expropriation of big capital in industry, banking, agriculture, trade and transportation, be it international or national capital. The real difficulties only arise when the borderline between that expropriation and the tolerance of small and medium-sized capital (with all its implications for economic growth, social equality and direct producers' motivation) has to be determined.

The historical record shows that a peculiar form of dual power of confrontation between the old and the new state order has appeared during all victorious socialist revolutions in underdeveloped countries: dual power reflecting a territorial division of the country into liberated zones in which the new state is emerging, and the rest of the country where the old state still reigns. This peculiar form of dual power expresses in turn the peculiar form of the revolutionary (and counter-revolutionary) processes themselves, in which armed struggle (guerrilla warfare, people's war) occupied a central place. In the cases of China, Yugoslavia, and Vietnam, this resulted from the fact that the revolution started as a movement of national liberation against a foreign imperialist aggressor/invader, while becoming increasingly intertwined with civil war between the poor and the well-to-do, i.e. with social revolution. In the cases of Cuba and Nicaragua, the revolution started likewise as armed struggle against a viciously repressive and universally hated and despised dictatorship, again growing over into a social revolution.

One should of course not simplify the pattern emerging from these experiences. At least in Cuba and in Nicaragua (to some extent also in the beginning of the Indochinese revolution and in several stages of the Yugoslav revolution) urban insurrections played an important role. A successful general strike and a successful urban insurrection decided the outcome of the Cuban and the Nicaraguan revolutions. The proponents of the strategy of armed struggle today generally adopt a more sophisticated and complex strategy than in the sixties, combining guerrilla warfare, the creation of liberated zones and the mobilization of mass organisations in urbans zones (including forms of armed self-defence) in order to lead the revolution to victory. This combination seems reasonable in many semi-colonial countries, where state repression under pre-revolutionary conditions leaves no other alternative to revolutionary strategy. We believe, however, that this pattern should not be considered unavoidable once for all in all Third World countries, regardless of specific circumstances and particular social-political relationships of forces at given moments.

V. *Political Revolution in So-called Socialist Societies*
The concept of political (anti-bureaucratic) revolution in the bureaucratized societies in transition between capitalism and socialism (bureaucratized workers states) was first launched by Trotsky in 1933. It resulted from the diagnosis of the growing contradictions of Soviet society and from the prediction that these contradictions could no longer be removed through reforms; and it was related, therefore to the prediction that a self-reform of the bureaucracy was impossible.[34] Most left tendencies considered this concept, and the premises on which it was based, as either a fantasy, or objectively a call for counter-revolution. The overthrow of the bureaucratic dictatorship could only lead to a restoration of capitalism: that was the assumption.

These objections were unfounded. Trotsky's prognosis of political revolution, like his analysis of the contradictions of Soviet society, appear as one of his most brilliant contributions to marxism. Since 1953, we have witnessed a chain of revolutionary crises in Eastern Europe: GDR June 1953; Hungary 1956; Czechoslovakia 1968, Poland 1980–81. One can discuss whether similar crises didn't also occur in China, both in the nineteen sixties and the nineteen seventies. (Mikhael Gorbachev himself calls his *perestroika* a revolution and compares it with the political revolutions which occurred in France in 1830, 1848 and 1870.[35]) In all these concrete revolutionary processes, there was no prevalent tendency to restore capitalism. This did not only result from the objective fact that the overwhelming majority of the combatants were workers who have no interest in restoring capitalism. It was subjectively determined by the very demands of these combatants, which in Hungary set up workers' councils with the Central Workers Council of Budapest leading the struggle. Similar development occurred in Czechoslovakia and in Poland. The line of march of the political revolution in the USSR will be quite similar.

On the other hand, it cannot be denied that attempts at self-reform of the bureaucracy have been many – the most spectacular of them being the introduction of workers' self-management at factory level in Yugoslavia in 1950. While often instrumental in triggering off a 'thaw' of the bureaucracy's stranglehold on society and enabling a revival of mass activity and mass politization at various degrees, these attempts have always failed to solve the basic ills of these societies. This was especially true for the historically most important of these attempts, the one initiated by N.S. Khrushchev in the USSR. Indeed, today most of the 'liberal' and 'left' Soviet historians and intellectuals agree that the reason for the failure of Khrushchev was insufficient activity from below. This, incidentally, is also Gorbachev's official version of the Khrushchev experience.

So the historical balance-sheet is again clear: attempts at self-reform can start a movement of change in the bureaucratized workers' states. They can even facilitate the beginning of a genuine mass movement. But they cannot bring about a successful culmination of such change and movement. For this, a genuine popular revolution is indispensable. Self-reform of the enlightened wing of the bureaucracy cannot be a substitute for such a revolution.

The bureaucracy is a hardened *social* layer, enjoying huge material privileges which depend fundamentally on its monopoly on the exercise of political power. But that same bureaucracy does not play any indispensable or useful role in society. Its role is essentially parasitic. Hence its rule is more and more wasteful. It tends to become the source of a succession of specific economic, social, political, ideological-moral crises. Hence the need to remove it from its ruling position is an objective necessity for unblocking the march forward towards socialism. For this, a revival of mass activity, in the first place political activity of the working class, is needed. While a revolution will have many implications in the field of the economy, it will basically consolidate and strengthen the system of collective ownership of the means of production and of socialized planning, far from overthrowing it. That is why we speak of a 'political revolution' instead of 'social revolution'.[36]

To a large extent, the bureaucracy rules in function of the political passivity of the working class; Trotsky even said through passive 'tolerance' by the working class. The historical-social origins of that passivity are well-known:

the defeats of the international revolution; the pressure of scarcity of consumer goods and of lack of culture born from the relative backwardness of
Russia; the consequences of the Stalinist terror; a disappointment of historical
dimensions, leading to a lack of historical alternatives to the bureaucracy's
rule. But the very progress of Soviet society during the last half century,
achieved on the basis of the remaining conquests of the October revolution and in spite of the bureaucracy' misrule, slowly undermines the basis
of that passivity. The stronger, more skilled and more cultivated becomes
the working class, the greater its resentments and expectations clash with
the slow-down of economic growth and the manifold social crises which the
bureaucracy's misrule and waste provoke. So conditions emerge which tend
to revive the working classes' activity.

Timothy Garton Ash quotes a remarkable memorandum by the new Polish
Prime Minister, Mieczyslaw F. Rakowski, which concludes with the prediction that if the 'socialist formation' does not find the strength to reform itself,
'the further history of our formation will be marked by shocks and revolutionary explosions, initiated by an increasingly enlightened people'. Indeed.
But as Ash himself clearly indicates, in spite of his favouring reforms moving
towards a restoration of capitalism tempered by a 'liberal' democracy, the
difficulty lies precisely in the social correlation of forces: the working class
is not ready to pay the price for a return to capitalism, i.e. massive unemployment and inequality. So you can't have generalized market economy plus
political democracy. You can only have partial market economy plus partial
repression. So you can't have radical reforms. So the likelihood that you'll
have a political revolution is growing. Ash himself rather cynically concludes:
'It seems reasonable to suggest that the reform has a rather higher chance
of minimal success – that is, of averting revolution – if only because of the
further diversification of social interests which it will promote. The freeing
of the private sector, in particular, means that Hungary might yet have an
entrepreneurial bourgeoisie that will go to the barricades – against the revolting workers. Capitalists and Communists, shoulder to shoulder against the
proletariat: a suitably Central European outcome for socialism. To estimate
the percentage chance of peaceful transformation, by contrast, requires only
the fingers of one hand'.[37]

Yet, precisely because the bureaucracy is not a new ruling class but a
parasitic cancer on the working class and society as a whole, its removal
through a political revolution by the workers does not require the type of
armed conflict which until now has accompanied revolutions in class societies, including modern capitalist ones. It is more in the nature of a surgical
operation. This was confirmed in the case of Hungary 1956 which went the
farthest towards a victorious political revolution. A significant part of the
CP apparatus and practically the whole army went over to the camp of the
workers (of the people). Only a tiny handful of secret police agents opposed
arms to the victorious masses in open provocations, thereby provoking an

overt conflict (and their own sad fate) which otherwise could have been avoided. In Czechoslovakia 1968 a similar trend was set in motion. In fact, in all cases of such political revolutions witnessed up till now, only foreign military intervention could prevent it from becoming victorious nearly without bloodshed. One does not see what force could replace such a foreign military intervention in the case of the USSR, probably not the Soviet army. And the capacity of the KGB to repress 265 million people seems dubious to say the least.

History has also confirmed the utopian character of the idea that the construction of socialism could be fully achieved in a single country or a small number of countries. It has confirmed that the USSR (and the so-called 'socialist camp') cannot escape the pressure of the world market (of international capitalism): the pressure of wars and of the permanent arms race; the pressure of constant technological innovations; and the pressure of changing consumption patterns for the mass of the producers. But far from being an unavoidable result of that pressure, the bureaucratic dictatorship undermines the revolution's objective and subjective capacity of resistance. A victorious political revolution in the USSR and Eastern Europe would strengthen considerably that resistance. It would make new advances towards socialism possible. But we should not fall into the illusion that it could even so, actually achieve a classless society on its own, independently of revolutionary developments elsewhere.

VI. *World Revolution Today*

The concept of the three sectors of world revolution refers to the different strategic-historical tasks with which the revolutionary process is confronted today. But this only represents the first step towards a concretisation of the concept of world revolution today. The question of these sectors and their interaction, and hence their growing unity, has also to be raised.

For decades, the apologists of the Stalinist dictatorship used to say that revealing the dark side of the Soviet (the Eastern European, the Chinese) reality discourages the workers in the West from fighting to overthrow capitalism. But history has fully confirmed that it is impossible to conduct a fight for a good cause on the basis of lies, half-truths or the hiding of truth. As it was impossible, in the long run, to hide the revolting aspects of Soviet reality, the mass of the workers in the West and Japan (including those adhering to or voting for the Communist Parties) ended by assimilating them. What really discouraged and demoralized them was not the revelation of these facts but the facts themselves – including their decade-long suppression by the Communist Parties and their fellow-travellers. One of the biggest subjective obstacles to a new development of revolutionary consciousness among the Western working class is the repulsive mask which Stalinism has put on socialism (communism). By contributing to tearing off that mask, a victorious political revolution in the East greatly advances the cause of socialism the world over. It strengthens the struggle against capitalism and imperialism, instead of weakening it.

The idea that, somehow, such a revolution would at least weaken the USSR (or the 'socialist camp') at state level and thereby change the military relationship of forces worldwide in favour of imperialism is likewise unfounded. It is an undeniable fact that the existence of the USSR in spite of the bureaucratic dictatorship and its policies of 'peaceful coexistence', objectively contributed to the victory and especially the consolidation of the Chinese revolution and to the downfall of the colonial empires in the subsequent decades. But parallel to that objective function must be seen the fact that the Soviet bureaucracy tried to obstruct the victory of the Chinese revolution through the strategy it advocated, and that it played a key role in the post World War II consolidation of capitalism in Western Europe.

Furthermore, it is impossible to disconnect military strength from its economic and social basis, and from the political nature of governments. A Soviet Union, not to say a 'socialist camp', governed through pluralistic socialist democracy and a broad consensus of the majority of the toilers, would be much more efficient economically, far more influential in the world, and thereby much stronger militarily than the USSR of to-day.[38]

The concept of unity between the three sectors of world revolution is supported by the fact that while victorious revolutions in Third World countries can weaken imperialism, they cannot overthrow it. In the epoch of nuclear weapons it is obvious that imperialism can only be overthrown inside the metropolis itself. But the main obstacle to that overthrow is not the objective strength of capitalism or the bourgeois state, nor the absence of periodically explosive contradictions inside the metropolis. The main obstacle is subjective: the level of Western (and Japanese) working class consciousness and the political quality of its leadership. Precisely for that reason, new qualitative advances towards socialism in the USSR and Eastern Europe, and the removal of the repulsive bureaucratic dictatorships, would greatly assist in the solution of the problem.

On the other hand, any leap forward towards a victorious proletarian revolution in the West or in the most advanced semi-industrialized Third World countries (like Brazil), which will occur under immeasurably more favourable objective and cultural conditions than the Russian October Revolution, will usher in material and social changes which will operate as a powerful stimulate for the toilers of all countries, beginning with the Soviet toilers if they have not yet overthrown the bureaucracy's yoke at that moment. To mention just one key aspect of any future victorious proletarian revolution in an economically advanced country: the realization of the half-work day would play the same role as the slogan 'Land, Bread, Peace' played in the Russian revolution. And if that were realized what sector of the working class the world over could stay impervious to that conquest?

The potential interaction – we say potential because it is obviously not yet

a fact to-day – between the three sectors of world revolution is premised
on the historical/social unity of the world working class and the strength
of the forces operating towards the development of conscious awareness of
that unity. We know perfectly well how strong the obstacles are on the road
towards that political consciousness. They have been enumerated and analyzed a thousand times. What we want to stress is that they can be overcome
by the operation of still stronger objective trends.

The unity of the process of world revolution is related to the growing
internationalization of the productive forces and of capital – exemplified in
the emergence of the transnational corporation as the typical late capitalist
firm predominant in the world market – which leads unavoidably to a growing
internationalization of the class struggle. Hard material reality will teach the
international working class that retreating toward purely national defensive
strategies (exemplified by protectionism) leaves all the advantages to capital
and increasingly paralyzes even the defence of a given standard of living and
of political rights. The only efficient answer to an internationalization of
capital's strength and manoeuvres is international coordination, solidarity
and organization of the working class.

During the last decades, the objective need for world revolution as a unity
of the three world sectors of revolution has received a new and frightening
dimension through the growth of the destructive potential of contemporary
technological and economic trends, resulting from the survival of capitalism
beyond the period of its historical legitimacy. The accumulation of huge
arsenals of nuclear and chemical weapons; the extension of nuclear power;
the destruction of tropical forests; the pollution of air and water the world
over; the destruction of the ozone layer; the desertification of large tracts of
Africa; the growing famine in the Third World: all these trends threaten disasters which put a question mark on the physical survival of human-kind. None
of these disasters can be stopped or prevented at national or ever continental
level. They all call for solutions on a worldwide scale. The consciousness
about the global nature of humanity's crisis and the need for global solutions,
largely overlapping nation-states, has been rapidly growing.

Mikhael Gorbachev and his main advisers and intellectual supporters tend
to draw from a correct perception of the globalization of problems and
of the absolute necessity to prevent a nuclear war the conclusion that
progressively, these global problems will be solved through an increased
collaboration between imperialist and 'socialist' states. They base themselves
on two assumptions in that regard. First they believe that a course towards
world revolution would exacerbate inter-state relations to the point where
the outbreak of a world war would become more likely, if not unavoidable.
Second, they tacitly presume that the inner contradictions of capitalism will
tend to decrease, that the real class struggle will become less explosive, that
trends towards increased class collaboration will prevail in the 21st century.
Both these assumptions are utterly unrealistic. They are of the same type as

the hope to achieve the building of a really socialist society in a single country, of which they represent in a certain sense the logical continuation.

The fact is that while victorious or even unfolding revolutions have undoubtedly led to counter-revolutionary interventions by imperialist powers, they have on several occasions prevented larger wars from occurring. Without the German revolution of 1918–1919, and the revolutionary general strike in that country in 1920, the preparations for a general strike in Britain that same year, a major war of all imperialist powers against Soviet Russia would probably have occurred. Without the victory of the October revolution, the first World War would probably have been prolonged at least for one if not for more years. The revolutionary upsurge in Spain, France and Czechoslovakia in 1936 significantly slowed down the march toward World War II. If it would have been victorious even only in Spain, not to say in France and Czechoslovakia as well, World War II could have been prevented. So to identify revolutions with unavoidable war is just a misreading of the historical record. In fact, a victorious revolution in France and Britain to-day, not to say in the USA, would be the surest way to make world war impossible.

The real reasoning of the neo-reformist Gorbachev version of 'globalization' is based on the classical reformist illusion of a decline in the explosiveness and intensity of the inner contradictions of capitalism and of bourgeois society. We have already dealt with the unrealistic character of that assumption. It errs especially by not taking into account the structural link between the destructive uses of technology and economic resources on the one hand, and competitive attitudes, competitive strife, private property and market economy on the other hand. Bourgeois society can never lead and will never lead towards a world without weapons and without technological innovations applied regardless of their costs to the natural and human ecology. You need socialism to achieve these goals. And you have to achieve these goals if humanity is to survive. The strongest justification for world revolution to-day is that humankind is literally faced with the long-term dilemma: either a World Socialist Federation or Death.

NOTES

1. Precisely because the marxist concept of revolution encompasses the necessary dimension of mass action, the concept of 'revolution from above' is not strictly accurate, although it was used by Engels and has, of course, a well circumscribed significance. Joseph II's reforms in Austria; Tsar Alexander II's abolition of serfdom; Bismarck's unification of Germany; the Meiji 'revolution' in Japan, were historical attempts to pre-empt revolutions from below through radical reforms from above. To what extent they were successful or failed in that historical purpose must be analyzed in each specific case. The same applies *mutatis mutandis* to Gorbachev's reform course in the Soviet Union today.
2. This was the epigramme of the weekly *Révolutions de Paris*, which started to appear from the end of August 1789 in Paris.
3. See Barrington Moore Jr., *The Social Bases of Obedience and Revolt*, M.E.

Sharpe, White Plains, N.Y., 1978.

4. This was the case during the days preceding the downfall of the Shah in the streets of Teheran, a spectacle largely forgotten because of the subsequent developments in that country.

5. This does not automatically flow from the disintegration and disarmament of the former army. The ruling class can make an attempt to substitute a new bourgeois army to the old one, as it did in Cuba after the downfall of Batista and in Nicaragua after the fall of Somoza, but without success.

6. This is the currently prevailing explanation of the reasons for the Shah's downfall: the combination of the 'white revolution' destabilizing traditional Iranian society and the savagery of SAVAK.

7. In Russia, the cause of the February – March 1917 revolution was the rottenness of tsarism and the tremendous parasitical weight of the peasants' exploitation upon the overall economic development of the country. The triggering factors of that revolution were hunger riots of the Petrograd women workers which the *cossacks* refused to repress. This expressed the emergence of a *de facto* alliance between the working class and the peasantry, contrary to what had occured in the repression of the 1905 revolution. There is, however, also a deeper dialectical mediation between structure and conjuncture. The specific social-political order in Tsarist Russia determined both its participation in the first world war, and its increasing incapacity to cope with the material and political prerequisites of successful warfare. This incapacity in turn deepened the social crisis in a dramatic way – leading to chronic food shortages, to hunger riots and hence to the decisive days of outbreak of the February – March 1917 revolution. A similarly multi-layered analysis is needed to understand contemporary revolutionary moments – including unsuccessful ones, such as May 1968 in France. What went on in France during the climax of the mass upsurge and the general strike deserves to be seen as a revolution, although it was defeated. And the triggering factor of the student revolt in Paris must itself be seen in the context of a deeper structural crisis of social and political relations. Useful here is the remarkable study by the Soviet sociologist, Alex D. Khlopin, *New Social Movements in the West: Their causes and prospects of developments*, which complements Western marxist analyses.

8. In Russia, the material interests of the *cossacks* as sons of peasants, the connections of these interests to political awareness on the one hand, and to the explosive crisis of the relations of production in the countryside on the other hand, all converge to explain the *cossacks'* peculiar shift in behaviour, at a given moment, in a given place.

9. It is, of course, possible that this breakdown is only temporary and only lasts some weeks or months. But this doesn't make the collapse less real. In Germany – not only, but of course especially in Berlin – this is what occurred in November – December 1918. In France, this is what occurred at the climax of May 1968. Indeed, it was recently confirmed that, at that moment, General de Gaulle couldn't phone General Massu, the commander of the French army in Germany: he had lost control of the whole telecommunication system in Paris as a result of an effective general strike. An anonymous woman telephone operator whom he finally succeeded in speaking to personally, refused to obey his order. The decision of the strike committee prevailed. These are the unknown heroines and heroes of revolution. This is the stuff proletarian revolutions are made of.

10. See Edward Luttwack, *Technique of the Coup D'Etat* (1968); cf. interview with *Stampa-Sera*, August 8, 1988.

11. Nevertheless Spinoza, who was himself sceptical about the outcome of revolutions, explicitly proclaimed the people's right to revolution, more than a century before that same right was ensconced in the Preamble of the American Declaration of

Independence first, in the French Declaration the Rights of Men and Citizens afterwards. To our knowledge, the Yugoslav Constitution is today the only one which not only contains explicitly that right, but even adds to it *the duty* to make a revolution under specific conditions.

12. The dogma of the basic 'evil' of humankind is based in the West on the super-stition of Original Sin. Of late, it has received a pseudo-scientific veneer with the Konrad Lorenz school of the alleged universal agressivity of human beings, which some psychologists then tend to generalize into a human trend towards self-destruction. Better psychologists, in the first place Sigmund Freud, pointed out that the human psyche combines both a trend towards cooperation and a trend towards self-destruction, Eros and Thanatos, to love and to kill. If only the second one would have prevailed, humankind would have disappeared a long time ago instead of showing an impressive demographic-biological expansion.

13. Two thousand years ago, the Jewish philosopher Hillel expressed the contradic-tions of individual scepticism in a succint way: 'If I am not for myself, who is for me? And if I am for myself alone, what then am I? And if not now, then when?' Kant tried to escape that dilemma through his categorical imperative, but failed to apply it convincingly to social conflicts (see his attitude towards the French revolution). Marx found the solution in his categorical imperative to struggle against all social conditions in which human beings are debased, oppressed, and alienated.

14. Revolutionary continuity was maintained by a handful of followers of Babeuf who, through the person of Buonarotti, helped to inspire Auguste Blanqui's *Société des Saisons,* which gave rise to a new revolutionary organization in the 1830s. But for nearly forty years, there were very few organized revolutionaries in the country which witnessed five revolutions in the course of a century.

15. The debate goes on, of course. René Sédillot (*Le coût de la révolution française,* Paris, Perrin, 1987) is the most brazen of the latter-day dragon-killers, who continue the good fight against the French revolution after two centuries. The sophisms on which he bases his argumentation are revealed by the fact that he adds the victims of counter-revolution, in the first place of the Napolean's wars, to the costs of the revolution. But he does not compare these 'costs' to those of the Ancien Régime's dynastic wars: the devastation of a quarter of Germany, the big famine in France at the beginning of the 18th century, etc.

16. The inclusion of Deng Hsiao-ping in this list is of course open to serious challenge. Mao was not Lenin; he was rather a unique combination of given traits of both Lenin and Stalin. Hence, Deng Hsiao-ping, in spite of many right-wing tendencies in his policies, cannot be considered the Thermidorian equivalent of Stalin of the Chinese revolution.

17. Incidentally, this is one of the objective bases for the second 'law of permanent revolution' formulated by Trotsky. For the revolutionary process to continue after it starts to recede in a given country, its centre of gravity must shift to another one.

18. Classical examples of defeated counter-revolutionary *coups* are the Kornilov one in Russia August 1917, the Kapp-von Luttwitz *putsch* in Germany 1920 and the Spanish military-fascist uprising in July 1936 in Catalonia, Madrid, Valencia, Malaga, the Basque country, etc.

19. A democratic counter-revolution is a counter-revolution which seeks to maintains essential features of bourgeois democracy, including a legal mass labour move-ment, universal franchise and a broadly free press, after having beaten back the workers' attempts to conquer power and to arm themselves. Of course, while engaged in suppressing the German revolution, Ebert, Noske and Co. system-atically curtailed democratic freedoms, forbade political parties, suspended news-papers, requisitioned strikers and even outlawed strikes, to preserve the bourgeois

state. Moreover, Ebert cynically lied before the All-German Congress of Workers and Soldiers' Councils (December 1918) when he denied having brought soldiers to Berlin for repressive purposes. He had actually done so, in direct connection with the Imperial Army's High Command, behind the back of his fellow 'people's commissars' (ministers) of the Independent Socialist Party. The repression started a few days later.

20. This occurred in Germany throughout the country starting with January 1919 in Berlin. It occurred in Barcelona after the May days in 1937, in Greece starting with December 1944, in Indonesia in 1965, just to quote some examples. Courageous left socialists like the prewar Austrian social-democrats and Salvador Allende in Chile did not refuse to fight counter-revolution arms in hand, but they refused to organize and prepare the masses systematically for this unavoidable showdown and deliberately left the initiative to the enemy, which meant courting disaster.

21. Revolutionists cannot 'cause revolutions', nor can they 'provoke' them artificially (this is the basic difference between a revolution and a *putsch*). Engels even went further and stated: 'Die Leute die sich ruhmen, eine Revolution *gemacht* zu haben, haben immer noch am Tage darauf gesehen, dass sie nicht wussten was sie taten, dass die 'gemachte' Revolution, jener die sie hatten machen wollen, durchaus nicht ähnlich sah' (letter to Verra Sassulitch of April 23, 1885, MEW, Band 36, p. 307).

22. The concept of 'combined revolution' is also applicable to some imperialist countries, but with a different ponderation of the combined elements from that of third world countries. E.g. the combination of proletarian revolution and self-determination of oppressed national minorities in Spain; the combination of proletarian revolution and black and hispanic liberation in the USA.

23. E.g. in Finland 1917–18; in Austria 1918–19, 1927, 1934; in Germany 1918–23; in Italy 1919–20, 1944–45, 1969; in Spain 1931–37; in France 1936, 1968; in Portugal 1974–75.

24. Some argue that the impossibility of escaping 'technology compulsion' *(technologischer Sachzwang)* constitutes today an unsurpassable obstacle on the road to proletarian revolution and 'Marxian socialism'. This is an unproven assumption, based upon the *petitio principii* that technology somehow develops and is applied independently from the social interests of those who have the means (under large-scale commodity production: the capital) to apply it.

25. See Eduard Bernstein: *Die Voraussetzungen des Sozialismus und die Aufgaben der Sozialdemokratie* (1899).

26. On Kautsky's evolutions away from revolutionary marxism in 1909–1910, its turning point (his capitulation to the *Parteivorstand* on the censorship that body applied to his booklet *The Road to Power*) and its political outcome in his opposition to Rosa Luxemburg's campaign in favour of political mass strikes, see Massimo Salvadori, *Karl Kautsky and the Socialist Revolution*, NBL, London, 1979 pp. 123 ff.

27. Karl Kautsky, *Les Trois Sources du Marxisme* (1907), éd. française, Spartacus, Paris 1969, pp. 12–13.

28. Kautsky's articles on ultra-imperialism in which he considered inter-imperialist wars more and more unlikely, started to appear from 1912 on. The final one had the unfortunate fate of appearing in *Die Neue Zeit* on the aftermath of the actual outbreak of World War I.

29. We have developed this idea further in our article 'The reasons for founding the Fourth International and why they remain valid today', *International Marxist Review*, Summer–autumn, 1988.

30. Ernest Mandel, *Revolutionary Marxism To-day*, New Left Books, London, 1979.

31. The case of the German workers' answer to the Kapp-Lüttwitz *coup* of 1920 and of

the Spanish workers' answer to the fascist-military uprising of July 1936–in a more limited way also the Italian workers' uprising of 1948–helps to integrate into this typology the question of the proletariat's capacity to answer massively counter-revolutionary initiatives of the bourgeoisie. This will remain on the agenda in the West in the future as it was in the past. But this does not justify any refusal to recognize that the process of proletarian revolutions likely to occur in the West and in Japan will most probably be quite different from these particular examples, as well as from the revolutionary processes which we witnessed in Yugoslavia, China, Indochina, Cuba, Nicaragua during and after World War II.

32. See Norman Geras, *The Legacy of Rosa Luxemburg,* (New Left Books, London, 1976) on this, and on Rosa being one of the founders, together with Trotsky, of a theory of dual power emerging from workers' mass strikes.

33. Trotsky, *Was Nun? Schicksallfragen des deutschen Proletariat,* January 1932.

34. Leon Trotsky first formulated that conclusion in 1933 in his article 'The Class Nature of the Soviet State' (October 1, 1933) *Writings of Leon Trotsky 1933–34,* p. 101 f.

35. On the question how far that characterization is legitimate, see Ernest Mandel, *Beyond Perestroika,* Verso, London 1988.

36. On the theoretical foundations of the definition of 'political revolution' and the analysis which leads to it, see Ernest Mandel, 'Bureaucratie et production marchande,' *Quatrieme Internationale,* No. 24, April 1987.

37. *The New York Review of Books,* October 27, 1988.

38. The Mexican sociologist Pablo Gonzales Casanova has tried to refute the legitimacy of the political revolution in the bureaucratized workers states on the basis of a hierarchy of revolutionary tasks on a world scale. As long as imperialism survives, revolutionists (socialists, anti-imperialists) everywhere in the world should give priority to the fight against that monster over and above all other struggles. (see his 'La Penetracion metafisica en el Marxismo europeo', in *isabado,* supplemento de Unomasuno, 8/1/1983). Underlying that reasoning is the hypothesis that an ongoing, not to say a victorious, political revolution in a bureaucratised workers' state somehow weakens the fight against imperialism. But that supposition is completely unfounded, for the reason we have advanced.

OUR MORALS
THE ETHICS OF REVOLUTION

Norman Geras

There were two 'Reigns of Terror', if we would but remember it and consider it; the one
wrought murder in hot passion, the other in heartless cold blood; the one lasted mere months,
the other had lasted a thousand years.

Mark Twain

The restraint of war is the beginning of peace.

Michael Walzer

In this essay I shall be concerned with what can be termed, broadly, the
ethics of revolution. I consider by what normative principles socialists might
be guided, whether in judgement or in action, when it comes to revolutionary
change. A comprehensive treatment of the issue would require more space
than I have here. It would involve not only a theory – be it of needs or of
rights or of justice – for the comparative assessment of social and political
institutions, a large enough desideratum, evidently, in itself; but also, with
it, the resolution of some deep questions in moral philosophy. I shall have
some things to say about all this. But I cannot deal with it, so to speak,
from the bottom up. In much, I have to proceed instead assertively, relying
where I can on the advocacy of others, or on the belief simply that a needed
argument could be supplied. The procedure allows me to use what space I
have for concentration upon a narrower purpose.

Roughly indicated, this is to argue that socialist discussion of revolutionary
ethics (or such of it as is known to me), and the discussion in particular of ends
and means, tends to be framed in abstract generalities of a sort which yields
neither specific rules or norms of conduct nor much practical guidance for
concrete cases; and to suggest that there is a lot to be learned here, by way
of trying to repair the deficiency, from another tradition of discourse altogether. The obvious relevance of this other tradition to the moral problems
of revolution makes it the more surprising that socialists have drawn so little
upon it.

I shall use the term 'revolution' as encompassing at once a standard Marxist
and a more limited meaning. That is, I intend by it the overthrow or very
radical transformation, within a relatively brief period, of the basic economic

185

and social relations of a society; or of its governing political institutions; or both. The definition is made to cover what are called political, as well as what are called social revolutions. So understood, revolutions need not involve the use of violence. But the problems to be discussed here arise from the fact that they generally do. By 'violence' I shall mean roughly the exercise of physical force so as to kill or injure, inflict direct harm or pain on, human beings. This is in one way narrower, in another broader, than alternative definitions. It is narrower by excluding damage to property; broader because it includes not just that killing, injuring and so on, which is illegal and/or presumed illegitimate, but all such action irrespective of the ends to which it is directed. Whatever may be said in other respects for competing definitions, the one chosen permits a focus on what is most contentious under the rubric of revolutionary means and without foreclosing the moral questions involved.[1]

My discussion is premised on the rejection of two attitudes. One of these is that the use of violence is never justified. The other is that, with regard to political or to revolutionary political violence, no question of justification arises. About the first attitude, I will only say that where it is genuine, held scrupulously, consistently, on pacifist-type grounds, it is a doctrine that would deprive people of all weapons save passive resistance in the face of any oppression or threat, however terrible. If that is not a sufficient case against it, I am unsure what could be. As to the second attitude, this can rest upon a certain kind of Marxist notion about the inevitability or 'immanence' of the ends and the means of socialism; or upon a would-be political realism such as goes back as far at least as Machiavelli. The politicians or soldiers, militants or supporters, of any revolution, it may be said on one or the other basis, will do what they must. All talk of justification, of norms of conduct or ethical appraisal in this area, is idle chatter. No treatment of the ethics of revolution would be serious, in my view, that did not give due weight to considerations of historical realism and to the operation of social determinants and constraints. But these never fully close down the space of political choice and individual decision. To that, moral as well as other standards of judgement are relevant.

I

I begin by providing some necessary context for the problem I wish to address. First, then, people may legitimately revolt against what used commonly to be known as tyranny and is now often termed political oppression. 'The tyranny of established governments,' as it has recently been put, 'gives rise to a right of revolution, held individually by each subject or citizen, rightly exercised by any group of them, of which they cannot be deprived.'[2] This is not a novel nor a specifically socialist thought. It was propounded by, among others, John Locke; who, to the anticipated line of criticism that it was 'destructive to the peace of the world', replied: 'they may as well say, upon the same ground, that honest men may not oppose robbers or pirates, because this may occasion disorder or bloodshed.' The analogy suggests both a notion of revolution as a defensive act and the basis on which it is held to be so and to be therefore justified (when it is). This is the basis – expressed also in the contemporary formulation just cited – of a concept of fundamental rights. As Locke immediately goes on to add regarding robbers and pirates, 'If any mischief come in such cases, it is not to be charged upon him who defends his own right.'[3] Moral justification for revolutionary violence against tyranny, however, does not have to rest on this basis. It can rest equally on a reckoning up of consequences, on the estimate that the costs in suffering of having to endure arbitrary or oppressive authority are greater than those of destroying it.[4] Irrespective of whether argument about these things is best made by formal appeal to a doctrine of rights, or by such consequentialist judgements, or by some combination of the two, I shall allow myself to speak loosely of a 'right' of revolution wherever revolutionary methods are justified – as they are in the case of tyranny.

Second, there is a right of revolution against grave social injustice: if the basic social relations of any order of society involve that, then a struggle for their expeditious transformation is legitimate. This entails that there is a right of revolution against any *state* which is a bastion against such effort to remove serious, systemic injustice. It entails it but is not equivalent to it. For, conceivably, the state itself might be able to be the instrument of revolutionary transformation. In other terms: where there is a right of social revolution on account of grave injustice there is not necessarily a right of political revolution; but there is one when the state is or becomes a bastion of that injustice.

Many people who call themselves socialists think capitalist societies are marked by grave injustice, and many of these many think also that some of it is systemic rather than incidental injustice. If we are right to think this, those of us who do, then the right of revolution against grave injustice yields a right of revolution against capitalism. Even so, the existence within some capitalist societies of institutions of parliamentary democracy, and of those other legal and civil institutions and norms now typically associated with it, leads to some familiar disagreements about what forms such a revolution might and should take in the societies in question. If, or where, parliamentary-democratic capitalist states are not – or are not necessarily – bastions of capitalist injustice but, as democracies, the possible vehicles of a social revolution against it, there is no need for political revolution and there is no justification for it. But if, on the other hand, even parliamentary-democratic capitalist states, as capitalist states, are such bastions, there is one.[5] I will return to this matter later. It suffices for my main purpose to say that there is a right of revolution against any bastions of capitalist injustice that there are, for there are some.

Note that in resting this right on grave injustice I do not ground it on any claim, such as is sometimes made in this sort of context, that all injustice is itself a kind of violence. Though backed by the threat and periodic use, now more, now less frequent, of violence, there are forms of injustice distinct from it. To put this differently, there are other evils in the world than violence. To argue that (some) violence is justified in a struggle against them, one has no need to extend its core meaning, as given above, to embrace them all. There are here, as Ted Honderich has written, '*two* orders of fact, each of them compelling, each of them terrible'.[6] That order of fact I am calling grave injustice may be formulated, as with tyranny, in terms of a notion of fundamental rights; or in terms of basic needs; or of exploitation; or of equality; or, as is in fact most usual owing to conceptual interdependencies here, of some combination of these. Once more, I set this aside. Capitalist societies, though there are great differences between them, ones that really matter, are gravely unjust on any of these criteria.

There is a right of revolution against tyranny and against any bastion of grave social injustice, including capitalist forms of it. Surveying the contemporary world for examples of these things, we are, unhappily, spoilt for choice. But an example that may be expected to carry the maximum possible number of readers along with the argument that revolution is sometimes justified is South Africa.

Now, what is morally permissible in the pursuit of a just revolutionary struggle? (By a 'just' revolutionary struggle I mean one to which there is a right, in my loose sense, however that right is founded as regards bedrock ethical theory.) What can be done, and what if anything may not be done? Are there limits to the means that may be used, and what, if so, are they? What are the broad principles by which we might try to decide them?

I dispose in short order of one kind of answer to these questions. This is that in any such struggle the means must be prefigurative of the ends in view. Setting aside some problems about its precise meaning – for what does a quantity of timber prefigure: a scaffold or a barn? and what the laying down of weapons: a return of peace? or impending massacre? – one may concede a value to some such rough idea. If we can exemplify, can display, our good ends in the good ways and means we use to achieve them, so much the better. But in the present context means cannot in general only reflect the ends in view, because they will also reflect their own beginnings, so to put it. They are doubly determined: not only by what they are intended to achieve, the putative goal, but by that situation which is their starting point as well. It is in the nature of the problem under discussion – of revolution – that this starting point has ugly features, including the mobilization of violence on its behalf. How could the means of opposing it not reflect some of that ugliness, how, even in trying to prefigure a better future, avoid being scarred by an awful past? Shooting at the direct agents of a hated tyranny is still killing people; it is a state of war and, as such, not 'prefigurative' of human harmony or even of reasonably tolerable social order, though it may be necessary in order to achieve that. To point this out is just to insist on an indispensable minimum of realism. All the same, it may then be said, revolutionary means must at least prefigure their intended ends to some, large extent. But to what extent? Which non-prefigurative means, if one is going to speak in this way, may, and which if any may not be used in a just revolutionary struggle? The notion of prefiguration gives no determinate answer to our question, merely another (and in my view unhelpful) language in which to formulate it.[7]

Let us see, then, if there is guidance to be had from what is perhaps the dominant form of argument in socialist discussions of revolution, and in the literature on justifications for political violence more generally. I refer to argument of a consequentialist kind concerning the costs and benefits of projected or anticipated violence relative to those of a continuation of the *status quo*. In the words of one writer, we can make 'rough consequentialist calculations' in the following spirit: 'revolutionary violence is only justified when, of the alternatives available, it will, everything considered, make for less misery and human degradation all around.' The common idea he so expresses is of what Barrington Moore has called a 'calculus of suffering'.[8] It should be noted, however, that consequentialist judgement in this connection does not have to rest, as these formulations suggest it at least might, on some form of philosophical utilitarianism. It need not be unified by reliance on the single measure of suffering/happiness. It could take a more pluralistic form, with the use of a number of indices (happiness/welfare *and*, say, freedom, or equality) not thought reducible one to another.[9] There is even possible here what I shall term a consequentialism of rights: that is to say, a view that there are basic rights, worth fighting for when infringed, but under a restriction of 'proportionality'; such as would oblige one to compare violations of rights likely to result from the fighting with 'those it intends to rectify.'[10]

Assume, anyway, that the sort of rough calculation envisaged points to a revolutionary struggle being justified. Then at least theoretically, two kinds of limit on the choice of means would seem to be derivable from these forms of reasoning, a qualitative and a quantitative one. It is not the case that anything whatsoever could be shown to be – though, of course, anything could be said to be – legitimate in a just revolutionary cause on the basis of consequentialist reasoning. For, first, the means chosen must be apt. They must be efficacious means (by which I do not mean they must be guaranteed of success, merely able in principle to achieve the projected end; every revolution runs some significant risk of defeat). As the point was put by Trotsky in a well-known discussion of these issues: 'That is permissible. . . which *really* leads to the liberation of mankind,' and 'Precisely from this it flows that *not* all means are permissible.'[11] Not anything, in other words, could work. Second, it is in the nature of the approach we are presently considering that from a range of alternative means all judged to be efficacious in principle, those that are least costly, by the indices of cost thought to matter, must be chosen. This would presumably exclude unnecessary or excessive violence: that is, all violence surplus to what is needed to win the struggle, even if such surplus violence would leave a balance in favour of revolution in the overall calculation. We have, then, a requirement of efficacy, with the attached proviso of minimum necessary force. If we now ask, however, what in particular is allowed and what ruled out by these two principles, or even what kinds of action or policy are permitted and excluded, the answer is far from clear. As Trotsky himself says in the same place: 'These criteria do not, of course, give a ready answer to the question as to what is permissible and what is not permissible in each separate case. . . Problems of revolutionary morality are fused with the problems of revolutionary strategy and tactics.'

But we must press the question, for we need more than this. That one's means should be efficacious and no more violent than necessary is, as a code of revolutionary ethics, a bit thin. So: what in particular, what in the way specifically of violence and its various forms, might be excluded by the two principles? Within the broad consequentialist framework we are exploring, there are in fact, if no precise answers here, at least responses in contrasting spirit. One of them is Trotsky's own: namely, that not very much can be excluded. Another is that some things – surely – must be. As to the first, Trotsky is quite forthright about it: 'the warring classes will seek to gain victory *by every means*.'[12] We may take it he does not intend by this to contradict his own emphatic statement that not all means are allowed; that he intends only, that beyond the requirement of their being efficacious for the end of liberation, the means of revolution cannot be further morally constrained. He is, at any rate, consistent in using formulations to the effect that the revolutionary class struggle is, or is always likely to become, a form of total war in which conventional moral limits go by the board. Thus he writes, 'The highest form of the class struggle is civil war which explodes into mid-air all moral ties between the hostile classes'; and 'To attempt to subordinate it to abstract "norms" means in fact to disarm the workers in the face of an enemy armed to the teeth.' The workers, Trotsky says further, must be free from the 'fiction' of 'transcendental morality.' His view, it will be evident, is harmonious with a famous formula of Lenin's about the dictatorship of the proletariat: 'The revolutionary dictatorship of the proletariat is rule won and maintained by the use of violence by the proletariat against the bourgeoisie, rule that is unrestricted by any laws.'[13]

In other socialist writing there has been a different inflection: even from within the overall consequentialist approach, a concern to uphold at least some general moral prohibitions. What is most illuminating about it, however, is the ambiguity of the terms in which it is typically expressed. Herbert Marcuse, for example, defending the rationality of historical judgement concerning the likely all-round effects of any revolution for human freedom and happiness, insists nevertheless on the unimpaired validity of certain 'general norms'. No matter how rationally one might justify revolutionary means by such historical reckoning, he says, 'there are forms of violence and suppression which no revolutionary situation can justify because they negate the very end for which the revolution is a means.' He mentions specifically in this connection 'cruelty, and indiscriminate terror'. Anthony Arblaster argues similarly. He affirms, following Trotsky, that the principle of efficacy (that the means chosen must 'really' be means to the end in view) will disqualify some putative means; and equally that this does not take us very far as a guide to action. Still, there are means, he holds, that so 'contradict' the ends of liberation that they must be ruled out for the Left. He mentions specifically 'cruelty or torture'.

The question here is what precisely the point is of saying that means such as these 'negate' or 'contradict' the given end. Is it that they could not contribute to its achievement? Or that they are 'never justified, however admirable the end they may actually advance'?[14] Are they disqualified because they could not work? Or even if they could? If the first, then we do not have a separate consideration from that of efficacy. We have no restriction upon the exercise of consequentialist calculation. One is bound to ask, therefore, why just these means – cruelty, terror, torture – are picked out by name for exclusion. Why could they not simply be reckoned up with everything else? If they were never efficacious in a just cause, that would ensure their exclusion. One gets the strong sense here of a worry lest this kind of reckoning should sometimes yield the wrong result, lest these means might turn out in some circumstances to be efficacious even in a just cause; and of an impulse, consequently, to put them beyond calculation. So they should be put. But placed as we are in this case before the second of the two possibilities, that these means are to be disqualified, then, irrespective of considerations of efficacy, we are bound to pose another question. Why should consequentialist calculation stop precisely here and not earlier or elsewhere, with other forms of violence? Why are just these the limits? If it is said, because the means in question are especially horrible, indeed they are. But neither of the writers whose views we are considering would be – or have been – willing to say that those forms of violence justifiable within a legitimate revolutionary struggle, killing, for example, or maiming by trying but failing to kill, are not horrible at all. So, by what criteria are we to say when horrible means have become too horrible to countenance?

There is insufficient determinacy in the positions we have had before us up to now. They give us only the most general of notions, whether about efficacy and the weighing of consequences or about some hypothetical but unexplained limits to this. General notions, to be sure, are better than nothing. But if they are too general to yield any more precise guidance, they may well come to nothing under the pressures of revolutionary conflict. Trotsky's approach states clearly one of the logics of a just revolutionary struggle: the moral importance of winning. What matters is what will succeed, and the indeterminacy lies in it being hard to say in the abstract what will. The other approach states another logic, that there must surely be moral limits of some kind to what could be justified, even in order to win. But it states it unclearly;

its indeterminacy lies in the difficulty of defining where such limits fall and why. Some effort of definition is, however, indispensable.

To appreciate more fully the need for it, one has only to reflect a moment on some typical circumstances of revolution. First, if it has indeed come to revolution, then an enormous amount is at stake. For, as not only Marx but also Locke pointed out, and contrary to a myth common with more vulgar forms of conservatism, revolutions are not easily stirred up.[15] Where it has come to a revolutionary struggle, the regime or order – the situation – against which this is directed is generally not just bad but terrible: whether in terms of basic rights, of misery and suffering, or other indices of human cost. And this is to say nothing about such further, often frightful, costs as may be imposed, in the event of a defeat, by the opponents of revolution. Second, and as nearly all theoretical reflection on political violence unites in emphasizing, against this backdrop there are also very large uncertainties. Which means will be efficacious and which not and which be counter-productive? What violence is necessary to the goals of revolution and what violence excessive? In general, how much confidence can there be in judgements about these matters made under great pressure? Two overarching questions may serve to organize the whole range here. Given what is likely to be at stake, can a revolutionary movement afford to forswear in advance the use of any means from which it might conceivably derive advantage? On the other hand, given the uncertainties, in what ways, and how far, may it legitimately by its actions put the lives or persons of others in jeopardy, how far contravene the general moral rules or norms which serve (when they do serve) to protect these?

The issues are extremely difficult. We need clearer lines. As one more way of bringing this into focus, the difficulty and the need alike, I want now to consider some arguments in Steven Lukes's recent, widely-noticed critique of the moral record of Marxism. The latter, according to Lukes, 'has from its beginning exhibited a certain approach to moral questions that has disabled it from offering moral resistance to measures taken in its name.' Having no satisfactory account of justice and rights; concerned, as a form of long-range consequentialism, with optimal outcomes rather than 'agent-centred restrictions'; morally blind, in the pursuit of large emancipatory goals, to the present interests of living persons; Marxism could not deal adequately with 'injustice, violations of rights. . . the resort to impermissible means'. It 'has never come properly to grips with the means-ends issue, and the problem of dirty hands.' I find much to quarrel with in the balance of Lukes's account but I shall pass over it, as some of the necessary critical points have already been well made by others. The problem of means and ends and ruthless solutions to it are not weaknesses special to Marxism, nor is subordinating the interests of living persons to a projected larger good or goal; they seem nicely distributed across the political spectrum. Many of the Marxist texts Lukes cites in support of his case evince a greater awareness of the complexity of these matters than he allows.[16] There is in the present context a more important thing to be pursued. Lukes makes a valid point, one which Marxists -- amongst others – ought to digest. But it is vitiated by the fact that he does not face up squarely either to the kind of background against which the questions here at issue arise or to the difficulty of proposing definite answers to them.

Marxist discussion of ends and means has been deficient; that is true. As was part of my purpose to illustrate in what has gone before, it has not produced an adequately determinate code of revolutionary ethics or conduct. It is also the case, as I go on to argue, that remedying this deficiency must mean giving weight to 'agent-centred restrictions': to individual rights. To the extent that Marxists have often been wary of or hostile to concepts of rights, they have not been well-placed to resolve these issues satisfactorily. Lukes's book valuably draws attention to this. The difficulty it fails to address is that of how far the oppressed are morally obliged to respect the rights of their oppressors. May slaves not kill their masters or overseers, or wound them in attempting to escape? May they tear them limb from limb? Or only seek to overpower them? Or what? There are rights – to life, against personal violation, and so on – involved here. How far must the victims and opponents of an unjust or tyrannical regime respect the rights of its defenders, supporters, beneficiaries? There is not an unlimited range of answers to this sort of question. We may take it, from the whole spirit of Lukes's approach, that he would not say these rights should be set at naught. The gross alternatives remaining are, then, to treat them as absolute, inviolable in all circumstances, or to give them some weight. Again, I discount the first of these alternatives: it appears clear from much that Lukes says that to put forward a variety of socialist pacifism is not his intention. The rights, therefore, even of oppressors, even of the defenders, supporters, beneficiaries, of injustice or tyranny, are to be given some weight.

How much? Which rights, all or only some of them, and what sort of weight? A general emphasis upon individual rights is, I have already said, of value in this context. But as an answer to the real problems posed by revolution, it is, in *so* general, so indeterminate a form, not only not better than the kind of consequentialism Lukes criticizes, it may turn out in practice to be no different from it. For, if all we can say is that (some?) rights must be taken seriously or more seriously than a lot of Marxists have been disposed to take them, that they must be given some or even a lot of weight, they are thereby in effect just thrown in with all other considerations, thrown into some overall calculation or comparison or judgement. When very much is at stake, in situations of dire pressure, they may not then count for enough, the broad emphasis on their importance notwithstanding. The point may be made clearer by adverting once more to Trotsky's contention that revolution comes down to a form of war and as such cannot be constrained by general or transcendental moral norms. Now, actually, revolution is not always or at once generalized war. Still, the relation between it, civil war and wider warfare has been close enough historically to highlight the obvious point that revolutions typically involve the most intense conflicts; conflicts as must make at least some rights and what they protect forfeit. Set against this background, there is nothing whatever specifically Marxist about Trotsky's reasoning. On the contrary, as Michael Walzer has written in a work systematically critical of such reasoning: 'Either fight all-out or not at all. This argument is often said to be typical of American (!) thought, but in fact it is universal in the history of war.'

Trotsky's view has, I believe, to be rejected. But we are better placed to reject it if we recognize it for what it is, not some specially Marxist form of ruthlessness, but an argument about human warfare which politicians and generals of every stripe have been known to voice: that 'for the sake of the cause', 'for justice', because of 'the moral urgency of victory', one must fight without restraint.[17] And we are better placed to reject it if we recognize also that where rights and lives and life chances are in general jeopardy, whether owing to war or to revolution or to those circumstances that make revolution justifiable, there general affirmations of the importance of rights are insufficient, as insufficient as the plea for prefigurative forms of struggle; more precise discriminations are required. The second recognition follows close upon the first.

It is for the same reason as I find Lukes's argument insufficient that I am unhappy also with the conclusion drawn by Kate Soper in the otherwise pertinent criticisms of it to which I have already once made reference. She too finds the bare appeal to 'respect for the principle of individual rights' inadequate. But she goes on to conclude, in a way quite as indeterminate as Lukes's own, that 'no absolute rule applies'; that 'all situations requiring moral decision are concrete and have to be judged on their merits'; that to act morally is 'to act in the light of general rules', but sometimes also 'in contradiction with one or other' of them. As she says further:

> I am put in mind here of E. P. Thompson's recommendation that humanist attitudes should find expression 'whenever and to the degree that contingencies allow', and of his come-back to his exasperated critics: 'what else can one say? That they must always find expression irrespective of contingencies?' The argument seems clumsy, somehow unsatisfactory – yet in essence I think it is the right one. On the other hand, the morality it implies is not easy to formulate or render into a coherent whole, since it requires us to combine respect for the individual with an agreement to waive that respect in certain conditions.[18]

Whatever might be said about this as a general observation on the nature of moral choice, for the sort of circumstances to which we here must apply it I think it is, and not merely seems, unsatisfactory. 'To the degree that contingencies allow': that is not a happy formula for a socialist or revolutionary ethic. Nor is: agreement to waive respect for the individual 'in certain conditions'. It is all too easy to envisage either of them as a recipe for complete moral cynicism. Of course, this is not the spirit in which Soper intends them; the very opposite. Even so, neither formula is helpful. By their nature they do nothing at all to delimit the ways in which, or the extent to which, 'contingencies' and 'conditions' may be permitted to displace 'general rules'. If such rules do not themselves incorporate at least the more likely, the more easily foreseeable, conditions and contingencies, then they are no good.

We only need to think about how these formulations, as well as all the others earlier reviewed, might bear upon a concrete case, to be brought face to face with their limitations. The South African state today is for the large majority of those subject to it a vicious tyranny. It is a bastion of grave injustice if such there be. The black people of that country are deprived of the most elementary political rights, and the violence mobilized against them, well-documented, widely broadcast – sjambok–wielding police violence and then more deadly than that; an epidemic of torture; 'accidental' death in police custody; one of the highest rates of judicial execution in the world, its victims nearly all black; Latin American style 'disappearances', the kidnapping and murder of chosen individuals by freelance death squads with who knows what degree of connivance and participation by the 'security' services of the state – this violence stands between an entire people and its goal of a more just and happier condition. That a counter-violence of opposition to such a regime could not be justified, because political violence in general cannot ever be, is a view I have already rejected. Here then, in turn, are some of the kinds of thing that occurred in South Africa during 1985 and 1986, years of a great wave of black resistance and struggle, before these were set back by the imposition of a state of emergency in June of the latter year. Bombs were placed in or near police stations, in the offices of the South African Defence Force, in one case in a shopping centre; the explosions caused death and injury. Black policemen and town councillors were attacked and killed. So were suspected police informers and collabo-rators, and individuals buying from certain shops in violation of a campaign of economic boycott. Sometimes such people were attacked in their homes and members of their families harmed. Often they were killed in shockingly brutal ways. 'One particularly cruel form of killing, known as the necklace, is to put a burning tyre around the neck of a victim who then dies a slow and painful death.'[19]

Now, how could we discriminate, on the basis of what we have from this discussion so far, of the putative ethic of revolution any of it might be thought to define, as to the legitimacy or otherwise of these several actions? Even if, as I suspect is likely, it may be said here that it is not for *us* so to discriminate, because it is not our struggle – a view I shall in due course also reject – still, how then could the participants in that struggle, or the leaders of it, discrimi-nate? How much would it help anyone to be told that the means of struggle must 'really' be means to the liberation of the majority of South Africans, or must not too obviously 'negate' or 'contradict' that end, or must take some significant account of individual rights, or must respect these to the degree that 'contingencies' allow, or must only waive them 'in certain conditions'? In truth, it would help them precious little; for all that some of these arguments do have a value as very general guidelines. The socialist discussion of ends and means is wanting in specificity. We need to look elsewhere.

II

Where I shall suggest we need to look is by now perhaps obvious. It is to the theory and practice of war: more specifically, to just war doctrine and, via that, to some of the rules of actual warfare. I introduce the topic on a semi-personal note. My own reason initially for looking to this material, what I sought there, and what on the other hand I found, are two different things. For, what I sought in starting to think again in a general way about the ethics of revolution were the considerations typically adduced to legitimate war, the commonest grounds for war being qualified as 'just'. I sought them as a way of focusing on the weakness in political viewpoints – some kinds of contemporary liberalism, most kinds of conservatism – generally hostile to revolution, yet at the same time more than willing to countenance the moral necessity, in certain circumstances, of war. In the event, that turns out to be light work. If war is sometimes justified, then so too is revolution, the reasons given on their behalf being of a kind: self-defence, autonomy, rights and freedoms, the throwing off of an oppressor, and so forth. All of this falls under the heading, one side of a distinction which is central in the literature, of *jus ad bellum:* the justice *of* war. What I found, however, not in the sense of having been altogether unaware of it before, but in the sense of coming to realize here was matter germane to the problems of socialist ethics and yet not much brought to bear upon them – what I found was the other side of the same distinction, namely *jus in bello,* justice *in* war: a body of doctrine concerning the methods of legitimate warfare, whether or not in a just cause; rules applicable to both parties; the obligation to fight even against aggression within certain moral limits.[20]

The most striking feature of this literature and indeed domain, coming at it from the angle we here do, is the contrast between the relative poverty, the underdevelopment, of socialist principles for revolutionary conduct, and the wealth of the rules of war, the fullness and determinacy of *jus in bello.* The number, the detail and the complexity of these rules, and of the qualifications to them, do stand out in the comparison. There are rules about combatant and non-combatant status, about the wounded and those rendered helpless in combat, about giving quarter to surrendering soldiers. There are rules defining the rights and obligations of prisoners of war, and concerning warfare at sea, and about the conduct of sieges. There are rules defining rights of neutrality and rules about partisan warfare. There are prohibitions on certain kinds of weapons. And so on. Such a list is in fact but a poor indication of the extent of the contrast: on one side, only the vaguest of notions; on the other, a vast and detailed literature, not to speak of well-developed international codes and conventions.

Now, it may be said that all these rules are much violated in the course of real war and so they are. But the point is that there exist, nevertheless, definite rules and that they are observed often enough to be of value. It is not difficult, again, to speculate on some possible reasons for the contrast. Wars are fought in the main between states and though states clearly have an interest in breaking the rules of war, otherwise they would do less of this than they in fact do, there must be enough of a common interest among them in having codes of rules for these to have evolved to the point they have. Few states, however, if any, can have an interest in drawing up, much less in observing, a comparable code of rules to govern possible revolutionary struggles against them. Oppressive regimes, it may therefore also be said, will use – do use, across the globe – the most savage forms of violence in the counter-revolutionary cause: use terror, torture, massacre. But those are *their* crimes. They are their morals; they cannot be ours. Whatever the interests of any state may be, there are reasons why a socialist ethic of revolution must embody a precise code of moral limits and moral rules.

Within the multiplicity of rules that apply to the waging of war, two principal types are relevant in the present context. One of them concerns the category of persons at whom violence may be directed: those who are legitimate targets of attack, who may be killed. The other concerns the manner of attack: how or in what circumstances they may be killed.[21] I shall consider each type in turn with a view to its bearing upon our subject.

Rules of the first sort draw a distinction between combatants and non-combatants. Under the concept of non-combatant immunity, they delineate a large area – the many people – off limits to any violent attack. In the context of war, this distinction, very roughly, is between soldiers on the one hand, and 'innocent' civilians on the other. It is important, however, that the notion of innocence involved in it is a special one. It has nothing to do with judgements of moral culpability. The soldier may be a reluctant conscript and the civilian an avid supporter of the war, even contributing time and effort to sustaining or boosting a war-fighting morale. The point is only that soldiers constitute, have made themselves or been made by others into, a threat. As, literally, the warriors of one or other side, those directly making war and so putting lives and persons in jeopardy, they are legitimately subject to violence themselves. There is an analogy with a justified act of self-defence outside of war: one may use deadly force against somebody threatening one's life if that is the only possibility of escape, irrespective of the attacker's motives or moral character, of whether or not he or she was egged on by others, and so on. Also important here is the circumstance that, as with many such distinctions, where the line falls exactly may be a difficult matter, a matter of some contention; the crucial thing is that there is a line. As Dr. Johnson said, apparently: 'the fact of twilight does not mean you cannot tell day from night.' So, in modern war the category of combatant has been extended to include munitions workers (but only as engaged in, when at their place of, work). It does not, however, include workers processing soldiers' rations. Manufacturing their weaponry counts as a contribution to the threat, while making what they need simply as human beings does not.[22]

Applying this now to the case of a regime against which, on account of tyranny or injustice, there is a right of revolution, the distinction must be made between its direct agents of oppression and everybody else. Here again there are likely to be difficult and contentious borderline instances. But the boundary needs to be quite narrowly drawn which defines such a regime's combatants. They are its leaders, soldiers, police, security agents, jailers, torturers; in general, those warring on its behalf, those involved in imposing and enforcing oppressive laws.[23] That would include, as in the South African case, known police informers and collaborators (a matter to which I return), but would not, without more ado, include just every kind of state employee; teachers, say, or health workers. And it would not include, either, the civilian population at large, even such sectors of this as may be open supporters or beneficiaries of the regime in question. If it is said here that political supporters or economic beneficiaries of an oppressive regime are *ipso facto* the enemies of its victims and therefore legitimate targets of revolutionary violence, it may be noted simply, in anticipation of the argument I later make against this, that much the same could be said about the civilians of an enemy power in time of war – in order to justify massacring them. It is a line of thought, of justification and of action that certainly occurs in war, but one also, I presume, that would give most socialists pause.

In its struggle for the liberation of Guiné from colonial rule, the PAIGC made a distinction between 'the Portuguese people. . . Portuguese individuals or families' and 'Portuguese colonialism': it was fighting, it said, against the latter and not the former. In the South African context there are public statements also from the ANC to the effect that the targets of its armed struggle are police and military ones; not civilians.[24] These discriminations agree with a 'political code. . . roughly analogous to the laws of war', one less respected, according to Michael Walzer, in our own century than in the last.[25] But it is a code, in any case, which many of us – overtly or not, some of us perhaps only half-consciously – refer to or make use of in a rough and ready way in thinking about these matters, and whether we are fully aware or not of the military analogy. It is a better instrument for the assessment of putatively revolutionary means than the various formulae I began by reviewing. It enables us to say, for example, that setting bombs against military and police personnel or installations is, where there is a right of revolution, a legitimate means of it, while bombing supermarkets or shopping centres, restaurants and other such venues is not. To be precise here: doing this is not, or is not only, a 'mistake', tactically, politically. It is a moral wrong, a crime. So clearly, according to a principle of non-combatant immunity adapted to the revolutionary setting, are the taking and killing of innocent hostages; making targets of people because of their country of origin, or of the airline they are travelling with, or of their destination; or because they are bourgeois, or are captains of industry, or settlers, or members of a particular ethnic group. So, generally, is terrorism in the true sense: the use of more or less random violence against whole populations. It is clearer to say of this, of indiscriminate terror, that it is wrong because it is making war on people who are not themselves making war, than that it negates the ends of revolution.

Trotsky, in *Their Morals and Ours*, mocks the distinction I here uphold, for his part defending, with reference to Bolshevik policy during the Russian civil war, the practice of taking hostages. The arguments behind the mockery, however, blur two significant points. Civil war, he contends, as the most severe of all forms of war, 'is unthinkable not only without violence against tertiary figures but, under contemporary technique, without killing old men, old women and children.' The difference between shooting soldiers at the front and shooting hostages, between open battle and 'the seizure of non-participants', he dismisses as 'a wretched and stupid evasion': many participants are just duped or unwilling conscripts; the means of modern war inevitably kill thousands of non-participants; those taken as hostages 'are at least bound by ties of class and family solidarity with one of the camps, or with the leaders of that camp.'[26] The first thing wrong with these arguments has already been spoken of. Because many who fight are blameless, more or less, for the war in which they fight, the boundary around the legitimate targets of war is quickly – massively – relaxed: to take in very large numbers of people whose existence and activities are not directly menacing. Innocence in one sense legitimates the deliberate killing of innocents in another. Trotsky's point is made in connection specifically with the practice of hostage taking. The formula, however, 'ties of class and family solidarity', is one, imaginably, of even larger-scale horror. It is an awful one.

Secondly, under the heading of 'contemporary technique', Trotsky too easily elides the difference between deliberately killing or injuring non-combatants and doing so unintentionally, even if as an effect of one's intended ends. I have not the space adequately to examine the principle normally adduced here, namely that of 'double effect', nor such related notions as 'collateral damage'. They give us no easy solutions anyway; can be, and are often abused. All the same, there is a line, a difficult one once more, which Trotsky's way of speaking casually dissolves. The principle of double effect, briefly and incompletely stated, permits an act likely to have some evil consequences, provided that these evils are not part of one's ends, nor means to one's ends; and – on an interpretation of the principle which I am persuaded of – provided also that one seeks to minimize the likely evils or the risk of them, at some cost to oneself.[27] In war, bombing an important military target with the foreseeable side effect of limited civilian casualties (against some rather rough notion of proportionality), this is one thing;

bombing whole cities in order to kill and terrorize civilians and so break
their morale is another. So too, arguably, in the sphere of revolutionary
struggle, is bombing or burning the home of a police or other official, and
(members of) his or her family with it.

A sense of proportion will not come amiss as regards the nature of
Trotsky's argument and the policies it defends. I say this not in order back-
handedly to condone the view I have just criticized, merely as a necessary
point in these times about Marxism's place in the world. The argument and
the policies tell against Trotsky and the Bolsheviks – just as equally brutal
arguments and, in cost of lives, worse measures tell against such statesmen
of the liberal democracies as Winston Churchill and Harry Truman. There
is a hard matter here. But it is about politics and war much more than it is
about Marxism.[28]

I turn now to rules of the second kind: concerning legitimate modes of
attack; setting limits to how those who are properly targets in war may be
killed. The basis of these rules, it must be said, is rather less obvious. It
may even be the case that the particular prohibitions obtaining at any time
against this or that sort of weapon have no other foundation than the formal
conventions agreed amongst states. There is a principle, nevertheless, which
seems to inform at least some of them and which is of relevance and value
in the revolutionary setting. It can be expressed in one way as a notion of
minimum force: one's weapons must be capable of stopping enemy combatants, which in the given circumstances involves killing them; but they should
not, beyond this, seek gratuitously to accentuate suffering. The same thing
can be expressed another way, in a formulation I have adapted from Thomas
Nagel, by saying that the weapons should attack the combatant and not the
person. They should not, therefore, be 'designed to maim or disfigure or torture' him or her.[29] Here again I think we have a clearer reason for ruling out
'particularly cruel' weapons and, more generally, cruel methods of killing,
the deliberate infliction and aggravation of pain, as in torture, than if we say
that these contradict the ends of liberation. Just as only the combatants of the
other side may be attacked, because they are the ones making war on you, so
too they may be 'stopped', killed, because that puts an end to the threat they
have been to you or their contribution to it. Extreme and purposeful cruelty,
beyond what is necessarily involved in any act of killing or wounding, is wrong
because it is more than their activities can justify – as it were defensively on –
your own part. Unless, that is, it is allowed that the ethics of socialism may
embody, as a component, some fairly terrible theory of retributive punishment. I assume without argument here that they may not.

A slow, painful death by burning, consequently, lies beyond the limits
of what is morally defensible in the light of an ethic of just revolutionary
struggle. Likewise, killing an old woman by forcing her to drink the bottle
of detergent or cooking oil she has bought in defiance of a shop boycott. (I
leave aside the question of whether this defiance can be taken to make of her

an agent of oppression, as I think it cannot. For, there are, anyway, forms of community pressure appropriate to meeting the specific nature of the threat she represents, her challenge to a boycott. This contemptuous cruelty far exceeds them.)[30] *Jus ad bellum* is in itself no guarantee of *jus in bello*. The justice of the cause does not make good, cannot transmute, moral atrocities committed in its name. In the case of South Africa, here chosen to exemplify these issues precisely because of the overwhelming justice of the revolutionary cause, the briefest description of certain episodes of violence suffices to communicate a sense of something in them other than the legitimate concerns of a just revolutionary struggle.

> They chased her across the veld, they beat her, they stoned her, they tore her clothes off, they set her on fire, they put a huge rock on her so that she couldn't get up and they rammed a broken bottle into her vagina.

> As the family cowered in the house, they saw the eldest son, who ran for help grabbed by the mob and dismembered in the street. As the mob burst into the house, [he] shot his younger son in the head to save him from a similar fate.[31]

At this point I anticipate two types of counsel: one, of historical realism; the other, to speak not of what does not concern you. There is more to be said for the first but I address myself to both. In any historically, or sociologically – or just 'humanly' – informed perspective, there must be an acknowledgement of some limits to the proper reach of moral discourse itself. To let an extreme case illustrate this: if a group of slaves or of prisoners in a concentration camp should, having the opportunity, suddenly get the better of a vicious overseer or guard and brutally slaughter him, it would not be apt to say they had gone too far or to reflect critically on the notion of 'cruel or unusual' punishments. *In extremis,* moral judgement fails. More generally, the violence of oppressors tends to breed violence amongst those they oppress. Their brutalities are brutalizing. A political or social order that must be overthrown by revolution will have generated, not only amongst its defenders but also with some of its victims, impulses of moral criminality and murderousness. An altogether morally 'clean' revolutionary struggle is probably rare, therefore, if it is conceivable. Even so, two points need to be emphasized about this.

First, the plea of *in extremis* is just that. It cannot too quickly or easily accommodate every horror generated out of situations of conflict. A young, defenceless woman (subject of the first description above), merely rumoured to be a police agent and perhaps not one, is not a sadistic concentration camp guard. The *son* of a collaborating official (subject of the second description) is not a ruthless slave-driver. Second, even if the perspective of historical realism may make certain occurrences understandable, it does not make them right. It does not make them right, in particular, in the perspective, as important this one as the other, of revolutionary policy and morality. The leaders, the militants, of a movement against injustice are obliged for their part to try, so far as it is in their power, to bring a disciplined, scrupulous, discriminating, ethical code into the dark history they are fighting to transform. Where understanding, on the one hand, and moral discrimination, on the other – or historical explanation and political choice; or sociological realism and the responsibility of individuals and movements for what they do – where these two meet, come face to face, there is a difficult philosophical issue indeed. Except, however, for the most extreme of determinisms, the first cannot altogether relieve the second of its burdens.

Only the discipline and scruple, incidentally, self-imposed by a revolutionary movement in the light of a defensible code of ethical principles and constraints can serve to mitigate a problem just alluded to and which, as far as I can see, has no genuinely satisfactory solution. This is that, in the context of a just revolutionary struggle, some of those rightly to be regarded as the combatants of tyranny or injustice will not be identified, as others of them are, by uniforms, insignia and the like, and will take some care not to be identified at all. At the same time the possibilities of sound judicial methods for establishing that they are informers, collaborators, agents or what have you, are either limited or non-existent. The danger of individuals being wrongly accused and killed are great. These dangers will be the more severe, obviously, as will be the chances of people resorting to violence to settle a personal score or for some other repugnant motive, if it is the anger of more or less spontaneously formed crowds and not any procedures informed by care or principle that determine an individual's fate.

As for the other counsel, against making judgements from outside on the struggles of others, what can be conceded to it, it seems to me, is only that opinion in these circumstances should not be hasty, but considered. Taken strictly, however, it is an admonition that would have forbidden Western socialists in the 1930s from expressing any criticism of the crimes of Stalin; or, more recently, would have excluded adverse comment upon those of Pol Pot and the Khmer Rouge. It is not a counsel to be heeded. Reflection on the Stalinist example reveals its effective meaning. For, it was doubtless one consideration in persuading many Western communists and socialists to maintain an uncritical, apologetic, attitude to Stalinist policies and practices which they ought to have condemned. It is a counsel, in fact, to refrain not from judgement as such but only from critical judgement.

Let us make explicit, then, the normative basis of the foregoing argument for extending central notions in just war doctrine to the case of revolutionary struggle. This basis is a principle that individuals have rights – against being killed or violated – rights that may not, in general, be set aside; unless they forfeit them by making war themselves in defence of tyranny or grave injustice. Here, I shall simply ignore the rather large question of whether such rights are the proper axiomatic starting point for an adequate moral doctrine or whether they are, rather, to be derived from other premisses. I bypass this question in a vulgar, practical manner. They are important for us one way or another: as axiomatic values; or because socialists generally profess a respect for human life and well-being, and rights are a crucial way of embodying that respect, of giving it normative or regulative force against this or that exigency or passion of the moment. As the point was expressed by Victor Serge, a point, in his view, to 'take precedence before all tactical considerations':

Defence of man. Respect for man. Man must be given his rights, his security, his value. Without these, there is no Socialism. Without these all is false, bankrupt and spoiled. I mean: man whoever he is, be he the meanest of men – 'class-enemy', son or grandson of a bourgeois, I do not care. It must never be forgotten that a human being is a human being.[32]

This is a necessary sensibility, that must inform every genuine struggle against oppression or injustice. In the circumstances and under the pressures of revolution, as of war, it can only be made effective at all if the conditions in which, and the extent to which the relevant rights may be forfeit are spelled out within very tight limitation. This must mean in an 'individualized' way. Otherwise, the rights, as individual rights, are not worth a fig. Whatever problems there may be, for example, in setting boundaries around the category of 'combatant', the principle from just war theory that 'no one can be forced to fight or to risk [their] life, no one can be threatened with war or warred against' if they have not 'surrendered or lost [their] rights' through warring themselves,[33] is a better one not only than Trotsky's 'ties of class and family solidarity'; but also than this, sequel to the passage quoted earlier, from Kate Soper: 'if one is a socialist in outlook then one feels obliged to recognize that individuals not only have immediate personal rights and duties but are also answerable for the larger social consequences of their collective individual acts, and that consistent failure to act on the obligations incurred at the social level is legitimate ground for challenging their entitlement to respect for their personal rights.'[34] This is far too open-ended in range of possible application. It is unthinkable that it was so intended, but it would legitimate the most widespread violation of personal rights, which means violation of individuals and of lives. How many people are not guilty of failing in their social 'obligations', in Soper's sense, in a world that is rife with avoidable miseries, inequities and iniquities? It cannot be right virtually to erase the distinction, as this argument by implication does, between those actively warring to sustain oppression, and others less directly related to it: supporters and beneficiaries, passive accomplices or mere bystanders; people who, whatever their moral faults, guilts or evasions, have not – or at least have not yet – made themselves into a coercive barrier against realizing the legitimate rights of others. Unless, once more, it is allowed that the ethics of revolution may be about the punishment of sin, rather than about the removal of armed obstacles to liberation or justice. I assume they may not.

These individual rights constitute a limit upon consequentialist calculation.

They cannot be disregarded in favour of, traded off against a hypothesis or speculation of there being, some greater benefit derivable from such trade – even if this supposed benefit is itself computed in terms of rights. That exercise might be legitimate, were the successful issue of revolutionary struggle millennial in character, a time and condition in which all would finally be well. We are surely over, if we ever really entertained, that kind of illusion. Whatever benefits real revolutions in a just cause may bring, each one is always a particular, a limited, even if it is a very large, step forward; and is a step always into new difficulties, new problems and conflicts, unforeseen and unforeseeable consequences; into uncertainties. That is if they win. Sometimes they lose, or lose for the time being. Against this background, these features of real as opposed to millenial revolutions, no one's life or person may be simply discounted for what are by their nature uncertain, sometimes highly speculative, projections; no one who has not taken the path of war by aggressing on behalf of tyranny or injustice – and in that case even they retain their rights against inhumane cruelty.

The question will be raised at this juncture whether individual rights against being killed or violated are then, in every other circumstance, absolute. They are all but absolute. If this answer is deemed to be insufficiently precise, its superiority over the meaningful alternatives to it appears to me compelling.[35] One such alternative is to say that the rights are indeed absolute, inviolable everywhere save when forfeited by their holders in the manner described. The trouble with this is that it is always possible to envisage cases (one has to kill an innocent person to avert a massacre of hundreds; or to save the population of a city; etc.) for which it would be conceded by all but a few doctrinaire fanatics that the moral horror of the consequences has – tragically – to be allowed to override the rights of the innocent. Examples like that are much rarer in reality than they are in philosophical discussion but cannot be excluded unfortunately from the situations of extremity which compose wars and revolutions. On the other hand, we make the force of these rights too weak if we say (something like): they must be respected by and large, or must be respected except when there are important or urgent competing considerations. That would render them, for present purposes, nugatory. For, the situations we are talking about just are, *ex hypothesi,* ones full of urgency, full of competing considerations of the gravest kind. In order, therefore, to have the necessary force to constrain and limit what is done in a just revolutionary cause, the rights must be treated as all but absolute.

That is to say that they may be overridden if and only if doing so is the sole means of averting imminent and certain disaster. I repeat: the sole means; and disaster which is otherwise imminent and certain. This is a proviso of impending moral catastrophe. What it permits is to do a moral wrong in order to escape some very terrible consequence. But it is, then, precisely a wrong that is done. Justifiable in one perspective, it remains unjustifiable in another. 'It does not become *all right*.'[36] It is produced out of an irresoluble conflict between two types of moral reasoning, the reckoning of consequences and respect for individual rights. Someone's rights *have* to be overridden; but *overridden* is what they have to be. It is a tragedy, an unavoidable crime. All the more reason so to specify the circumstances of exception as maximally to ensure that people's rights against violence may not be disregarded lightly. And if it is said that even the stipulation of impending catastrophe cannot eliminate difficult borderline cases and, therewith, the possible commission of avoidable under the heading of unavoidable crimes, that cannot be denied. All the same, it does put much, and quite clearly so, beyond acceptable limits: the acceptable limits of a just revolutionary struggle.

In his argument that revolution, as tendentially a form of war, cannot be limited by 'abstract norms', Trotsky derides 'the bourgeois pacifist who wants to "humanize" warfare by prohibiting the use of poison gases, the bombardment of unfortified cities, etc.' The argument backfires. It acquits those engaged in warfare of any responsibility for what they do by blaming the phenomenon – war – itself. It is a variant of the 'war is hell' theme and, as such, anticipates arguments of the same general form which were to be used, a few years later, by Harry Truman and his advisers to justify the atomic bombing of Hiroshima and Nagasaki.[37] It is too easy. That a revolution is likely to involve violence; that the opponents of freedom and equality, democracy or socialism, are generally ready to use massive, horrifying violence; that the struggle against them is then a war, and as a war, a realm of the most brutal necessity; none of this can legitimate a way of thinking, or at least of speaking, which would relax all moral limits by making the activity of war itself the culprit for anything that the participants in it might do. If there are indeed circumstances to make some moral crimes unavoidable, it is still necessary to have the rules and restraints which define them as crimes and which serve as a barrier against the avoidable ones. Socialists surely have good reason to be on their guard against forms of argument that are used to throw off all ethical constraints from around the conduct of war; and that were used, specifically, to justify opening the latest and potentially the most lethal chapter in the history of human warfare.

III

Where there are established parliamentary democracies, with a set of basic civil and political rights and freedoms protected under law, there is no right of revolution on account of tyranny. There is a right of social revolution – on account of grave injustice – against the capitalist forms of power, wealth and privilege over which these democracies preside, but the thing is complicated by the claim the latter make to democratic legitimacy. For, the claim rests upon a presumption, explicit or implicit, of popular consent, and the presence of consent – even be it granted that it is less than full-blooded or universal, that it is qualified in all sorts of ways, shades into mere acquiescence or apathy, and so on – must partially weaken the force of any judgement of grave injustice.

I carry water every day a long distance to your house and at some cost in time and energy to myself. You say, 'Thank you very much.' I do it under threat of violence and would not otherwise. The relation is exploitative. Now, on the other hand, I carry the water every day because, even though it takes time and is hard, you are a weak and aged friend and cannot do it. I do it willingly, as a favour. There is no injustice in the relation. These are deliberately simple, extreme, examples. It is possible to construct a range of intermediate ones in which the ingredients of force and consent are more mixed and are thrown together with others still: habit and custom, ideology or illusion, etc. But further examples are unnecessary to my point: that the stronger the basis for a presumption of freely given consent to some particular set of social relations, the more qualified must be the practical conclusions that can be drawn from any judgement of injustice pertaining to them. In the present case, no revolutionary attempt, especially as involving violence, is justifiable in the light only of a philosopher's – or revolutionary's, or political group's – judgement that the social order is unjust. That judgement needs to be 'proven', in a manner of speaking, by a recognition, on the part of those on the receiving end of the unjust relations, that such is indeed their character.

This amounts to saying, first, that any project of social revolution has to demonstrate its democratic credentials; and second, that if it is to contest the democratic legitimacy of those limited types of democracy that exist in some capitalist societies, it will have to offer, and then win democratic support for, an alternative form of democratic legitimacy. The road of social revolution cannot therefore simply bypass the institutions of parliamentary democracy. It either runs through them as a gateway or, being blocked in the attempt, shows in practice that they are not one, but are a fortress rather, a bastion against social revolution, just or democratic as may be; and shows the location of a genuine gateway at the same time.

We come here upon old and well-known arguments. This road, in theory and dispute, is a much beaten track. I tread it myself again now briefly, in order only to make one observation pertinent to the ethics of revolution. I am concerned, then, with two broad types of strategic viewpoint, which may be called, for short, the 'gateway' and the 'bastion' hypotheses. (I reject a more familiar terminology of 'parliamentary' versus 'extra-parliamentary' roads to socialism, for reasons to be set forth in a moment.) In either case, though, it should be emphasized, it is the ethics of socialist *revolution* that are under discussion: I set aside the viewpoint sometimes known as gradualism. According to this, there is no need for revolution at all because socialism can be achieved bit by bit over a very long period. At the end of the line, there will have been a radical transformation but there will have been no revolution in the sense that matters here, because of the long drawn out, the piecemeal, albeit cumulatively fundamental, nature of the process.[38] I set this conception aside as irrelevant to the ethical issues involved, irrespective of whether or not it offers a feasible path to socialism; that is, even if (as I doubt) it does. For, 'can' does not imply 'ought'. If capitalist societies are gravely – integrally – unjust and a democratic basis can be won for their more or less rapid transformation, it is not then clear what moral consideration would speak in favour of preferring a process which might take two or three hundred or more years.

I now set aside, also, extreme variants of the 'gateway' and 'bastion' hypotheses. It does not matter whether or not anyone really subscribes to these in such an exaggerated form, though the opponents of each can be found who will so present or caricature the view they reject. The two extremes are, in any case, limit positions to be set aside in trying to delineate the strategic terrain in a more realistic way. Let us call them, respectively, 'pure' parliamentarism and 'pure' insurrectionism. According to the first, socialist transformation can be achieved by a political process in all essentials identical to the normal passage of parliamentary legislation. A socialist party is elected on the basis of its revolutionary programme and this is carried through into law and public policy. Its implementation is the socialist revolution. The state that sees it through remains intact. According to the second conception, by contrast, the battle for socialism takes place outside the (bourgeois) parliamentary arena and against the existing state. It is a mass, extra-parliamentary struggle, throwing up alternative democratic institutions and, with them, a situation of dual power. The victory of this new democracy over the old state, which is destroyed, is the indispensable condition of social revolution.

Now, given both the enormity of the tasks entailed in any socialist transformation of society and the extent of probable opposition to it, it is unthinkable that the project could be accomplished on pure parliamentarist lines. It would require as a complement the most intensive commitment and participation, active struggle, by very large numbers of people outside parliament; and in a sufficiently structured and organized way that there is good reason to stress the vital role of an extra-parliamentary democracy alongside the parliamentary one. However composed, moreover – of workers', consumers' and neighbourhood committees, local or regional councils, campaign bodies, minority movements, or whatever – if it is indeed socialism that is brought into being, then much of this other, participatory democracy, of the structures and the spirit of it, would have to survive the work of revolution itself, as the material of a more democratic political order. To put the same thing otherwise, even if there is some historical continuity between the parliamentary democracy at the origin of this whole process and the polity that emerges from it, this could not be exactly the same state, unchanged in its fundamental features. If not, as in the Leninist canon, 'smashed', it would have been significantly transformed.

On the other hand, the pure insurrectionist approach will be embarrassed to explain how a socialist party, or coalition of parties, or movement, which

had been capable of guiding a struggle for socialism to the point of dual
power, had been able to win a democratic mandate for its revolutionary
project within institutions of workers' or popular or participatory democracy lying across the territory of an entire country – how such a political
formation could be incapable of winning significant representation within an
existing democratic parliament. If it can begin to found a new democratic
legitimacy, it must have some possibility of creating a space, a platform,
a point of struggle for it within the old. Simply bypassing the democratic
institutions that exist is not, therefore, a serious hypothesis. In addition, the
insistence, under the rubric of 'smashing' the state, on a total discontinuity
between bourgeois-democratic and projected socialist polities has tended to
obscure for too many revolutionary socialists the value of certain norms and
institutions which any real socialist democracy would need to incorporate:
amongst them, a national representative assembly elected by direct universal suffrage, some separation of powers, the independence of judicial from
political processes, the protection of basic individual rights, a constitutionally
guaranteed political pluralism. Even if a socialist democracy can only emerge
by replacing the institutions of the old state, there is reason to dwell on a line
of continuity here all the same.

Thus qualified, the 'gateway' and the 'bastion' hypotheses remain different. Each now comprehends, as is necessary in the given context for any
minimally serious strategic approach, both a parliamentary and an extra-
parliamentary dimension to socialist revolution, both a continuity and a
discontinuity of political forms. But they still differ, and critically, in this:
the former hypothesis forbids, what the latter one countenances, a point of
constitutional rupture. For, in the 'gateway' view socialist transformation
must, while in the 'bastion' view it need not, derive its legitimacy from the
parliamentary source.

I defend the ethical basis of the 'bastion' view. The other one says
more, probably, or at least implies more, than it knows. By treating the
prevailing, parliamentary legitimacy as the single acceptable origin of any
projected socialist legitimacy it places allegiance to an existing state above
considerations of democracy or justice. To see the point, one only has to
allow here what has been much emphasized in the earlier part of this
essay: the inherently, the deeply, uncertain character of all revolutionary
situations. So, try to envisage the broad lines of such a situation with both
its parliamentary and extra-parliamentary facets. These two democracies,
let us concede, under some conditions could cohere into a more or less
well-articulated assault on the positions of capitalist power and wealth;
into a successful assault. But how, other than dogmatically, could it be
ruled out in advance that they might not so cohere? That, for example,
a particular parliamentary assembly might try to use what was left of
its present term – which could be some *years* – to resist very urgent
demands coming with clear, formally expressed and overwhelming support

from the extra-parliamentary democratic institutions? Or that other forces, including other forces within the state, might move, and some of them violently, to block the parliamentary gateway? One only has to allow the possibility. Must the justification, the legitimacy, of socialist revolution in the parliamentary-democratic capitalist countries, come from one specific kind of institutional link with the past? It will come, if it does come, from securing a democratic foundation for putting an end to social relations that are unjust.[39]

NOTES

1. It follows Anthony Arblaster, 'What is Violence?', in Ralph Miliband & John Saville (eds.), *The Socialist Register 1975*, London 1975, pp. 227–39.
2. Michael Walzer, 'The Moral Standing of States', *Philosophy and Public Affairs* 9, 1979–80, p. 215.
3. John Locke, *The Second Treatise of Civil Government*, Chapter XIX, paragraph 228. And see paragraphs 149, 199, 201, 212, 229.
4. See Barrington Moore jr, *Reflections on the Causes of Human Misery*, London 1972, pp. 25–28.
5. As this contrast may also be expressed, 'Are capitalist states capitalist because there has been no socialist revolution, or has there been no socialist revolution because they are capitalist?' I owe the formulation to Göran Therborn who used (something like) it at a colloquium some years ago.
6. Ted Honderich, *Violence For Equality*, Harmondsworth 1980, p. 35. (Emphasis in the original – as generally here unless stated otherwise.) The sentiment vaguely echoes that of Mark Twain I have used as epigraph. Honderich has some compelling ways of focusing one's mind on the 'other' compelling order of fact. See, for example, pp. 16–20, 26; and p. 141, lines 16–21. On the definitional point, see again Arblaster, 'What is Violence?', pp. 239–43.
7. I discuss and criticize the notion of prefiguration at length in *The Legacy of Rosa Luxemburg*, London 1976, pp. 133–173.
8. See, respectively, Kai Nielsen, 'On Justifying Revolution', *Philosophy and Phenomenological Research* 37, 1976–7, pp. 527–8, and Barrington Moore jr, *Political Power and Social Theory*, New York 1962, p. 206. See also the same author's *Reflections on the Causes of Human Misery*, pp. 25–30; Mihailo Markovic, 'Violence and Human Self-Realisation', in his *The Contemporary Marx*, Nottingham 1974, p. 169; and David Miller, 'The Use and Abuse of Political Violence', *Political Studies* 32, 1984, p. 417.
9. This might well be the sense of Herbert Marcuse, 'Ethics and Revolution', in Richard T. De George, *Ethics and Society*, London 1968, pp. 139–40, 142–6; and is the sense of Honderich's argument in *Violence For Equality*, pp. 45–51, 163–5, 182–7; albeit that Honderich, for his part, is explicit in rejecting the terminology of 'calculation' or 'computation' for one of 'comparison'.
10. The view is put forward apropos war by David Luban, 'Just War and Human Rights', *Philosophy and Public Affairs* 9, 1979–80, pp. 174–6.
11. Leon Trotsky et al., *Their Morals and Ours*, New York 1966, p. 41. And cf. Marcuse, 'Ethics and Revolution', p. 146.
12. 'The Moralists and Sycophants against Marxism', in Trotsky, Ibid., p. 48 – and see his earlier *Terrorism and Communism*, Ann Arbor 1961, pp. 22, 58, for similar arguments: 'Who aims at the end cannot reject the means. . . If the socialist revolution requires a dictatorship. . . it follows that the dictatorship must be

guaranteed at all cost'; '. . . the revolution does require of the revolutionary class that it should attain its end by all methods at its disposal.'

13. *Their Morals and Ours*, pp. 19–20, 46–7, 53; and Lenin, 'The Proletarian Revolution and the Renegade Kautsky', *Collected Works*, Moscow 1960–1970, Volume 28, p. 236. Cf. Barrington Moore, *Reflections*, p. 39.

14. Arblaster tentatively offers both possibilities; in Marcuse the point is unclear. These arguments are from: Marcuse, 'Ethics and Revolution', pp. 140–1, and two as yet unpublished essays by Anthony Arblaster, 'Bread first, then morals' and 'Means and Ends in the Struggle for Socialism'. The first of the two is due to appear in David McLellan (ed.), *Socialism and Morality*, London 1989; it is the second that has the specific exclusions. Cf. also on this matter Kai Nielsen, 'On the Ethics of Revolution', *Radical Philosophy* 6, Winter 1973, p. 19.

15. See Locke, *The Second Treatise of Civil Government*, Chapter XIX, paragraphs 223, 225, 230.

16. Steven Lukes, *Marxism and Morality*, Oxford 1985, pp. xiii, 141–2, 146–8; and see Arblaster, 'Bread first, then morals', in McLellan, *Socialism and Morality*; and Kate Soper, 'Marxism and Morality', *New Left Review* 163, May/June 1987, pp. 111–3.

17. Michael Walzer, *Just and Unjust Wars*, New York 1977, p. 227.

18. Soper, 'Marxism and Morality', pp. 112–3.

19. The description is from Phillip Van Niekerk, 'Ends and Nasty Means', *New Statesman*, 8 November 1985, p. 19. In general, my information is from newspaper coverage of the period. I have confined myself to using only what was widely reported.

20. See Walzer, *Just and Unjust Wars* (cited hereafter as Walzer), p. 21. The extent of my debt to Walzer's book will be plain to anyone familiar with it, as it will from the frequent reference here made to it. I should like, all the same, to acknowledge the debt more formally.

21. Walzer, pp. 41–3; and cf. Thomas Nagel, 'War and Massacre', *Philosophy and Public Affairs* 1, 1971–72, pp. 133–4.

22. Walzer, pp. 137, 144–6; Nagel, 'War and Massacre', pp. 139–40. For argument about the notion of 'innocence', see further George I. Mavrodes, 'Conventions and the Morality of War', *Philosophy and Public Affairs* 4, 1974–75, pp. 117–31, and Robert K. Fullinwider, 'War and Innocence', *Philosophy and Public Affairs* 5, 1975–76, pp. 90–97.

23. See Walzer, pp. 199–204.

24. Amilcar Cabral, *Revolution in Guinea*, London 1969, pp. 103–5; and Basil Davidson, *The Liberation of Guiné*, Harmondsworth 1969, pp. 96, 146–7. PAIGC: the African Independence Party of Guiné and the Cape Verde Islands. ANC: the African National Congress. For statements of the latter, see, for instance, the interview with Oliver Tambo in *The Guardian*, 5 November 1985, and the speech of his reported in the same paper, 10 January 1986. The second of these, it has to be said, is less unambiguous than the first.

25. Walzer, p. 198.

26. *Their Morals and Ours*, pp. 31–2, 46–7.

27. Walzer, pp. 151–9.

28. As well as his book, there is also a shorter piece by Michael Walzer addressed to it: see 'Political Action: The Problem of Dirty Hands', *Philosophy and Public Affairs* 2, 1972–73, pp. 160–80.

29. Nagel, 'War and Massacre', pp. 140–1.

30. See reports by David Beresford in *The Guardian*, 15 February and 29 May 1986.

31. From, respectively, David Beresford, 'The Killing of Maki Shosana', *The Guardian*, 26 July 1985, and Allister Sparks, 'The Road to Revolution', *The Observer*,

28 July 1985.
32. Victor Serge, *Memoirs of a Revolutionary 1901–1941*, London 1963, p. 282. The passage is also cited in Lukes, *Marxism and Morality*, p. 122.
33. Walzer, p. 135.
34. Soper, 'Marxism and Morality', p. 113.
35. I here follow, yet once more, Michael Walzer; for this and the next paragraph, see Walzer, pp. 228–32, 251–5, and *passim*; and also his 'Political Action: The Problem of Dirty Hands', pp. 171, 174.
36. Nagel, 'War and Massacre', p. 136–7; and cf. pp. 126, 142–3.
37. Trotsky, *Their Morals and Ours*, p. 47. Walzer, p. 265; and see also pp. 32–3.
38. See my definition of revolution at the beginning of this essay.
39. In thinking about the issues that occupy the major part of this essay I was helped by some discussions I had with friends. I thank them all, Paul Cammack, Mary Simons, Hillel Steiner, Ralph and Angela Young; as well as my closest friend, Adèle. Given the subject matter, I am more than just conventionally obliged to add here that none of the above necessarily agrees with the views I have expressed.

FATHERLAND OR MOTHER EARTH?
NATIONALISM AND INTERNATIONALISM FROM A SOCIALIST PERSPECTIVE

Michael Löwy

Two hundred years after the call for a universal brotherhood of all humankind issued by the Great French Revolution and seventy years after the foundation of the Communist International, what remained of the great dream of internationalist solidarity of the oppressed? Hasn't nationalism always been the main moving forces of world politics? And how should socialists relate to it?

The contradictory rôle of nationalism is one of the great paradoxes in the history of the 20th century, which is now approaching its end.

At the service of the State and of reactionary forces, the ideology of nationalism fostered and legitimised some of the worst crimes of the century: the two world wars, the genocide of Armenians, Jews and Gypsies, the colonialist wars, the rise of fascism and military dictatorship, the brutal repression of progressive or revolutionary movements from China in the 20s to Indonesia in the 60s and Argentina in the 70s.

On the other hand, in the name of national liberation, the colonised people gained their independence and some of the most important and radical socialist-revolutionary movements were able to win popular support and triumph: in Yugoslavia, China, Indochina, Cuba and now Nicaragua. . .

Another puzzling paradox: although nationalism has been the dominant factor in shaping 20th century politics, the greatest revolution of our times, October 1917, owed nothing to nationalism and was explicitly directed against the 'national defence of the Fatherland' in the war with Imperial Germany. Moreover, there has never been in the history of the labour and socialist movement a mass world organisation so thoroughly committed to internationalism as in the 20th century: the Third International (at least during its first years of existence).

How to understand these paradoxes? Can Marxism furnish the theoretical tools for such an understanding? Have the workers and the exploited really no Fatherland, as Marx thought in 1848? How far can Mother Earth become the concrete horizon for social liberation? And what are the perspectives for nationalism and internationalism in the next years of this *fin de siècle*?

Any attempt to answer these questions has to start with a dialectical approach to the problem: the national question is *contradictory* and its

212

contradictions are not the expression of some eternal trait of human nature, but of concrete *historical conditions*.

First of all, what *is* a nation? This problem has plagued many generations of Marxist thinkers and leaders.[1] They hoped to find the *objective criteria* permitting them to define whether a collective body of people was or was not a nation. For Karl Kautsky the nation was essentially the result of a common *language*. For Otto Bauer, each nation had a peculiar 'national character'. Anton Pannekoek considered the nation as merely a 'bourgeois ideological phenomenon'. Others suggested geographical or economic criteria.

The most systematic attempt to build such a classificatory theoretical framework is of course Stalin's famous essay from 1913 (*Marxism and the National Question*). Compounding all 'objective' criteria – common language, territory, economic life, and 'psychological make-up' – in one single definition, he insisted that it is 'only when all the characteristics are present together that we have a nation'.[2] This rigid and dogmatic frame was a true ideological Procrustean bed, and became for many decades a huge obstacle for the understanding of 'heterodox' national communities like the Jews, or the US Blacks, etc, etc. It cannot explain how Germany, long before its economic unification through the Customs Union, became a nation or why French speaking Belgians or Swiss are not part of the French nation.

In contrast to such abstract and 'closed' conceptions, Otto Bauer made a very significant contribution to an 'open' Marxist analysis of the nation by his *historicist* approach: without ignoring the various other criteria (language, economy, etc) he defined the nation as being above all the product of a *common historical destiny*. In other terms: the nation is not only a crystallization of past events, a 'frozen piece of history' but also the 'never-finished outcome of a constant process'. This historical method permitted him to avoid mistakes such as Engels' neo-hegelian theory of the 'non-historic nations' (Czechs, Roumanians and others) doomed to disappearance. . .[3]

It seems to me that this kind of un-dogmatic analysis leads logically to the conclusion that a nation is not simply a collection of abstract, external, 'objective' criteria. The *subjective* dimension, i.e. the consciousness of a national identity, the vitality of the national culture, the existence of a national political movement, is no less important. Of course, these 'subjective factors' do not come out of the blue; they are the result of certain historical conditions: persecution, oppression, discrimination, etc. But this means that in the last analysis no doctrinaire 'expert' armed with a list of 'objective' characteristics will determine whether a community constitutes a nation or not, but *the community itself* (or that part of it which considers itself as belonging to a nation).[4]

It is important to distinguish very carefully between the feeling of national identity, the attachment to a national culture, the consciousness of belonging to a national community with its own historical past – and *nationalism*. Nationalism as an ideology is composed of all these elements but also of something else, which is its decisive ingredient: the choice of the nation as *the* primary, fundamental and most important social and political value, to which all others are – in one way or another – subordinated. Hans Kohn, the well known historian of modern nationalism defined it as 'a state of mind, in which the supreme loyalty of the individual is felt to be due to the nation-state'.[5] This is a quite adequate definition – if one includes in it also the struggle *for the establishment* of the nation-state – even if one has to admit that there exist at least some (moderate) nationalist movements who aim only at cultural or territorial autonomy.

It is not easy to find out exactly how and when nationalism was born. Some authors see it as contemporary with the emergence of the modern nation-state in the 15-16th centuries (Machiavelli!). Others, like Hans Kohn, relate it to the first great bourgeois revolutions; in England in the 17th century and France in 1789 for the first time the state 'ceased to be the king's state: it became the people's state, a national state, a fatherland'.[6] More recently, Tom Nairn tried to prove that nationalism emerged in the 19th century (as a result of the uneven development of capitalism) in the peripheral countries (Germany, Italy and Japan), and only later attained the 'core-areas' (England, France),[7] but this strange chronology is too arbitrary and seems to ignore such well known historical facts as the patriotic dimension of the French Revolution and of the Napoleonic wars. . . In any case there is no doubt that for many centuries the political ideal was not the nation, or the nation-state, but other forms of social and political organization: the clan, the city-state, the feudal lord, the church, the dynastic kingdom and the multi-national empire. And although some precedents can be found in the past (the ancient Hebrews or the ancient Greeks), they are of a quite different nature and substance from modern nationalism.

Marxist socialism is fundamentally opposed to nationalism. First of all because it refuses to see the nation as an undifferentiated bloc: all nations are divided into *different social classes*, with different interests and different conceptions of the national identity. But above all it rejects the nationalist ideology and its scale of values because its supreme loyalty is not to any nation, but to an international historical subject (the proletariat) and to an international historical aim: the socialist transformation of the world. It is internationalist both for ethical and for material reasons.

The ethical motives are important: for the Marxist world-view, materialist and atheistic, the only value which can be considered 'sacred' – i.e. absolute – is humanity itself (of which the exploited and the oppressed are the emancipatory force). In this sense, the motto 'Proletarians of all countries, unite!' is not only a practical proposition for action, but also the socialist ethical answer to the 'Amour sacré de la patrie' of the nationalist ideology. Socialism is therefore an internationalist movement by the universalist and humanist character of its values and its aims. Without this ethical appeal it is impossible to understand the total commitment and sacrifice of many generations of activists from the labour movement of many countries to international socialism (or communism). As the old bolshevik Adolf Yoffé wrote in his last letter (before committing suicide in 1927) to Trotsky: 'Human life has no meaning unless it is at the service of an infinite, which for us is humanity'.

However, if internationalism were only a moral principle, a categorical imperative, it would be easy to dismiss it as a beautiful utopia. If this is not the case, it is because proletarian internationalism draws its political force from *objective, concrete, and material* conditions, already analysed by Marx in the *Manifesto*: the economic unification of the world by the capitalist system.

As any dialectic totality, world capitalism is not the addition of its parts, the national economies – nor is the international class struggle the addition of the national struggles. They constitute an organic whole, with its own forms of motion, distinct from the peculiarities of its component elements. Georg Lukács insisted in *History and Class Consciousness* that the category of totality was, on the methodological level, the carrier of the revolutionary principle. From the dialectical standpoint of totality, any local or national situation cannot be grasped in theory and transformed in practice, if one ignores its articulation with the whole, i.e. with the world economic, social and political movement.

As a matter of fact, far from being anachronistic, Marx's analysis in the *Manifesto* is much more adequate *in our times* than in 1848: imperialism has imposed on the world capitalist system a much higher degree of integration, the control of the market by multi-national monopolies is incomparably greater; in short, the unification of the planet by the capitalist mode of production has achieved today a qualitatively higher level than in 1848. And this economic unity has also its political and military expression in Western atlanticism, US interventionism, etc. This means that internationalism has its roots in the structure of world economy and world politics; socialist internationalism is *also* the consciousness of this objective reality.

Which is the decisive factor in class struggle: the national or the international conditions? Should one privilege the importance of the world process, or, as Mao once wrote, the internal factors and the national (endogenous) causes? In this problematic, the question itself is misleading. It supposes an abstract, metaphysical and static separation between the national and the international, the 'internal' and the 'external', the 'inside' and the 'outside'. The dialectical standpoint is precisely based on the understanding of the *contradictory unity* between the national economy and the world market, the national and the international class struggle – unity which appears already in the fact that the (economic and social) national specificity is the product of the unequal development of international capitalism.

What *is* wrong in the *Manifesto* and other of Marx's writings is the idea that modern industrial capitalism is essentially a *homogenizing* force, creating *identical* conditions of life and struggle among the exploited of all countries.

In an essay written in 1845 (recently discovered) he wrote this astonishing sentence: 'the nation of the worker is not French, nor English, nor German, it is *toil, the wage slavery, the selling of oneself*. His government is neither French, nor English, nor German, it is *Capital*. His native air is not French, English nor German, its the *factory air*. The land which belongs to him is not French, nor English, nor German, it is a few feet *below the earth*'.[8] This thesis has a large part of truth, but it ignores not only the cultural specificities of each nation (which capitalism does not abolish at all) but also socio-economic differences between the proletarians of different nations, which result from the *uneven and combined development of the world capitalist system*. Moreover, one cannot neglect the importance of the national peculiarities for the 'making of the working class' in each country and for the development of its own tradition of anti-capitalist resistance and struggle.

In other words: although capitalism creates both in the industrial metropolis and in the dominated countries a modern proletariat which fights against the same enemy and has the same objective historical interests, this does not mean at all that the material and social conditions of life (not to mention the national cultures) are identical. . . As Leon Trotsky once wrote: 'If we take England and India as the two poles of the capitalist type, we must recognize that the internationalism of the English and Indian proletarians is not at all based on the *identity* of their conditions, tasks and methods, but on their *unseparable interdependence*'.[9] World capitalism creates incredible inequalities and brutal differences in life-conditions between centre and periphery of the system: only the complementarity, the reciprocal relation of the struggles in the different countries can generate internationalist solidarity. Thus the anti-war movements in France in the 50s and in the USA in the 60s and 70s were a powerful contribution for the struggle of the Algerians and of the Indochinese people – and vice-versa: these colonial struggles helped to ignite radical contestation in the metropolitan centres.

The same logic of complementarity applies also, but in a different context, to the link between the struggle for socialist democracy in the West and the post-capitalist societies of Eastern Europe: it is not the identical situation which creates a relationship of reciprocity and mutual reinforcement, but the *common aim*. The events of Czechoslovakia in 1968 were the beginning of such an internationalist dynamic, but it was thwarted by the Soviet invasion, before it could unfold all its potentialities. In any case, there is no doubt that the existence of the (bureaucratised) post-capitalist States creates a new international dynamic (unforeseen by Marx and classical Marxism) and a new form of internationalism which cannot be deduced only from the unity of world capitalism. This new form results from the common interest of the labour movement, East and West, to see bureaucratic dictatorship abolished in the post-capitalist societies, thus destroying the most efficient ideological argument of the Western ruling classes against radical (i.e. socialist) change.

To sum up: internationalism is not the expression of the identity in life-conditions of the exploited and oppressed of all countries, but of a *dialectical* relationship of complementarity between at least three very different kinds of struggles: the socialist labour movement in the advanced capitalist societies, the social and national liberation movement in the dependent (or colonial) capitalist countries, and the anti-bureaucratic movement for socialist democracy in the post-capitalist societies.

Marxists have often under-estimated the importance of the national question, the decisive significance of national liberation for the dominated people. This is part of a general pattern of blindness, neglect or at least insufficient attention to *non-class* forms of oppression: national, racial or sexual. It is not that Marxism as such is unable to take into account these dimensions, but the economistic approach which dominated much of Marxist thinking (and also some of Marx's own writings) led to a tendency to disregard them.

Marxists have also very frequently under-estimated the power of nationalism. A peculiar combination between economicism and the illusions of linear progress (inherited from the Enlightenment) led to the wrong belief that nationalism would inevitably and soon decline. For instance, in the *Communist Manifesto*: 'National differences, and antagonisms between people, are daily more and more vanishing, owing to the development of the bourgeoisie, to freedom of commerce, to the world market, to uniformity in the mode of production and in the conditions of life corresponding thereto.'[10] The Second International also believed that nationalism belonged to the past and Karl Kautsky dreamed of a socialist future without nations and with one single language: 'In a painless way, the nations will fuse with each other, more or less in the same fashion as the Roman population of the Grisons canton in Switzerland, who, insensibly and without resistance, is slowly germanizing itself because it discovers that it is more advantageous to speak a language that everybody understands in a vast area rather than a language that is only spoken in a few valleys'.[11] Obviously, equipped with such ideas, Marxists were little prepared to confront the fantastic upsurge of nationalism after August 1914, which took over the labour movement and led to 'Sacred Unity in Defence of the Fatherland' – and to the mutual slaughter of the workers of all countries. Kautsky himself rallied to the 'National Defence' of Imperial Germany, arguing that the Socialist International was an instrument suited only for peaceful times, and had to be put gently aside during the war. . .

The first condition for an effective confrontation with nationalism is therefore to give up the illusions of linear progress, i.e. the naive expectations of a peaceful evolution, and of a gradual 'withering way' of nationalism and national wars, thanks to the modernisation and democratisation of industrial societies, the internationalisation of productive forces, etc.

How can one explain this incredible force of nationalism in the course of 20th century history? A first answer would be the classic Marxist argument:

nationalism is a bourgeois ideology and its power over the popular masses is one of the main forms taken by the ideological domination of the bourgeoisie in capitalist societies. This analysis is not wrong, but insufficient to explain the power of attraction of nationalism, sometimes over significant sections of the labour movement. Other causes have to be taken into consideration:

1) Concrete material and economic conditions: the competition between workers of different nations (or States), resulting from the nature itself of capitalism. It is a question of short-range interests – for instance, to prevent the entrance of foreign commodities which can provoke unemployment – but their real weight can hide from the competing workers their common historical interest: the abolition of exploitation. This, incidentally, happens also inside one single nation, when unemployed workers volunteer to replace striking ones. Marx himself recognized in the *Manifesto* that the competition among workers constantly threatens to divide and destroy their common organisation.

2) Irrational tendencies, similar in chauvinist nationalism, religious fanaticism, racism and fascism: a complex psychical phenomena, which still has to be studied. Reich's work on the mass psychology of fascism, Erich Fromm's on the 'escape from freedom' and Adorno's on the authoritarian personality are among the first important contributions for an explanation. Nationalism is by its own nature an irrationalist ideology: it cannot legitimate the privilege of one nation over the others with any rational criteria – since substantive (i.e. not purely instrumental) rationalism is always tendentially universal. It must therefore make appeal to non-rational myths like the divine mission attributed to the nation, the innate and eternal superiority of a people, the right to occupy a larger geographical *Lebensraum,* etc. However, it may also make use of pseudo-rational and pseudo-scientific forms of legitimation: geo-politics, racial anthropology, etc. Often it does not correspond to any deep historical and cultural unity, being just the official ideology of more or less artificial states, whose borders are the accidental product of colonisation and/or de-colonisation (in Africa and Latin America for instance).

But there is another reason for the upsurge of nationalism, which has to be taken very seriously by Marxists and Socialists: the struggle for liberation of the oppressed or colonised nations. Although Marxism is as such opposed to the nationalist ideology, it must very clearly distinguish between *the nationalism of the oppressors and the nationalism of the oppressed.* It has therefore to support all struggles for national liberation, or for the right of self-determination of the oppressed nations, even if their ideology (or the ideology of their leaders) is nationalist. Of course, Marxist internationalists taking part in a movement for national liberation should keep their independence, and try to persuade the exploited popular masses of the need to develop the struggle (in an uninterrupted way) beyond the national aims, towards a socialist-revolutionary transformation. But they cannot ignore or under-rate the significance of the popular demand for national self-determination.

The reason for this is not only that Socialists are opposed to *all forms of oppression* (national, racial, sexual or class) but also because there is a *dialectical relation* between internationalism and national rights. Socialist internationalism cannot develop without the recognition, by the socialist movement, of the equal rights of all nations. In the same way as the unity and solidarity of the workers of one and the same nation cannot be established except on an egalitarian basis – without any distinctions or privileges of profession, religion, race, sex or branch of production – the internationalist unity of the exploited can only be built on the recognition of the national rights – and in particular the right to self determination – for all people. When Lenin insisted that the Russian Workers Party (the POSDR) should recognise the right of self-determination of Poland – i.e. the right of the Polish people to decide for themselves if they want or not to establish a *separate State* – he did it not only because the struggle of the Polish nation against tsarism was historically progressive (the argument used by Marx and Engels) but above all because it was the pre-condition for the establishment of an internationalist alliance between Russian and Polish workers. The recognition of national rights is an essential condition for international solidarity, insofar as it permits the dissolution of suspicions, hatreds and fears which oppose nations and nourish chauvinism. As Lenin wrote, without the right to divorce – i.e. to have a separate State – there can be no truly free marriage – i.e. unity or federation between nations. Unfortunately, the policy of the Bolshevik government (including Lenin) after October 1917 did not always correspond to this principle: invasion of Poland in 1920, occupation of Georgia in 1921 etc. . .

One of the most negative aspects of Stalin's famous pamphlet from 1913 is that – in contradiction to Lenin – he makes no distinction between Great-Russian oppressive nationalism and the nationalism of the oppressed nations of the Tsarist Empire. In a very revealing paragraph of his essay, he rejected in the same terms the 'warlike and repressive' nationalism 'from above' – i.e. of the Tsarist State – and the 'wave of nationalism from below which sometimes turns into crass chauvinism' of the Poles, Jews, Tatars, Ukrainians, Georgians, Ukrainians, etc. Not only did he fail to make any distinction between nationalism 'from above' and nationalism 'from below', but he aimed his most severe criticism at social-democrats in the oppressed nations who had not 'stood firm' in the face of nationalist movements.

By making the capital distinction between oppressed and oppressor's nationalism, socialist internationalists do not have to adhere to the former. But they perceive its contradictory nature: its emancipatory dimension as a rebellion against unjust oppression, and its limits as a particularistic ideology. It is therefore logical that all truly social-revolutionary movements in an oppressed nation necessarily put national liberation at the centre of their struggle, while linking it to the social emancipation from capitalist exploitation – Nicaragua is the most recent example – while in the imperialist metropolis, it is the rejection of nationalism which is at the heart of all radical confrontation with the established order – from the anti-war movement in the USA to the French Mai 68 (whose main slogan was 'les frontières on s'en fout!').

This being said, it should be stressed that the distinction between the two kinds of nationalism is a *relative* and not an absolute one. First, because very easily the oppressed from yesterday become the oppressors of tomorrow: there is no lack of historical evidence, in our own times. . . Secondly, because the nationalist ideology (or movement) of oppressed nations has often a double cutting edge: liberating against their oppressors, but oppressive towards their own national minorities. And thirdly, because one can find in both forms of nationalism elements of chauvinism, global rejection of the 'other' and (sometimes) racism.

Lenin was probably the 'classic' Marxist thinker who best understood the dialectics between internationalism and national rights. However, in certain passages of his writings he presents the democratic rights of the nations as a *part* which has to be subordinated to the *whole* which is the world democratic and socialist movement. This formulation seems to me dangerous and some-what mechanistic. If socialist revolution is the self-emancipation of the pro-letariat – in alliance with all the other exploited and oppressed social groups – it is intimately linked with the democratic self-determination of the nation. A people to whom 'socialism' would be imposed from outside, against its will, would only know a caricature of socialism, inevitably doomed to bureaucratic degeneration (many Eastern European countries illustrate this rule!). In my opinion it would be more adequate – and corresponding better to the spirit of most of Lenin's writings on the national question – to conceive the socialist revolution and the international fraternity of the proletariat as the *aim* of Marxists, and the self-determination of the nations as a *necessary means* for implementing it. Means and aim are dialectically articulated, in such a way that the subordination of the national dimension to internationalism excludes the possibility of 'sacrificing' the first to the second one.

If socialist internationalism is opposed to nationalist ideology, this does not at all mean that it refuses the historical and cultural tradition of the nations. In the same way as the internationalist movements in each country have to speak the national language, they have also to speak the language of the national history and culture – particularly, of course, when this culture is being oppressed. As Lenin acknowledged, each culture and each national history contains democratic, progressive, revolutionary aspects which have to be incorporated by the socialist culture of the labour movement, and reaction-ary, chauvinistic and obscurantist aspects which have to be uncompromisingly fought. The task of the internationalists is to fuse the historical and cultural heritage of the world socialist movement with the culture and the tradition of their people, in its radical and subversive dimension – often deformed by bourgeois ideology, or hidden and buried by the official culture of the ruling classes. In the same way as Marxists must take into consideration, in their revolutionary struggle, the decisive importance of the national specificity of their social formation, in their ideological struggle they cannot ignore the national peculiarity of their own culture and history. This is what the FSLN did in Nicaragua, articulating Marxism with the Sandino heritage, a radical tradition alive in the collective memory of the Nicaraguan people. And a similar process took place in Cuba, with the democratic and anti-imperialist tradition represented by José Marti, in South America with the Indian rebellious past embodied by Tupac-Amaru, etc.

If socialism, in the Marxian sense – i.e. a class-less and state-less society – can exist only on a world scale, what would be the place of the nations in the future 'Socialist Mother Earth'? This is not a purely utopian and irrelevant question, since the internationalist nature of the final socialist-revolutionary aim should inspire, to a certain extent at least, the present forms of struggle.

For historical materialism, the nation-state is not an eternal category: it is not the result of 'human nature' nor of any biological law of nature (a thesis advocated by certain ultra-reactionary 'socio-biologists' who pretend to deduce the nation from the 'territorial principle' of certain animal species. . .); it did not always exist in the past and nothing forces one to believe that it will always exist in the future. In one word: it is an historical product and can be historically superseded.

The necessity of some form of structured (or 'institutional') *organization* is a universal need of all civilized human societies. This organization can as well take national forms, as infra-national (the clan, the tribe) and supra-national ones (the religious civilizations). Medieval Europe is a characteristic example of a social and political organization combining local structures which are 'pre-nation' (the fiefs, principalities, etc) and universalistic structures which are 'beyond the nation' (the Holy Roman Empire, the Church). The modern nation-state emerged around the 14–15th centuries, – with the rise of capitalism and the formation of the national market – precisely through the destruction/decomposition of these two non-national structures.

There is therefore no reason *a-priori* to deny the possibility, in the future, of a new supra-national organisation of human society, a World Socialist Republic, which, unifying economically and politically the human species, would reduce the nation essentially to its cultural dimension. The universal culture which would arise in such a framework would peacefully co-exist with the rich multiplicity of the national cultures.

This is probably what Marx and Engels had in mind when they wrote in the *Communist Manifesto* that the proletarian revolution would abolish 'national differences (*Absonderungen)* and antagonisms between peoples'.[12] As the well known Marxist historian Roman Rosdolsky rightly stressed, this means 'certainly not the "abolition" of existing ethnic and linguistic communities (which would have been absurd!) but of the *political* delimitation of peoples. In a society which (in the words of the *Manifesto*) "the public power will lose its political character" and *the State as such will wither away*, there can be no room for separate "national States'". Of course, as Marx acknowledged in the *Manifesto*, the proletariat must first seize power within the framework of a national State, but this separate proletarian State *'will be only a transitional stage towards the future classless and Stateless society*, since the construction of such a society *is possible only on the international scale'*.[13] There is no doubt that one can find in Marx and Engels' writings (particularly during the years 1845-48) the hope of a future communist *cosmopolis*, a 'world city' without frontiers, a universal *Gemeinschaft*, an international socialist federation, in which not only national antagonisms and conflicts would disappear but also the *economic, social and political* (but not cultural) differences between nations.[14]

This issue has been quite controversial in 20th century Marxism. One can find basically two tendencies: 1) Those who favoured (or considered inevitable) the future *assimilation* of all nations in a universal common socialist culture: Kautsky, Lenin, Stalin, Pannekoek, Strasser. Kautsky's theory of the single international language is the coherent expression of this position. 2) Those who believed in the *free development* of all national cultures in an integrated universal community: Otto Bauer, Trotsky and Rosa Luxemburg. For instance, Leon Trotsky wrote in an essay from 1915: 'The nation is an active and permanent factor of human culture. And in a socialist regime the nation, liberated from the chains of political and economic dependence, will be called to play a fundamental rôle in the historical development. . .'.[15] A third position, 'national neutrality', is implicitly sketched by Vladimir Medem, the leader of the Jewish Bund: it is impossible to predict whether future historical development will or not lead to the assimilation of the Jewish nation. In any case, Marxists should neither prevent nor stimulate this process of assimilation, but remain neutral.[16] If one generalizes this position to all national cultures (which Medem did not) one would have an original and new conception of the problem.[17]

What happened to socialist internationalism in the 20th century? August 1914 brought a catastrophic breakdown of internationalism, when the great majority of the socialist labour movement (leadership as well as rank-and-file) was engulfed by the immense wave of nationalist (and chauvinist) hysteria, in the name of 'national defence'. However, this was not to be the end of internationalism, but the beginning of a *new* internationalist upsurge in the socialist movement; at first limited to small circles of revolutionaries or pacifists, and then, after October 1917, growing into an impressive mass movement – the Communist International. The existence of the Comintern, a world movement genuinely committed to proletarian internationalism (at least during its first years), is a powerful historical proof that the international solidarity of the exploited is not just a utopia, an abstract principle, but that in given circumstances it can have mass appeal among the workers and other exploited social layers. In several key European and 'colonial' countries, the

Third International soon rallied the majority of the organized labour movement, invalidating the conservative myth that the great masses of the working
people cannot transcend nationalist ideology. This is a decisive evidence that
internationalism – and revolutionary class consciousness in general – is an
objective possibility, based on reality and its contradictions; of course, its
concrete implementation depends on historical circumstances, and on a political battle of the revolutionary forces to win the people and liberate them
from the blinkers of nationalism. In other words: Marxist internationalism –
as well as the hope of revolution – is based not only on an objective analysis of
world economy and world politics, but also on a *historical wager*: a wager on
the rationality of the working people, on the capacity of the popular masses
to understand, sooner or later, their objective historical interests.

However, this extraordinary upsurge of internationalist faith and action –
without precedent in the past history of socialism – the incredible capital
of internationalist energy and commitment represented by the Communist
International was wasted by Stalinism. It channelled this energy at the service
of bureaucratic nationalism, its state policy and its power strategy. Internationalism became the maid of Soviet diplomacy, and the world communist
movement an instrument to help building 'socialism in one country'. The
most obvious example is the policy of the Comintern towards German naz-
ism, from 1928 until its dissolution in 1943: its strange turns and about-turns
had little to do with the life-and-death interests of the European workers
and peoples, but were exclusively determined by Soviet (Stalinist) changing
diplomatic and military alliances.

Nevertheless, during the thirties Europe saw *the* most impressive example of *internationalist practice*: the International Brigades in Spain, and
the general mobilisation in solidarity with the anti-fascist struggle during
the Spanish Civil-War. Tens of thousands of volunteers – communists,
socialists, anarchists, trotskyists, independent marxists, radicalized liberals
and anti-fascists of various tendencies – from dozens of nationalities came
from all over the world in order to help the Spanish people in its desperate
war against fascism. Thanks to Hitler and Mussolini's help to Franco (and
the so-called 'non-interventionist' policy of the Western democracies) this
war was lost, but the fight of the International Brigades – many of whose
volunteers fell in the battle-field – remains one of the highest manifestations
of internationalism in our century.

After (and also during) the Second World War nationalism became again
the dominant ideology – even among the 'really existing socialist countries',
who engaged in a process of nationalist confrontation (USSR vs. China) or
war (China vs. Vietnam). What remained as 'internationalism' in the world
communist movement after the dissolution of the Comintern was only a
blind fidelity to the Soviet Union and its leadership (now in the process
of vanishing too). The only exceptions were small revolutionary tendencies, among whom the Fourth International, who remained committed to

the original internationalist aims of the Comintern, but their influence was limited.

This decline in communist internationalism left an ideological void which very quickly was to be filled by nationalism. Today, as in the past, nationalism can be found with very different political contents. Reactionary nationalism is alive and well in the advanced capitalist metropolis, both in the traditional form of colonial or imperial hegemonism and in the more recent form of anti-immigrant racism. The immigrants from the former colonized people who were recruited as cheap labour force in Europe during the years of the economic boom are now being presented as the scapegoat for all social ills resulting from the crisis (unemployment, criminality, etc) by semi-fascist nationalist (racist) forces, particularly in France, Great Britain and Germany. But also in the Third World one can find reactionary forms of nationalism, in the ideology of various military regimes (particularly in Latin America and the Middle-East). Nationalism can also be used to legitimize wars of territorial or political expansionism, like the Indonesian invasion of Timor, and the Iran-Iraqui war – the bloodiest and most absurd national conflict in recent history. Finally it can be used to justify the oppression of national minorities, like the Kurds in various Middle-Eastern countries, the non-Muslim African population in Sudan, the Eritrean people in Ethiopia, etc.

But there are also, nowadays as before, forms of nationalism which have – whatever their limitations, shortcomings and contradictions – an emancipatory dimension. First, the anti-imperialist and anti-colonial nationalist movements of liberation in Latin America, Africa (Namibia, South Africa), the Middle-East (Palestine), etc. Secondly, the movements against national oppression in the post-capitalist societies: the national minorities in the USSR (Jews, Tatars, Armenians, etc) and the oppressed nations of East Europe: Poland, Czechoslovakia, etc. And finally, the various national minorities or national cultures in the main European nation-states which are struggling for their right of self-determination or at least for various forms of national autonomy (Basques, Catalans, Andalusians, Northern Irish, Scots, Welsh, Bretons, Corsicans, etc).[18]

While the old internationalism identified with the Soviet Union is in decline, there are new forms of internationalist fraternity which emerge in our times. The 60s produced already a big and unexpected wave of internationalism among the younger generation, taking the form of anti-war movements, solidarity with Third-World revolutions and the rejection of nationalist chauvinism. The French Mai 68 saw hundreds of young people chanting 'Nous sommes tous des juifs allemands' – a slogan which expressed this spontaneous and massive internationalist feeling.

To-day a *new internationalist culture* is in the making. In the Third-World it results from the convergence between a new Marxist Left – which refuses the disastrous Stalinist tradition of blind allegiance to a 'Socialist Fatherland' (USSR, China, Albania, etc) – and the christian socialists linked to Liberation Theology. The 'catholic' – i.e. international–character of religion has entered, thanks to Liberation Theology, in a relation of elective affinity with Marxist internationalism. . . Whatever the limits of their international outlook, Sandinismo in Nicaragua and the Brazilian new *Partido dos Trabalhadores* (Workers Party) are some examples of this.

Among the new European generation this new internationalist culture in process of constitution is the product of various components, which combine and fuse with each other in various proportions:

1– What remained from the older socialist tradition of proletarian and revolutionary internationalism – kept alive among left-socialists, critical communists, anarchists and in such organisations as the Fourth International – and from the new-leftist culture of the 60's.

2– Pacifism, the vast anti-nuclear movement which rejects the armament course, the logic of cold war (in both military blocs) and imperialist (or nationalist) militarism. Whatever their disagreements, pacifist movements from both Western and Eastern Europe are united in the common aim of preventing the nuclear holocaust and saving humanity from 'exterminism'.

3– Ecology, whose struggle to protect Nature and 'Mother Earth' from destructive 'progress', industrial waste and ecological disaster knows of no borders, and relates to a common interest of all humankind.

4– Anti-racism, a spontaneous movement of fraternity with the (African, Arab, Asiatic or Turkish) immigrant population, refusing the nationalist/racist logic of exclusion. One of the most important issues raised by this movement (particularly in France) is the separation between nationality and citizenship: all inhabitants living in a country should be considered citizens (with the right of vote) independently of their nationality.

5– Feminism, which subverts the traditional patriarchal culture of aggressive nationalism, 'male' military virtues and 'heroic' patriotic violence. If there is an elective affinity between patriarchy and the reactionary cult of the imperial 'Fatherland', there is also a similar link between the feminist politics and culture and the pacifist (or ecological) defence of 'Mother Earth [19].

6– 'Third-Worldism', i.e. the sympathy and solidarity with the struggles of Third-World people to liberate themselves from imperialist oppression, native dictatorships, hunger and misery. Although less political than the anti-imperialist movements from the 60's, this current–today frequently composed of radicalised christian activists – is genuinely committed to internationalist fraternity.

An objective factor contributing to the rise of internationalist tendencies in Europe is of course the development of the European Common Market, which renders increasingly obsolete many old nationalist quarrels (France vs. Germany) and creates favourable conditions for common European social struggles – for instance the trade union fight for a 35-hour week. However, in the short range, the so-called 'objective economic constraints' of the international environment and in particular of the Common Market have been used as one of the main arguments of social-democratic governments in Europe (France, Spain, Greece, etc) to justify the lack of any radical social measures on the national scale. The well known socialist historian Daniel Singer answered very accurately to this kind of self-legitimating discourse by pointing to the present dialectics between national and international change: 'The fact that the medium sized nation-state is historically doomed in its present form does not mean that it does not provide for the time being the first platform for social transformation. Indeed, it still provides the only possible initial terrain. To deny it is to oppose the very idea of radical change. The question must still first be put within national borders even if the answers are already international, European to begin with. (. . .) Similarly, only a western Europe forging a different type of society stands a chance of preventing our future from being American. The growing economic interdependence, the inevitability of a rapid expansion of the movement from a national to a European scale does not condemn individual countries, as it is being suggested, to permanent submission to the rule of capital. It simply condemns a socialist movement, however deep its national roots, to internationalism'[20].

It is too soon to predict if these various ingredients will be able to combine harmoniously, and if the new internationalist culture will unfold as a unified mass movement in Europe (or the world). But it may be that these are the modest beginnings of what will be the socialist internationalism of the 21th century. . .

NOTES

1. For an historical survey of the debate see my article 'The Marxists and the National Question', *New Left Review* 96, March–April 1976.
2. J. Stalin, 'Marxism and the National Question', *Works*, vol. 2, Moscow, 1953, pp. 300–381.
3. Otto Bauer, *Die Nationalitätenfrage und die Sozialdemokratie*, Vienna, 1924, pp. 239–272.
4. Cf. Trotsky on the Blacks in the USA: 'An abstract criterion is not decisive in this case: much more decisive are historical consciousness, feelings and emotions'. *Trotsky on Black Nationalism and Self-Determination*, N. York, Merit, 1967, p. 16.
5. Hans Kohn, *Nationalism*, Princeton, Von Nostrand, 1955, p. 9.
6. H. Kohn, *Op. cit.*, p. 15.
7. Tom Nairn, 'The Modern Janus', *New Left Review* 94, London, November–December 1975, p. 15.
8. Marx, 'Ueber Friederich Lists Buch. . .' (1845) in *Sozialistische Politik*, Berlin, 1972, no. 19, p. 103.

9. L. Trotsky, 'Vorwort zur deutschen Ausgabe', *Die Permanente Revolution*, Berlin, Verlag Die Aktion, 1930, p. 11.

10. Marx and Engels, *Communist Manifesto* in *Revolutions of 1848*, London, Penguin-NLR, 1973, p. 85. For an interesting criticism of this aspect of the Marxist tradition, see T. Nairn, *Op. cit.*, pp. 19–21, 26–27.

11. Karl Kautsky, 'Die moderne Nationalität', *Die Neue Zeit*, V, 1887, p. 451.

12. Marx, Engels, *Werke,* 4, Berlin, Dietz-Verlag, 1959, p. 479.

13. Roman Rosdolsky, 'Worker and Fatherland: A note on a passage in the Communist Manifesto', *Science and Society*, Summer 1965, vol. XXIX, no. 3, pp. 335–337.

14. For a more extensive treatment of this idea, see my article 'Marx and Engels: Cosmopolites', in *Critique. A Journal of Socialist Theory,* no. 14, 1981.

15. L. Trotsky, 'Nation et Economie', 1915, in *Pluriel-Debat,* Paris, no. 4, April 1975, p. 48. Our analysis is borrowed from Enzo Traverso's excellent paper 'Socialismo e nazione: rasssegna di una controversia marxista', *Il Ponte*, XL, 1984, no. 1, p. 60.

16. Vladimir Medem, *The national question and social-democracy,* Vilna, 1906, quoted in Arieh Yaari, *Le defi national. Les théories marxistes sur la question nationale à l'épreuve de l'histoire*, Paris, Anthropos, 1978, pp. 186–187.

17. E. Traverso, *Op. cit.,* p. 61.

18. For an interesting and provocative analysis of this new upsurge of the national minorities against the established nation-states, and its anti-capitalist potential, one should see the recent work of a Basque Marxist: Gurutz Jauregui Bereciartu, *Contra el Estado-nacion. En torno al hecho y la cuestion nacional,* Madrid, Siglo XXI, 1986.

19. By the way: *Mother Earth* was the name of an internationalist journal founded in the USA before World War I by the well known anarchist leader Emma Goldmann. . .

20. Daniel Singer, 'Radical Change and Europe's Nation State', paper presented at the 1987 Cavtat Conference (Yugoslavia) on *Socialism, Nations, International Cooperation*, p. 10.

REVOLUTION TODAY
THREE REFLECTIONS

FRIEDER OTTO WOLF

For Eva

Preliminary remarks

Today, on the threshold of the 1990s, rethinking the very idea of revolution has turned into an urgent task.

There is double urgency about it – an urgency of re-thinking of our conceptions of revolution, some of which have become outdated, and an urgency of the 'thing itself', of revolution as a real process.

Our current ideas on 'revolution' have been first fashioned by the great divide of the late 18th century, i.e. by the French Revolution, the 'political revolution' against late feudalism, with its popular uprising against the established powers, as well as by the British 'Industrial Revolution', the economic revolution that brought about the world-wide dominance of capitalism, which caused deep structural transformations of society, comparable only, it seems, to the 'neolithic revolution' that ended nomadic modes of production. The series of defeated proletarian uprisings since the early 19th century that culminated in the victorious Russian October of 1917 has radicalized our thinking on Revolution by bringing those two aspects much more closely together, but has not altered the basic formula which could be resumed as 'Jacobinism plus structural transformation'.[1] The Stalinist deformation of the post-revolutionary Soviet Union – and the ensuing deformations of the Communist movement – has, then, oddly blurred our perspectives: by claiming its monopoly on the very idea of revolution, while turning it into an ideological tool in the service of another system of domination. Less spectacularly, although probably still more profoundly, our thinking on revolution has been influenced by the historical destiny of the competing 'evolutionary' approaches to social transformation – from Austro-marxism via Sweden's 'middle way' to the post-war 'welfare state': their 'failure in success' has been in fact the vital factor to put the idea of revolution on the agenda of history again, in the centres of a world-wide system of capitalist domination, in a new beginning of revolutionary politics in the 1960s.[2] Still less visible, however, but maybe still more effective, has been the impact of the 'passive revolutions', which have shaped the last hundred years far more deeply than the active ones, the – sometimes rather radical[3] – changes by which ruling classes or dominant, imperialist states have prevented real revolutions from effectively sapping their domination, reaching from the political 'reforms' of Louis Bonaparte via Bismarckian social reforms to the 'New Deal', and to the post-war blends of 'Fordism' and 'Labourism' in Western Europe or to the Bretton Woods system of international economic relations, with the neocolonialism it helped to bring about.

This has been a century, so far, that has been more deeply shaped – if not traumatized – by active and passive revolutions than any other century before. And yet, the implications of this simple truth for the future of humankind are far from clear. It has become difficult to write about revolution. Not just because it is suspected, in the eyes of so many new anti-totalitarians (who have come out of the rebel generations of the 1960s) of lapsing into the cardinal crime of a 'will for power'.[4] And not at all, because it is, in fact, offensive to a dominant common sense of 'published opinion' in our Western capitalist countries[5] which excludes even the possibility of a revolution. The real difficulty lies in a – quite justified – popular diffidence which forms a subterranean counterpart to the claims of the ruling classes of having achieved, as a result of their past active and ensuing passive revolutions, a final state of history, where the main task at hand is 'to end the revolution'. Not only the peasants or the housewives, even large strata of the working classes have made a historical experience that makes it a real question for them, whether another revolution could do them any good. And without the exploited and dominated classes and categories of our societies a revolution is not even thinkable.[6]

At the same time, within the process of real human history, those contradictions have been exacerbated, that have served as a foundation for the plea, as well as for the hope, for a revolutionary transformation since it first came into being: and it is not just the unaccounted, almost uncountable past and present victims of the kinds of modern imperialist regimes[7] that have been surpassing everything that came before them in terms of genocide, of civil and military destruction[8] – it is even more their growing capacity of mortgaging the future for their present expansion. This is achieved via an expanding, increasingly flexible system of credit money that helps gigantic re-allocations of capital; and via 'economies of constant capital'[9] which serve as a central condition for an industrializing upsurge without precedent. This second aspect has been taking different forms, the most important certainly being a type of economic growth that has not only squandered the larger part of the energetic and mineral resources of humankind within the lifespan of two generations – and that has not only destroyed an entire heritage of 'informal' traditions that had been handed down mostly on the female side of humankind in the process of the 'Sonyization' and 'MacDonaldization' of every-day life, but that has doubly put the very survival of humankind in jeopardy; by provoking a global ecological crisis that has begun to sap the natural conditions of human civilization and survival, and by executing the biggest military build-up of history that makes a 'total war' on a planetary scale a real possibility. Humankind is, already, paying most dearly for not having succeeded in ending these dialectics of destruction a long time ago, when they became first apparent in the second half of the 19th Century, by a thorough-going socialist revolution.[10] As a result of this development, the urgency of a social revolution has merged with the urgency of simply guaranteeing the very survival of mankind: The newly discovered 'common interests of mankind' do, therefore, in no way divert us from the true class interests of the dominated classes – they just have to be understood in their radical implications, which are no less than a revolution ('perestroyka') in the East and a radical break with the logic of imperialist destructiveness, i.e. decisive steps towards a real socialist transition, in the West.[11] This new urgency of revolution does not, however, invalidate the apparently opposed consideration that the situation had developed into presenting such a serious threat to the survival of humankind that there is no more time for experimentation – and has not the slogan 'no experiments!' always served to argue 'no revolution'? Can we afford to spend our time in a revolutionary process that may turn out to be as long-winded as the passage from feudalism to bourgeois class dominance which took, roughly, five centuries? And what, if there are any, are the alternatives to such a revolutionary process?

First reflection:
revolution as a millenary task

We do think, hence we are revolutionaries
(L.M. Batkin, in: Afanassyev, Y., ed., There is no alternative to perestroyka, Moscow 1988, German edition, p. 217)

Nobody else but a person, a subject, her-or himself can judge what she or he thinks to be true, what he or she feels to be right. She or he may rely on others, trust their authority, but it is always her-or himself who has to be the ultimate judge of this authority, revoking it without any warning, if she or he feels like it. Domination, as any authority over others that is *not* based on their consent[12] nor revocable[13] in this way, is seen as *ab initio* illegitimate in the light of this evidence – however good, well-meaning or superior it may be in other respects.

Historically, the spelling out of this basic evidence by the poets, comedians and tragedians of the Greek Fifth century B.C., has been the prelude of the central philosophical thesis of the Sophists[14] that there is no other way of judging, what is true, right, or beautiful, except through every person's own judgement, as well as of the stance of Socrates to prefer capital punishment to conformist subordination to the mores and views of his fellow citizens.

These elementary claims against all kinds of domination that were directly

derived from this elementary evidence – although they had an indirect historical occasion in the crisis of ancient society that was at the basis of the
short flowering of the Greek democratic city state – were soon silenced
and perverted by a metaphysical philosophy that made the justification
of 'order' and, quite explicitly, of 'domination' its pivotal task. It is true
that these early, philosophical claims of 'enlightenment' against any kind
of domination had the major weakness of not yet being capable of linking
themselves to a 'science of history',[15] and, therefore, were quite unable even
to approach the problem of defining the conditions of their realization within
the real history of humankind. The development of modern economic, social,
and political theory, from Renaissance political prudence to Enlightenment
political economy, however, and its scientific reformulation in the critical out-
lines elaborated by Marx, have accompanied a profound change in the real
historical situation – in which the old claim of liberation from domination,
of emancipation, began to be incorporated by a real social movement, by
the class struggles of the exploited class the bourgeoisie was constituting in
its very rise. The elementary evidence that any domination of humans over
humans is basically illegitimate did not, by this new incorporation lose its
force. Quite to the contrary: by being able to indicate the conditions of
its historical realization in combining philosophical critique with scientific
discovery and the practical experience of real revolutionary movements, it
gained additional force: effecting its metamorphosis from a philosophical
anticipation to a real historical project, and, thereby, finally overcoming
the subaltern position to which 'materialist', anti-domination philosophy had
been relegated since early Hellenism by the effects of dominating ideology.[16]

In our type of society, because of its elementary structures, an economy
regulated by a market mechanism,[17] and a state constituted as a representative democracy[18] with its perpetual changes of government by general
elections, makes 'revolutionizing' a permanent feature of these societies as
they are, these structures themselves bringing an end to the very idea of a
revolution: why should anybody ask for a revolution, let alone practically
participate in one, in a state of affairs where revolutions have become
commonplace or, better still, where orderly social innovation and orderly
political changes have, once and for all, made any revolution superfluous?

These contemporary objections can be dealt with by carefully reexamining
the arsenal of traditional marxist analysis and argument.[19] *First*, the market
as the basic economic regulatory mechanism of a society, and not as a
simple distributive device, is necessarily linked to generalised commodity
production. This is, in turn, inseparable from the capitalist mode of production – with its characteristic combination of the exploitation of wage
labour and material expansion.[20] As the market mechanism, therefore, is,
as a basic regulatory mechanism of social production,[21] a structure of class
domination (as even the most methodically individualist analytical *marxists*
will have to agree), there are structural limits to its 'revolutionizing': as a

basic structure of capitalist domination it is revolutionizing anything but this domination itself. Second, the state as a political form of concentrating power, especially by monopolizing the use of violence over and above society[22] and by reproducing and articulating the material institutions and procedures effecting the hegemony of dominant ideology over all its 'subjects', is essentially a structure of domination. This is also true for modern representative democracy, although domination does take here the outward appearance of a rule of the dominated themselves. In fact, there can be no radical grass-roots democracy, where 'representation' does not include concrete control, implying, at least, instant and simple revocability. The same is true, however, where the capitalist class is still, if only economically, dominant – which means, under the structures established by the capitalist economic revolution, that central areas of decision on the development of society are 'out of reach' of the democratic political process.[23]

A project of revolution which is at the same time 'radically contemporaneous', and uncompromisingly radical, taking up the old dream of humanity by meeting the pressing current needs for structural transformation in a way that takes them to their full emancipatory consequences, will have to find answers to the elementary questions of why people need to get rid of the effects of capitalist domination once and for all, by getting rid of the capitalist mode of production itself, and how they can go about achieving this, without at the same time simply reinforcing the political power of a state they are themselves unable to control. These questions lead us to the double problematic of the necessary depth of the transformation process required to overcome the capitalist mode of production, in a society bearing its direct or indirect imprint in every single fibre,[24] and of the restructuring of the process of reproduction of society, including its regulating institutions, that will allow the empowering of concrete individuals and collectives in a development towards direct democratic regulation.[25]

What is still being sought is nothing less than a 'social revolution' which goes beyond the double, political and economical, revolution of the bourgeoisie. And that goes beyond it in a peculiar way: without reproducing its characteristic 'blind spots' and illusions, and yet without neglecting the deeper reasons that underlay their ideological appeal even to the dominated masses, i.e. without neglecting their (false) promise of ending all domination of humans over humans. What is needed is a political project of real historical change that takes up the task of concretely[26] abolishing all structures of such a domination – in the words of the young Karl Marx: 'hence with the categorical imperative that all relations in which man is an debased, enslaved, left alone or despicable being have to be overthrown.' (Contribution to a Critique of Hegel's Philosophy of Right, Marx-Engels, Werke, vol. 1, 385). This again must not be read as promising a future society that is liberated from the material need of reproducing (and, eventually, safe-guarding) its own conditions of existence, i.e. of economical (and ecological) considerations. Nor is it to advance to a specifically post-political, 'anarchist'[27] or 'technocratic' state of history, where everybody would simply decide for himself, or where 'scientific authority' would settle any questions that may arise, deciding in the place of everybody, without any need to engage with others into a collective, political process of perpetually defining and redifining the needs that may be fulfilled, and those that must be postponed, or even neglected, as well as the cost in terms of human effort and ecological change that a given society should allocate to them.[28]

Second reflection:
revolution after the crisis of statism and technolatry[29]

> The causes for the defeat of the working class are to be sought for much deeper than in the tactics of its parties, evidently deeper than in single tactical mistakes.
>
> (Otto Bauer (1934), in Werke, vol. 3, p. 990)

Today, in a historical situation, where the post-war achievements of Western European social democracy have not only shown their severe limitations, but also have almost generally given way to a renewal of quite un-socialized forms of capitalist regulation, and where the crisis of Eastern European regimes has become so deep, that a revolutionary transformation from above seems to be the only possibility of re-opening a process of socialist transition that is left to them, it is, certainly, more pertinent than ever to observe that it is by analyzing its *errors* that historical, human projects may arrive at correcting their available knowledge. The historical project of revolution that is to be actualized in the present situation is that of *proletarian* revolution – at least, where ever[30] the aims and effects of bourgeois revolution have been institut-ionalized in their characteristic, rather peculiar way.[31] Actualizing the project of revolution begins, therefore, by identifying and analyzing the deeper causes of that generalized defeat of the working class movement Bauer was farsighted enough to see in 1934, before it has been doubly compounded first by the rise of fascism, and then by the rise of the Fordist USA to world-wide hegemony after the Second World War.

The theoretical and philosophical debate around the deeper causes of this defeat had been vivid and brilliant in the time of its very beginnings, the Soviet Union functioning as a 'laboratory' for a creative and critical Marxist debate, and new, independent theoretical initiatives springing up among the various traditions of the working class movement, in its social-democratic tradition as well as in it newly forming Communist branch, (from the Italian *consigli* to Austro-Marxism), while at the same time an auton-omous theoretical and philosophical practice of Marxism came into being with the first beginnings of what was later to become 'Western Marxism'.[32] With the Stalinization of the Communist movement, however, and with the

marginalization of social democracy in the remaining parliamentary democratic Western countries, together with the exile and the persecution of
the European left intelligentsia, the debate became muted, exactly when
its urgency was greatest. For a long period, relatively isolated figures like
Trotsky, Thalheimer or Otto Bauer represented a potential of self-criticism
of the working class movement outside of its mainstream, while Gramsci (as
rendered by Togliatti), or Mao stood for theoretical innovation from within
the Stalinized Communist mainstream, and the philosophical despair of the
Frankfurt School in its US exile, or the open renegation of authors like
Arthur Koestler, represented a potential of intellectual criticism the working
class movement itself had lost.[33] The road to a self-critical and productive
marxist debate had to be reopened again, with great difficulty, in a rather
devious way, reaching from the ambiguity of the philosophical project of
'de-dogmatizing' marxism (Lefebvre, Goldmann, Kosik, the early Budapest
school) to the apparent dogmatism of Althusser's philosophical theses, which
led up, in the late 1970s, to a violent diagnosis of the crisis of the Communist
movement. Twenty years of debate only to arrive at a full-fledged diagnosis
of the crisis of marxism, that had been repressed by official marxism since the
1930s?

Today, a decade later, the balance of this development may be drawn
in a more positive way: once the liberating step of acknowledging the
repressed crisis had been taken, not only new philosophical and theoretical
work became possible,[34] it also was increasingly seen that the scattered,
marginalized or muffled self-critical labour of Marxists since the 1930s had
become open to a new reading, as it were, to a re-appropriation within a
suddenly widened horizon. In this double process two new axes of marxist
theoretical self-criticism emerged and gained theoretical consistency: the
diagnosis of the 'state trap', in which preceding marxism had been caught,
led to a new understanding of the political tasks to be mastered within a
revolutionary process, and the diagnosis of the neglect of the determination
of the productive powers themselves by the capitalist accumulation process
and its imperialist modes of regulation[35] brought marxist analysis to a meeting
ground with the 'new social movements' that had begun to develop in the
meantime, by opening a much more radical perspective on the necessities of
material transformation involved in any sustainable revolutionary process.

Both axes of marxist self-criticism have immediate implications for the
conception of 'social revolution': first, the diagnosis of the 'state trap' has
likewise refuted all conceptions of simply using the existing state, with its
complex networks of institutions, to 'implement' a revolutionary process,
and all conceptions of doing so by means of a 'new state', to be constructed after smashing the present, bourgeois one. Revolutionary processes, in
order to be politically and socially sustainable, have to reach into the very
'molecular' fibres of the social reproduction process as a whole, in all their
variety – and this cannot be done via the two elementary media of constraint

which characterize the action of any state as such, via commands backed by violence, or via promises of compensation backed by tax money.[36] It can only be achieved through appealing to the individual and collective subjects concerned, i.e. regarding subjects themselves constituted under the dominant ideology, by inducing and reinforcing anti-ideological, anti-domination effects of resistance, rebellion and revolt *within* the network of ideological practice, determined in the first instance by dominating ideology. This result of theoretical analysis, in turn, precludes, at the same time, any relapse into the ideology of the 'sovereign subject',[37] underlying the seeming evidence of 'spontaneist' or 'movementist' alternative conceptions of a revolutionary process. In the field of ideology this means to be sensitive to the real resistances and rebellions that happen[38] among concerned subjects, being able to respond to them in articulating demands and struggles, constructing social and political movements and powers that challenge the efficacy of dominant ideology. This cannot be done by using the means of the state machinery, be it the existing one, or embryonic (or full-fledged) future ones. Only the self-activity of the concerned subjects is able to provide such a process with a sustainable basis that is able to grow, until it can, more partially, or more globally,[39] challenge the efficacy of the dominating ideology.

Second, to take a point of departure in a central piece of marxist theory that has been somewhat neglected within the marxist tradition: the transformation of 'labour power as a commodity' into 'labour potential' of 'associated free individuals' is a historical process that does not only go beyond mere property relations, but also involves two distinct processes of transformation – the conversion of the 'objective' productive forces, of the entire 'machinery' of economic and extra-economic production, produced by the capitalist mode of production, by capitalist accumulation, into material instruments and conditions of a conscious regulation of the material exchange of humankind with nature; and it also involves the collective and individual appropriation of the 'subjective' productive forces, of the capacities the exploited classes already and still possess[40] to re-shape and to re-use these objective instruments of the material reproduction of society in a way corresponding to their self-defined needs,[41] in order to make them the instruments of their own full and sustainable development, individually and collectively, as well as of the capacities that have been separated for them, relegated to the exclusive control of scientific experts.[42]

These efforts of theoretical criticism have been accompanied by the development of new practical sensitivities and initiatives, by the emergence of new practices of opposition on a mass scale, as those of the 'civil rights movement' in the USA of the late 1950s and early 60s, or of the 'anti-colonial movements' that emerged in Western Europe at the same time – or, later, the student and youth revolt of the 1960s, and the 'new social movements' of the 1970s. This practical movement of criticism,[43] which has begun with the emergence of a new left since the 1960s, has, since then, taken the shape of definite grassroots political projects. Some of them influenced the appearance of new parliamentary parties[44] within specific national situations:[45] like the People's Socialist Party in Denmark, the 'rainbow coalition' in the USA, the 'women's party' in Iceland, or the Greens in West Germany. These four examples represent, as it were, specimens for different types of development that have been taking place: a former Euro-communist party transformed by the impact of new mass movements, a political project mainly based on the struggle against race discrimination, and operating within a two-party system of low social efficacy, a social movement which was invigorated by new impulses to the point of developing something like a parliamentary branch, or a new party formed by a difficult convergence of new social movement and self-critical new left activists under the pressure of an exclusive electoral device – which could not legitimately be changed after having been overcome.[46]

In a different way, however, this movement of criticism has also affected some of the larger organizations coming out of the political tradition of the working class movement: the PCI's move towards 'eurosocialism'[47] is one example of this, the recent struggles for a renewal of the British Labour Party is, certainly, a second one, and the SPD itself, with its attempts at programmatic renewal (cf. the so-called Irsee programme draft, 1988), in order to halt the rise of the Greens, may be cited as a third one.

What I think paramount in these developments is neither a return of the working class movement to a revolutionary purity it never possessed, nor an advance towards a kind of political unity it will never achieve. It will rather be a painful process of recomposition which will define new cleavages cutting across old ones, making e.g. the ex-Stalinist whose self-criticism has brought him to a position of grassroots democracy and political control of the development of the productive forces side with the ex-hippie, the ex-trotskyite, and the ex-social-democrat against people coming from the very same origins, but having drawn opposite conclusions, i.e. defending centralized state control and the latest 'technological revolution'. And the diversity of political conjunctures and party systems will certainly lead to the necessity of a new kind of 'poly-centrism' – while the transnational strategies of leading capitalist groups and imperialist state alliances will rapidly force these organisations and movements to develop a new kind of internationalist practice. What will certainly emerge more clearly in coming years is the obsolescence of some traditional dividing lines concerning tactical differences – while the new cleavages and alliances will be organizing around the strategic problematics of a radical transformation as such and not around the question of the adequate means of building a social movement and counter-power that will be able to start and to sustain such a process of transformation. This is not to say that 'social revolution' or 'reforming capitalism', i.e. active revolution, from below, or passive revolution, from above, have ceased to be alternatives. It has, however, become far more difficult to distinguish the respective practices and forces within a concrete conjuncture – and the possession of traditional ideological *shibboleths* has ceased to be of any use in such a critical ideological and political process.

Third reflection:
revolution on the brink of human self-destruction

> Is there any science that seems less apt, by virtue of its innocent approach, to fill the world with apprehension? Those young men and women. . . who are. . . inventing counting traps for prairie mice. . . – they do not resemble at all those exiles who had been preparing, in Zurich, Vienna, and Munich, ..., the downfall of a world. And yet, suddenly, the mice counters transgress a boundary.
> (Carl Amery, Natur als Politik, Reinbek 1978, p. 43)

So far, I have been discussing the contemporary problematics of revolution in a perspective of continuity, however broken. This would be insufficient, because today's conjuncture is also determined by a number of new factors which are not contained within this continuity, nor to be derived from it in some way. Schematically speaking, I can see three such new elements of today's global situation, presenting us with corresponding new, real challenges in rethinking the idea of revolution for our own times:

First, the *ecological crisis*, with the new urgencies and responsibilities it is imposing;

second, the current *crisis of traditional military strategies*, which urges us to call into question the traditional link between revolution and war;

third, the ongoing *struggle for democratic rights* to new nations, and to new social categories – defined by gender, race, and age – and the challenge this is presenting to the 'digestive' capacities of the dominant ideologies, as well as to working class organizations patently under their influence.

With regard to these elements, two aspects have to be considered here:[48] On the one hand, it will be necessary to grasp the specificity of their novelty, on the other, to draw out the consequences they entail for an actualized conception of a revolutionary process. As to the first aspect, one property can be underlined which the three elements seem to share: being, all of them, although in different ways, irreducible to the specific objects of the emancipatory class struggle of the working class, they pose a new problematic of alliances, which is qualitatively different even from a rectified version of the alliance between the proletarian and the peasant class: the alliance to be articulated does not only concern individual and collective subjects that are objectively included within the exploited working class: it is also necessarily of a long-term character, without a tangible perspective of the different categories to be articulated in it vanishing in a process of social change or with no realistic perspective of being overcome by such a process in the short or medium term. For instance, those concerned with an ecological alteration will necessarily be, at least in part, other working class subjects, their immediate interests standing against the interests of those committed to a certain branch of production,[49] and there is not the slightest perspective that this difference of approach will wither away by virtue of some future social process. Even though the militarist deformation of our societies, certainly will be effectively engaged before the turn of the century[50] – it will probably be with us for some considerable time, and a comparable opposition holds between those within and those without the 'military – industrial complex'.[51] And as long as international relations of dependency and discriminatory structures based on gender, race, or age will persist or will still be perceived as a possible danger – which, given the deep material roots of such practices within the global reproduction processes of contemporary capitalist societies, will be for a long period – the same holds true for differences and oppositions resulting from them.[52]

Moreover, the risk, and the urgency, involved in all three of these elements do entail a number of constraints on responsible revolutionary tactics – and, to some degree, even on revolutionary strategy: certain types of industrial disruption, like e.g. nuclear power plants or certain chemical plants getting out of control, cannot be accepted as an inevitable side-product of class conflicts, and even the amount of ignorance we have, e.g. concerning the climatic and ecological consequences of large-scale deforestation, has to serve as an indication of avoiding types of action that may accelerate such processes.[53] Certain types of military conflicts, not only nuclear war, but also chemical and biological warfare, or 'conventional' war in densely industrialized areas, will also have to be excluded from the options of a revolutionary political practice[60] – as will be the recourse, in socialist transition processes, to violent and/or industrializing ways of birth control and 'demographical politics', not just because of the destruction of possible alliances across the gender division they entail, but also because of the risks to which they, maybe unintentionally, expose the very biological process of human reproduction.

Finally, the very difference of these issues and problems, which are irreducible to each other in theory as in practice, imposes a structure of internal plurality on any realistic, adequate revolutionary strategy and tactics if the specific contradictions which concern ecological, peace, or woman's liberation movements are not and cannot be addressed in an autonomous way, derived from the specific theory and practice they develop in their struggle; and if, on the other hand, the specific tasks of industrial workers fighting capitalist exploitation cannot be addressed quite as specifically, then the whole movement risks failure. If they are not able to present the practical credentials of concrete, specific emancipatory struggles, resistances, and rebellions, opposition movements will always be weaker than the reproduction mechanisms of dominant ideology – which simply cannot be confronted effectively on the level of general ideological discourse.

As will easily be seen from these short remarks, the 'overdetermination' of anti-capitalist, revolutionary struggle, serves to reinforce the effects of the critique of the 'state-trap' and of a too simple, technocratic conception of the material transformations involved in a revolutionary transition. I would go as far in this direction as to maintain that, indeed, the 'new social movements' concerned with these specific contradictions have a tendential 'liberating effect' on a working class movement, that has been caught in many ways by the 'passive revolutionary' mechanism and processes of the last hundred years of capitalist history.

Concluding remarks.

The project of a contemporary revolution that has overcome the ambiguities of statism and technolatry will have to take shape concretely in the project of an ecological, feminist, and socialist revolutionary process. The construction of such a project on sound foundations, and yet in an imaginative way, adequate to the real tasks it faces, and attractive to the minds of many who still are under the influence of dominant ideology, can be helped by theoretical analysis, and may be furthered by philosophical interventions that succeed in addressing the right, sensitive problems. When the continuing attractiveness of the latest *aggiornamento* of dominant ideology – in the form of neo-liberal ideology and politics – fades in the 1990s, all those who have begun to see the real urgency of such a revolution will need such theoretical analysis and philosophical intervention.[61] But it is as will not be forget that the inventiveness of masses in revolt has been and will continue to be beyond the imagination of the most sensitive philosopher.

NOTES

1. Molina (*L'Etat du Monde,* Paris 1986) has shown that even this idea of revolution, dated though it certainly is, is not nearly as dead, as established French ideology has it since the late 1970s.
2. Subsequent defeats, as well as later parochialism, have somewhat blurred the fact that this began – although with rather shaky connections – as an international, world-wide process, stretching from Shanghai via Berkeley to Berlin-West, Paris, and Turin shaking the latter-day strongholds of fascism in Europe on its way round the globe: Lisbon, Madrid and Athens.
3. Out of the ten revolutionary demands of the *Communist Manifesto* (Marx/ Engels, Werke, vol. 4, p. 481s.) only three – the expropriation of landed property, the abolition of the law of inheritance, and the creation of an equal constraint to work for all – have not been at least partially tackled – in however perverted ways – by such initiatives as a preventive restructuring from above.
4. It would be wrong to treat anti-totalitarianism as a pseudo-issue. After the 'night of the century' (Mandel) it is a real pertinent question to ask for the conditions of the rise of such absolute, and lethal, however different forms of state power as that of the Nazis or that of Stalinism. This is, however, no reason at all to accept the theoretical and political distortions present in much anti-totalitarian theory (cf. e.g. the international committee that led Polish defenders of Solidarnosc to demonstrate alongside with upholders of Somozist nostalgia in Nicaragua). Nor is it any reason for neglecting the differences between e.g. the French 'antitotalitarians' like Glucksmann who have come to side with reactionary conformism and their German counterparts like Cohn-Bendit who have turned

ordinary 'reformists', constituting the spearhead of the 'Realist' wing within the West German Greens.

5. As it had been *de facto* under the Stalinist system of domination in the East, until Gorbachev proclaimed his 'revolution from above', calling to be relieved by a 'revolution from below' (Gorbachev 1986) – while maintaining at least some of the ambiguity of an 'official' use of revolution by the holders of state power with regard to any revolution that is not effectively controlled by themselves, and therefore, in the last instance, a passive one, as Gorbachev himself is aware.

6. This real difficulty has led a number of more imaginative thinkers to look for sub-stitute 'historical subjects' of another revolution in the psycho-socially deprived marginals or in the 'world-village' of an imperialist periphery. These attempts, while in fact helping to understand new – or neglected – contradictions within contemporary social formations, could never offer a satisfactory solution to the question of how any sizable transfer of power from its present centres to revo-lutionary counter-powers could ever be brought about without actively involving masses of those exploited and dominated social classes and categories.

7. It seems to me necessary to maintain – and even to stress – the basic conceptual linkage between the capitalist mode of production and historical imperialism as well as its successors that has been established by Hobson, Hilferding and Lenin, and which has often been neglected in 'phase models' of the development of capitalism. This has the theoretical implication, which I accept, that we cannot analyse the crimes of Stalinism under the category of imperialism. We rather have to analyse it under a new category for processes of socialist transition that went wrong in some radical way. Even Soviet authors are now beginning to discuss the category of counter-revolution for what happened in the Soviet Union with the implementation of Stalinist politics.

8. To indicate this context is not to trivialize the uniqueness in terms of human destruction of German fascism – it rather is a first step of grasping its multiple determination by concrete historical situations as well as by more general, struc-tural effects.

9. Using resources – like air, soil, water, or wild animals – that on a societal or glo-bal level have to be reproduced or substituted at considerable cost, constituting 'external costs' of production, (if they can be substituted at all) as 'free goods' for capitalist production.

10. This is not to say that the problems of ecological sustainability or of women's liberation would not have arisen, as it is sometimes implied – they simply would have arisen under far more propitious conditions, without having to counter the double, civil and military impact of capitalist exploitation and imperialist domina-tion structures.

11. Of course they are enunciated in an ambiguous way, putting 'humankind' against 'class emancipation'. But this false, 'humanist' wording should not deceive us about the substantive content of these claims of 'new thinking' – which has to begin, in fact, by putting aside false definitions of class interest in order to become able again to pose the real problems of class struggle of our times, which are no less than struggles with the survival of humankind at stake.

12. This has to be more than the traditional categories of 'tacit consent' or of 'trust' the subtle John Locke introduced to justify the domination of the modern bourgeois state; something like 'potential active consent' – which may be measured by the potential of active and effective dissent that is in the hands of any individual – may serve as a provisional formula.

13. It has not been by accident that the problematics of the 'imperative mandate' has been central to every practical experience of grass-roots democracy – from the Paris Commune to the 'citizen's initiatives' of the 1970s.

14. Who started from making their own the task of educating good citizens only to arrive at the radical demand of the equality of all human beings.
15. Cf. however the important advances made into that direction by e.g. Thucydides, Ibn Khaldoun, or, opening on a new development, Machiavelli.
16. What the effect is of this new situation for the ulterior development of philosophy is one of the less clear issues within the marxist tradition. The only element that seems to be established by now, is the important fact that the 'theoretical counter-revolution' of the Stalinist 'emendation of marxist reason' (as DIAMAT) is certainly no legitimate part of it.
17. What a market mechanism is – and could be – comes out most clearly in the recent controversy between Mandel, Nove, and others.
18. Norberto Bobbio has been foremost in posing the problem of representative, constitutionally institutionalized democracy within the marxist debate again, where it had been neglected as it were by common consent between statism and movementism. Which is, however, not to say that the underlying assumption of Bobbio and his followers – i.e. that marxists should give up their criticism of the state as a separate political form of domination resting upon a real autonomization of the rulers against the ruled – and their plea for the specific institutional forms of representative democracy are themselves above criticism.
19. Such reexaminations are now beginning to be available, in French, in George Labica's and Gerard Bensussan's 'Dictionnaire Critique du Marxisme', Paris 1982, 2nd. rev. ed. 1986 (German ed., Berling, Argument, 1984ff.), and in German, in W.F. Haug's and others' 'Neues Worterbuch des Marxismus', which will begin to be published in 1989.
20. Capitalist modes of production have to accumulate, which necessarily entails intensive and extensive forms of material expansion – even if the individual interests of capital owners as human beings dependent on certain natural resources would go against it.
21. This qualification is important – there is nothing that precludes an *accessory* use of a market mechanism even under fairly advanced socialist relations of production, as long as it is certain that it will not get out of the conscious control by the political choices of society.
22. This is not to be misunderstood as maintaining that there is no more social violence outside the state – as there certainly is, e.g. in modern gender relations or in organised crime – , nor as the contention that in pre-capitalist societies there were no 'separate' concentrations of power, in the hands of the ruling classes. I think it is the most adequate way of stating the implications of the separation of 'economy' and 'politics' characteristic of capitalism for its 'political form' itself.
23. The catch-word 'self-production of society' seems to be the best available formula for politics in a class-less society, which has abolished capitalist domination and exploitation, when attention is given to the three simple facts (a) that 'society' is never a real historical agent, nor (b) ever producing its own conditions of existence, nor, finally, (c) the society that produces is ever really identical to the society that is produced. To use it for societal processes under capitalist domination, however, seems to be at least preparing oneself for falling victim to the mystifications of capitalist ideology.
24. It is not just shyness to talk about revolution which has made the metaphor of 'reconstruction/conversion' – as in the 'Umbau' – programme of the German Greens, or as in the debate on 'perestroyka' – so popular in referring to this problematic – it certainly also is an expression of an awareness of the complexity of the task involved.
25. Such a restructuring certainly includes a significant element of 'regionalization' – not because of any romantic attachment to the narrow traditions of backward,

closed regions, dominated by local 'notables', but because of the necessity to bring real power of decision making back into the hands of those immediately concerned. It also implies, in other respects, the overcoming of still existing regional and national boundaries, like e.g. in finding a peaceful and ecological way of living around the Mediterranean. The attitude of the regionalist parties of the 'European Free Alliance' who aim at some kind of independence within a larger, European framework seem to reflect this necessity – although with the limitation of not clearly confronting the dangers of an EC-centred imperialism and chauvinism.

26. Which implies that there can be no short-cuts, no 'domino theory' of revolution: there is no automatic sequence between e.g. overcoming capitalism, and overcoming patriarchy – although the two have become increasingly linked to each other.

27. In the historical sense that expression has taken by the interventions of Stirner, Bakunin, and Kropotkin – which should not keep contemporary revolutionaries from carefully examining the always extremely instructive experiences of historical anarchist practice, especially if it was the practice of a mass movement.

28. Such a basically Saint-Simonian illusion has been inherent in some of the classical marxist formulations on class-less society, as well as on the 'withering away of the state'.

29. The term 'technolatry' seems to be the least inadequate designation for an attitude which did not only project the development of the (technologically defined) productive forces into the position of an (automatic) 'subject *of* history', neglecting class struggle as the elementary form of human historical practice, but which has also tended to define the material societal process of reproduction exclusively in economic terms ('economism') and the economic categories of wealth, need, and cost as exclusively in terms of produced goods ('productivism'). As the critique of 'economism' and 'productivism' have, however, sometimes been used to argue in favour of abandoning such elementary insights of marxist theory as the 'determination in the last instance' or the theoretical primacy of production (in its full sense, including the production of children or of discourse) in, e.g. a materialist theory of needs, I prefer a designation which does not lend itself so easily to misunderstanding.

30. This is not only to be interpreted geographically, but also referring to areas of the social reproduction process, like the area of gender relations, which have remained on this side of bourgeois constitutionalism – and where, accordingly, demands for guaranteed individual rights and enforceable norms and procedures, i.e. demands for an egalitarian state intervention, are still a central point.

31. Care should be taken not to confuse typical situations of bourgeois post-revolutionary structures of domination – like e.g. the existence of a legally unfettered capitalist despotism within the process of production, a generalized venality of politicians, or the existence of uncontrollable secret services, as being situations of a non-realisation of bourgeois revolution: exactly these are the situations by which it is realised as such, bringing and maintaining the bourgeoisie in the position of the ruling class.

32. Perry Anderson's later critique of it does not only start from false hopes of a return to revolutionary purity – and therefore misrepresents a good deal of the real links these thinkers had with the class struggles of their times – , he fails to understand that an autonomous existence of a marxist theoretical and philosophical debate, without an institutionalized subordination to working class organizations (and, therefore, necessarily a subordination to tactical concerns) is, indeed, a key condition for any living marxism, as it is for any kind of living theoretical and philosophical activity.

33. The later intellectual fate of Karl Korsch may be taken as an instructive example

of this regressive development.

34. In which approaches that had fought or ignored each other in preceding phases began to recognize the need for reformulating their basic assumptions in learning from each other, while discovering new, more interesting, but also graver differences within their own tradition.

35. There is more than one such mode of regulation, consecutive in time (like colonialism and neocolonialism) or competing for world hegemony, like the New Deal 'fordism' and German fascism, or like, contemporarily, an emerging neoliberal mode of regulation in the USA, under growing competition from a Western European and a Japanese variant of bargaining corporatism.

36. Of course, the situation is, in reality, more complex, due to the existence of the state as a complex of ideological institutions alongside its networks of coercion and bribery. This does not, however, change the situation, I am trying to focus: either the struggle within this network of institutions is taken up in statist terms – then the issue is getting to the central positions of control which try to run these institutions via these more elementary 'media' of statist action – , or it is granted that the point is, with regard to this network, to win consent, against the dominating ideology, which cannot de done by occupying any 'posts of command', but requires a different strategy, involving necessarily the critical 'self-activity' of the individuals and concrete collectives concerned.

37. Which is itself an effect of bourgeois juridical ideology.

38. Against a certain voluntarism (and corresponding determinism) within the marxist tradition the aleatory aspect of such elementary ideological events is to be stressed.

39. In this protracted process, which is decisive for the fate of any revolutionary development, there is no final victorious battle, although there may be defeats which may break the dynamics of a revolutionary process for a given period – especially, when concerned subjects become convinced that their struggle will only lead to an exchange of the persons ruling over them.

40. Experiences like the 'popular planning' of the Greater London Council have shown the impressive nature of this capacity.

41. Which always, under conditions of a socialised way of production, include a consideration of proportionality between expenditure – in terms of human effort or natural resources – and the satisfaction to be gained.

42. The real tendencies to a proletarization also of scientific wage labourers have not yet abolished this still quite real separation – and it is doubtful that they ever will: new elitist mechanisms of separating theoretical from practical knowledge seem to be invented by the dominating class any time the two get 'too close' to each other.

43. I do not want to imply in any way that this has been something like 'an implementation' of the theoretical and philosophical developments I have alluded to in the preceding paragraph. It sprang up, rather, in unexpected ways, at least for the traditional left, from very concrete practical occasions of rebellion, or, simply, of concern, like the early anti-nuclear movement in Western Europe, or the resistance to the draft in situations of colonial wars.

44. It is to be noted that the concept of a party as inherited from the Marxist tradition is not immediately applicable to such parliamentary parties: they neither are simply 'partisan movements' as the 'communist party' of the manifesto, nor strongly cohesive, disciplined political organisations of activists, as in Lenin's conception of a revolutionary party. They are a political phenomenon specific to a historical conjuncture in which, on the one hand, the social efficacy of the ideological system of dominating politics is so strong – which is rather simply verified by low ratios of abstentionism – , that there is no space for political organisation without it, and where, on the other hand, alternative political organizations which do not, or not

entirely, conform to some main mechanisms of this dominating ideological system of politics and of the mass media linked to it, are not excluded from participating, by electoral devices (as in the UK) or by political interdictions (as in the case of KPD in the FRG).

45. Although their concrete social composition differs, none of these parties is, in a significant sense, except, maybe, ideologically, 'middle class'. All of them represent, in their activists as in their voters, rather certain strata or sectors of the working class the 'old' working class parties failed to organize in a significant way.

46. After the FRG Greens had overcome the 5%-clause of electoral law, there was some discussion in right wing or conservative circles about how to eliminate them again – by opting for a first-past-the-post electoral system (which was unacceptable to the small liberal party, in government since 1969), or even by illegalizing the Greens, which would have made representative democracy a rather thinly disguised farce. Instead, the mass media mounted a continuous campaign against this radical opposition party, trying to block its message from passing, and putting all types of pressure on it to 'grow up', to 'accept the rules of the game'. So far, they have not prevailed.

47. An institutional expression of this is the recent decision of the PCI to leave the Communist group of which it has so far been a member within the 'European Parliament', in order to join the socialist group, with the West-German SPD.

48. I have tried to outline a theoretical approach to the links between capitalist accumulation and the ecological crisis in 'Actuel Marx', No. 3, Paris 1988.

49. Even, when taking away the spurious argument from job (=income) security, which could be made irrelevant under non-capitalist social relations, those who are interested in producing some concrete 'use-values' will tend to underrate the cost in terms of risks and alterations this production may socially or ecologically imply. And this tendency will have to be counter-balanced by giving voice and influence to those concerned by these effects in such decisions on production.

50. To be furthered by unilateral initiatives, as those asked for by the more radical peace movements, and, recently, tentatively put into practice by the Gorbachev administration.

51. Of course, there is no reason to suppose that this opposition will not be overcome by a sufficiently radical social transformation. However, it may be presumed that a tension between whose who support more expeditious ways of solving social conflicts, and those who defend a more radically non-violent way of acting them out will be a long-term constant of future human history – even after the institutionalized violence of the state as a form of social regulation has one day been overcome.

52. Differences between ethnical traditions, however, between gender practices, and age-bound forms of life will certainly continue to be a constant of human social life – they only will have ceased to take the form of a struggle for elementary democratic rights, while 'race', which is itself an ideological category produced by racism, will in fact vanish from human history.

53. I.e, basically, that any revolutionary action has to answer to the same standards of social rationality as any other action of human production, making allowance, of course, for its specific urgency.

60. Non-violence, which had been a pacifist utopian idea in the past, therefore becomes, in a specific interpretation that does not close its eyes before the necessity of effectively countering state violence, a real issue even for revolutionary strategy and tactics.

61. And if they do not rise to the occasions, others will try to make use of it, radicalizing the anti-democratic tendencies contained within dominating ideology itself in the direction of the new right that has begun to take shape over the last decade.

FEMINISM'S REVOLUTIONARY PROMISE[1]
FINDING HOPE IN HARD TIMES

Johanna Brenner

Being a socialist-feminist activist has never been easy. We occupy a stony ground between the popularity of liberal (and social-democratic) feminism's apparently practical reformism and the heady appeal of radical feminism's claim to a female moral/spiritual superiority. Especially in these not so very revolutionary times, to write about the meaning of revolutionary change from the point of view of socialist-feminism seems to be more an exercise in myth-making than analysis, more an expression of utopian hope than an outlining of political strategy. Ironically, just at the moment that socialist-feminists are trying to cope with what we experience as decline if not defeat of feminism, or at least of feminism as a grass-roots movement within which radicals could organize, some on the left are finding in feminism – and other 'new move-ments' – revolutionary subjects to replace the working-class.

Feminism certainly has much to contribute to expanding what marxism understands to be human liberation and to creating the kind of movement that could possibly bring it about. Feminism insists that we take as a field for theory and political intervention domains of social life that marxism has fundamentally ignored: sexuality, intimacy, raising children, the care and nurture of adults. In so doing, feminism has allowed us to think far more extensively than before about the material basis of socialism – about the best way to organize social life to 'make' socialist people and to foster relationships of equality and respect. In confronting the pain and rewards of motherhood in contemporary society, and in understanding mothering as a kind of work, feminism has allowed us to redefine what we mean by both alienated and unalienated labour. In revaluing those human capacities and activities that have been defined as belonging primarily to women, feminism has fundamentally challenged any vision of socialism that fails to re-integrate the dimensions of human life that capitalism has so radi-cally separated. Feminist theory has helped to undermine the system that marxist theory had become: its economic reductionism, its productivism and uncritical approach to technology; its narrow definitions of work, worker, and working-class; its reification of the capitalist split between 'public' and 'private' and the privileging of the public as an arena for theoretical analysis

245

and political organization; its impoverished understandings of consciousness, particularly its inattention to the way that emotional needs shape political understandings, the relationship between gender identities and the construction of political and economic 'interests.' Feminism, in its theory and in its political practice has been a rich resource for the renewal of marxism – for recapturing and developing its radically democratic liberatory vision.

Feminist organizations have wrestled with questions that the marxist left rarely recognized: the tension between process and product, between leadership and inclusiveness, between building collectivity and encouraging critical debate, between creating consensus and appreciating differences, and so forth. Certainly, in our struggle to find 'pre-figurative' forms of organization, the feminist movement hasn't come to easy answers. Indeed, most of the questions feminism raises can only really be answered through a broad process of dialogue and experiment engaging the creativity and experience of many diverse communities of resistance. But if these tensions can't be easily resolved, confronting them has allowed feminism to develop ways of discussing, acting together and deciding (or deciding not to decide) that could help to counter the bureaucratic tendencies that have plagued left organizations, small and large.

The Contribution of 'New Movements'

Contemporary left critics[2] who draw inspiration from the 'new movements' and argue for a politics based on radical democracy rather than on class exploitation have identified a crucial question facing revolutionary socialists: how to move the demand for democratic participation and the struggle against forms of domination other than class from the margins of socialist politics.[3]

Further, while they aren't the only ones making this point, these critics are certainly right, I think, to argue on the one hand for the subversive potential of protests against domination, ecological destruction, nuclear annihilation, and on the other hand that a revolutionary socialist bloc is a political creation: no demand, including the demand for democratic participation, is necessarily subversive and any struggle can be articulated to an incorporationist project as well as a revolutionary one.

Laclau and Mouffe argue:

> All struggles, whether those of workers or other political subjects, left to themselves, have a partial character, and can be articulated to very different discourses. It is this articulation which gives them their character, not the place from which they come. There is therefore no subject – nor, further, any 'necessity' – which is absolutely radical and irrecuperable by the dominant order, and which constitutes an absolutely guaranteed point of departure for a total transformation.[4]

Many of us would agree with their salutary focus on the political, on the constructed and contingent character of revolutionary consciousness. But what are the strategic conclusions to be drawn? Because there is no subject which is necessarily radical, does that mean that revolutionary worldviews are as likely to be constructed and adopted by one social group as another? To be sure, needs and interests are socially and historically constructed and counter-hegemonic worldviews are part of this process. Radical discourses redefine needs and identify interests in ways that illuminate the interconnection of different needs and interests and link those needs and interests to a vision of transformed society. But worldviews are carried by groups who by their social location and experience, their everyday experience as well as their experience in reform movements, are more or less open to one set of ideas or another.

Moreover, the struggle against exploitation and the struggle against domination, ought not to be counterposed. If the new movements have shown us the importance of other dimensions of oppression and other identities as sources of radical protest, their evolution has also demonstrated how structures of capital accumulation, when unchallenged (either politically or economically), limit and distort these possibilities. While there are still some activist 'new movement' groups, in general the new movements have failed to extend their social base and, at least in the U.S., increasingly rely on strategies such as lobbying and providing expertise within existing political structures. Their move toward more conservative reform strategies cannot be explained simply by a failure of political imagination. The leaderships of these movements have responded to a political climate whose hostility to reform is definitely shaped by an international capitalist offensive against labour and the defeat and disorganization of the trade unions.

These pressures – and their political consequences – are quite clear in the successes and failures of feminism. A consideration of this one new movement perhaps can make clear the enduring necessity for socialist revolutionaries to base our politics (organizations, activities, as well as programme on the self-activity of those people we can broadly call the working-class.[5].

Feminism After the Second Wave

In the 1960's and 1970's feminism had an historic role to play as a 'cross-class' movement for democratic rights. For it is only in our time and through feminist organizing, that the bourgeois revolution has been completed and women have become not only citizens but also owners of their own person and truly free sellers of their own labour power. The entire edifice which legislated women's subservience in marriage, denied us control over our bodies and reproductive capacity, and legalized our economic marginalization has been substantially dismantled. This victory has helped to force a reorganization of the gender order – materially, culturally, politically. The terms of this reorganization are now a matter of contest. In this struggle, women face not only a reactionary right that romanticizes the patriarchal family but also a modernizing right which celebrates meritocratic values and individual choice, understood to reside in the market.

As its opponents are changing, so too is feminism. Feminism began as a real social movement. The autonomous, grass-roots, local organizations which were the hallmark of second-wave feminism – and the locus of its creative genius – have been replaced by feminism as organized interest group. While feminists (in the broadest sense of advocates for women) have entered and begun to affect conservative as well as liberal and social-democratic parties, business and professional organizations as well as trade unions, the major contemporary inheritor of second-wave feminism is to be found in what I would call 'social welfare feminism' – a loose network of individuals and organizations inside and outside the state apparatus who seek to represent the interests of women, including working-class and racially oppressed women. Feminism in advanced capitalist countries today is much more a network of organizations for lobbying than for grass-roots organizing. The membership provides money, sometimes votes, sometimes letters and phone-calls, but very little local activism.

Like their counterparts in the trade unions, although perhaps even less organizationally tied to their social base than trade union officials and staff, the women who make their living one way or another as representatives of women's interests (what Australian feminists have called 'femocrats') have particularly strong connections to the political parties that have historically supported the expansion of the welfare state – the social-democratic parties (and the Democratic Party in the U.S.). While feminists have been able to wield considerable influence within these parties, and within their governments when in power, they have also been bounded by their dependence on these parties and the state apparatus, and by the vulnerability of their own organizations with their relatively weak social base. Thus, in general (and depending on the relative strength of the political parties to which they are tied) feminists have been pushed onto the defensive politically.

Where, then, lies feminism's transformative promise? I would argue that the same social, economic, and political changes that have led to the institutionalization of feminism and its cultural incorporation have created the possibility of a new kind of feminist organization – one based on the self-activity of working-class women. Rather than a cross-class movement for democratic rights, such a women's movement would be based in organizations of and for women which are allied to and part of other struggles and located organizationally within working-class movements, whether these are based in communities or workplaces. Such a movement would not necessarily be revolutionary – any more than trade unions or other working-class organizations are. Nonetheless, by both their structural position and experience working-class women are best placed to create and respond to a political practice that does go beyond reformism to bridge socialism and feminism. The realization of this potential depends in part on whether the revolutionary socialist left will embrace, in its vision of revolution and modes of organization, the insights and experience of feminist theory and practice.

The Impact of Increasing Class Divisions Among Women

As an organized self-conscious political movement feminism has been largely middle-class and white. Women of colour certainly made crucial contributions to feminist theory in their writing and to feminist politics in their community organizing. But only in the 1980's and mainly through the trade unions have working-class women become organized with a consciousness of their special capacities and needs. This is not to deny the participation of women workers, both unionized and not, such as teachers, in the feminist movement of the 1960's and 1970's, but only to argue that organized feminism remains over-whelmingly white and middle class.

In the 1960's and 1970's working class women (white women and women of colour) entered politics as members of families and communities. They were at the core of the civil rights, welfare rights, school integration, tenants, and other movements. In those struggles, women often transformed their con-sciousness, developed a sense of their personal effectiveness and their right to respect in personal and public life, learned to value women's leadership, and some even contested with men in their movements over programme, demands, strategy. But they did not, for the most part, identify their organi-zations and struggles with feminism or women's rights. They spoke as women of an oppressed class, or race, or community, while the feminist movement spoke of Woman.

This feminist movement, for its own part, made historic gains for women, including working class women. But working class women were not the major actors in making reform nor its primary beneficiaries. Feminist demands for equality have been culturally incorporated and institutionalized as the right to compete and to contract. Old assumptions about the natural basis of the sexual division of labour have been challenged. Women are free to negotiate relationships and parental responsibilities with men, to choose 'life-styles' and 'careers.' This new gender ideal reflects real changes, especially in the lives of middle class women who have the resources to negotiate the class and race-biased systems of education, cultural formation, employment, etc. Indeed, women have become more class divided – and it is even less the case today that a middle-class movement can speak for all women.[6] Although almost all working women have double responsibilities, either because they do not get equal participation from male partners or because they are single parents, women in managerial and professional work can find individual solu-tions to combining waged work and family care. Their higher incomes makes it possible to buy their way out of household responsibilities and especially to have quality childcare; they have more bargaining power as individuals to negotiate benefits like paid parental leave; they have more control over their job conditions, and thus more flexibility at work; their higher status jobs place them in less dangerous and vulnerable positions.[7]

The majority of women cannot achieve equality through individual solu-tions. Most crucially, so long as caring for other people is the private responsibility of individual households, women will find it difficult to break out of the vicious cycle in which their relatively low wages reinforce the sexual division of labour within the family, and their domestic responsibilities disadvantage them in the labour market. In addition, for most women, single parenthood will continue to spell hardship and poverty. It is hardly surprising if many working-class women, even those who share feminist aspirations for respect and equality, feel very ambivalent about feminism. Women's increasing freedom seems to have come at the expense of decreasing protections – in a society of atomized individuals who regard each other as means to end, many women can only be the losers. The drudgery of a double day is hardly liberation; and identities realized in expanded consumption, in appropriating marketed lifestyles and images, can't fill our need for social recognition and effective participation.

However, the reforms necessary to promote most women's equal participation in work and public life and thus women's equality in personal life, have proven to be much more difficult to win than the legal and cultural changes that are the legacy of second wave feminism. As a movement for legal reform, feminism was able to make gains in the 1960's and 1970's without really taking on capitalist class power. That is not to say that it was easy to force managers to stop discriminating in hiring or to pay women and men equally for equal work, or to legalize abortion. Nor is it to say that these gains are even today uncontested. But a movement that was predominantly based in the middle class – educated women, students, affluent housewives, professional women – could still compel legislatures to pass anti-discrimination law, compel the police and the courts to enforce it.[8]

To change the situation of working-class women, however, will require a significant redistribution of resources. Working-class women require, at minimum, quality affordable childcare (and eldercare) and paid time off for parental responsibilities (including meeting children's educational and emotional as well as physical needs) and in the longer run, shorter work days – not only so that parents can enjoy relating to their children but also so that they have time in their lives for activities other than meeting responsibilities in paid work and domestic work. Most crucially, women need time for organizing a politics to rediscover, re-name, and combat women's oppression.

Yet, any substantial reorganization of social reproduction represents a serious claim on surplus wealth – and therefore runs up against the interests and demands of capital (expressed in both the power of individual employers and the resistance by the state to providing the material basis for women's equality). Even in relatively wealthy countries with strong social democratic parties, state provisions – family allowances, paid parental leave, state subsidized childcare – are still not extensive enough to undercut the logic of a sexual division of labour. One year paid parental leave, and a week or two's worth of paid family leave a year, makes doing two jobs easier, but households still need lots of unpaid labour to sustain themselves. Responsibility for dependent people (children, the ill, the elderly, etc.) requires time, emotional effort and physical work from household members. While some women can demand equality of sacrifice from male partners or manage well alone, most end up in arrangements where they are the primary caregivers, achieving a decent living standard through the contributions of male partners whose greater income earning capacities underwrite their privileged primary 'breadwinner' status. Moreover, the scope of subsidies and government provisions is always constrained by the demands of capital accumulation – economic downturns lead to state cutbacks, often most severely in highly labour intensive areas of personal services and in those services that meet the needs of the least politically well-mobilized constituencies, in other words, in those services most important to women and especially mothers.[9]

I am not arguing that the persistence of the sexual division of labour in the occupational structure and in the household is simply the outcome of rational responses by men and women to material difficulties they face. Clearly, women's life goals, their desires for children, their sense of responsibility for elderly parents are socially shaped, and women enter into and stay in relationships with men for reasons other than economic survival. Further, had women not to contend with men's resistance, the possibilities for changing the sexual division of labour in the household or in the workplace would be much greater even within the limits set by the protection of capital accumulation and the privatization of social reproduction. Nonetheless, these structural limitations are important barriers to women's self-organization and points of resistance to feminist projects.

The Political Drift to the Right
Once we consider this point, it becomes easier to understand why a fundamentally minoritarian political movement, the new right, has been so successful a counter to feminism. The appearance of a right-wing opposition was only to be expected in reaction to feminism's challenging the traditional gender order. However, there is nothing inevitable about the right's capacity to define the terms of political discourse, to put feminism on the defensive, especially because most women reject the right's vision. Indeed, the right appears so influential not because it reflects majority sentiment but because there is no politics and no political organization that articulates a compelling alternative worldview. Without the capacity to construct personal dilemmas as political issues, feminism is necessarily on the defensive as it confronts an opposition whose political influence reaches far beyond its numbers. Rejecting a mainstream feminism that over-values male-defined success, accepts the competitive and hierarchical structures of capitalist society, uncritically supports the technocratic welfare state, yet repelled by the right's repressive moralism, most women have turned away from participation in organized political life. It is not only the pressures of everyday survival but

the barrenness of politics that pushes women to seek solutions in a perfected personal life.

Still, feminism remains very much alive, institutionalized in a vast network of organizations which together create a kind of 'woman's lobby.' Configurations reflect national political structures. In the U.S., this network includes organizations that are part of government at local and national levels – women's commissions and task forces, affirmative action offices, parts of the social welfare bureaucracy, etc.; traditional political organizations (e.g., the Congressional Women's Caucus, the National Women's Political Caucus, organizations within the Republican and Democratic Parties, the National Organization for Women); lobbies for almost every women's issue from welfare rights to tax reform to abortion; organizations who work in and around in the judicial system, primarily lending legal support to anti-discrimination and other hopefully precedent-setting cases. The lobby also includes groups that are not explicitly political, such as the official associations of predominantly women professions (social workers, librarians, nurses, etc.); women's caucuses and organizations of women in traditionally male professions; organizations of women trade union officials; organizations of social service providers, and so on. This women's lobby functions as a traditional political interest group aligned primarily with the Democratic Party.

Of course, political differences remain within mainstream feminism. The old style liberal feminism, focussed primarily on legislating equal treatment rather than expanding state services, unwilling to address class and race differences among women, is still quite powerful. Indeed, this brand of feminism has been increasingly incorporated into political discourses of the centre and all but the extreme right. The debate about whether mothers should work, whether children should be in day care, whether women ought to be able to compete with men in economic and political life, has been pretty much won by the 'feminist' side. The argument now is over whether the state should take responsibility for creating the conditions for 'equal opportunity' or whether that can all be left to the competitive incentives of the marketplace.[10] In North America, for instance, the debate on childcare legislation revolves not around whether mothers should work, but how much the government should spend on daycare, and for whom, and whether the state should subsidize private providers (through vouchers or tax-credits, for instance) or develop public childcare.[11] Social-welfare feminists argue for state intervention and effort, and many have come to elaborate a politics that looks to the state for much more than anti-discrimination legislation and enforcement.[12] If not by their own experience, then through the lives of women they try to help and, perhaps most important, through pressure from organizations of trade union women and Black women, these social welfare feminists have organized campaigns for government intervention to help working-class women: e.g., paid parental leave, quality child care, subsidized health care, pay equity.

However, given a) the tremendous resistance in this decade to expanding government spending in general, b) the powerful industrial and regional interests who defend the current distribution of state funding, e.g., the military-industrial complex, and c) the much greater political resources of middle-class as compared to working-class/poor constituencies, most of these efforts have either been completely defeated or the legislation finally passed has benefited primarily middle-class women and had a negligible or in some cases even deleterious impact on working class and poor women.[13] Moreover, facing these very powerful constraints, social welfare feminists (who because of their political worldview and structural location are in any case much more at home with legislating benefits for women than with helping women to organize themselves) have failed to expand their grass-roots activist base.

Without that kind of support, however, they have been especially vulnerable to pressures from the right. This is nowhere more visible than in the attempt to re-appropriate 'the family' from the right, primarily by recasting demands for expanded state benefits for women as a programme to strengthen the family.[14] In the spring of 1988, for example, Representative Patricia Schroeder, co-chair of the U.S. Congressional Women's Caucus, organized a 'Great American Family Tour,' in which she and other speakers campaigned across the U.S. for parental leave, childcare, housing, and health care legislation. In conjunction with Schroeder's campaign, the Coalition of Labor Union Women organized a demonstration in Washington, D.C. on these same issues, calling the demonstration 'Celebrate the American Family: Working Together for Change.' This strategy has been especially disastrous in marginalizing the issue of compulsory heterosexuality on the feminist political agenda and thereby strengthening the influence of conservatives on issues such as abortion, teenage sexual rights, lesbian/gay rights, AIDS.[15] Organizers of the CLUW demonstration refused to include gay/lesbian rights or abortion rights as family issues, would not accept speakers from organizations involved in those campaigns, and attempted to keep gay/lesbian organizations from displaying their literature at the rally.[16] Demands for reform that increase women's sexual independence and that directly contest male domination in personal relationships cannot be so easily recast as 'really' programmes to improve the lives of children and men – which is what 'pro-family' politics is all about. Moreover, justifying benefits to women in this way further delegitimizes women's claim to autonomy, self-development, and individuality, undercutting the very ground on which the project of women's liberation has to rest.

From this analysis, the counterposition of feminism and marxism, of the feminist movement to the trade union movement, appears particularly absurd. Feminism as a mass reform struggle with radicalizing potential cannot be renewed on the basis of its old middle-class constituencies but depends on the rebuilding of working-class self-organization. By working-class self-organization, I mean the collectively-structured process of engaging in resistance to and making demands on corporate capital, whether that is done directly (strikes) or indirectly (campaigns for government intervention), by people who do not exercise power in their daily working lives and who are situated economically so that they don't control very much of their own time on the job or off it. Without the capacity, *in practice*, to take on the limits set by the demands of capital accumulation in a period of increasing international competition, feminism will continue to be vitiated of its radical potential, capitulating to the right, and unable to mobilize broad layers of women.

The Self-Organization of Working-Class Women

The fate of feminism as an actual *movement*, then, is tied to the fate of trade unionism and other forms of collective resistance to corporate capital. If it was possible for 'new movements' to flourish in the 1960's and 1970's alongside an essentially bureaucratic and de-mobilized trade unionism, this is no longer the case. But the decline of the old trade union movement is not the end of the working-class, or of trade unions, as agents of social change. It is the exhaustion of a kind of unionism and a kind of industrial organization – the 'social contract unionism' based in heavy industry that became dominant after World War II. To confront an increasingly centralized and mobile capital, many organizers and activists look to a social and political unionism based in solidarities beyond the workplace – linkages with communities, across industries and sectors, etc.[17] Obviously, one key strategic issue is how to rebuild involvement and organization at the base of a kind that can sustain militant resistance under conditions of an intense employers' offensive substantially underwritten by the state.

In this effort, working-class women can make a crucial contribution as organizers in communities and workplaces. Historically, trade union women, and perhaps especially Black trade union women, have fought for women's equality in their unions and in their workplaces; but so long as women were a minority within the workforce and therefore within the trade union movement, they could be marginalized. Mainstream feminism's success in legitimizing the ideal of equality and the massive entry of women into waged work have created the conditions for the development of a working-class feminism, one that integrates itself not only politically but organizationally with other movements of the exploited and oppressed.

The action and politics of working-class women in their trade union and community organizing have forced socialist-feminists to re-think our categories – even how we define 'feminist'. Are Black women organizing for better pre-natal health care, or for neighbourhood watches to prevent rape, doing feminist organizing, even if they locate themselves within the anti-racism movement and don't identify themselves as feminist? Are working women organizing for higher pay as family breadwinners feminists even if they define themselves as trade unionists? Out of these activities, many working-class women activists become conscious of their oppression and of their need to organize as women *not in opposition to but in relation to their membership in unions or oppressed communities*.[18] They must therefore find forms of organization and political expression that reject the practice and politics of both the traditional left and of feminism. Both movements have tended to find common ground by universalizing similarities ('we are all workers' 'we are all women') without recognizing and incorporating differences, whether these be differences of gender, race/ethnicity, sexual orientation, etc. What the organizational forms might be, it's hard to say. One model, perhaps, would be a geographically based (local, regional, national) confederation of grass-roots women's groups based in unions, workplaces, communities, that are organized around certain projects and which bring women together frequently to socialize, make decisions, act.

At the moment, of course, organized working-class women are in the minority. Still, they represent a potential leadership, not only for a renewed feminism but for a renewed trade unionism, one that no longer concerns itself only with public issues and public life, that no longer narrows its scope to workplace/industrial as opposed to community/personal issues.[19] Women's lives bridge, in ways that men's do not, the divide between work and community. Working-class women cannot create, as men have often done, a union culture that builds solidarity through exclusive bonds and loyalties and that regards families and communities to be auxiliary rather than central points of support and power.[20] Dependent on sharing networks of kin and neighbours to negotiate their double day, working-class women are likely to define independence in ways very different from men and to be less vulnerable than men to the bourgeois ideal of themselves as freely contracting citizen workers and independent wage earners. Finally, in their workplaces and occupations women are less racially segregated, than they are in terms of where they live. At work, white women and women of colour might find common ground as they discover that they share the experiences and dilemmas of meeting their obligations and interests not only as workers but also as kin, friends, members of communities.

Reform and Revolution

An effort to elaborate a socialist-feminist reform strategy for a working-class women's movement, to contest the emerging leadership of women politicians and trade union officials, to develop grass-roots organizations of working-class women that are prefigurative in their demands as well as in their organizational forms, should be at the centre of any discussion of revolutionary strategy in the late 20th century.

It may be that in the long run advanced capitalist societies could re-organize social reproduction in ways that would substantially decrease the burdens of care now carried by households and by women. But socialized forms of care would still inevitably be delivered, like other welfare state services, in a class and race biased and highly bureaucratic system. Nonetheless, such an expansion of the welfare state would substantially underwrite further change in gender relations and gender ideology.[21] In any case, it is certain that, while it may be possible for capitalism to absorb gender equality in the long run, significant shifts away from the privatization of social reproduction will have to be forced upon capital, in the same way as universal male suffrage, the recognition of trade unions or the welfare state were won through struggle. And women's struggles to create the material basis for gender equality has the potential to go far beyond its incorporationist ends. That potential lies in the movement itself – in its creation of aspirations that transcend any particular reform – and especially in the capacity of revolutionary socialists to deepen grass-roots organization and broaden the political understandings of women activists.

As a movement for equality and against male domination, feminism is not inevitably radical or socialist. Social-welfare feminism has a reform vision that can be very attractive to working-class women: a workplace attuned to family needs, a benevolent and expanded welfare state, and a democratized nuclear family. This vision is not contradictory to capitalism. It accepts the split between public and private in which the social relationships and culture of the workplace remain structured by hierarchy and competition. The mainstream feminist vision would reduce the penalties for losing and insure that women could fairly compete, but not change the essential organizational structures nor eliminate the labour market.[22]

The social-welfare feminist vision contains little critique of the bureaucratic welfare state and maintains a liberal faith in the welfare state's ability to equalize the unequal. Childcare might become a general entitlement, like public education. But, as with public education, class and race inequalities will produce vast differences in the quality of care and in the capacity of parents to negotiate the system: both to ensure that their children's needs are met and to protect themselves from unwanted intrusions. The modernizing right's attack on the welfare state draws heavily on these legitimate concerns.

Reforms that expand state supports for family households (subsidies to family care-givers, tax credits for childcare costs, etc.) assume that they will continue to be the primary units for providing care. While such policies might help the family (at least more families) better deliver on its promise of fulfillment and self-expression, they pose no challenge to the individualism and alienation that defines our experience of public life in advanced capitalist societies. They thus reinforce the existing cynicism about the possibilities for participatory democratic alternatives.[23]

In order to address the central dilemmas in working class women's lives – and in particular the felt counterposition between autonomy and collectivity, between freedom and security, between self-development and nurturance – we have to not only project an attractive socialist vision but also develop a strategy for reform that transcends rather than capitulates to existing political worldviews. This strategy has to include, first, a reform programme which is self-conscious about the changes called for, the language in which we justify our claims, and the necessity to link always short-run goals to visions of a radically re-organized society. Second, the strategy has to support and try to bring into being political organization and institutional reforms that allow individuals to develop and control collectively their own objectives and activities, to increase their personal capacities and to enhance their sense that even larger changes would be possible if they joined their efforts with those of others. Commitments to a radically democratic and participatory society can more easily be built out of some practices than out of others.

Once we focus on this issue, however, the importance of revising marxist theory to integrate socialist-feminist analysis also comes to the fore. Marxist politics, even in its most democratic and visionary tradition, does not speak to the key contradictions of women's everyday lives. Just think, for example, how much time the democratic socialist tradition in marxist politics has spent debating workplace democracy, planning and participation, addressing issues such as how to combine expertise with workers' control of production, authority with democracy. But hardly a word has been spoken on the problems of organizing social reproduction, the renewal of life daily and intergenerationally.

How, for example, do we provide security and continuity for children without replicating the intense, exclusive relationships of the nuclear family? We know that women and children need to be liberated from each other. But, once we recognize that motherhood is not only oppressive but also a kind of skilled work and that parents derive pleasure from children, what implications does that have for how we organize participation in other work, in production? Does creative work require complete freedom from the obligations and restraints that caring for someone else necessarily entails? Finally, how can we organize collectivities in a way that reduces, if not ends, the tension between self-development and collective obligation? Ignored by marxists, such questions have been extensively explored in socialist-feminist writing and politics.

In response to the right's romanticized evocation of 'the family,' socialist-feminists have argued for a strategy of 'deconstruction.' Kinship, love, and good things to eat tend to go together in our society, but that's not inevitable. How then do we want to 'deconstruct' the family? Should households continue to take responsibility for children and the daily physical needs of adults, or should we meet more of our needs outside the place where we sleep and enjoy privacy? How might we differently arrange living spaces? What kinds of bonds will connect people who share them? Where will children live and how might they be cared for? Can we find inspiration in the open and fluid networks of adults and children cooperating across households that constitute the survival strategies of the very poor?

There is no feminist agreement on these issues, no socialist-feminist ortho-
doxy to be absorbed into marxism.[24] But these debates have to be considered
central questions on which any good marxist must be well-educated – as
well-educated as on debates in political economy. This is not only because
socialist-feminist theory allows us to present a much richer and broader
vision of what socialism might be. It is also because socialist feminists have
been concerned with whole areas of human experience in capitalism that
marxism never really considered as a field for political action – sexuality,
intimacy, motherhood, gender identity. Moreover, socialist-feminist analysis has demonstrated the profound impact of gender relationships, gender
identity, and gender ideology on Marxism's traditional territory – trade
unionism, parliamentary and extra-parliamentary politics, state policy. In
defending feminist gains against the attack from the right, socialist feminists have been forced to confront, to analyze, and to try to respond to the
powerful relationship between sexuality, gender identity, and political commitments and worldviews. In identifying the longings and anxieties on which
anti-feminism draws, socialist-feminism has strengthened marxist analysis of
conservative politics and laid the ground for a more effective response.

Crafted differently depending on the issue, this strategy might follow some
general guidelines. Today women (and men) are forced to sacrifice one
human need in order to fulfill another. Our politics ought to centre on
concrete reforms which allow people to get beyond these dilemmas. Further, the reforms we propose and the way we organize for them (the kinds
of movements we build) ought to prefigure the social/personal relationships
and reordered priorities we want to achieve through socialist revolution.

First, we need to reappropriate the issue of control from the right – which
has so effectively counterposed the market and the family (as arenas subject
to individual control) to the welfare state. Instead of simply defending existing services, we should be proposing democratically run (worker and client
controlled), de-centralized and collective alternatives to the unpaid domestic
work of women. For example, working-class mothers have good reason to
feel reluctant about turning their children, or their elder parents, over to
the expert domination of the bureaucratic welfare state or to the exploitative profiteering of the marketplace. Women from oppressed racial/ethnic
communities have every reason to regard with suspicion institutions that
systematically deny the value of their culture, suppress their history, and
undermine their children's self-regard. On the other hand, neighbourhood
childcare centres cooperatively run by parents and workers support and
require participation and involvement. In addition to building the experience
of democratic participation into individuals' everyday lives, they could be one
base for collective action, e.g., to join with other centres to increase funding.

Second, we need to reappropriate the issue of choice. In the liberal lexicon, choice is only guaranteed negatively – i.e., as the right to act without
interference. For affluent middle class women, negative freedom may be

sufficient. But working-class women need much more. We ought to define choice positively – i.e., as the right to have good alternatives to choose from. And we want to make sure that good choices for some women don't rest on the exploitation of others – as domestic servants, low-paid childcare workers, fetal incubators, test cases for new contraceptives or whatever.

Third, we need to integrate women's right to autonomy, self-knowledge, and self-development into every argument for reform. We can make this claim, first, on the ground simply of our humanity but second on the ground that it will make for better communities. We should avoid any temptation, for example, to defend women's access to decent jobs or living wages only on the ground of their family obligations – their husbands don't make enough, they have no husbands, therefore they 'need' to work. Liberals define autonomy in the language of contracts and limited liability, while conservatives invoke the values of interdependence and long-term commitments within the confines of traditional community. Our goal is not to 'free' women from commitment and obligation, but to insure that we enter those compacts from a position of equal access with men to economic survival and political power.

Fourth, we have to contest the marginalization of sexual politics from the feminist agenda, and most particularly, the defensive silence on abortion and lesbianism. These issues raise, more directly than almost any other, men's anxiety about losing the love and care of women and raise women's fears of evoking these anxieties in men. They also challenge, perhaps most deeply, women's gender identities. Rather than ignoring them, because they make people uncomfortable, we can discuss them in the context of arguments for giving women choice and control. For example, we locate abortion within a broader constellation of 'reproductive rights' which create the conditions for women to control our reproductive lives – to choose to be as well as not to be mothers. We include, along with adequate housing, a living wage, adequate parental leave, shorter workdays with no loss in pay, etc. the freedom to express sexual preference. Women can't be said to choose to share parenting with a man until women are free to raise children by themselves or with another woman. The value of freely chosen relationships, the wish to give and receive sexual intimacy by desire, not by constraint, are values women hold deeply, often without ever questioning how compulsory heterosexuality denies them.

Finally, we have to become far more self-conscious about creating pre-figurative political relationships and political cultures in our grass-roots organizing and in socialist groups. Socialist-feminism has struggled with concerns about political organization that traditional marxism considered long since settled. To name a few: what modes of decision-making will include the less knowledgeable, less experienced, and less assertive in equal participation? What kinds of leadership will generate thoughtful self-activity and discourage passivity? Which of their needs and to what extent should members expect an organization to meet? Are some kinds of organizational structure and political actions more likely to encourage members to become more confident and more capable? What goals should we use to measure success? These questions are so familiar they would hardly bear repeating, were it not for the fact that they are still largely disregarded on the left.

There has been considerable experimentation with modes of group organization, decision-making structures such as consensus, forms of political education, efforts to create non-hierarchical political communities. Much of this has occurred in the eco-feminist, radical-, spiritual- and anarchofeminist, and direct-action peace movements.[25] Many of their techniques could be translated into revolutionary socialist organizations, particularly at the local level.[26] Of course, there is no perfected feminist process that will resolve all our organizational dilemmas. But to recognize that these dilemmas exist and to commit ourselves to exploring solutions is absolutely essential. That political organizations of the Left have been so resistant to this project, perhaps more than anything else, is an indication of how far we have yet to travel.

NOTES

1. I'd like to thank Jan Haaken, Nancy Holmstrom, Alan Hunter, Leo Panitch and Bill Resnick for their thoughtful comments. Although I couldn't respond to all of their suggestions, the article has been much improved by their critiques.
2. For instance, Samuel Bowles and Herbert Gintis, *Democracy and Capitalism* (New York: Basic Books, 1987); Ernesto Laclau and Chantal Mouffe, *Hegemony and Socialist Strategy: Towards a Radical Democratic Politics* (London: Verso, 1985).
3. Thoughtful critiques by Ellen Wood, Alan Hunter and Norman Geras have delineated most of the problematic aspects of these works. Ellen Meiksins Wood, *The Retreat From Class: A New 'True' Socialism* (London: Verso, 1986); Alan Hunter, 'Post-Marxism and the New Social Movements,' *Theory and Society*, forthcoming; Norman Geras, 'Post-Marxism?', *New Left Review*, no. 163 (May/June, 1987).
4. *Hegemony and Socialist Strategy*, pp. 169 – 170.
5. Because the definition of working-class is so contested these days, one can't assume a commonly held meaning. For purposes of this article, I'm using the term middle class as a catch-all to include groups often defined as 'new middle class', such as higher salaried professionals, middle to upper managers, and the old middle class of the self-employed and small businessmen/women. By working class, I mean all other wage and salary workers.
6. On this point for England, see Elizabeth Wilson, 'Thatcherism and Women: After Seven Years,' *Socialist Register: 1987*, eds. Ralph Miliband, Leo Panitch and John Saville (London: Merlin Press, 1987).
7. While sexual violence – sexual harassment, rape, wife-beating – is a cross-class and cross-race phenomenon, nevertheless, income, occupation, age, and race certainly differentiate women's vulnerability.
8. Some of these programmes, of course, were severely eroded under the conservative governments of Reagan and Thatcher – especially enforcement of anti-discrimination policy in education and employment. Still, overall, even under conservative regimes, the movement of women into management and

the professions has continued, while in areas such as changing local police and court practices in cases of rape and domestic violence there has been marked improvement, at least in the U.S.

9. On the impact of welfare state cutbacks on women, see Jennifer G. Schirmer, *The Limits of Reform: Women, Capital and Welfare* (Cambridge: Schenkman, 1982), pp. 133–135; H. Heclo and H. Madsen, *Policy and Politics in Sweden* (Philadelphia: Temple University Press, 1987), pp. 165–173; Borchorst, A and B. Siim, 'Women and the Advanced Welfare State – A New Kind of Patriarchal Power?' in A. Showstack Sassoon, ed., *Women and the State: The Shifting Boundaries of Public and Private* (London: Hutchinson, 1987); Mimi Abramovitz, *Regulating the Lives of Women* (Boston: South End Press, 1988); Anna Yeatman, *Feminists, Femocrats, Technocrats: Essays on the Contemporary Australian State*, Chapter 7 (Allen & Unwin, forthcoming). I am very grateful to Anna Yeatman for sharing her manuscript with me.

10. For an excellent analysis of Thatcherism's 'modernizing' gender ideology, see Wilson, 'Thatcherism and Women: After Seven Years.'

11. On Canada, see Jane Stinson, 'Window On The North: Women's Issues and Labour in Canada,' *Labor Research Review* no. 11 (Spring, 1988), pp. 46–47. On the U.S. see the comparison of Democratic and Republican party platforms on childcare in *Ms.* (October, 1986).

12. Political/state structures have very much shaped the strategic issues facing 'social-welfare' feminist organization and politics. As both Siim and Hernes point out, in the Scandinavian countries with highly corporatist systems, all parties have assumed that the state has a responsibility to help *women* cope with a 'double day,' but feminists (and women generally) have been marginal to the centralized decision-making structures within which state policy is crafted. Berte Siim, 'The Scandinavian Welfare States – Towards Sexual Equality or a New Kind of Male Domination,' *Acta Sociologica* v. 30, nos. 3/4, pp. 255–270; H. Hernes, 'Women and the Advanced Welfare State – the Transition from Private to Public Dependence,' in H. Holter, ed. *Patriarchy in a Welfare State* (Oslo: Universitetsforlaget, 1984).

13. For example, Child Support Enforcement has been the only major legislation coming out of the 'feminization of poverty campaign,' which sought a broad range of programmes: childcare, increased services and income for elderly women, increased access to quality health care for women and children, etc. Whatever their impact on increasing the collection of support awards from affluent men (and the evidence is mixed at best) these laws have led to increased harassment of women welfare recipients without any improvement in their level of income. See, Wendy Sarvasy and Judith Van Allen, 'Fighting the Feminization of Poverty: Socialist-Feminist Analysis and Strategy,' *Review of Radical Political Economics*, 16 (4), 1984, pp. 89–110.

14. See, for instance, Betty Friedan, *The Second Stage* (New York: Summit Books, 1981) and Jean Bethke Elshtain, 'Feminism, Family, and Community,' *Dissent* (Fall, 1982).

15. For an analysis of how this political adaptation undercuts the organization of poor Black women, see Barbara Omolade, *It's A Family Affair: The Real Lives of Black Single Mothers*, (Kitchen Table: Women of Color Press, 1986).

16. Although the 1984 CLUW Convention reaffirmed support for women's reproductive freedom, the CLUW leadership obviously may choose when to publicly endorse reproductive rights. An organization of women trade unionists working *within* the structures of the AFL-CIO, CLUW is one of the most integrated women's organizations: 50% of its leadership and membership are women of colour. Although it has/had tremendous potential for mobilizing rank and file

trade union women, CLUW is today, for the most part, little different from the highly bureaucratized union organizations of which it is a part. For a history of CLUW, see Diane Balser, *Sisterhood and Solidarity* (Boston: South End Press, 1987).

17. For a discussion of alternatives based on recent U.S. experience see, 'Dare to Struggle: Lessons from P–9,' Phil Kwik and Kim Moody,' 'Watsonville: A Mexican Community on Strike,' Frank Bardacke, 'Keeping GM Van Nuys Open,' Eric Mann all in *Reshaping the U.S. Left: Popular Struggles in the 1980's*, eds. Mike Davis and Michael Sprinker (New York: Verso, 1988).

18. The grass-roots organizing of women within the Nicaraguan agricultural workers' union (ATC) is one example. In addition to increasing the education and involvement of women in the union, and putting demands like paid maternity leave on the bargaining agenda, this project has sent delegates to national women's conferences and to international meetings. At the request of the Nicaraguan women, feminists in Spain are mobilizing to send spanish language pamphlets about contraception, contraceptives and instruments for performing abortion to women in the ATC. (Personal communication from Norma Chinchilla). On the potential and problems of working-class and peasant women in the Nicaraguan revolution, see Maxine Molyneaux, 'Mobilization Without Emancipation? Women's Interests, the State, and Revolution in Nicaragua,' *Feminist Studies*, v. 7, no. 2 (Summer, 1985).

19. For some examples of women's impact on the trade union movement in the U.S. and Canada see, *Feminizing Unions: Labor Research Review*, no. 11 (Spring 1988). For an instance of the impact of women's networks on workplace organizing, see Karen Brodkin Sacks, *Caring By the Hour* (Urbana and Chicago: University of Illinois Press, 1988).

20. I wouldn't deny the historical importance of community ties – friendship, kinship, neighbourhood – to men's trade union militancy. But I would argue that these reinforcing ties outside the workplace and the union hall were both in practice and subjectively created in a separate and exclusive male sphere.

21. Some feminists, drawing on the experience of the Soviet Union and Eastern Europe, are sceptical that providing more social supports to working women will have much impact on gender inequality. This is an issue that can't be settled here. But I would make three general points: 1) these societies in fact are still very far from freeing households substantially from the burdens of providing for their members; 2) the lack of political freedom in general tremendously inhibits the self-organization of women; 3) the bureaucratic and coercive character of public life leads to a romanticization of family and private life as domains of freedom, undermining women's aspirations for alternatives to traditional gender roles.

22. For an elaboration of this point, see my article, 'Feminist Political Discourses: Radical versus Liberal Approaches to the Feminization of Poverty and Comparable Worth,' *Gender & Society* v. 1, no. 4 (December, 1987), pp. 447–465.

23. On this point, see especially, Michele Barrett and Mary McIntosh, *The Anti-Social Family*, (London: Verso, 1984), Chapter IV.

24. See, for example, Barrett & McIntosh, *The Anti-Social Family*; Judith Stacey, 'Should the Family Perish?', *Socialist Review* 14, 2(March–April 1984); Martha A. Ackelsberg, 'Sisters or Comrades? The Politics of Friends and Families,' in Diamond, ed., *Families, Politics, and Public Policy*, (New York: Longman, 1983), Johanna Brenner and Nancy Holmstrom, 'Autonomy, Community, Women's Rights,' *The Year Left: Volume I*, eds. Mike Davis et al., (London: Verso, 1985); Denise Riley, 'The Serious Burdens of Love?: Some Questions on Childcare, Feminism and Socialism,' in Lynne Segal, ed. *What Is To Be Done About the Family?* (London: Penguin, 1983).

25. Although, for an inspiring example from the revolutionary socialist left, see 'City Life: Lessons of the First Five Years,' Kathy McAfee, *Radical America*, v. 13, no. 1 (January/February 1979).

26. See, for example, Michel Avery, Brian Auvine, Barbara Streibel, Lonnie Weiss, *Building United Judgment: A Handbook for Consensus Decision-Making*, (Madison, Wisconsin: Center for Conflict Resolution, 1981). Other techniques and modes of organization might not translate so well from one kind of movement to another. For instance, where the 'group' is locally based, even if it is large, some forms of decision making might work better than where the group is geographically dispersed (compare, for example, the possibilities at Greenham Common and those in the miners' strike). For other considerations along these lines, see Barbara Epstein, 'The Politics of Pre-Figurative Community: The Non-Violent Direct Action Peace Movement,' *Reshaping the U.S. Left: Popular Struggles in the 1980's*, eds. Mike Davis and Michael Sprinker (London: Verso, 1988).

RELIGION AND REVOLUTION
A BRIEF FOR THE THEOLOGY OF LIBERATION

Lawrence Littwin

I

Revolution is a total and ongoing process. All aspects of society, civil, as well as political, are affected. Base, superstructure, praxis must all change. The revolutionary experience indicates that these changes are always uneven: unequal development, resistance to change, counter-revolution have been the rule. Such generalizations aside, the revolutionary universe is murky, fraught with questions, besieged and confounded by debatable answers. Such is our burden, in particular, when we approach the problem of the relation between religion and revolution, and perhaps nowhere more so than in respect to Latin America.

Marx and Engels' systematic and emphatic rejection of religion as a source of revolution has added to this burden. In attempting to establish socialism on a rational and scientific basis, they in essence obviated religion as a valid concern. Scientific socialism could not accept religion as the moral and ethical fount of revolution and liberation. Although Marx understood religion as a necessary palliative for the alienation felt by men in class dominated societies, it could play no role in societies liberated from the false consciousness necessary for such domination.

Engels, who treated religion, especially Christianity, more explicitly than did Marx, appreciated it as a powerful motivating force except for the fact that it led men in the wrong direction.[1] The salvation which it promised was to come in the afterlife. The modern workingmen's movement, in contradiction, held salvation to be an earthly task with earthly fulfillment. God and the Kingdom of Heaven were false and irrelevant goals upon which to build a revolutionary movement.

For Marx and Engels, religion and revolution were antithetical both as concepts and as realities. Revolution, as a resolution of class conflict, must be driven by class consciousness. Religion obscures such consciousness. Its palliative role has been a weapon of class domination. It has taught acceptance, passivity and fatalism on the one hand, and on the other justification for those who dominate. Religion as a formal structure has traditionally been associated with the status quo and reaction.

The classical revolutionary indictment of religion would certainly seem to hold true when applied to much of Catholicism's history in Latin America. For three hundred years of colonial hegemony, the church had contributed to a culture of domination. Its symbols and beliefs filtered Latin America reality. Anyone acculturated to that reality, religious or not, could not avoid being in some way molded by church perceptions. This was true in the secular realm as much as it was in the religious. The ultimate separation of church and state in the mid- and latter- 19th Century, encouraged by various liberal and radical movements, could not totally separate the religious from the now rational, positivistic profane. Church symbols were still everywhere. The church established the first and most prestigious universities. It built and serviced hospitals and charities. It blessed new governments. The cardinal appeared with the President and the leaders of the military in public ceremonies. Catholicism's influence continued to be intimate and integral to social life. To be sure, religious beliefs and practices have had a bifurcated development in Latin America. For the rich and the middle sectors, the church remained the religious medium. The poor took a more individualized, less regulated path. When for various reasons a shortage of clergy occurred, many, especially the poor, remained uninitiated in the recognized rites and sacraments. These unevangelized people maintained more personal, more fatalistic, and passive ways. The rich and poor often worship different saints, or call the same saints different names. The poor have syncretized the Catholic pantheon with their own pre-Columbian gods. This dualized religious structure conformed nicely to a basically Thomistic world view wherein religion and social structure (very much inclusive of class relations) were meant to confirm each other in a perfectly hierarchical architectonic universe.

What was imported from Iberia for the purpose of domination thus has remained an integral instrument of hegemony to this day. Roman Catholic themes, such as hierarchicalism, corporatism, the relationship between faith and reason, a certain Manicheism leading to totalism and maximalism continue to pervade Latin societies today, extending from a religious core to deep involvement in the profane life of the people. Yet, paradoxically, just as these concepts were intensely important in the structuring of societies of domination and subjugation since the conquest, they also remain emergent and influential in some transformed state even where revolutions have taken place. This is so in Nicaragua. It is also so in El Salvador, where religion has an enormous influence over the revolutionary process and has provided the inspiration for many contemporary revolutionaries.

In general the Catholic value system is more pervasive in Latin America than the identifiable institution of the church and has become more complex and varied, especially in the last three decades, since the emergence of the

Theology of Liberation. Religion today plays a role as a moral and ethical fount of revolution and liberation. How are we to understand this development?

Pre-Liberation Catholic thought and values, emanating from 13th century Thomistic ideology seasoned with a number of Iberian ingredients, coincided well with the need to justify conquest, enslavement, hierarchical colonization and the peculiar love-hate relationship with Europe and the United States that characterizes Latin America's dependent role in the world economy. Although it cannot be argued with Latin societies were ever really closed systems, the challenges of rationalism, liberalism, empiricism, positivism and Marxism have never successfully overwhelmed this Catholic value set. Religious elements in Latin cultures have been so pervasive that Catholicism's challengers have themselves taken the guise of secular religions so that struggles for hegemony have always been intensely maximalist and asserted as non-debatable ideological rationalizations.

Because the church, as a political-economic institution, as well as ideological legitimator, has been so central to Latin American life, it has always been the primary focus of attack by those who wished to 'modernize' the society. In the 19th century, when liberalism was seen as Latin America's path to modernization, it was an anti-clerical liberalism that was used to justify the placing of church lands in the private domain. This assault ultimately left the church separated from the state in most Latin nations and moved most civic matters, such as marriage, burial, and education to the secular realm. All of this was a real defeat for the church. But the Catholic value system, firmly planted during 300 years of conquest and colonization, remained entrenched in the Latin mentality as a basic structural form within which secular concepts would find their transformational cues and their validity as a reference for acceptable practices.

Religion, in this structural sense, is a language. It has its own vocabulary, grammar, and history. It is a language used to relate God, people, and society. Catholicism, as such, infuses the secular languages spoken in Latin America. It is more pervasive than Spanish or Portuguese. It is integral to the many tongues used by Latin Americans. It is a bridge uniting in many perceptions, people of diverse backgrounds and ethnicities. It has its local ethnic and class nuances and more obvious distinctions. But that which occurs to people will be perceived and discussed using in some part Catholic vocabulary and grammar and will happen within the limits and to the extent established by its conceptual boundaries. It may be a more pervasive element in some Latin societies than in others, for some groups more than others. This is for the researcher to investigate. But it is there and an element to be reckoned with if what happens and what is possible in Latin American societies is to be understood.

Capitalist and Marxist economists, or even revolutionaries, may be able to conjure up the most objective, logical, rational and empirical pictures of the

political economy along with all the imperative prescriptions for its amelio-
ration. But these prescriptions will not be feasible if 'objective' conceptions
exclude the consciousness of the people for whom they are designed. In Latin
America, an understanding of this 'consciousness' must include a grasp of the
struggle for ideological hegemony that besets the Catholic Church today.

II

This Latin American conflict emerged and coincided with Catholicism's
overall attempt to respond to the challenges of the modern world. The
European Church made this attempt in Vatican II in the first half of the
1960s.[2] Although many Latin American priests and bishops attended its
sessions, this essentially European conclave responded to modern challenges
in a language which did not correspond to the Latin reality. Neither were the
challenges perceived always the same as those which confronted the Latin
Americans.

The ostensible problem for the Church of Rome was how to confront a
Europe of science, reason, atheism, and Marxism with an institution and
a theology constructed in the Middle Ages. Churchmen wondered if their
church had anything to say to this world. The more basic question was
whether a loving and just God was still a tenable concept in a Europe that
had experienced two world wars, including the Holocaust, and the possibility
of nuclear annihilation. This essentiality European church also faced and was
forced to respond to the fact that by the end of the century a majority of its
adherents would be Third World people. In light of this, the church had to
supply some answers to the increasingly impoverished lives of this evolving
majority. The church responded using the vocabulary of the Catholic Social
Justice Tradition which owed much of its approach to the work of Pope Leo
XIII and European churchmen who followed in his path. It should be remem-
bered that Pope Leo made St. Thomas the official philosopher of the Catholic
Church and extolled the 13th century as the finest. In this light, Vatican II's
responses were traditional. However, the Church accommodated the modern
world by stating that science and technology were no longer enemies but
instead partial answers to the world's problems. This technology developed
in the First World was to be extended to the Third. With so much focus on
material deprivation and material productive capability, the church would
supply the spiritual counter to materialism. In sum, the rich were implored
to give technology to the poor in the spirit of charity and justice. In that
man cannot live by bread alone, faith supplied by the church would be the
transcendant factor, faith beyond reason.

The Third World bishops who attended this council generally encouraged
its concern for issues of social justice and its more progressive responses.
But, for the Latin Americans a different approach was imperative. Fidel
Castro's success had encouraged a Marxist revolutionary process throughout

Latin America. Hardly a country had been spared the activities of urban guerrilla cells and rural *focos*. The Central American uprising, including the Sandinistas and the Salvadorian movements, had their genesis in the early 60s. In addition, a severe shortage of clergy and a growing Protestant evangelical pressure challenged the continued dominance of Catholicism. Many Latin American Catholics now perceived their church to be in crisis.

This crisis of the Church was rooted in the crisis of Latin American societies themselves. The demography of Latin America was changing. Population was increasing at a phenomenal rate. The agriculture base, continually super-exploited to produce export crops or huckstered in speculative deals, or explored and mined for mineral exports, was no longer hospitable to the growing numbers of the rural poor. They left the land and migrated to the cities in increasing numbers. Foreign investment, especially from the United States, required the urban concentration of cheap labour. But, not all who came were to be fully employed. The shantytowns housing these poverty stricken people proliferated. As a rationale for continued exploitation and in response to a real concern about the revolutionary possibilities in these countries, the U.S. encouraged a two-pronged development scheme. Couched in academically concocted terms, such as 'meeting the needs of the revolution of rising expectations,' 'reaching the point of takeoff,' 'modernization,' the U.S. encouraged the Latins to welcome further investments, and especially to modernize the military to maintain the stability necessary for development.

Encouraged by Vatican II's new focus on the poor, and so the universal Church's awareness of the growing importance of its Third World population, the Latin American Church began to take measures and became increasingly open to struggles which in turn began to transform Latin American Catholicism itself. Latin American churchmen knew that the analyses and answers supplied by a European conclave did not apply to their reality as they were beginning to understand it. Thus the Church in Latin America, although it also faced a contemporary crisis, remained a more important actor, than the European Church, and the population, for the most part, were believers.

Secondly, the language of developmentalism, along with its emphases on technological solutions and its reliance on the primary role of the First World, contradicted the reality of Latin American experience. In most cases, the burgeoning poor of Latin American seemed light years away from being able to appropriate the use, let alone the benefits, of advanced technology. Furthermore, Latin American analysts were aware that when technology arrived in their world, it came as part of capitalist investment, seeking capital intensive methods which exacerbated unemployment and poverty. Along with this awareness was a growing understanding of the satellite status of the Latin economies in the world market system. The Latin role was to enrich the First World at the intensifying expense of its own populations. This had been so since the conquest and was no less so in the modern era. Rome's encouragement of this relationship indicated a deep lack of understanding of the Latin American situation. Therefore, as the European Church seemed to refocus its mission in enunciating 'a preferred option for the poor,' its solutions seemed completely contradictory to that preference in Latin America.

III

The Latin American Bishops addressed these contradictions as they met in Medellín, Colombia, in 1968.[3] They also attempted to understand the dismal state of their own political, economic, and spiritual reality. For a number of Bishops, the facts of Latin impoverishment, as demonstrated by their own social scientists, were new and shocking. Although the bishops legitimized a quest for answers, the responses which were to have a profound impact on Catholicism came from among the lower clergy and laity. These responses emerged, at one level, in the individual activities of Catholic revolutionaries; at another level, they took the form of the creation of theologies of liberation; and at a third level, they could be seen, pastorally and collectively, in the establishment of Base Ecclesial Communities.

Nestor Paz exemplified the individual response: the Catholic, inspired by religious principles, who becomes a guerrilla fighter.[4] On October 8, 1970 this ex-seminarian died of starvation on the banks of the Mariapo River in Bolivia. He was about to turn 25 the next day. His 'nomme de guerre' had been Francisco after the great Saint Francis of Assisi whose love for the poor had inspired the young guerrilla to martyr himself. The kind of thinking that led to such individual behaviour was enunciated two years before Paz's death in a document submitted by 900 Latin American priests to the Latin American episcopate meeting in Medellín. In this document (which came to be known as 'Latin America: A Continent of Violence') the priests discussed the frustrations of people living under conditions of underdevelopment. They emphasized the growing desire of the people for fundamental change in the socio-economic structures of the continent. They Catholicized this process by stating:

> . . . Because the privileged few use their power of repression to block this process of liberation, many see the use of force as the only solution open to the people. This same conclusion is being reached by many militant Christians whose own lives faithfully reflect the light of the Gospel.[5]

Nestor Paz viewed his revolutionary involvement as imperative to living life according to the Gospel. Becoming a guerrilla, fighting against those who oppressed the poor, was his attempt at discipleship. He saw himself in a line descending from Christ through his Colombian predecessor, Fr. Camilo Torres. His message on leaving to join the guerrillas in Teoponte begins with a quote from Camilo: 'Every sincere revolutionary must realize that armed struggle is the only path that remains.'[6] Camilo, who was killed in a guerrilla action four years before his Bolivian disciple, had also concluded that the oligarchic forces of repression had a stranglehold on Latin American societies.[7] He also believed that the only path to liberation was armed force. Both Nestor Paz and Camilo Torres died shortly after taking up arms. Neither was a great warrior. Neither engaged in extensive combat. Yet both are considered heroes and martyrs in an era that has seen only a small number of priest-guerrillas, but an all too large number of tortured and murdered religious people.

Enrique Dussel, among others, argues that Catholics, such as Nestor Paz and Camilo Torres, are just as much a part of the Catholic tradition as Fr. Sepulveda and the many Catholics who have stood for oppression or passive quiescence.[8] It is true that the thread of progressive rebellion has run through the larger garment of retrogression and hierarchical hegemony from the first days of the conquest to the present. What distinguishes the rebellion and martyrdom of the last two decades is that it has become a pervasive and qualitative challenge to traditional Catholicism. Pragmatic steps taken by the church, conjoined with the revolutionary possibility first advanced by Cuba in 1959, have prompted a genuine and viable struggle to restructure the Catholic 'language.'

Although Colonial predecessors of Torres and Paz differed from these latter-day martyrs in a significant way, their resistance to injustice also was based on existing Catholic tradition and their individual compassion for the oppressed. The well-spring of this compassionate resistance is as old as Christianity itself. The loving rebel/martyr witnessing evil and denouncing it is Christ's example throughout the Gospels, and is, of course, a major theme of his sacrifice on the Cross. For the thin line of Catholic martyrs marching through history, this confrontation and sacrifice is *the* categorical imperative. It is at the heart of a certain Catholic existentialism which preaches, 'See evil. Denounce it with your bodies. This is your only choice.' It began in Santo Domingo in 1510 with the scathing sermons of the Dominican priest Montesinos and continued with the struggles of Bartolome de las Casas. It has never ceased.

The emergence of the Theology of Liberation has changed, however, the context of these denunciatory acts. It gives to the act of rebellion a new systematic base. In essence, it rationalizes rebellion, by shifting the focus and method of the church. This shift derived its basic orientation from the opening statement of Vatican II's *Pastoral Constitution on the Church in the Modern World*: 'The joys and the hopes, the griefs, and the anxieties of the men of this age, especially those who are poor or in any way afflicted, these too are the joys and hopes, the griefs and anxieties of the followers of Christ. . . . this community realizes that it is truly and intimately linked with mankind and its history.'[9] This reference to mankind and its history is encapsulated in John XXIIIs term, 'the signs of the times', first used in his encyclical *Pacem in Terris* and repeated in the *Pastoral Constitution*. The concern for the 'signs of the times' expressed in these important documents signifies a change in the way theology is supposed to be done. Theology is now to be stood on its feet, based on an inductive analysis of the conditions of people's lives. This is a 180 degree turn from a theology formerly derived from the deductive reference to first principles. This archaic method had been used to judge society, not on its reality, but on ideals generated in another age.

Gustavo Gutierrez conceives of the Theology of Liberation as a *'new way to do theology'*: he maintains that 'Theology as critical reflection on historical praxis is a liberating theology, a theology of the liberating transformation of the history of mankind . . . part of the process through which the world is transformed.' Of course for Gutierrez, as for other theologians of liberation, this liberating praxis is to be performed in the Latin American reality of underdevelopment.[10] A basic credo of this theology is that faith evolves and has meaning as it relates to the life of the poor – *as they understand it*. This reference to understanding by the poor does not imply some mystical investment in a benighted and superstitious perception of reality. It is a reference to an active understanding honed through praxis. The term 'understanding' here also refers to the poor participating in the construction of their own reality. In the language of liberationism, the poor are to transform themselves from 'objects,' the passive recipients of history, to 'subjects'.

In this new Catholic language, 'the poor' has a much more extensive meaning, rooted in Latin America reality, than the Marxist term 'working class.' Although recognition of class and class conflict are integral to liberationism, massive unemployment and underemployment, and the size and suffering of a rural population which hardly resembles the proletariat, traditionally conceived, would make a focus on the working class much too narrow and exclusive. The really important point is that class conflict, broadly defined, is seen as a social reality. Liberationists, such as Gutierrez, deny that they prescribe this conflict. They merely recognize its existence as a function of unjust economies. And they side, in that conflict, with the poor who are the ones who will both interpret and create the 'signs of the time.'

A related theme involves the need to understand, for the purposes of action, the conditions of underdevelopment. Keys to this understanding come through an adaptation of certain constructs supplied by neo-Marxist and Marxist thought. The first of these is dependency theory. Without undertaking a deep and critical application of this theory, liberationists nevertheless generally contend that the overall impoverishment of their populations has been caused by the relegation of Latin America to the historical role of peripheral capitalist economy. Simply stated, their argument is that Latin America from the time of the conquest to the present has never been allowed to develop economies of productive and distributive justice. Instead, they were created and developed to serve a narrow spectrum of society, as this spectrum is linked to the internationally based economies of the first world.

Out of this recognition of class conflict and dependency emerges a tripartite analysis of violence. Not only liberationists *qua* liberationists, but the bishops who met at Medellín, understood that the poor live regularly under conditions of 'institutional violence.' This is, first of all, violence implicit in physical, mental, and spiritual deprivation. This deprivation does violence to the humanity of the poor. It destroys the living and those not yet born. It is as simple as the impact that a mother's lack of protein has on the development of her fetus. It is as complicated as the refusal of a peasant to allow himself permission to recognize oppression for fear of the implications of that recognition. This violence destroys the bodies and inhibits the consciousness of the poor.

Secondly, it is recognised that when the poor attempt to organize in any way to confront these conditions, even peacefully and minimally, their attempts are smashed with the 'violence of oppressive reaction.' This dimension of violence has been a fact of life, whether the authorities are ostensibly civilian or military. It has been the reflexive reaction of an oligarchy who sees its status only in terms of the absolute subjugation of the poor.

'Revolutionary violence,' the third element in this trinitarian analysis, initially emerges as the poor's attempt to defend themselves. In a certain sense, revolution here is not prescribed. It is a natural and defensive outcome of insufferable conditions. It is certainly not a first choice. Reform, if it could come about, even in the minimal sense of allowing the poor to formulate and solve some of their immediate problems, and thereby gain a sense of dignity, would be much preferred. But liberationists recognized how threatening this reform is perceived to be by society's hegemonic forces.

The recognition of violence as a structural problem is followed by an interesting deviation from Catholic traditions in the portrayal of both sin and salvation as collective possibilities. Liberationism does not dismiss the possibility of individual sin, nor does it reject individual salvation. But, locating the source of this new theology in objective reality leads to the inevitable understanding of the impact of this reality on those who share it. If violence is primarily institutional and this violence brutalizes the humanity of both the poor who suffer and the rich who are bound by definition to perpetrate this violence, than this structure cannot help but produce a dialectic of sin. This sin is not minor and personal, it defines life. Likewise for salvation; if a society of oppression were to be transformed to one of distributive justice, the sinful imperative would be obviated and salvation from sin would be structural, and, therefore, collective.

In light of this emerging consciousness of the collective destiny which is structural, liberationism is elevated and developmentalism is rejected. This latter solution, so celebrated by western foreign policy-makers and social scientists alike, is seen by liberationists as just more of the same. Its trickle down potential is just as hierarchical as any structure of the past. It voids the basic emphasis on the need for the poor to define their own destiny, and, as was stated above, to transform themselves from objects to subjects. In addition, developmentalism intensifies the key dependency relations between metropolitan and peripheral economies. It also promotes technological answers to what liberationists understand to be profoundly human questions. At the centre of liberationism is the quest to liberate the whole human: body, soul, and mind. This is admittedly a slow and initially small scale project. But, societies beset by collective sin were a long time in the making.

V

If tainted and brutalizing structures produce collective sin, liberation and collective salvation can only be achieved by the development of new structures. Liberationists call for 'ecclesiogenesis,' the birth of a new church.[11] This church, like the early Christian Church is to grow from the 'faith-practice' of the people. It is to be a grass roots church. It will meld the faith of early Christianity with the experience of the poor as they live their lives today. Its motor force is the praxis of people in struggle using the gospel as the core of this praxis. This church is to spin out of a continuous circle of observing, acting, and judging.

But what shape is this struggle to take? Here we come finally to the third level where pastoral and political work are combined in collective organization. There is the hope that the thousands of Base Ecclesial Communities, active throughout Latin America, will provide the nucleus for this 'ecclesiogenesis.'[12]

The BEC was not an idea prescribed by the Theology of Liberation. These communities were first established before liberationism was conceptualized as a theology. The method employed in the first BECs and adapted by many since was based on the thinking of Paolo Freire, the Brazilian educationist who designed literacy programmes for Brazilian peasants and who was involved in setting up the first base communities in Brazil in the early 60s and soon after in Chile.[13] His goal was to teach progressive consciousness through literacy training by teaching the people to read using a vocabulary integral to their lives. This method has come to be known as 'conscientization'.

Ideally, a Base Ecclesial Community consists of a group of neighbours who meet regularly to pray and to reflect on biblical passages as these passages elucidate problems these people face in their daily lives. Essentially, these are action oriented spiritual groups. Problems addressed range from the personal to the political. Alcoholism, marital infidelity, garbage collection, unemployment, the need for a well or a school, are all problems addressed by these groups. Although the bishop of a diocese and local clergy are instrumental in establishing these communities, the leaders of individual groups come from the laity. The original purpose for the establishment of BECs was to overcome a shortage of clergy and to evangelize the enormous number of marginalized poor who had migrated to the cities. The BEC was not conceived of as an entity separate from the parish nor was it ever thought to be the initial stage of the hoped-for ecclesiogenesis. However, the BEC emphasis on the grassroots poor, the methodology used in its meetings, and the oppressive and chaotic atmosphere of Latin America, have inspired visions of a reborn church revolutionizing the society at large. The pedagogical methodology used in the idealized BEC, plus the metaphor of an early Christian Church of oppressed and imperialized people, contribute to this liberationist eschatology.

Thousands of BECs now operate throughout Latin America and have made starts in other parts of the Third World as well as in the Southwestern United States. They are not all the idealized conscienticizing cells. Some are. Many are merely community prayer meetings. In some, themes drawn from Exodus, Isaiah, and Luke inspire activities that are explicitly political. However, individual BECs are not designed to act as political units beyond the point of interacting with local authorities for local improvements. The basic function of a BEC is religious. It is meant to evangelize the unevangelized and to integrate marginalized neighborhoods into parish networks. It is the conscienticizing methodology used within the BEC and the focus on problems, many of which have political implications which help to form individuals who may then involve themselves as political party activists, unionists and join the ranks of protestors or even become guerrilla fighters. Work with these communities has also radicalized clergy.

As a result, in countries such as El Salvador, Nicaragua, Chile and Brazil, activist laymen, and clergy have been harassed, jailed and are murdered. By contrast, because the term BEC has been touted at episcopal conclaves, nothing more than praying the Rosary by a group of elderly women will be labeled a BEC meeting by a proud parish priest. Because of this variegated approach to community and because little research has been done, it is difficult at this time to know whether the BEC is really the foundation of ecclesiogenesis or merely a metaphor for such a birth in the minds of theologians of liberation. It is probably both.

V

The advent of Camilo Torres and his disciples, the birth and unfolding of the Theology of Liberation, and certain activities and expectations of Base Ecclesial Communities, have caused an ongoing troubled reaction by the Vatican. Even if one were to be sceptical about the revolutionary potential of all of these developments and dismiss them as a limited rebellion in an otherwise enormously conservative institution, it is still notable that Rome has seen these developments as a real threat.

Soon after the Second Council of Latin American Bishops began to focus on the need for change in Latin America, the Vatican began to replace progressive bishops with conservative ones. This has taken place in country after country so that the overall hierarchy has begun to take on a much more conservative posture. Recently a leading Brazilian theologian, Leonardo Boff, was called to the Vatican and after a lengthy inquisition was sentenced to a year of penitential silence. Boff was a leading proponent of ecclesiogenesis and had compared the structure of the church to capitalist structures of domination and exploitation. Cardinal Joseph Ratzinger, Prefect of the Vatican's Sacred Congregation for the Doctrine of the Faith, has authored two instructions on Liberation Theology, both highly critical. The Pope himself has issued words of caution and criticism. On his trip to Nicaragua, he openly admonished the Sandinista priest, Ernesto Cardenal, to obey his bishop and remove himself from politics. He has elevated contra defender Archbishop Obando y Bravo to Cardinal.

Although church scholars today believe that a certain *modus vivendi* has been reached between the Vatican and liberationists, a number of Rome's basic criticisms of the new theology still stand.[14] These criticisms are interesting because they reveal the extent to which liberationists have identified with movements for change. They also provide some insight into the expectation held by both the Vatican and liberationists, that changes in Latin America Catholicism might have implications for revolutionary changes in society at large.

A primary criticism is that the Theology of Liberation depends on Marxism for its basic concepts.[15] The Vatican's major fear is the identification of class conflict as a central characteristic of Latin societies. The church maintains that all classes must exist in harmony. This is a major thrust of the official Catholic Social Justice Tradition. The idea of class cooperation is at the heart of Christian Democracy.

The Vatican also rejects what it sees as a willingness to cooperate with Marxists on the part of liberationist factions. This combination of Marxist concepts and joint activity with Marxists leads Rome to fear that the Theology of Liberation, as expounded by some priests, is a prescription for revolution and the total demise of Catholicism in Latin America. In addition, the Vatican feels that the Theology of Liberation de-emphasizes the eternal spiritual message of the Church in favour of a materialistic focus on the here and now. Rome does not reject the material needs of people, but feels that true liberation will be achieved only as 'liberation from death through salvation in Christ.'

Aside from liberationism's proximity to class analysis, the Vatican reproaches this theology for what it claims is a total emphasis on the poor and its exclusion of the wealthy. It is interesting that in Guatemala, for example, the greatest defection to Protestantism has come from the middle sectors. In El Salvador, members of the wealthy right wing have indicted the Church for its communism and have encouraged the killing of priests. A number of Salvadoran officers have converted to evangelical Protestantism.

A key structural problem identified by Rome and emerging from the praxis of the Base Ecclesial Community is the growth of a 'parallel magisterium.' The Vatican claims for itself the role of primary teacher. It is to be the ultimate authority within the church. If, as happens in Base Ecclesial Communities, ordinary people are allowed to interpret the Bible in terms of their own experience and believe and act on the basis of that interpretation, the primary authority of Rome is nullified. The role of the priest sanctioned by this authority is also undermined.

As a result, the hierarchical nature of Catholicism is in danger of collapse. In effect, a new religion, a religion of the people and without Rome's authority, fundamentally challenges the role and power of the Roman Church. Linked to its response to this challenge is Rome's rejection of the idea of sinful structures and collective salvation. A powerful centralized and hierarchical church maintains its authority because it is the vehicle that determines individual sin and the path of salvation. Therefore, the Vatican asserts that it is not structures that are sinful and produce evil people, but sinful people who use otherwise neutral structures to evil ends. It is these individuals who must be saved.

At the core of all these objections is a conflict over the role of theologians and theology itself. Rome, in spite of Vatican II, maintains that the Vatican teaches and theologians explain and propagate. The source of theological innovation must be centralized. The Theology of Liberation and the praxis of the BECs allow for myriad possibilities of decentralization.

All of this indicates that a profound and historic struggle is taking place within the church. In Latin America, where Catholicism is co-extensive and integral to the lives of the people, this struggle is crucial for society at large. If Catholicism has been a fount of civic values since the conquest, there is nothing to indicate that it will cease to be so. This is ever more so in that the Theology of Liberation is very self-consciously designed to be socially invasive. The conscientization, which takes place in many of the thousands of BECs, is meant to assault the parochial nature of the people and orient them toward social involvement. For a people who are basically religious, the sacred nature of their social involvement sanctions selfless activism in ways that transcend normal ideological commitment.

One cannot predict the outcome of this institutional conflict and reformation. But one can certainly say this. Where a revolution has occurred, as it has in Nicaragua, or where popular revolutionary struggles are still in motion, as in El Salvador and Guatemala, or even where the political scene is dominated by reformism or temporarily stable dictatorships, no serious analysis can be made if the role of religion is ignored. The emergence of the Theology of Liberation, and the role it plays in the struggle for ideological hegemony in Latin America, is transforming old notions of both religion and revolution. The impact of that transformation will be felt, indeed, it is already being felt, far beyond Latin America itself.

NOTES

1. Karl Marx, *Toward the Critique of Hegel's Philosophy of Right* and in Engels, for example, see *On the History of Early Christianity*.
2. All documentary references to Vatican II are from Walter M. Abbot, S.J., General Editor, *The Documents of Vatican II*, (New York, 1966).
3. For the English version of the Medellín document, see 'The Church in the Present-Day Transformation of Latin America in the Light of the Council' (1973).
4. Nestor Paz, *My Life for my Friends* (Maryknoll, 1975).
5. *Ibid.* pp. 4–5.
6. *Ibid.* p. 21.
7. For a brief biography of Camilo Torres and a presentation of his work, see *Revolutionary Priest. The Complete Writings and Messages of Camilo Torres*, edited by John Gerassi (New York, 1971).
8. Enrique Dussel, *A History of the Church in Latin America* (Grand Rapids, 1981).
9. *Documents of Vatican II*, op. cit., pp. 199–200.
10. Gustavo Gutierrez, *A Theology of Liberation* (Maryknoll, 1973).
11. Leonardo Boff discusses this concept at length in his very controversial work, *Church: Charisma and Power*, the writing of which caused this Brazilian theologian to be censured by the Vatican.
12. For a good summary discussion of the BEC, see Phillip Berryman, *Liberation Theology* (New York: 1987), pp. 63–70. This work is also a good general introduction to the Theology of Liberation. Pablo Galdamez, *Faith of a People* (Maryknoll, 1983) describes the life of a BEC in El Salvador. For a discussion of the BEC in Chile, see Lawrence Littwin, 'Base Ecclesial Communities in Chile,' unpublished paper delivered at the Latin American Studies Association Congress, Mexico D.F. 1984. Gustavo Gutierrez delivers a theological view of the BEC in his *We Drink from Our Own Wells* (Maryknoll, 1984). See also Leonardo and Clodovis Boff, *Introducing Liberation Theology* (Maryknoll, 1987).
13. See his *Pedagogy of the Oppressed* (New York, 1972) for a description of the methodology of 'conscientization.'
14. The evolution and nature of this *modus vivendi* is partially explained in the July 9–16, 1988 issue of *America* by Arthur F. McGovern and Thomas L. Schubeck in their article 'Updating Liberation Theology.'
15. These criticisms can be found in the 'Instructions' on the Theology of Liberation issued by the Sacred Congregation for the Doctrine of the Faith and authored by Cardinal Joseph Ratzinger in 1984 and 1986 respectively. The second instruction is considered by some to be a more conciliatory document.

NOTES ON THE CUBAN REVOLUTION

Saul Landau

I

I recall standing high on the tribune in the Plaza of the Revolution on January 2, 1961[1] just as I did twenty-eight years later and straining my neck unsuccessfully to see the end of the crowd. And Fidel, with five microphones, the number he still uses to ensure that his words will reach even the far end of the rally, denouncing the imperialists with the same fervour and some of the same language as he used on December 5, 1988.

So much in Cuba has changed in thirty revolutionary years. Fidel at 62 and gray in hair and beard no longer shows that spontaneous grin of wonder. The casinos, beggars, sex shows and aura of free and dirty third world capitalism remain only in the film archives, captured on celluloid.

So much remains the same, not just the same as before the revolution, but the same as the 19th Century, and even before. Cuba is Spain and Africa, the old world and the new. It is U.S. gangsters and gamblers, baseball players and novelists. A little of Cuba is the Soviet Union, much of it is Caribbean and Latin American. It is culturally diverse and provincial. It is also, in Fidel's mind, the last bastion of socialism left in the world. The visitor sees the superficial, members of the Cuban militia – more than a million strong throughout the nation – fastidiously dressed, occupying the front position of the crowd, the crack troops, including the Special Forces marching by with precision movements, as they do every five years. Under thousands of the neatly pressed military blouses militia members wear *santeria*[2] beads.

In the countryside new homes for peasants dot the landscape, some of them five story apartment buildings. But try, as I have done several times, to use the bathroom in one of the new peasant flats; inevitably the peasant will regret that the facilities are not working. I discovered after several rural refusals that breakdown is a result of the pig being illicitly kept there, despite clear 'health' prohibitions.

Bohios, the thatched huts that Columbus found and that the settlers copied because they kept out heat, still remain in the countryside. In the Plaza of the Revolution the cold and white architecture (built before the revolution) presents a façade of European civilization. Watching the goose-stepping troops or

278

the MIG's flashing by overhead, one would not think that Cuba is just out of underdevelopment.

The mass meeting on December 5, 1988, marked the thirty second anniversary of the landing of the *Granma,* the yacht on which Fidel and 82 guerrillas embarked from Mexico to Cuba to launch their war against the Batista regime. Normally, every five years missiles and tanks pass under the reviewing stand. Not in 1988. They were not necessary. Cuba had won major battles against South Africa[3] in Angola, and 500,000 Havaneros showed up to watch the troops march and listen to Fidel speak – for four hours, the last one in a pouring rain. The parade and the people were symbolic reminders to the White House and Pentagon that an incursion against Cuba would be costly; and to Soviet President Gorbachev that Fidel's brand of socialism – not *glasnost* or *perestroika* – has wide popular backing.[4]

Underneath the display of military power, the symbolic demonstration of support for the Commander-in-Chief, lies a complex, troubled, confused and still superstitious population. The Cuban Revolution is, on the one hand, a glaring success. Compare Cuba's current health and education statistics to those of the Dominican Republic, or to pre-Castro years. Or consider the foreign policy accomplishments of an island nation of ten million people. Cuba today has relations with more than 110 nations, including most from Latin America, which the United States has tried to prevent for twenty five years. Beneath the surface, however, the revolution is in trouble.

The economy is not performing as Fidel expected. Although some sectors remain productive, others falter. The distribution of goods and services to the city dwellers is a source of despair, both for those who must wait for hours for buses, months or even years for certain home repairs, and those who have organized the economy. Fidel knows and feels the pain when the Cienfuegos oil refinery due to be finished in 1985 is still not finished in 1989, or when a Pinar del Rio hospital takes eleven years to complete, because of forms of economic organization and use of the labour force that would drive an ordinary person to madness.

Construction enterprises would contract with other parts of the economy to build an edifice, which is to cost, say 5 million pesos. The housing is pronounced completed, the construction firm declares itself to have made a profit of say 3 million pesos and the recipient of the housing declares that its plans have moved ahead. In reality, the housing is inadequate, and therefore useless. For purposes of show, however, both the construction firm and the recipient declare success.

On other occasions, construction enterprises begin operations and then cease. The excuse may be lack of necessary parts, or tools. Half-done structures became common from the mid 1970s on. And with this kind of systematic fraudulence, which the Soviet Union knew too well, and which in part it had exported (the system) to Cuba, comes demoralization, corruption and the variety of cover-up schemes that inevitably accompany crime. The system breeds contempt for the kinds of ideals that Fidel has proclaimed, for the image of a self-sacrificing Che Guevara. Yet, the managers and executives of the companies that perpetrated fraud were often in the vanguard of slogan shouting and outward displays of revolutionary fidelity.

Sectors of the labour force work in ways that would make efficiency experts despair. I witnessed a team of sweepers at an outdoor site at the Cienfuegos oil refinery. From afar I saw them sitting in the shade of a storage tank. When they saw the film crew approaching they became very busy sweeping dirt from one place to another. The wind would come up and blow it back, but they kept sweeping.

At stores a passive-aggressive attitude often characterizes the personnel. In December, 1988, I stopped to film a long line of people, waiting to buy green vegetables. At the front of the line sat two lethargic clerks torpidly making change with computerized cash registers. A woman shopper noticed the video camera and shouted at me in Spanish: 'Look at the crap we have to put up with.' I asked the cameraman if he had caught it, but since he spoke no Spanish he didn't see any significance. I asked her to repeat what she had said. She asked me if I was with Cuban TV. When I told her I was a foreigner she said forget it. 'I wanted Fidel to see what we have to go through to get a few greens. For foreigners, no.'

Like other Cubans I have talked to, this woman is defensive before outsiders. If proof were needed that Fidel has at least brought a feeling of nationalism, pride in country, experience of the collective 'we', just try to get critical Cubans to voice their complaints to the outside world. And it is not for fear of repercussions so much as it is fear of revealing the depth of the problems after thirty years of revolution. Cubans have long pretended that the problems didn't exist or were easily soluble. In fact, such a façade worked to confuse their own situation.

Who or what is to blame for the fact that goods don't reach the stores, that people have to stand endlessly in line, especially for transportation, that home repair is almost impossible to get in a short time, for the low quality of parts of Cuban – produced goods, and for the amount of corruption that people privately acknowledge? The CIA can no longer be held responsible.

Cuba's enemies have begun to call it the Albania of the Caribbean. That is unfair, given the immense international connections that Fidel has forged. But the odious comparison contains a germ of insight about the inflexible nature of the Cuban revolutionary government. While hierarchies break down even inside some multi-national corporations, they maintain their rigidity inside the Cuban bureaucracies. Cuba at the end of 1988 is not experiencing the information revolution. Only the top is let in on information; even minor decisions are made at the highest levels.

When I landed in Cuba, in late November, 1988, I had already read in the Miami press that Fidel would attend the transfer of presidential power in Mexico. But members of Cuba's Foreign Ministry did not – or they lied – have that information. It had not appeared in *Granma*, the official Party daily. In Cuba, routine information exists on the street, in buses and barbershops, but not in the media – unless it is officially authorized.

While routine information – much of it idiotic – floods the rest of the western and considerable areas of the third world, and Soviet leaders encourage it, Cubans operate on war psychology – need to know. The notion that information-sharing will aid the enemy still dominates the consciousness of revolutionaries. And Fidel use military language when he talks about the obligations of the Cuban work force. 'Cada trabajador a su puesto de trabajo,' Fidel exhorted the half million people.

At certain ministries the telephone is answered 'Ordenes.' Cubans remain suspicious of all non-routine activities. For twenty years I have had similar experiences filming on the streets of Havana. A citizen spies the camera, calls the police and I am told that I need official permission to film on the street. At first, I accepted this, but was told by a government official that there was freedom to film.

So, in 1974, when a policeman asked me for my authorization document, I asked him what law said that I needed one. He replied that everyone knew about the law requiring permission to film on the street. I persisted, so he went to his patrol car and asked the sergeant, who told him to tell me that there was such a law and that I had better obey it or else. I demanded that the sergeant read me the law. Exasperated, he radioed to headquarters, telling the lieutenant of my absurd request. Some thirty minutes after all this trouble began, the policeman approached me and ordered: 'Film,' making a motion with his hand and arm as if to start the cameras rolling.

A similar experience occurred in 1988 outside a suburban supermarket, with the police and citizenry gathering around the film crew angrily demanding to see our filming permit and finally having to retreat in sullen defeat when a patrol car unit affirmed the right to film on the street without permission.

In June, 1987, I requested to film Cuba's nuclear facilities, due to go on line in 1990. The foreign ministry official assigned to the film crew laughed at the idiocy of my request. 'No way,' he told me. When Fidel met us on the day of the interview, he asked if we had filmed the nuclear plant. Upon hearing that it was off limits to cameras, he frustratedly replied: 'What idiocy. With the cameras on the satellites, the CIA can photograph an individual hair on my beard, and yet with your primitive equipment you are denied access. Well, these ways of thinking, derived from earlier periods, are hard to break.'

One of the roots of Cuba's difficulties is the reign in certain sectors of a kind of military stupidity, founded on experiences of the 1960s. Workers have learned that safety and job security lie in not taking initiatives. A dramatic case occurred, while oil was being pumped from a tanker to the land storage tanks of the Cienfuegos refinery.

The monitoring operator noticed indicators of a spill and tried, unsuccess-fully, to find his supervisor. So, he waited, as the oil leak into Cienfuegos Bay increased, until, hours later, someone with authority ordered him to turn off the pump. By that time 1,200 tons of fuel had seeped into Cienfuegos Bay, doing immense damage to the flora and fauna. In an ensuing trial, revelations emerged about a work process that lacked the soldier's attention to duty, but did imitate the military establishment's (anywhere) propensity for waste and bureaucracy.

Fidel, initiative-taker par excellence, has taught that each worker should be in his work post and follow orders, while at the same time he has tried to encourage the people to use their common sense, when such incidents occur. Fidel, who makes all the key decisions, is acknowledged throughout Cuba and much of the third world – even begrudgingly in the United States – as a political magician, having survived thirty years of U.S. aggression. Fidel is the commander-in-chief of the armed forces, and everything else. He has made Cuba into an important player on the world stage. But the proverbial military mentality, a direct opposite of Fidel's flexible and imaginative think-ing about foreign affairs, prevails as a kind of left-over from the days when a U.S. attack may have been imminent.

Guards with rusty old rifles patrol buildings that once may have been mili-tary targets. Cuban citizens assume that saboteurs and subversives from the CIA are ever present and intend to destroy their revolution. The CIA has obligingly provided ample evidence for that assumption over the past thirty years.[5] As Cuban counter intelligence continues to play its spy games with its counterparts at the CIA, that conspiratorial world outlook will retain credibility.

Throughout 1987 and 1988 the antagonistic yet strangely symbiotic CIA and Cuban counter-intelligence played out this spy silliness. A Cuban DGI official stationed in Eastern Europe defected, along with a decorated Air Force general, who was a hero at the Bay of Pigs.[6] Both defectors offered stories about Cuban intelligence's penetration of every nook and cranny of the 'free world.' They also described the 'totalitarian horrors' of life in Cuba. The Cuban government responded by defaming their characters and presenting an embarrassing TV show, filmed by hidden cameras, that portrayed much of the activities of the U.S. Interest Section in Havana, as being devoted to planting high tech gadgets to spy on Cuba, or paying off Cuban agents to do this or that piece of naughtiness. The faces of some 70 current and former State Department officials were held on the TV screen and identified as nefarious CIA officials. The programme lasted an entire week, and while much hoopla was made about the infiltration by DGI of CIA activities, the foreign media's response was a loud yawn. Cuba lacks the kind of spin doctors that attract the press to such stories. Had the CIA carried off a similar coup, would the journalists have been so cavalier?

Cuba's spy concern arose because of a real need to protect its revolution against the plotting 90 sea miles away. From the first days after the triumph, the best and the brightest of Cuba, not counting those who left or whose loyalty was thought to be dubious, found themselves involved with one or another form of Cuban defence. Fidel developed intelligence and counter-intelligence agencies. By 1960, he began to fashion a formal military force to replace the guerrilla army. Those smart and revolutionary youngsters from the university, even teachers' schools and high schools, from government ministries and from the professions, were recruited into the defence establishment. By 1962, as Cuba became dependent on the Soviet Union for its defence supplies, Cubans routinely went to Moscow for formal training.

Instead of the best minds working on planning, culture and education, they were put to work in the less productive, but obviously necessary and murky field of national security. Cuban intelligence probably saved the revolution from destruction and its leader from assassination on numerous occasions. The best and the brightest also cleverly designed the reproduction of their agencies and, like national security bureaucrats everywhere, help to maintain the aura of emergency and crisis, the *sine qua non* for spy vs. spy atmospherics. They did not put their intelligence toward the positive and difficult task of building a socialist society with strong spiritual values. They became the core of the repressive apparatus.

After 30 years, symbiotic links exist between the prestigious political leader of the island and the majority of the Cuban people. The ties have withstood the test of time, sacrifice, and much joy, pain, success and failure. The ritual of Fidel interacting with hundreds of thousands of Cubans has remained intact. As has the ritual of great expectations and daily sacrifice, the promise of utopia large and small and the delivery of a bureaucratic quality of equality that meets the letter but not the spirit of Fidel's promises.

In October, 1987, Fidel offered in a speech to a Cuban congress of workers his ideas on the virtues of eating vegetables. He extolled the health and nutrition qualities of vegetables, and then proceeded to offer recipes on how to prepare them. Castro wanted Cubans to discard the habit of eating greasy and fried foods and instead enjoy healthy and tasty vegetables. Fidel went through some twenty varieties of green and other crops grown in Cuba, paying special attention to broccoli and egg plant. The audience responded with good humour and seemed genuinely impressed with Fidel's knowledge. An elevator operator was talking about the speech later with another hotel employee, both amazed at Fidel's comprehensive knowledge not only of vegetables, but of cooking. 'The only thing he didn't tell us,' she said, 'was how to get the vegetables.'

Distribution problems have plagued Cuba, as they have other socialist countries. Most of the city dwellers are convinced that the goods exist, but are either rotting in some warehouse, or being hoarded by some corrupt officials to sell later on the black market. The ubiquitous bureaucracy is blamed. And, logically, Fidel has decided periodically to launch campaigns against bureaucracy and inefficiency. These campaigns appear to alleviate some of the popular anxiety, but have not resulted in serious improvement over the past decade.

In late 1986, he declared that there must be a massive rectification. The Cuban economy, he acknowledged at a Communist Party Congress, required serious reform, and, he emphasized, 'there is a lot that needs correcting.' No more half-done jobs, mindless bureaucracy, wasteful habits. No more institutionally condoned stupidity. Wage rates should be decided according to actual work, not some abstract design hatched in a Planning Ministry. Equality and justice must be the actual rules at work, not slogans that bear no relationship to the reality of daily work.

Everyone agrees. But, warns Fidel, the campaign will not lead to a loosening of socialist principles, to revisions of Marxism-Leninism, to a permissive atmosphere that would allow elements of capitalism to enter the Cuban economy. No way. Cuba does not need glasnost or perestroika, said Fidel. There is a story making the Cuban rumour rounds. Fidel supposedly visits the same barber each week, and while seated in the chair, he is asked: 'Fidel, what do you really think of *glasnost*?' Fidel does not respond. The barber repeats the question each week, and finally Fidel responds annoyedly, 'Why do you keep asking me that question?'

'It makes your hair stand on end,' replies the barber, 'and it's easier to cut.'

The Rectification Campaign, however, is taken as Fidel's substitute for the Soviet reforms. Each Cuban, by following the example of the legendary Che Guevara, will help to solve Cuban's problems. Some Cubans told me that they could not believe their ears when they heard Fidel in October 1987, twenty years after Che's death in the Bolivian mountains, call upon Cubans to imitate the Argentine martyr, to think and act as he did, to emulate his behaviour at work and as citizens.

'Che was a saint,' one government functionary confessed to me. 'I am not a saint. I can work hard, but I cannot do what Che did. Anyway, I have been working overtime most of the last twenty nine years. I am tired. All that extra work has not made me more efficient. I have attended endless meetings where we discuss and agree that steps must be taken to make sure that Fidel's programme of rectification is carried out.'

By 1986 few in Cuba would disagree; something must be done. Words of solid support ring out from every corner of Cuba. We must rectify. Slogans are prepared, posters are painted, commentators analyze and exhort on TV and radio. The rectification campaign is on. But what is done? The sloppy work continues, the bureaucracy remains in its comfortable and mean mode, the goods that are produced somehow do not reach the stores, transportation is worse than ever and idiocy continues to rule in many work-places as a daily norm.

After thirty years of revolution, the economy does not function as Fidel expected. The pieces are in place. The roads and dams built, the people educated and healthy, high levels of skill and technology abound, factories are in place, energy sources produce, the trains run through the island, but somehow the pieces do not fit together. Cubans see all this, participate in their own way in the malfunctioning of the system, complain about the imbecility, and feel compassion for Fidel, who must bear the weight of imperfection – not failure. Yet, in daily life it is the Cuban people who suffer from the poor bus service, the difficulty of obtaining goods and services, the bureaucratic nightmares involved in transactions that require official seals.

The apocryphal joke made about other socialist countries has made the rounds in Cuba as well. There's no unemployment, but no one works. No one works, but everyone meets his quota. The quotas are met, but there are no goods in the stores. The stores are empty but everyone seems to be well fed and clothed. People have what they need but gripe constantly about the poor leadership. Yet, when Fidel speaks people pour out in droves and applaud everything he says.[7]

Fidel refuses to concede that the form of socialism as practised in Cuba, not all that different from the form practised in the Soviet Union, has inherently impossible features. Never has a massive state bureaucracy been able to manage with efficiency a small restaurant or barber shop, provide for the kind of distribution in which capitalism by its very nature specializes. Nor is there space in Cuba for public political opposition to positions announced by the Party or government.

Cuba's incapacity to embrace *glasnost,* however, derives not from a particularly sectarian or rigid party but from the nature of its leader. Fidel Castro is not just the President of Cuba, the head of the Communist Party and the Commander-in-Chief of the armed forces, militias and the public in general. He is also the living myth or legend, treated as if he were the redeemer and Saviour. How can free discussion take place when such power resides in one man – and with the apparent consent of the majority of Cubans?

Thus the handle of reform in Cuba is elusive – or perhaps illusory. The system that was imported from the Soviet Union, mostly during the Brezhnev era, and modified by Cubans to conform closer to their reality, is not one with great flexibility built in. The central state controls all the outlying areas of the economy and politics.

Cuba has more pressing reasons for fearing reforms that would allow for the re-entrance of capitalism. The United States, one of the few countries in which capitalism has performed for a substantial sector of the population, held Cuba as an informal colony for some sixty years, and should Cuba make itself vulnerable to the repenetration of U.S. economic power, its independence, sovereignty, might also falter.

Fidel and other leaders as well as rank and file communists are well aware that capitalism has not worked well for the majority in most of the world. Latin America not only staggers beneath its immense debt, but is unable to feed, clothe, house, educate and provide medical care for a substantial part of its population. In most African countries, capitalism has become a sick joke.

Socialism, a young and inexperienced way of organizing resources and people, has had to operate in limited space and with undeveloped resources; it has also had to face counter-revolutionary attack and war – and the fact that it developed in the European nation least suited to experiment. The model that Stalin developed became the only one available to nations like Cuba, whose precious independence, fought for over a period of more than 100 years, demanded that it extract itself from the clutch of U.S. domination. When nationalists in Cuba or elsewhere in the third world sought language to elaborate their goals of sovereignty and social justice, Marxism-Leninism appeared as the one mode of discourse available that encompassed the national needs and the social demands.

Fidel told me that he began to revere Marxism from the time he first read the *Communist Manifesto*, when he was 18, a university freshman. But he was not a communist then, or immediately after the triumph of the revolution. He believed that revolution could accomplish nation-building goals, and allow for necessity to determine the economic and social policies. So, Fidel, who told Jean Paul Sartre in 1960 that the Cuban revolution would function on the basis of providing for people's needs, as they arose objectively and subjectively, was expressing his own wish, to bring a classless utopia to Cuba. Sartre approved of this existential experiment that would not fall into either the U.S. or Soviet camp.

But Fidel found that Soviet aid did not replace U.S.-managed capitalism, and that unlike the market system that prevailed under capitalism, the Soviet-based aid model offered little room in which to manoeuvre. The resource restraints under socialism put fetters on Fidel's ambitious and urgent development plans. He hoped to gather capital by using the Cuban labour force for an extraordinary effort: producing 10 millions tons of sugar cane, a quarter more than had ever been refined.

The failure to meet his goal of 10 million tons in 1970 was also a symbolic end to Fidel's 1960s utopianism. Fidel had no options. The Soviet system could provide expertise in military and educational affairs, set up accounting systems that would facilitate the new trade links between the countries, provide Cuba with energy supplies, wheat and the infinite amount of needs that Cuba had as a nation. Individual need had to be delayed indefinitely. Socialism as it was used to develop Cuba had a national priority. The Cuban people appeared to have understood this, made the sacrifices necessary and postponed their individual appetites. But for how long can such a delay be justified by appeals that this is the necessary cost of development?

After seventy years, the Soviet leadership declared that its system suffered from major inherent defects – some that had been exported to Cuba – and that major reforms were needed. Fidel must have feared that such an admission in Cuba, and the allowance for private capital's entrance into the island economy, could have put in jeopardy the core of the revolutionary programmes. So in 1989, as the Soviet intellectuals experience an opening somewhat akin to what the West went through in the 1960s, Cuba remains under the informational and ideological harness of the hierarchical and inflexible system that the Soviets helped implant there.

II

Revolutions begin as liberating acts. In January 1959 Havana rocked with a sense of free rhythm. Celebrations marked the overthrow of a nasty dictatorship and the expectations of eternal democracy and freedom, although few had any notions about what forms the new order would take. I recall a funeral procession in the summer of 1960 on the day the telephone company was nationalized. Workers carrying a coffin with a phone on it cha cha cha'd down the street and dumped the box into the ocean with great fanfare. How many of the demonstrators were thinking that ITT had invested heavily in Cuba as its third world communications experiment centre, and that its executives would never forgive or forget the impudent challenge to its property, its power?

In 1959, Fidel nationalized the Mafia-owned hotels and casinos, another bold and popular move that would have serious repercussions for the revolution. The Mafiosos, like their corporate colleagues, did not look kindly on acts that dispossessed them. It was not only the lost money, but the example-setting that bothered the criminal and corporate dons. Shortly after the expropriations, ITT and Mafia executives cooperated with the CIA in attempts to destroy the revolution and assassinate Castro and other revolutionary leaders.[8]

One of the nationalized hotels was the Havana Hilton, renamed the Havana Libre. In the late 1970s, Paul Jacobs, a reporter, fresh from a two-week trip to Cuba, chanced upon the Hilton heir, Baron Hilton, at a dinner party and described to him, much to Hilton's dismay, how the hotel had changed since the days when the Hilton family owned the Havana franchise.

'The place is full,' Jacobs informed Hilton, trying to disguise his glee. 'Maybe the clientele has changed a little, but every room is taken. And you should see the way they've maintained the place. The logo HH is still on the door, and some of the glasses still have the old markings.' Baron Hilton was not enjoying this as Jacobs sang the praises of the hotel workers who had taken over the management. 'The casinos are shut down of course, but the big sign over the hotel is still lit up. But your name isn't on that one anymore.'

Baron Hilton could stand no more. 'Well, one day our name will be back up on that sign. You can bet on that.'

'You may be right,' Jacobs answered, 'but I think you might have to change your name to Baron Libre.'

Jacobs was right. The Cuban revolution is thirty years old and no one expects the Libre to be renamed Hilton. Castro did to the American property owners what no one had dared do to them in this part of the world. He took away their property without asking permission and didn't pay for it. He stuck out his tongue at them and for thirty years at the powerful in the U.S. government.

I first went to Cuba in June 1960, when the revolution was still in its *pachanga* stage, a feeling of dancing and party, of mind-bending change and continuous excitement. No one knew what was going to happen next.[9] Cuba and the United States were well along the road of hostile relations. The tit for tat behaviour had already produced considerable nationalization of U.S. property.

U.S. officials did not find this behaviour the least bit amusing. In fact, the rapid unfolding of the Cuban Revolution after January 1959 brought a sense of rising panic to national security officials in Washington, months before Fidel had opened diplomatic relations with the Soviet Union. Revolution, even without fundamental change in property relations, had caused alarm bells to ring in Washington's national security circles. The Cuban case involved basic economic reorganization, a clear claim to national sovereignty, and a direct poke in the eye to U.S. power. In just the first few months of revolution, Castro made it clear that the revolution would be run for the majority of poor Cubans, not for U.S. interests, or for that matter, to please U.S. public opinion.[10]

By 1960, Castro brought most of Cuba's labour force, non-land resources, and markets under state control, and some under state ownership. With each diplomatic move by the State Department, the Cuban leader intensified his anti-Yankee rhetoric, and action. 'Cubans,' he announced, 'shall own Cuba, and Cubans shall dictate what becomes of the resources and wealth on the island.'

The state 'intervened' in those U.S.- and Cuban-owned enterprises that were reportedly violating the new revolutionary rules on labour relations, resource utilization, and marketing. Some firms and lands were nationalized outright, with agrarian reform bonds offered as partial compensation. In 1959 and 1960, Cubans held street celebrations whenever the government announced that it had 'intervened' in a U.S.-owned enterprise. 'Intervention' was the legal name given to the transition stage between private ownership and nationalization, used to justify state intervention while proceedings took place to determine whether or not the targeted company had violated revolutionary laws. Most of them, of course, had. The most important political fact on the island changed on January 2, 1959. From that point on, the U.S. Ambassador could no longer consider himself the most important man on the island.[11]

SAUL LANDAU 289

In 1989 a U.S. Interests Section sits in the place where the U.S. Embassy once housed over 400 functionaries. The lonely handful that now occupies the building overlooking the sea on one side has to look at a poster on the other side. A bearded cartoon character is advising Uncle Sam: '*Señores Imperialistas*, We're not scared of you one bit.'

It does bother the senior staff at the U.S. Interests Section. Mr. John Taylor had served a term in China before moving to the island enemy as Chief of Mission. From his office, he can see the colourful poster, which lights up at night. In the space between the Interest Section and the billboard, kids play baseball. The Marine guard looks through the blinds and indicates that the pitcher and centre fielder are considerably older than the other players. 'They're DGI [Cuba Intelligence],' he confides. 'We've seen them before in other costumes.' (When the interview with Taylor was over we tried to photograph the ball game below. The pitcher grinned at the camera, but the centre fielder glared and with his hand indicated no picture taking).

Mr. Taylor likes the Cubans he deals with, finds them quite Spanish, 'not really third world at all,' and clearly would like to see a return to formal relationships. He is treated like the ambassador at diplomatic functions, but does not bear the title since the U.S. Interests Section in Havana is formally run by the Embassy of Switzerland. (In Washington, Czechoslovakia plays that role for the Cubans.) He takes some credit for the improvement in human rights in Cuba, the release of hundreds of political prisoners, who were allowed to emigrate to the United States, and a general routinization of relations.

Like all those who have met Castro, Taylor thinks that Fidel is special, but that this sway over the masses and his extraordinary abilities, have not produced anything to gloat over. The revolution, Taylor says, really hasn't accomplished anything. If one compares Cuban health and education statistics from 1958 with those of Costa Rica, one finds that both nations developed at approximately the same rate. So, he concludes, with or without the revolution, Cuba would still probably have the lowest rate of infant mortality and the highest literacy rate.[12] This approach to the Cuban revolution – grant them nothing – may serve as more of an answer to the anti-Yankee sign below the U.S. Interest Section building than it is a statement of truth or belief. Taylor's remarks may respond more to the childish poster, than to Cuba's reality, or to serious interests of the U.S. government. The Cuban revolution is not only permanent, but has created a nation out of an informal U.S. colony, a unified and coherent state that plays a world role far beyond that which its size and economy should permit.

Cuba has proved vulnerable in the human rights area, especially as defined by the western media, whose definition of human rights usually refers to the procedural, not the substantive freedoms laid out in the United Nations Covenants. Reagan's Assistant Secretary of State for Inter-American Affairs, Elliot Abrams, pushed the line that Cuba was a prime human rights violator, and gained considerable international attention on this issue. After Cuba released most of its political prisoners by mid-1988, Abrams picked up another line, that the revolution was a failure in all areas. A position that is designed to undermine Fidel's most recognized accomplishments.

Since the mid-1960s, Cuba's number of political prisoners has decreased from perhaps as high as 20,000 down to less than 150 by 1989, according to monitoring organizations like Americas Watch and the UN Human Rights Commission. The limits on speech, press and assembly, the power of state security to deprive citizens of liberty without due process, and some cases of unusually harsh treatment that remain in Cuba's prisons continue to draw the legitimate fire of human rights watchers. These critiques of Cuba are rooted in fact. But Cuba allowed a U.S. team to inspect six of its prisons, without restrictions, while the United States denied Cuba's reciprocal request to look at U.S. prisons. No human rights team, nor journalists have inspected U.S. prisons and jails and then compared the abuses in them to those found in Cuban penal institutions. None of the human rights agencies however, compares Cuba to the United States in relation to human rights like housing, medical care or right to a job, areas where Cuba would win easily.[13]

Most European governments and even intellectuals appear to accept the Cuban Revolution as one more fact in the long decolonizing process of the 20th Century. In Latin America, Fidel and the revolution are seen not only as possible development models, but as symbols of Latin courage and will. In Quito, for the inauguration of Ecuador's new president, Fidel was treated with reverence by the other heads of state and by the media. In Mexico at the transfer of power from de la Madrid to Salinas, Fidel was a conquering hero, with heads of state and media trying to be near him, with crowds on the street trying to touch him and get his autograph. In Caracas, in 1989, Fidel held discussions with several leaders from around the world.

In much of Africa, Fidel Castro is not only a hero for saving Angola from the clutches of South Africa, and Ethiopia from a Somali invasion, but for having the courage to send some 60,000 troops, a good part of them black, as an act of international solidarity.

While Europe uses Africa as a dumping ground for toxic waste, Cuba sends people to help defend, educate and cure the sick of the world's sickest continent. And Mr. Abrams also understands that Fidel has been able to keep those troops in place, defeating the mighty and arrogant South African forces in the battle of Cuito Cuanavales, sending the blue eyed, blond haired youth to a humiliating retreat – many of them in body bags. Castro calls the battle the Bay of Pigs of Africa.

By 1989, the United States, which refuses to recognize its island neighbour, appears petulant to much of the world diplomatic community. The reasons behind U.S. intractability bear some scrutiny.

Throughout 1959 and 1960, Castro pushed radical reforms: he slashed rents, nationalized utilities, and carried out a massive agrarian reform, which resulted in the expropriation of more than six million hectares by mid-1963.

These moves violated a rule that Secretary of State John Foster Dulles enunciated to an oil company executive in 1956: '. . . the United States would not acquiesce in the rights of nationalization' because of an 'international interest [which] goes far beyond the composition of shareholders alone, and should call for international intervention.'

By 1960, despite the rapid deterioration in relations, American investors in Cuba still clung to the notion that the United States would not permit expropriations of its citizens by an upstart nation. Dulles' Doctrine was well known to those who had made investments abroad. Dr. Rene Vallejo, a Cuban gynaecologist who in 1958 had joined Castro's guerrilla force in the mountains, was subsequently appointed to direct the Agrarian Reform Institute in Oriente Province. In this capacity, in 1960, one of his tasks was to deliver the order nationalizing the King Ranch, whose thousands of acres were located in eastern Cuba. The Cuban government offered agrarian reform bonds as symbolic compensation. The U.S. could have decided to honour the bonds and thereby offer the Cuban government credit, or not honour them and thereby render them worthless.

Vallejo described the attitude of disbelief on the part of the Ranch manager, whom Vallejo had known and whose wife had been a patient of his. At first the American thought the Cuban doctor was playing a practical joke, but when he realized the seriousness of the mission, he told Vallejo: 'You can't do this, you know. You are taking away property of U.S. citizens and every time that has happened the U.S. marines come in and get it back. And that's the way it's going to be again.'

From late 1959 on Castro's policies became an area of national security 'crisis.' Since there was insufficient public support for direct intervention, Cuba became the concern of a secret task force set up under Vice-President Nixon, whose job was to destroy the revolution and replace it with a pro-U.S. government.

But unlike other nationalistic reformers who thought they could bargain with the United States, Castro assumed that Washington would meet the Cuban revolution with implacable hostility. He armed the populace by forming militias, and quickly carried out the basic reforms, guaranteeing job and wage security and offering education and housing programmes that gave millions of Cubans a material and moral stake in their revolution.

As the United States cut off its trade, commercial and military relations, Castro reforged links with the Soviet Union. By early 1960, it appeared clear to American political leaders that Castro was trying to prove not only that revolution could succeed on the U.S. doorstep, but that it could be done with Soviet aid. In July 1960, Washington threw down the gauntlet by encouraging U.S.-owned oil refineries in Cuba to refuse to process Soviet oil, and by cutting off the Cuban sugar quota.[14]

No one who had followed the unfolding conflict was surprised by the invasion of the island in April 1961. The strike force was composed of Cuban exiles trained, financed, and controlled by the CIA, and launched from the east coast of Nicaragua with the full support of Nicaraguan President Luis Somoza. But after less than 72 hours, the Cuban exiles that had landed in the Bay of Pigs on the south coast of Cuba had either been killed or captured by the country's volunteer militia and army.

Castro had proven false two of Latin American revolutionaries' absolute truths: 1) Revolution can be made with the army or without the army, but never against the army; 2) Successful revolution can never be made without U.S. permission. The Batista army was leaderless, without morale and easily dispersed. Those who retained the will to counter-attack joined the CIA's Bay of Pigs army, and found themselves either dead on the Giron or Largo Beach or in prison.

Castro later traded most of the prisoners to President Kennedy for some medical supplies. Today, when he is attacked by the U.S. government for being a human rights violator he recalls the treatment of those prisoners.

'The mercenaries that invaded us in The Bay of Pigs, almost fifteen hundred mercenaries, were paid and directed by the CIA, in the service of a foreign power. They came here to bomb, using the Cuban flag to attack us traitorously and they took the lives of dozens and dozens of *compañeros*, hundreds of injured and we took more than one thousand prisoners at the Bay of Pigs.'

Castro's eyes reflect his grappling with memory, searching for details that will dramatize his point. 'The mercenaries were all over the place and had to be rounded up. One troup fought for almost seventy two hours straight, saw its compañeros die, and then they caught the invaders one by one and took them prisoners and didn't even lay one finger on them. When we brought together all the captured mercenaries from the Bay of Pigs not one of them could accuse us of any human rights abuse.' Castro hits a righteous stride and continues with his factual analysis.

'We took them prisoners despite the hatred which the people held for them. This is one irrefutable proof of our correct conduct, because our men were in the heat of battle and we could have finished off many of them as soon as the battle ended. They wouldn't have had time to surrender; yet we captured some one thousand two hundred and most of them are still alive and healthy in the U.S.'

Twenty eight years have gone by since the Bay of Pigs fiasco, as the Kennedy historians name it. That fateful April date is frozen in the memory of many of the Miami-based veterans. In the coffee shops, bars and restaurants, at dinner tables and on Miami's Spanish language radio, the Bay of Pigs veterans relive those fateful 72 hours. Fidel Castro to them is more than a man. He is a mixture of God and Satan, Hercules and Attila. Hundreds of the now late middle aged men continue to vow that 'one day' they will. . .

The Bay of Pigs marked the first defeat of the United States in its dealings with the lower continent. The scars have not healed among those who took pride only in victory: to the ageing CIA crowd, to the men who lost estates and sugar mills, to the ideologues of U.S. supremacy and to the anti communists, Fidel Castro turned history. After the Bay of Pigs, the U.S. suffered its agonies in Southeast Asia, watched scores of countries turn socialist in Africa, Asia, and even in our own backyard the Sandinistas dared to pronounce that Nicaragua was free from Yankee control, and that the Yankees were 'the enemy of humanity.' President Reagan could not even force a U.S. puppet, Panamanian strongman, General Manuel Noriega, from his post of power.[15]

A critical factor in determining policies in Cuba and the United States involved the refugee population. The United States, from the day the revolution triumphed, has opened its doors to anti-communist Cubans, who sought refuge in the United States, secure in the knowledge that the marines would land, overthrow the bearded guerrillas and reclaim the seized property. In a period of less than two years Castro had exported his enemies to the United States, thanks to the welcome mat offered by Washington, and had transferred thereby the centre of counterrevolution from Cuba to Florida.

III

Castro has built an island power in three decades, with the single-mindedness of a Napoleon or a Simon Bolivar. He has been firm, tough, decisive. The entire politicized world thinks of him as a Jack the Giant Killer. He has watched seven U.S. presidents pass through the White House, while he retains a quantity and quality of power that no person should be allowed to attain. Some Cubans argue disingenuously that they are fortunate that Fidel has presided for so long, and that if Mexico had been lucky, Fidel would have been born there. Fidel, as most of those who have associated with him would have to agree, has not abused power as the traditional *caudillos* did, but rather, because of the amount of authority he possesses, has undermined all other potential leaders and institutions – even ones he has created. The view from Washington, under at least three presidents – Eisenhower, Kennedy and Nixon, who authorized assassination plots – has been that Fidel is a serious enemy, without whom the revolution might disintegrate.

If Fidel was a petty man, he might have felt some sense of satisfaction in knowing that while Kennedy tried to assassinate him, an assassin's bullet struck Kennedy instead. Yet, his feelings for Kennedy are quite the opposite. In 1974, Fidel described the events, from his perspective, surrounding the Kennedy assassination, and of one particular meeting that was happening at the very moment Kennedy was shot.

'I was meeting with an emissary that Kennedy had sent when the news came over the radio that Kennedy had been shot in Dallas.' The messenger was French journalist Jean Daniel, who had brought to Castro a list of subjects for possible discussion with the U.S. president. Castro said he felt profoundly upset when he heard about the news, and some concern about his being accused of responsibility for the deed.

He told about how Lee Harvey Oswald was denied a visa to come to Cuba before the assassination, 'thanks only to bureaucratic routine.' He explained how he was philosophically and morally opposed to assassination. 'It would have been much easier to try to assassinate Batista than to wage a guerrilla war in the mountains for more than two years. But when you assassinate a figure you remove only him, but do not change the system that he represented.'

Castro paused, lit a Cohiba, and continued: 'Kennedy was a known adversary. We had confrontations with him at the Bay of Pigs and during the Missile Crisis. We knew how he thought, how he behaved, indeed, what to expect from him. Why should we trade a known adversary for an unknown one?'

Warming to the subject, Castro talked about the consequences of getting caught. 'The repercussions, should we have actually perpetrated such an act and been discovered, would have been horrendous. The United States could simply destroy us. In short, we had nothing to gain and everything to lose from the assassination of Kennedy.'

Fidel continues to hold a special place for the Kennedy family and even granted an interview to NBC's Maria Shriver because, although undistinguished as a reporter, she was a member of the clan. 'Kennedy was a brave man,' Fidel stated, 'one who accepted responsibility for the Bay of Pigs, instead of trying to put the blame on others.' 'Victory,' John F. Kennedy had declared, with both resolve and sadness in his voice, 'has a thousand fathers; defeat is an orphan.' Courage is a subject Fidel likes to discuss, and he claims to hold no grudge against Kennedy; rather he praises him as being a model of a courageous man. 'Courage in politics is the ability to change your mind, to admit that the investment made in this or that direction was a wrong one and to admit it and alter one's course.'

In Fidel's hierarchy of values, bravery stands above competence. And that has been one of his criteria for selecting leadership during thirty years of revolution. It has also been one of the revolution's major problems. Those who performed with valour and courage on the battlefield, those who could endure the incredible rigours of guerrilla life, those who had an intuitive sense for battle, could not convert those extraordinary qualities into administrative skills and managerial wisdom. On the contrary, the men who landed with Fidel on the Southeastern shore of Cuba on December 2, 1956, aboard the yacht *Granma*, from Mexico, have distinguished themselves by failing to run their ministries efficiently or fairly.

Yet, Fidel continues to transfer them after ministerial failures to head yet another ministry. In all fairness, these once great guerrilla fighters should not bear all the blame. Who could successfully run a major government department with Fidel's shadow cast over the daily work plan? Fidel, not government bureaus, is the repository of political legitimacy; he, not the lesser known figures, owns the monopoly on authority.

Fidel is one of the few genuinely charismatic leaders that the world has known in this century.[16] He is endowed by many Cubans with extraterrestrial qualities. He is called 'the horse,' in street conversation. This reference is to his religious incarnation. Fidel is seen as the redeemer, the Saviour, the man who, if he wills it, can solve impossible problems, perform Herculean tasks. And he has. He is not only the most powerful, once in a Century character to have appeared, but he has used his position to make himself relatively immune from the resource constraints on all other individuals and institutions on the island.

This has been a blessing and a curse for the Cuban people. Fidel has used his attributes to build a viable political organism: a nation.

Building a nation in the mid and late 20th Century is a different task than in the 19th Century. The Garibaldis and Bolivars, who brought the masses to consciousness of national identity, did not face the technological chasm that 3rd world leaders encounter 150 years later as they attempt to mould colonies into coherent entities, whose people share fealty to common symbols and abstractions.[17]

The Cuban revolution has been a marriage between Castro and the masses, for the purpose of building nationhood, and, for those that stayed, a social system rooted in the quest for equality. Underneath the layer that Cubans have placed over their revolution for a variety of purposes, there exists a profound historic and religious drama, whose unfolding involves heroes of almost God-like proportions. Fidel is such a hero. Fidel is *obatalá*. The faith of the Cuban people is not Catholicism, as even the Cuban priests will admit, but *santeria*. Fidel's role in this African-based religion is little known outside of Cuba.

Cuban santeria is mysterious, exotic, compelling as is Haitian voodoo and other Caribbean rites and rituals that have been made into religions over the nearly 400 years since Columbus happened upon the territory generically known as America. *Obatalá*, is one of the messengers of a deity that would be sent to save the island. The messenger would have unusual, almost super-human qualities. He would possess the strength and stamina of the horse, the determination and presence of a stallion. The figure would be a spellbinding orator who could lead Cuba from its demoralized, discombobulated state into unity, power, greatness on the world stage. *Obatalá* would redeem the island's people, save its soul and dignity, forge the populace into a mighty engine of moral force.

Fidel's ways, secretive, single-minded, firm, unflappable, determined, brilliant, invincible, fit the description that the *santeros* had passed down – or perhaps some of this was invented post hoc.

How much of Cuba practises *santeria*? No polls have been taken, but estimates run to as high as one quarter of the population. Another 25% may believe, but not practise. After 30 years of revolution, Cubans of all colours and classes visit the healers, often after or before they see the doctors.

In Guanabacoa, a predominantly black neighbourhood of Havana, a *santero* sang and spoke his polyglot of Arabic, Swahili, Latin and Spanish in a minor key. The woman he was treating had a pain in her chest. The doctors said exploratory surgery was indicated. She went to the *santero*.

On the wall of the modest apartment hung photos of Michael Jackson, ET, Che Guevara, Christ and Fidel. An African deity, a burning candle and a display of fruit and beads adorns a makeshift altar. The *santero* puts the burning end of a cigar in his mouth and blows smoke over the woman, now wrapped in a white sheet. He rhythmically intones as great gusts of smoke pour from his mouth. The woman is touched and gently massaged – not erotically.

Some phrases from Catholic mass are spoken, admonitions to the evil spirits, encouragement to clean karma and a few Arabic phrases complete the final stage of the healing ceremony before the coconut is thrown onto the floor and cracks open. The woman told me that she believed in the power of the *santero*, but that she also had faith in the doctor. She saw *santeria* as her chance to avoid the surgery.

Cuban doctors, now 25,000 strong, the majority of the new graduates women, tolerate *santeria*; the more experienced ones try to cooperate with the *santeros* in certain cases. Indeed, there are Cuban doctors who wear the telltale beads under their white coats. It is widely rumoured that Fidel's long time close companion, Celia Sanchez, was involved in *santeria*. Rene Vallejo, sympathetic to the religion, told me that *santeria* had to be studied because it had produced remarkable results in healing, when traditional medicine failed. Vallejo himself was a spiritualist. Like Celia Sanchez, he was closer to Fidel than anyone else during the difficult years of the mid and late 1960s. Vallejo died in 1969, Celia in 1982.

Without Vallejo and Celia, his constant companions, Fidel has been alone and perhaps quite lonely. His intimate personal life is not a subject he discusses. It is presumed that he has a *compañera*, but the depth of relationship he shared with Vallejo since 1958 and Celia since the guerrilla days, cannot be replaced.[18]

Fidel the lonely messenger of African and Caribbean deities, the world acknowledged stateman and strategist, finds himself in 1989, at age 62, with ever more levels of responsibility, commensurate with ever greater personal power.

IV

THE CULT OF CHE GUEVARA

It was the summer of 1974. We were riding in Fidel's black Soviet limousine and Kirby Jones had asked Castro what had gone wrong with Col. Camaaño's plan to retake the Dominican Republic. With Cuban backing, Camaaño and his guerrillas left Cuba to attempt to reclaim power in Santo Domingo. Fidel attributed Camaaño's rapid demise to recklessness. 'He took his troops to the highway,' Fidel said, almost sneering.

Then he turned to a more important subject. 'Che was *temerario* (reckless),' Fidel explained. 'It was his one flaw,' Fidel admitted. 'He was so brave that he would stand up in the middle of a fire fight. I told him that his value was inestimable and that it was irresponsible to behave that way. I believe he was wounded on several occasions, precisely because of that reckless quality.' Fidel said that one reason for Che's demise in Bolivia was his lack of concern for safety and security.

In the summer of 1968 Fidel blamed the Bolivian Communist Party for having betrayed Che. He insisted that guerrilla warfare was the only means by which Latin Americans could liberate themselves. He blamed the Soviet line for diluting revolutionary thought, insinuating that the orders to sabotage Che's mission came from Moscow, not La Paz.

The ensuing years, however, had changed his perceptions. Cuban foreign policy by 1974 no longer focused on extending the Cuban guerrilla war model to all other Latin American countries. Events had overshadowed the model that Fidel had proved in practice, but that no one else, including Che Guevara, the ablest revolutionary, could repeat.

The death of Che Guevara, Latin America's most romantic martyr, in a remote Bolivian ravine in October 1967, meant more to Fidel than the loss of a close comrade and friend. Fidel had staked Cuba's foreign policy, its posture before the world, on the belief that the guerrilla *foco* could serve as the source of revolution throughout Latin America. And what better emissary, what more imaginative lieutenant, than Che Guevara to carry it forth?

Che had written his guerrilla diary during the two plus years with Fidel in the mountains of Oriente Province (as he wrote one in Bolivia as well). He had continued to make his notes as he led the 200-man column down from the Sierra and through the centre of the island to inflict upon the Batista army the coup de grace in the battle of Santa Clara during Christmas 1958.

During the first five years of revolutionary power, Che played decisive roles, both institutionally and ideologically. In 1960, when Fidel had to appoint a new Bank President, a popular joke began. At a meeting of the rump cabinet Fidel inquired if there was an economist in the room. Che responded affirmatively and Fidel appointed him. After the meeting Fidel said: 'Che, I didn't know you were an economist.'

'Economist?' replied Che. 'I thought you said communist.'

In 1960, Fidel had not yet acknowledged publicly that the Cuban revolution had a socialist character, and some members of the 26th of July Movement, the broad coalition that collaborated in the cities with the mountain guerrilla warriors, still denied that Marxism-Leninism could take over the free and democratic spirit of the Cuban Revolution. In that year, two books, one by C. Wright Mills and the other by Jean Paul Sartre, affirmed the non-communist nature of the zany Cuban experiment, and of its leader, who spent several days with each author in Cuba.

Che had the reputation of being the hard liner, the real communist, although he had no known affiliations with the Communist Party (PSP). Fidel's younger brother, Raùl, had ties to the Cuban Party and had attended several international communist youth meetings. But these formalities effectively ended when he accompanied Fidel on the 1953 assault on Fort Moncada. The Cuban Communists called Fidel a *golpista*, a *putschist*. Che boasted that he was a communist, but not a Party member. He was thought to be more a Luxemburgist or some sort of purer breed of revolutionary than those found inside the Moscow-dominated structures.

As President of the National Bank and Minister of Industries, Che Guevara set out to make socialism – and maybe even communism, in his lifetime – function in Cuba as it had not elsewhere. Che wanted to see every Cuban worker become an active participant in the great transformation that Marx and Engels had predicted and that Lenin had launched in 1917, but not lived to see actualized. Che wanted a socialism that elicited from each individual a spiritual effort, not the imperfect model of massive state bureaucracies that characterized the model from the USSR and Eastern Europe. It was not the nationalization of property that Che faulted, but the cold divorce between Party and masses that existed in the Eastern Bloc countries, the impersonality of State managerialism.

Yet, the only models available to the head economist and planner of Cuba, were these imperfect ones developed in the grim days of Stalin, and modified in the ten years after his death. Borrowing pieces from the Soviet, Czech and East German planning systems, Che helped create a melange, one that probably could have worked had all of the administrators and middle level personnel been like Che himself. Che dramatized the notion of voluntary work, or real social work. He became the living example of sacrifice by the individual for the collective. He himself chopped sugar cane, seemingly tireless for a long day, or days. He spent his Sundays in the factory, observing, working, talking with the proletariat that he believed would become the agency of social transformation from capitalism to socialism, of psychological change from individualism to collectivism.

Che was convinced that Cuba could both industrialize and diversify its agriculture within a short period of time. Fidel's experimental boldness and Che's utopíanism, were based on logic and the intuitive impulse that Cuba had to get out from under the curse of single crop sugar cane. In a 1962 experiment to convert sugar cane acreage to other crops, and simultaneously to initiate light industry, and expand nickel production, Che and Fidel discovered that what looked promising on paper did not correspond to Cuban reality. The skills, coordination and levels of infrastructure that Western Marxists assumed – and convinced the Cuban leaders of – did not exist. The experiment damaged the economy and weakened Che's ideological position with the political elite in Cuba.

Che became, for Fidel, a model of the thinking man who never flinched from doing an efficient hard day's worth of labour. He was medical doctor as guerrilla fighter, polemicist as cane cutter; commander of troops as President of the national bank. Che was the poet administrator. He drove his own car, lived modestly, uninterested in worldly possessions.

Almost any system could work if manned by Che Guevara clones. What worker would not feel the innate sense of satisfaction of falling into the rhythm of Che on the job; what administrator would not welcome his rational, just and confidence-giving presence in an office or ministry? What young revolutionary, would not find his romantic model in this modern version of Quixote with 20–20 vision?

But since there was only one Che, the diversification effort failed initially. Farmers did not have experience growing diverse crops. Some destroyed too much of the cane fields. And, in addition, there developed an acute labour shortage in the countryside, since people flocked to the cities to take advantage of the new opportunities offered to citizens by the socialist revolution. And Cubans did not have easily transferable skills sufficient to make new industry work on the first try. Most of Cuba's educated and professional population had fled to the United States. No matter how hard Che worked, no matter how much confidence he inspired, he could not by himself, or even with Fidel's mighty assistance, transform Cuba miraculously from an underdeveloped country, whose economic system had suffered a severe warp over the past centuries, to a developed one in a few years time.

What a loss when Che left Cuba to act as Fidel's chief missionary abroad! In the Congo, in Vietnam, as proving grounds, to make one, two, many Vietnams! Fidel blessed Che's mission, agreed to finance his revolutionary expedition to Bolivia, and thus to sacrifice his most ardent revolutionary, his most brilliant aide, the man of wit and charm, who dared to speak out against stupidity, banality, violation of principle when others held their tongues for fear of annoying, angering or disappointing *el maximo lider*. Or for fear of risking their jobs – although these same *barbudos* had risked their lives.

Che understood that it is easier to risk one's life, a simple, singular act of commitment, the ultimate male act, the bonding experience par excellence, than it is to risk the less tangible, less noble, less dramatic elements that revolve around position, status, prestige and, of course, the quickly acquired habits of comfort and pleasure, the security of routine – even revolutionary routine.

Che was to Fidel what Sucre was to Bolivar. Che was Lord Byron, a rootless, cosmic man, who could never feel at home in provincial Cuba. Few foreigners with a global communist vision could co-exist with the venality of the Cuban Stalinists whom Fidel appointed to fill the gaping holes inside the fledgling administrative apparatus of the revolutionary state. Che found it easier to relate to the dock workers, most of them deeply involved in *santeria*, than to engage in the dull bureaucratic infighting with the elusive old guard of the PSP.

Che believed in debate, in free discussion among comrades, in the free and frank exchange of views and counter views. The old PSP had learned differently. Those who taught them the texts of the Little Lenin Library did not believe as Lenin did in the need for open discussion; such notions became, under Stalin, bourgeois at best; perhaps even Trotskyite. But the aura around Che, the halo that seemed to radiate from his face, did not afford the plotters a clear target. Che was too popular, too many people seemed to want to protect him, and understand revolution from his words and deeds.[19]

For Che, the Soviet notion of material stimuli being offered to the agency of social and moral change was a negation of the working class role in the great scheme of revolution. And he wrote, in *Cuba Socialista*, cogent arguments for rejecting the Soviet and East European models of bureaucratic administration and material manipulation of the work force. Che was a democrat, a bit of a Trotskyist, a smidgen of a Maoist, a Gramscist, and a Fidelista. His thinking and being was much closer to Fidel's than any of the old Communists. The other noble samurai who attacked Moncada, washed ashore on the *Granma*, and fought valiantly in the Sierra did not publish their thoughts, or make them known in speeches or public gatherings.

From 1959 until he left Cuba to become the apostle in 1965, Ernesto Che Guevara epitomized the beauty and purity of Cuba's revolutionary experiment. Like Fidel, whom he always understood to possess, in his character, the seed of Latin American destiny, Che saw the Cuban Revolution as a step toward making a hemispheric revolution. In this process, he accepted his role as lieutenant to the commander-in-chief, to the one whose vision was matched by the qualities needed for the most detailed planning and calculation, a mind that could analyze and compute each and every specific, human and natural, that could enter into any given situation, a battle plan or a conception for a national economy. Che could understand, discuss and help to carry out even the most complicated of political and military schemes, but his egalitarian impulses, his inability to overcome his natural valour made him less than able to carry on as the maximum leader. Che understood the qualities that were unique to Fidel, and recognized in his goodbye letter to his comrade that 'my only serious fault was not to have trusted in you more from the very first days in the Sierra Maestre, and not to have understood clearly enough your qualities as leader and revolutionary.'

In death, Che Guevara has become not the wonderful but flawed warrior, the doctor who used medicine for revolution, the man who could not be tied to family or nation, but the virtual saint of Cuban revolutionary lore. Revolutionary youth make pilgrimages to the site of his death, although the Bolivian forces, commanded by CIA officials, made sure that there would be no body or grave marker.[20]

In October 1987, in Pinar del Rio, Fidel delivered a three-hour speech on the virtues of Che Guevara. Some twenty years earlier, just after Che's death, the slogan 'Be like Che' dominated walls and billboards throughout Cuba. If the words were taken literally the slogan could paralyze the average citizen. Who could hope to aspire to Che's level of achievement, discipline, commitment, determination, intellect? Surely, when Fidel urged the people to think like Che and model their lives after him he was only using a metaphor – or was he?

After thirty years of revolution, Cuba had a Constitution, an electoral system, a penal and judicial system, a developed Communist Party, and mass organizations, designed to mobilize the population around work and defence tasks. Yet, Fidel stood for three hours urging each individual Cuban to reform himself to be like Che. The President of the Republic and Commander-in-Chief of the Armed Force, The Secretary General of the Communist Party and universally acknowledged leader of the revolution continues to use his charisma to mobilize, inspire and mould the population. And the crowd responded, with applause, cheers, occasional slogans. They stood for three hours and listened, signalling their agreement. Then they returned home and continued to behave in exactly the way they had before the speech. Their work habits were often inefficient and careless. But each one would take up arms to defend the revolution, or stand endlessly listening to Fidel's speeches. On their walls they might very well have Che's picture hung, with the slogan, 'Be like Che.'

In 1968, I travelled for nearly a week with Fidel through the mountains of Oriente. I sat in his jeep by day; at night we dined in his tent. The entourage that accompanied him, and the film crew, consisted mainly of comandantes and other leaders. By experiencing the underdeveloped conditions of the island, talking to the local inhabitants of villages and farms, Fidel was demonstrating a method of governance, one in tune with the model dramatized by Che's life. But Fidel had more endurance, not just for the difficult and often tedious daily jeep treks through rocky and muddy roads in intense heat, but for the methodical discovery process about the multiple layers of underdevelopment.

'Underdevelopment,' Fidel explained to me in 1968, as the jeep bounced and squirmed through rut and mud, 'is first an economic problem. The nation lacks the infrastructure, the industrial underpinning. Cuba also lacked the trained, educated, confident people necessary to develop.' And, Fidel added, 'underdevelopment is a psychological problem. The population needs to be able to believe that it can accomplish tasks that seems impossible.' Fidel's method of forging a nation included forging confidence, and mass meetings, at which upwards of a million bodies could congregate and generate that sense of strength and possibility.[21]

The light in Fidel's tent stayed on late each night. He was reading textbooks on agricultural sciences, history books, biographies. Almost twenty years later, in 1987, we travelled together for a day around the outskirts of Havana. He had the same insatiable curiosity, the same pace and rhythm, getting out of the jeep quickly, chatting with people, and rapidly reentering the jeep for the next location. He controlled, or tried to, every detail of every operation. His mind was like a strategic computer. He was surrounded by people – there was no longer an entourage of comandantes – who treat him as if he was his Babyship, a kind of obsequiousness that seems to irritate him; and yet he has permitted or encouraged it for more than two decades.

In 1989, Fidel holds more power than ever. He works longer hours, oversees more operations and acts not only as Cuba's beloved, revered and legendary-in-his-own-lifetime ruler, but as trouble shooter, chief ideologue and long-term planner. The mature Cubans that have grown up with Fidel understand that the institutions and Constitution that he created and shaped will not function until he is gone from the scene. Without wanting to, he undermines all other leaders, all institutions, all decisions that are not his – because he can, at will, change a law, a ruling, an economic plan – or the design for the construction of a house for the family doctor.

Fidel hears the complaints of the populace, sees some of the malfunctioning parts of the system, and observes the repeated failures of his guerrilla comrades and old Communists to run ministries efficiently. He also knows that revolutions break more than eggs, and that socialism is a young system, one which is intimately linked to Cuba's future. Socialism cannot fail in Cuba, without having the long hard years of struggle by so many millions of people dissipate. Fidel feels this responsibility and lives each day to see his work and his aspirations realized by a people. Yet, as long as he, and he alone, must bear this responsibility – and assume the power that goes with it – the Cuban people and their institutions will not have a chance to test themselves.

Fidel, said one Cuban official, is not of the same species as the rest of us. He introduced us to socialism when neither he nor anyone else on the island understood much about what it was. He led an experiment with most of us consenting. Sometimes it worked; sometimes not. He has led the Cuban people to nationhood and as soon as he is gone, we will see – whether we have the cohesion to stay together without him, whether we can have a discussion about how we want to live together. He has done a monumental job. When he leaves – we will see.

NOTES

1. His speech on that balmy winter day in Havana provoked President Eisenhower to break diplomatic relations. Fidel demanded that the United States reduce its Embassy staff from over 400 down to 11, the number of Cubans operating at their Embassy in Washington. Fidel strongly implied that the U.S. diplomats were CIA and added that 'if all of them want to leave, let them go.'
2. Santeria is a form of religion developed from African and Catholic heritage, but far more pagan than Roman. Variations of African gods are objects of worship, but they take on the names of Catholic saints. On this subject Nelson Valdes is preparing an original and insightful essay and has shared some of his immense knowledge with me. Miguel Barnet, a Cuban writer and anthropologist, has also enlightened me on this theme, as have several *santeros*.
3. To compare revolutionary Cuba with the United States or the Soviet Union makes little sense – with one exception. Cuban military forces have remained in Angola for more than 13 years, out-doing the U.S. in Vietnam or the Soviets in Afghanistan. And, unlike the super powers, Cuba has apparently been able to force its version of peace through negotiations on South Africa. In 1988 Cuban troops, MIGs and artillery routed South African forces at Cuito Cuanavale in southeastern Angola. The victory helped push South Africa into accord.

   The Cuban public has supported the expeditionary forces since the Fall of 1975, when Fidel made public the decision. He explained in March of 1977 how he made the decisions. With maps in front of him, Castro took Bill Moyers and myself through a step-by-step process, from the time that Angolan Prime Minister Augustin Neto appealed to Cuba to send forces to stop invasion by Zaire from the East and South Africa in the South. Castro, as he told it, convened the Politburo and obtained unanimous agreement to try to honour Neto's request immediately. The logistics problem required imagination: how to get Cuban planes, loaded with troops and weapons, to Luanda. Fidel telephoned Jamaican Prime Minister Michael Manley, who offered full support for the Cuban expedition, but refuelling at the Kingston airport didn't gain Fidel much advantage because of its proximity to Cuba. But, with Manley's help, Castro did get Guyanese prime minister, Forbes Burnham, to offer his airport for Cuban refuelling, and thus the Soviet made jets could ferry the troops into Angola.

   Next, Fidel dispatched his brother, Raul, to Moscow, to alert the Soviets of Cuban plans and to get Soviet moral and material support for the effort. The Soviets approved Fidel's move, after the Cuban victory over Zaire's army. By December, 1975, Cuban troops stopped the South African advance, routed the Zairean forces, and then protected Gulf Oil properties in Cabinda, which had been under threat from Zairean troops.

   Thirteen years later, on December 5, 1988 Fidel declared that Cuba was prepared to remain in Angola five, ten, fifteen even thirty more years, if necessary to the independence of Angola and its security from a South African invasion. 500,000 people stood in a pouring rain, in Havana's Revolution Plaza, applauded and chanted appropriate support slogans.

   Neither U.S. Presidents nor Soviet Premiers have been able to marshal such public backing for overseas undertakings.
4. There is also considerable opposition to the path chosen by Fidel, and Cubans tell a joke, which, although ostensibly about the Soviet system, is meant to describe conditions in Cuba as well. Former Soviet Premier Brezhnev is finally persuaded to meet an elderly peasant woman who has been waiting for months to ask him a question. 'Comrade General Secretary,' she asks, 'you people who made the

revolution, were you revolutionaries or were you scientists?'
Brezhnev laughs and exclaims, 'We were revolutionaries of course, why do you ask?'
'Oh,' says the woman, 'that's exactly what I thought, because if you had been scientists you surely would have tried this experiment on rats first.'

5. The CIA operation against the Cuban revolution was the largest ever mounted, and it was done from Miami. Hundreds of houses (safe houses) were bought, a massive payroll (thousands of anti Castro Cubans) was recruited, most to join the invasion brigade, but a considerable number to do more dirty operations. Under Jimmy Carter, the Agency refrained from violent clandestine operations, but certainly excelled in the disinformation category.

6. Valentin Azpillaga, the intelligence official, stationed in Prague, revealed some 500 names of Cuban intelligence operatives throughout the world – a remarkable feat of memory for any person. General del Pino, who accomplished heroic feats during the Bay of Pigs invasion in 1961, stole a plane and flew it to the United States, where he made across the board denunciations of the Cuban Revolution. A U.S. intelligence officer of many decades responded to these events to the author: 'Intelligence and military people defect for three reasons: because they made serious errors and would have received poor fitness reports that would damage their careers; because they are offered some immense sum of money; or young nooky – usually provided by rival services.'

7. The revolution has transformed the island, built thousands of schools, through university and medical schools, (Cuba claims 25,000 doctors in 1988, compared to 6,000 in 1959, of whom 3,000 fled to the United States) hundreds of clinics and hospitals, roads, day care centres, factories and apartment houses. Because of Fidel and the revolution that he has led since he first launched a daring raid against Fort Moncada, Cuba's second largest army base, Cuba is a physically and psychologically new country. It is not only a young country but an ardently communist one – at least as far as Fidel and the members of the Party are concerned.

8. The assassination attempt that came closest to success, according to Castro, involved a 'pernicious poison.' Castro admitted, in 1974, to have been almost addicted to chocolate milk shakes, and the best ones in town back in 1960 and 1961 were made at the Havana Libre hotel. The CIA, as Castro told it, smuggled this venom into the hands of the ice cream scooper at the hotel, who hid the chemical in the freezer, next to the chocolate ice cream container. As luck would have it – and Fidel has had his share – the poison container froze against the inside wall of the freezer, and rather than risk alerting Fidel's body-guards, the would-be assassin did not insert the material into Fidel's milk shake. Soon after, through infiltration, the assassin was caught, confessed and the poison was sent to a laboratory. 'It was quite a clever concoction,' Fidel commented. 'I would have become very ill, my beard would have fallen out, and the poison would not be traceable in my body.'

9. By the end of 1965 more than 500,000 Cubans had fled the island, most of them settling in the Miami area. With exceptions they shared a collective expectation that the U.S. marines would oust Castro and reinstate a regime that respected private property.

10. Just as U.S. citizens were unaware of the role of their country for the past sixty years in Cuba, Cubans were super aware of U.S. intervention in the 1895–98 war of liberation against Spain, the imposition of the hated Platt Amendment, giving the Americans unilateral intervention rights, the Marine occupation of the island for six years before 1920, and other abuses of Cuban independence, ranging from U.S. sailors urinating on a Jose Marti statue to the U.S. backing of Batista.

In March, 1960 some 500 former Batista military and police officials were shot after a Kangaroo Court convicted them of having committed horrible crimes. The Castro government said that some 20,000 Cubans had been slain by the Batista apparatus. These summary trials and firing squads turned the U.S. media, hence U.S. public opinion, against the revolution.

11. Before the revolution the saying went that Batista was the second most important man on the island, next to the U.S. Ambassador.

12. This view of the revolution is disingenuous at best. Costa Rica has a different history, a population of less than 3 million (compared to Cuba's 10 million) and is home for many thousands of retired Americans, who insure a constant inflow of dollars into the country. It has not been the object of U.S. attack for thirty years and is a recipient of U.S. aid. Its revolution did not change property relations, nor bring about the kind of counterrevolution which creates a need to invest in a military establishment to protect itself. Costa Rica is the one fortunate nation in Latin America to have escaped the pestilence of an on-going military apparatus.

A more accurate comparison could be made with the Dominican Republic, like Cuba a sugar-based island, with a similar history. It had a dictator, Trujillo, who like Batista was a long-time darling of Washington. After Trujillo was assassinated, and the Dominican people elected a leftist government under Juan Bosch there was a military coup and when the Dominicans rose up to defend their elected government, in 1965, President Johnson sent 22,000 marines onto the island to ensure that no repetition of Cuba would take place.

13. The Western media assume that the definition of human rights is restricted to the political and legal, or procedural questions, regarding free trial, maintenance of minimum prison conditions, freedom of speech, press and assembly etc. . . The Cubans, like most of the socialist bloc, emphasize the economic and social or substantive clauses in the UN Human Rights documents, which list as fundamental rights food, shelter, education, medicine etc. . .

Cuba, lacking the public relations apparatus necessary to respond to the State Department's spin experts, inevitably fares poorly in the media, although not necessarily with the international diplomatic community. When Reagan appointed Armando Valladares as the U.S. Ambassador for the UN Human Rights Agency in Geneva many allied and friendly diplomats were horrified. Valladares apparently used threats and intimidation as tactics against other diplomats.

Valladares had been arrested in late 1960 on charges of terrorism. The evidence presented showed that he had been in possession of explosives, disguised as cigarette cartons. He was tried and convicted by a revolutionary court and sentenced to twenty years in prison. Upon his release, he published a book about his prison experience which Cuban writers questioned, speculating that someone had ghosted it. Valladares had worked for the Batista security forces, up to January, 1959. The revolutionaries reviewed his file and found him fit for employment. At the time of his arrest, he was working for the Post Office.

14. The Soviets had made their first official visit to Cuba just ten months after the triumph of the revolution, and, after the United States and its allies, under U.S. pressure, had refused to sell arms to Castro, offered Fidel both arms and oil, if he needed it. Both offers were accepted by Spring, 1960.

15. A reporter asked Fidel if he considered Noriega to be an honest man. 'General Noriega,' Fidel replied solemnly, 'is a very brave man.'

16. I mean what Max Weber meant by the word charisma, God-like, special qualities, ones that differentiate the leader from all the rest. Modern use of the word often refers to anyone who is a good public speaker, or appears strong and determined, people in general with leadership qualities. Fidel, of course, possesses all of those attributes – and much more.

17. Fidel has fought his share of the age-old Cuban struggle with the demons, holding

reason aloft against superstition, even as the leaders of organized superstition declare him one of their own, indeed, the highest of the order of living Gods. While Fidel was making a speech in Havana shortly after the triumph of the revolution, two white doves perched on his shoulder. This seemingly miraculous occurrence made the *santeros* (faith healers or priests of the *santeria* religion) believe that Fidel was a messenger of *obatalá*, the African God that has survived in Cuba long after the abolition of slavery.

Tomas Gutierrez Alea made a film in 1971, *La Pelea Cubana contra los Demonios*, which lays out the contemporary struggle of reason against superstition against the backdrop of such a battle in the 17th Century.

18. Those who now accompany him on his rounds, Pepin Narranjo and Jose Chome Millar, do not possess the special qualities of Celia or Vallejo.

19. After two hectic months of activity by Fidel and his *barbudo* lieutenants to reorganize the state, Che fell ill, and became the subject of a veiled attack in a gossip column, printed in *Carteles*, a popular, but decidedly capitalist magazine. The columnist said that 'Comandante Guevara has established his residence in Tarará', a resort area outside of Havana. Che wrote a letter to the editor of *Revolucion*, to 'inform the readers. . . that I am ill, that my illness was not contracted in gambling dens or staying up all night in cabarets but in working more than my constitution could take for the Revolution.'

Che also made public his salary as an officer of the rebel army, 125 pesos a month, which did not allow him to rent a house large enough to house his entourage, work team and body guards; so the Rehousing Agency lent him one that was deserted by a Batista follower because the doctor ordered him to rest. 'The fact that this is a house belonging to an old Batista follower makes it luxurious; I chose the simplest one I could, but even so it is an insult to the people's sensibility. I promise. . . the people of Cuba that I shall abandon it as soon as I am recovered.' Letter from Guevara to *Revolucion*, 10 March, 1959.

20. Che was murdered by orders of a U.S. adviser, Felix Rodriguez, the man who later emerged as a CIA player in the Iran contra scandal.

21. Fidel spoke of underdevelopment as he gave me an illustrated tour of what it looked like, how it smelled and sounded. By day we bounded through the rutted tracks, sloshed though the sometimes flooded dirt trails that the people of the Sierra Maestre called roads. We met peasants coming down the hills with burros loaded with coffee beans. Parasite-infected children, twenty-five year old women who looked sixty, illiteracy, tuberculosis, severe gastro-intestinal disorders – this was life in the mountains before the revolution and for at least a decade after it as well.